Military Justice in America

Military Justice in America

The U.S. Court of Appeals for the Armed Forces, 1775–1980

Revised and Abridged Edition

Jonathan Lurie

University Press of Kansas

Originally published by Princeton University Press in 2 volumes, *Arming Military Justice: The Origins of the United States Court of Military Appeals, 1775–1950* (1992), and *Pursuing Military Justice: The History of the United States Court of Appeals for the Armed Forces, 1951–1980* (1998).

Published by the University Press of Kansas (Lawrence, Kansas 66049), which was organized by the Kansas Board of Regents and is operated and funded by Emporia State University, Fort Hays State University, Kansas State University, Pittsburg State University, the University of Kansas, and Wichita State University

Library of Congress Cataloging-in-Publication Data

Lurie, Jonathan, 1939–
    Military justice in America : the U.S. Court of Appeals for the Armed Forces, 1775–1980 / Jonathan Lurie.—Rev. and abridged ed.
        p. cm. — (Modern war studies)
    Rev. ed. of 2 previous titles by same author: Arming military justice. ©1992.; and Pursuing military justice. ©1998.
    Includes bibliographical references.
    ISBN 0-7006-1080-4 (pbk. : alk. paper)
    1. United States. Court of Military Appeals—History.   2. Courts-martial and courts of inquiry—United States—History.   I. Lurie, Jonathan, 1939– Arming military justice. II. Lurie, Jonathan, 1939– Pursuing military justice.   III. Title.   IV. Series.

KF7667 .L873 2001
343.73'0143—dc21   2001017534

British Library Cataloguing in Publication Data is available.

Printed in the United States of America

10 9 8 7 6 5 4 3 2 1

The paper used in this publication meets the minimum requirements of the American National Standard for Permanence of Paper for Printed Library Materials Z39.48-1984.

Again for Mac, David,
Deborah, and Daniel,
and also for Jason

Contents

Preface

The United States Court of Appeals for the Armed Forces (USCAAF) is housed in a small but stately building located along with several other courts in an area of Washington appropriately called Judiciary Square. Erected in 1910, the structure is now listed on the National Register of Historic Places and has been the home of USCAAF since 1952. Upon entering, a visitor sees the ever present security guard along with the usual scanning and screening monitors. The visitor notices the shining marble floors, the high ceilings, and the large, well-lighted corridors. On the first floor are located several important offices, such as the Clerk of the Court and the Docket Room, where all incoming cases must first be filed. Often these offices are busy, and one hears echoes of voices and footsteps drifting down the hallways. Upon moving to the second floor, however, in front of the entrance to the courtroom, the atmosphere changes.

Here, the visitor stands in an impressive foyer, replete with high columns and ornate chandeliers. Two large portraits, of George Washington and of Robert Anderson at the battle of Fort Sumter in 1861, hang on the wall above the marble staircase. In the center of the foyer, and in sharp contrast to its grandeur, is a set of double doors, simply marked "court room." Going through these doors, which are actually at the back of the chamber, one enters a functioning courtroom restored to what existed early in the twentieth century, when the building was first constructed. A large skylight in the center of the ceiling filters light through the entire room. At the far end, one notices a massive mahogany bench, along with several desks for court staff. Directly in front of the bench one also sees a small mahogany lectern, where lawyers stand (or lean, depending on their mental state) as they argue their cases before the judges. Because this is an appellate court, there is no jury box.

In back of the large seats behind the bench hang high, heavy, dark red drapes, which separate gracefully as the judges move to their seats. On the back wall at the rear of the courtroom there are portraits of all former judges appointed since 1951. Several of them—including those of the first chief judge, Robert Quinn, and Paul Brosman, the last of the initial three appointments—face the current members of the court, looking out, as it were, toward their successors. Unintentionally perhaps, the location of the portraits reflects a sense of linkage between past and present judges, as the court continues to function. One can almost hear the silence in this empty courtroom; an air of permanence and inevitability seems to hang over it.

At the appropriate time, the Court bailiff will strike his gavel and demand that "All rise!" "Hear ye, hear ye," he chants. As if responding to a cue, the curtains in back of the bench part so that five judges in black robes can take their accustomed seats on the bench, the chief judge in the center and the remaining judges to his right and left in order of seniority. Like many opening rituals of appellate courts, this is an impressive ceremony to observe. Indeed, there are seats for about 140 visitors, but in fact, they are rarely filled. For most appeals there are more participants present than spectators. With few exceptions, such as a newsworthy case or an admissions ceremony for new members of the Court bar, the appeals attract little attention. The absence of both jury and witnesses helps inhibit any lawyer's tendency toward excessive legal theatrics, and to the outside visitor observing an appeals argument, the impression created may be one of legal mumbo-jumbo, of minor interest if not boredom. Such a perception is probably characteristic of appellate courts in general.

But this particular court has special functions, unlike other federal courts of general jurisdiction. Though its authority is limited by statute to cases arising from within the armed services, in fact it has jurisdiction over millions of Americans. That is because their service in our armed forces subjects them to the Uniform Code of Military Justice (UCMJ), which, among its many provisions, established a court of military appeals. Created during the aftermath of World War II, the Court was intended to ensure a civilian appellate bench for the military, that it too might function (to cite a famous phrase) as a government of law and not of men to the greatest extent possible—even within the admittedly unique and restrictive parameters of military life.

Justifiably labeled as an experiment by its creators, USCAAF has been in existence since 1951. More than two generations of litigants have appeared before it, and over thirty thousand lawyers have been admitted to its bar. Its decisions now fill more than seventy-five volumes, and its interpretations of both the UCMJ and the Manual for Courts-Martial (MCM) are for the most part definitive. On the federal level, this judicial experiment is now a permanent part of the judicial establishment, and its history raises a number of important questions.

Why did Congress establish the tribunal in 1950? Why not in 1919 or even 1861? What did the legislature intend as its mission? What tradition, if any, of military appellate procedure had developed within the armed services? How did congressional preferences and the political process affect the new legislation?

How have the armed services reacted to the Court? How have its members been selected, and how have these choices reflected political considerations usual for such presidential appointments? How has it operated since 1951? Finally, what mandate has the Court exercised and with what degree of success or failure?

In seeking to answer these questions, a number of themes—separate yet sometimes intertwined—have emerged. First is the tracing, over time, of appellate jurisdiction within American military justice. Second, there is a related theme of the interplay between military justice and civilian judicial activity. Although episodic throughout our history, several such incidents have raised troublesome questions concerning the extent of civilian control over the military. The development of an appellate procedure within the military and the role civilians might play in it represented an important dimension of this issue.

One must also keep in mind the continuing tension between military justice and its civilian counterpart. Military justice is virtually inseparable from military discipline, which seeks attainment of specific objectives, gained by a military force prepared for death if necessary. Our civilian justice system aims primarily to safeguard the rights of property, community, and the individual. Basic differences between the two systems are immediately apparent, but the extent to which they should be separate from each other remains a source of continuing controversy.

A third theme is the interplay of politics on the course of legislation, not only in its early stages but more obviously when it reaches Congress. Unusual efforts were made to keep the drafting of the UCMJ nonpolitical. Yet, like most legislative efforts, even this statute was not immune from political considerations. Issues of presidential authority as well as congressional preferences affected the code's final form.

A number of additional themes emerge from the history of the Court after 1951. First is the maturation of the Court as an institution with its own procedures and personality. Related to it is an issue of the Court's identity, both from within and without. The way the judges saw themselves—especially in the Court's early years—differed from the perceptions of other agencies of government, including the military. Nagging questions concerning the "extent" to which USCAAF was supposed to be an actual court, similar to other federal tribunals, have troubled its judges. Did Congress intend the Court to be part of the federal judiciary? Or rather was it an administrative agency within the executive branch? Answers to these questions invariably raised the fundamental problem of the Court's legitimacy—a matter about which its judges, at least, had no doubt whatsoever.

Directly related to this problem has been another matter of vital concern to the Court. Since 1951, its judges have made extraordinary efforts—thus far unsuccessful—to persuade Congress to grant them life tenure. For reasons to be explored in some detail, the USCAAF jurists concluded early on that such permanence was essential in order to function properly as an independent federal appellate tribunal. Why have they maintained this position with such consistency, and why has Congress been equally consistent in its refusal to depart from the 1951 decision to provide for specific judicial terms, even as the lawmakers have reaffirmed the independence and standing of the Court—comparable in prestige and salary to any other federal appellate court?

A second major theme in USCAAF's history has been its relationship to the military, in particular the Judge Advocate General (JAG) Corps. There is no doubt that Congress was concerned about this issue. What did the lawmakers intend this relationship to be? While mandating cooperation between judges and JAGs, the UCMJ virtually guaranteed conflict as well. Although the code charged the JAGs with the task of making "frequent inspections in the field in supervision of military justice," it made no mention of any such similar function for the Court.

Yet an appellate tribunal described by its creators as the "Supreme Court of the military" would of necessity claim for itself ultimate supervisory jurisdiction of military justice. And in actual fact, the relationship between these two bodies of leadership in this field has ranged from ill-concealed antagonism to grudging acceptance, with an occasional spasm of approbation. It has always been guarded. One can argue that this unstable synthesis may indeed have been what Congress anticipated, if not intended. More important, however, is less the intention than the result, which the following chapters explore in some detail.

Finally, there is the emergence over time of a substantial body of military appellate case law. And although the above themes are all independent, they rest on this common base. Since 1951, USCAAF has been deciding cases—delineating the permissible limits of acceptable military judicial conduct. How the military and Congress reacted to its key decisions sometimes affected their relationship to the Court. While of necessity a number of important cases are discussed in this study, my focus is not legal doctrine as much as institutional evolution. The formal decisions of this Court are readily available for all to study, but tracing its path from a new experiment to an established civilian federal tribunal is a more difficult historical challenge.

Indeed, I hope that this book will lessen an unfortunate though understandable impression that the system of military justice is "fundamentally arcane and inaccessible." It does not need to be so, and perhaps outside accounts of its origins will "encourage the free flow" of ideas, analyses, and innovation between the military and civilian justice systems. Both can gain from such interaction. In the long run, being subject to rigorous scholarly scrutiny may be of significance in seeing that military justice attains the highest possible level of performance. Most important, I believe that effective civilian control of the military—including military justice—depends on civilian interest, awareness, and involvement to a much greater extent than is now the case. A history of USCAAF from 1951 to 1980 may shed some light on how this development has occurred.

My history of the U.S. Court of Appeals for the Armed Forces was originally published by Princeton University Press as *Arming Military Justice*
(1992) and *Pursuing Military Justice* (1998). In order to prepare a paperback
edition that would not be of unwieldy length, all footnotes have been deleted,
and some portions of the text have been omitted or abridged. The basic account
and analysis of the Court's history, however, remains unchanged. The original
annotated volumes are readily available from Princeton University Press and
most university and law school libraries.

The Court first invited me to research its history in 1987, and the resulting volumes as well as this paperback would have been impossible without its
continued support and cooperation—even as its judges, both current and former, have consistently distanced themselves from my efforts to explore their
Court's history. Because I am certain that they may well not agree with all my
conclusions, some of which tend to be critical, it should be emphasized here
that these remain my responsibility. On the other hand, freely admitting that
inexplicable and inexcusable lapses in military justice have indeed occurred
and doubtless will again in no way diminishes the significance of impressive
changes that have taken place since 1951.

In the course of more than a decade devoted to researching and writing the
Court's history, I have received much assistance from many individuals. They
have been acknowledged in previous prefaces to the earlier volumes, and I
thank them all once again. Mention should be made of the judges with whom
I have worked since 1987: the current chief judge, Susan Crawford; her colleagues Eugene Sullivan, H. "Sparky" Gierke, and Andrew Effron; and Senior
Judges Robinson Everett and Walter Cox Jr. I also remain indebted to the Court
clerk, Thomas Granahan, and his entire staff, especially Sherry Arter, Robert
Bieber, Gail Bissi, Kathy Cassady, Connie Crozier, and Joe Lusk. The Court
librarian, Agnes Kiang, has been consistently invaluable as well as tolerant.

As my research and writing progressed, John Holt, Chris Sterritt, and
Robert Mueller have listened, reacted, questioned, counseled, and encouraged.
Their insights are scattered throughout these chapters, but they are in no way
responsible for the conclusions I have drawn. A special word of thanks must
go to Eugene Fidell, a distinguished practitioner and scholar in the field of military justice. Over the years, he took the time to read and critique every chapter of both volumes. His fortitude has been remarkable, and the value of his
scholarship much appreciated.

Finally, I am grateful to my good friend Michael Briggs, editor in chief at
the University Press of Kansas, who first suggested the idea of an abridged
paperback edition. It has been a pleasure to work with the staff at the press,
while the cooperation of Princeton University Press in facilitating a paperback
edition is acknowledged with many thanks.

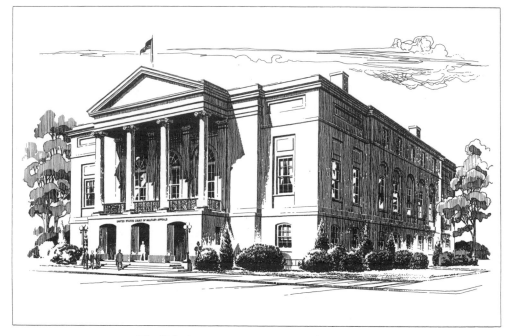

The U.S. Court of Appeals for the Armed Forces

1

Military and Civilian "Review" to 1815

The idea of an appellate procedure vis-à-vis American constitutional and political history is of venerable ancestry. Between 1650 and 1775, the thirteen original colonies all developed systems of judicial administration that implied, if not employed, an appeals process. The seeds of both a separation of powers doctrine as well as judicial review can thus be seen in the frequently complex relations between colonial legislatures, royal governors, and the Royal Privy Council. The council, in addition to reviewing much colonial legislation, could and did veto certain laws. By the time of the Revolutionary era, from 1775 to 1787, some sort of appellate review had become a virtual given in terms of American *civilian* political institutions.

Of necessity, the colonial figures who orchestrated the revolution in political terms also had to confront governance of the army. Leaders like John Adams and Thomas Jefferson, both acutely aware of the possible contagion of revolutionary sentiment but from very different philosophical viewpoints, were also concerned with the establishment of a workable system of military justice. Of minimal importance were the "rights" of the American soldier, which included any appellate procedure. Of crucial importance was a set of regulations that would ensure discipline and effective control of the armed forces. For all their political and philosophical differences, Jefferson and Adams could both support two early versions of the Articles of War (1775 and 1776) that together constituted the official foundation of American military justice.

TOUGH TALK FROM JOHN ADAMS

Those who drafted the 1775 articles, including John Adams, drew heavily upon the existing British rules, rules admittedly harsh but, at least from Adams's viewpoint, historically effective. Thus the regulations provided for both regimental and general courts-martial. In certain cases, the latter could serve as an appeals body from the former. Moreover, an officer who felt himself "to be wronged by his Colonel, or the Commanding officer of the Regiment" could "complain to the General or Commander-in-Chief . . . in order to obtain justice, who is hereby required to examine into the complaint and see that justice be done." Similar provisions were available for "any inferior Officer or Soldier." Punishments meted out both by regimental and general courts-martial could not take place until confirmed (and thus presumably reviewed) by the commanding officer. "All the Members of a Court Martial are to behave with calmness, decency, and impartiality." Article 25 provided that "whatsoever officer or soldier shall shamefully abandon any post committed to his charge, or shall speak words inducing others to do the like, in time of an engagement, shall suffer death immediately." No provisions for any sort of judicial procedure, let alone inquiry, were provided.

Of special interest, in terms of the evolving system of American military justice from the 1775 articles to the 1951 Uniform Code of Military Justice, were articles 46 and 49. One provided for the dismissal of a commissioned officer convicted by a general court-martial "of behaving in a scandalous, infamous manner, such as is unbecoming an Officer and a Gentleman." The other stated that "all crimes not capital, and all disorders and neglects which Officers and Soldiers may be guilty of, to the prejudice of good order and military discipline, though not mentioned in the Articles of War, are to be taken cognizance of by a General or Regimental Court Martial, according to the nature and degree of the offence, and be punished at their discretion." These two articles, often described as "catchall" articles, have remained part of American military justice for more than two centuries. As will be seen in a later chapter, controversy surrounds their continued presence. But the military has consistently, and thus far successfully, insisted on the absolute military necessity for their retention, even though such necessity is increasingly of dubious validity.

The 1776 revision deleted the article calling for immediate execution, noted above. It also provided that "no sentence of a general court-martial shall be put into execution, till after a report shall have been made of the whole proceedings to Congress, or to the general or commander in chief of the forces of the United States, and their or his directions be signified thereupon." Furthermore, this individual "shall have full power of pardoning or mitigating any of the punishments ordered to be inflicted, for any of the offenses" mentioned in the articles. On the other hand, the limit on lashes to be inflicted as punishment was raised from thirty-nine to one hundred.

By 1776, Congress had established military courts-martial. They predate our federal district courts by more than a decade and thus can accurately be said to have been among the first, if not *the* first, federal courts authorized by the United States. They were drawn from a set of military articles, admittedly severe, and thus the question arises why two practical patriots such as Adams and Jefferson—the one with his well-known lawyer's respect for due process, the other with his passionate belief in self-government—could both support regulations that can be considered antithetical to much of what they stood for.

The answer probably lay in their belief that governance of the military was based on needs very different from those of a civilian polity. Adams took it for granted that the militia had to be governed by different standards than those applicable in civilian society. His concern for a disciplined army overshadowed the issue of due process within the military itself. In one form or another, although not without some modifications, this concern and its attendant preference continue to the present day. But there was also a practical side to be considered. As a group, revolutionaries generally are not happy with the prospect of losing. The way the army was governed could only affect the way it fought, and whether it won or lost might have overwhelming personal consequences for men like Adams and Jefferson.

"I saw very clearly," wrote Adams, "that the ruin of our cause and country must be the consequence if a thoughrough [sic] reformation and strict discipline could not be introduced." Indeed, in his correspondence, Adams made frequent reference to the need for discipline. In 1777, he wrote to his wife Abigail that "if I were an officer, I am convinced I should be the most decisive disciplinarian in the army. . . . Discipline in an army is like the laws in a civil society. There can be no liberty in a commonwealth where the laws are not revered and most sacredly observed, nor can there be happiness or safety in an army for a single hour when discipline is not observed." For Adams, liberty and discipline represented two sides of the same coin. To him, "the *unum necessarium* to our salvation" was discipline in the army—together with strong and effective state governments. The two were inseparable.

Adams's ideas about military discipline were important in legitimating the doctrine that military justice was to be an entity in itself, separate from civilian practice. Yet the 1776 articles made it clear that Congress was to play some sort of supervisory/review role in regard to military justice. How closely civilian (congressional) supervision was to be applied to the army remained unclear. Less than three years after the formal conclusion of hostilities between the United States and England, the American Congress had to confront this problem. How much information concerning courts-martial was to be reported to Congress, when, and with what result?

CONGRESSIONAL CONCERNS, 1786–1815

Early in 1786, Secretary of War Henry Knox received a report from Major John Wyllys, assigned to a post on the frontier of Pennsylvania. Seeing his command shrink due to blatant incidents of desertion, he convened a court-martial of five officers to try several soldiers for this offense. To be sure, the 1776 articles called for "a panel of 13 officers for capital cases, obviously impossible in a peace-time army which," according to Richard Kohn, "contained less than 40 officers in toto." The men were convicted, whereupon Wyllys forwarded the findings and sentence to the War Department, as required by the Articles of War. He also made the sentences public, hoping that they would have a dramatic effect upon other members of his command. They did; immediately three more soldiers deserted. This time, Wyllys did not hesitate. The men were promptly captured and executed, with neither trial nor prior notification to Congress. "No deser-tions," he wrote to Knox, "have happened since & he thinks this instance of severity will probably preclude the necessity for executing the deserters now in confinement." Wyllys was "fully convinced that nothing but such exemplary punishment could produce the desired effect," and he hoped that his course would meet with the secretary's "approbation."

Ultimately, Knox exonerated Wyllys, but he was shocked by the incident. He informed Congress that a commanding officer "cannot inflict the capital punishment of death for desertion contrary to the established forms. To super-sede the laws in this respect is to assume the sovereignty and annul the com-pact, which the public have made with their troops, that they shall be governed by the rules and articles of war." He asked that Congress investigate the entire incident and, pending the outcome, suspended Wyllys "from all command in the troops of the United States."

Congress responded with some revisions to the articles, which were adopted on May 31, 1786. The new rules provided that general courts-martial could consist of "any number of commissioned officers from five to thirteen inclusively." Of greater importance, another article stated that no sentence of a court-martial could be executed "until after the whole proceedings shall have been laid before the said general or officer commanding the troops." Moreover, no sentence of a court-martial "in time of peace, extending to the loss of life, the dismission [*sic*] of a commissioned officer, or . . . either in time of peace or war . . . a general officer [shall] be carried into execution until after the whole proceedings shall have been transmitted to the Secretary of War, to be laid before Congress for their confirmation, or disapproval, and their orders on the case."

In the 1786 changes, Congress also authorized the commanding officer to establish a court of inquiry and provided that "the parties accused shall also be permitted to cross-examine and interrogate the witnesses, so as to investigate fully the circumstances in question." It should be noted here that the court of inquiry served as the military equivalent of a grand jury proceeding. Yet the right to cross-examine witnesses, as indicated above, went far beyond any compara-ble privilege granted in civilian practice. Even today, grand jury proceedings are usually secret, and the objects of their scrutiny are not permitted to cross-examine, let alone hear, other witnesses. In this respect, military justice—and this before adoption of the federal Constitution, to say nothing of the Bill of Rights—afforded, and presumably still does afford, a greater measure of due process to an accused than in civilian court procedure. It is not too early in this book to caution that one should be very careful when generalizing about the comparative merits of judicial procedure within military and civilian justice.

The adoption of the Constitution replete with the modern system of congressional, judicial, and executive functions came and went with no appreciable impact on the existing Articles of War. Clearly, Congress could establish rules and procedures for courts-martial. Could the president do the same? Was a court-martial executive or legislative in origin? Not important in 1800, the question would be of much greater concern when a secondary issue arose: the problem of the relationship between actions of courts-martial and other federal tribunals. Were decisions of military courts reviewable outside of the very limited steps under the articles, and if so, by whom? As will be seen in later chapters, much of American military-legal history has focused on the efforts to answer these questions.

By the early nineteenth century, American military law was well established. More important, a tradition had already evolved that reflected political inclinations not to apply civilian standards of justice to military procedures. This is not to imply that presidents tended to shirk their responsibility to review certain court-martial cases seriously. But they operated within a set of assumptions that, as time passed, would make it virtually impossible to expect courts-martial to receive the same kinds of review usual in civilian trials. Further, such a viewpoint typically applied to civilian judges when they were asked to intervene in a military proceeding.

Yet the theoretical foundation for civilian supervision, if not control, of military justice remained strong. Concrete application of this doctrine, however, was difficult. During the nineteenth century, when military necessity collided with civilian due process, the results tended to be either inconclusive or inconsistent, usually at the expense of civilian authority. These incidents raised important questions. Why should either a justification for martial law or a declaration of military necessity be immune from civilian judicial examination? Could a citizen, not a soldier, be tried by a military tribunal, and if so, with what procedural safeguards? What due process rights did a member of our armed forces retain? One episode, an 1815 case that pitted the most popular military hero of his day against an obscure federal district judge, brought the first two of these questions into dramatic focus.

THE GENERAL AND THE JUDGE

Andrew Jackson's career can be described as a classic example of the American civilian-military synthesis: the civilian who in times of crisis becomes a military leader, only to return to civilian life after the crisis has passed. With the possible exception of George Washington, probably no American president before or since Jackson has personified this perception with such popularity. Thus, the episode that ultimately involved him as a supreme military commander, a defendant in federal court, and finally a venerated elder statesman in retirement reflects the peculiar American ambivalence toward military necessity and civilian control in the context of American politics. Its outcome indicates that in the American experience, civilian control of the military cannot always be separated from the political process; a fact that may well render such control less effective than might otherwise be the case.

Prior to the famous battle of New Orleans in January 1815, Jackson had placed the city under martial law. With the incredible victory over a much larger British force, he was regarded as the city's—to say nothing of the nation's—savior. Yet Jackson believed that the great celebrations in his honor had ended neither the war itself nor the necessity for martial law. Until he received *official* word that a treaty had been signed (as in fact had actually happened even before the battle), Jackson insisted on the retention of the status quo ante. During the next two months, tensions between Jackson and New Orleans's leaders were exacerbated, to say the least. Declining to release the militia, he even went so far as to order the deportation of numerous French-speaking citizens. This order caused his ultimate confrontation with federal civil authority.

In response to his "edict," a French-language newspaper printed an editorial very critical of Jackson's conduct. "We do not feel much inclined, through gratitude, to sacrifice any of our privileges, and, less than any other, that of expressing our opinion of the acts of his administration." With the British now in open retreat, Jackson's continued authoritarianism was neither appropriate nor acceptable. The general's response to the editorial was both rigorous and rapid—two characteristics usually associated with military justice.

The editor of the newspaper was brought before Jackson and forced (it is not clear upon the threat of what penalty) to identify the author of the offending editorial. This gentleman was one Louis Louailler, who in addition to his proclivity with a pen was a member of the Louisiana legislature. Jackson ordered his arrest both for inciting a mutiny and for spying. In New Orleans, Louailler was picked up a couple of days later by a unit of troops and apparently yelled to some observers that he was being kidnapped by armed men. A lawyer in the crowd offered his services and rushed to the home of federal judge Dominick A. Hall, who promptly issued a writ of habeas corpus, returnable in open court the next morning. Just as promptly, Jackson ordered the judge arrested for "aiding, abetting and exciting mutiny within my camp." The next day found Louailler not before Judge Hall but rather locked in the same barracks with him, presumably not what the judge had envisaged in issuing the writ in the first place.

Jackson convened a court-martial to try Louailler, but the defendant challenged the authority of the court to try him at all, arguing that in fact he was neither a member of the army nor the militia. As for the charge of spying, what spy would go to the trouble of making his views known through a newspaper column? The court dismissed the charges, whereupon Jackson dismissed the court and commanded that Louailler be returned to prison.

The general's use of the court-martial in this case was understandable. However, it was far from clear if the Articles of War actually applied to a civilian such as Louailler. What Jackson needed was a military mechanism designed to deal with civilian offenses. By the eras of both the Mexican and Civil Wars, one had evolved—known as the military commission. Unlike a court-martial, a military commission could focus on military wrongs committed by civilians. Many such tribunals functioned during the Civil War; the most famous probably was the panel convened to try the individuals accused of Lincoln's assassination.

Under existing rules of war, the verdict of a court-martial was not binding upon the commander, also known as the convening authority. He could, and sometimes did, order the court to "reconsider" its verdict, often indicating whether it was to be increased in severity. He could also disregard the verdict, if so inclined. Since the commander selected the members of the court in the first place, the potential for what is now known as "command influence" was self-evident. In 1818, for example, while in Florida campaigning against the Seminoles, Jackson ordered the arrest and court-martial of two British subjects—Arbuthnot and Ambrister. He believed that speedy trials and even speedier punishments were warranted. The entire procedure from court-martial to consummation of sentence took two days. The court ordered Arbuthnot to be hanged and Ambrister to be shot, but at the request of at least one member, the officers reconsidered Ambrister's fate and ultimately voted for "fifty lashes on the bare back, and confinement with ball and chain to hard labor for one year." Jackson disregarded the recommendation and ordered both executions. "These unprincipled villains," he later wrote to Secretary of War John Calhoun, "were legally convicted . . . legally condemned, and most justly executed for their iniquities." Their cases, he continued, presented scenes of "wickedness, corruption, and barbarity at which the heart sickens."

Jackson, himself a lawyer and a former judge, may well have hesitated over the matter of Judge Hall, for he never convened a court-martial to try the case. Instead he ordered Hall to be marched out of New Orleans "beyond the limits of my encampment to prevent you from a repetition of the improper conduct for which you have been arrested and confined." One day later, on March 13, 1815, Jackson received official word of the peace treaty. He immediately revoked martial law, freed Louailler, and permitted Hall to return to the city. The judge's response was not long in coming. But for the moment, as had also been the case immediately after his initial military triumph two months earlier,

Jackson was once again the city's hero; he had won the war and now heralded the peace.

In responding to laudatory remarks proffered by one group of soldiers, Jackson referred indirectly to the recent period of martial law. An extremely able politician, he fully realized the strong opposition that his measures had provoked. When constitutional rights were threatened by invasion, certain basic privileges "may be required to be infringed for their security. At such a crisis, we have only to determine whether we will suspend for a time, the exercise of the latter, that we may secure the permanent enjoyment of the former." Should the legal order sacrifice "the spirit of the laws to the letter," and thus "lose the substance forever, in order that we may, for an instant, preserve the shadow?"

In 1861, Chief Justice Roger Taney denounced the suspension of habeas corpus by President Lincoln. Later, in justifying his action to Congress, Lincoln sounded very much like Jackson. In the midst of the secession crisis, he asked, "Are all the laws, but one, to go unexecuted, and the government itself go to pieces, lest that one be violated?" Although Judge Hall certainly suffered a loss of dignity, he was very lucky compared to other members of the Maryland judiciary during the Civil War. One circuit judge, Richard Carmichael, "was arrested while conducting court at Easton, and when he refused to submit, was clubbed over the head with a revolver and dragged off the bench."

Jackson had no doubt that "laws must sometimes be silent when necessity speaks." Robert Remini has well described Jackson's argument as one that "can justify monstrous misdeeds as well as noble acts of patriotism." Reliance on "military necessity" has been used to justify Lincoln's suspension of the writ of habeas corpus in 1861, treatment of American soldiers in World War I, and the exclusion of Japanese Americans during World War II, to say nothing of more recent examples during the Vietnam War and its aftermath. The zeal of military commanders to carry out their mission is understandable. On the other hand, the role of the courts in this process is open to criticism. "Too often," according to the *New York University Law Review,* "courts have responded to announcements of military interests with supine deference rather than with a careful assessment of the legitimacy of those claims." This trend has accelerated in recent years.

On March 21, 1815, Judge Hall issued a show cause order for Jackson to appear before him to explain why he should not be held in contempt of court for the Louallier incident. Hall probably was determined to punish Jackson for the outrage perpetrated against this federal judge as much if not more than for the treatment meted out to the unfortunate columnist-legislator. It would seem that in making himself judge, prosecutor, and jury in a matter involving, again, himself, Hall came perilously close to judicial indiscretion if not impropriety. At any rate, in response to the writ, Jackson appeared before the judge on March 24, accompanied by two attorneys and an admiring crowd of sympathetic spectators. According to Remini, one of this number sidled up to Jackson and whispered, "General, say the word and we pitch the judge and the bloody courthouse in the river." Jackson declined the offer and, turning to Judge Hall, who may well have observed the incident with some consternation, intoned, "There is no danger here. . . . the same arm that protected from outrage this city . . . will shield and protect this court, or perish in the attempt." Of course, Hall had already received a personal example of Jackson's "protection."

Jackson's counsel immediately raised a number of legal objections to the entire proceeding. They ranged from the claim that although witnesses against Jackson had been summoned, no actual suit had been commenced—to the assertion that because Hall had not been in court when he issued the writ, none of Jackson's alleged contempts were offered in any cause or hearing *before* the said District Court—to the argument that Jackson's response might well require investigation of Hall's conduct while martial law was in effect, a proceeding over which Hall could not preside "without violating one of the first and clearest maxims of all law."

The judge rejected all these challenges, whereupon Jackson sought to read a lengthy justification and explanation of his actions beginning prior to his imposition of martial law. Hall, convinced at some point that the arguments essentially came down to military necessity alone as justification for Jackson's conduct, refused to hear the complete statement. The general insisted that "necessity then, may in some cases, justify the breach of the Constitution; and if, in the doubtful case of avoiding confusion in a court, shall it be denied in the serious one of preserving a country from conquest and ruin?" As for an apology to the judge, the powers Jackson exercised "have saved the country; and whatever may be the opinion of that country, or the decrees of its courts, in relations to the means he has used, he can never regret that he employed them." The case apparently was put off for one week.

When the case came up again on March 31, the government attorney attributed Jackson's "arbitrary proceedings" not to "his conviction of their necessity," but rather to the "indulged infirmity of an obstinate and morbidly irascible temperament, and to the unyielding pride of a man naturally impatient of the least show of opposition to his will." Again, Hall refused to hear Jackson's defense. Instead he asked the general to respond to nineteen specific interrogatories. Now it was Jackson's turn to refuse. He would not answer because the court "would not hear my defense," and thus Jackson awaited sentence "with nothing further to add." On the other hand, "as no opportunity has been furnished me to explain the reasons and motives which influenced my conduct, so it is expected that censure will form no part of that punishment which your Honor may imagine it your duty to perform."

Hall responded with an equally dignified statement. Jackson's service to the country was obvious; a jail term was inappropriate. But for this judge, described by one contemporary as "a magistrate of pure heart, clean hands, and a mind susceptible of no fear but that of God," the only question was "whether the Law should bend to the General or the General to the Law." For Hall, the answer was never in doubt, the most convincing evidence being his own experience. He found Jackson in contempt and fined him one thousand dollars, a sum that the defendant promptly paid. Moreover, Jackson delivered a mini discourse on civic obedience to the crowd that escorted him from the courtroom: "Considering obedience to the laws, even when we think them unjustly applied, as the first duty of the citizen, I did not hesitate to comply with the sentence you have heard, and I entreat you to remember the example I have given you of respectful submission to the administration of justice."

Why did Jackson pay the fine? He never wavered in his belief that his treatment of Judge Hall was fully justified. Yet it was not in character for him to give in on what he considered an important matter of principle. Remini notes that the conflict had gone on too long, and that Jackson "was not prepared to defy Hall; [and also was] unwilling to blemish his victory with a quarrel he was certain to lose." On the other hand, Jackson may have realized that he was not altogether blameless. After all, it was Jackson who earlier had refused to "render obedience to the laws" upon Hall's issuance of the writ.

Although the federal authorities in Washington took note of the Hall-Jackson incident, neither Madison nor his cabinet, nor—upon reflection—even Jackson himself, had any desire to keep the incident alive. Indeed, during an emotional visit to New Orleans in 1816, the judge and the general crossed paths again. Jackson savored the experience: "When he offered me his hand, I received it and in the gratification of my friends on this occasion my mind receives its reward and tells me I have done right. I have in some measure added peace to his bosom, tranquility to my own and restored him to the social circle of his former friends. . . . On my part the hatchet is buried in oblivion."

Had Jackson retired from the military and resumed his career as a southern planter, his statement might have been accurate. But he went on to provoke further controversy concerning his military conduct in Florida, entered into national politics in 1824, and ultimately served two terms (1828–1836) as one of the most popular presidents thus far in our history. Externally, with the exception of occasional references during political, partisan debate, the incident was buried in oblivion. Internally, it continued to rankle within Jackson's memory. But not until 1842, with the former president retired, in failing health and serious financial difficulties, did Congress review the episode.

In June of that year, Jackson's congressional supporters introduced a bill to remit the fine levied in 1815, plus accrued interest. They framed their proposal as a simple refund of a fine, without getting into the very controversial question concerning whether either Jackson or Hall or both had been justified in their actions. The proposal immediately fell victim to partisan wrangling. In December 1842, President John Tyler urged that the fine be refunded, again without "any reflection on the judicial tribunal which imposed" it. Tyler, one of our less distinguished presidents, in this case at least showed himself to be well aware of the underlying issues concerning civilian authority over the military.

As Tyler wrote, "The voice of the civil authority was heard amidst the glitter of arms, and obeyed by those who held the sword." Conceding that Jackson had certainly not obeyed the initial issuance of the writ, Tyler still insisted that even "if the laws were offended, their majesty was fully vindicated." Concluding that a refund would be "gratifying to the war-worn veteran, now in retirement and in the winter of his days," he added that "if the civil law be violated from praiseworthy motives, or an overruling sense of public danger and public necessity, punishment may well be restrained within that limit which asserts and maintains the . . . subjection of the military to the civil power."

Delayed by continued partisan bickering, the refund was finally approved early in 1844 by decisive votes, 30 to 16 in the Senate, 158 to 28 in the House. The Whigs, typified by John Quincy Adams, whose admiration for Jackson was less than excessive, had persisted in their efforts to make political capital out of the inevitable. Adams urged that Congress not set a precedent of "pensioning off an ex president." Rather, Adams would "make up a subscription among the members of Congress to make a present to the old man in his last days." From his plantation in Tennessee, the old general felt "truly gratified at the vote . . . reversing the fine imposed by that vindictive and corrupt Judge Hall." On February 27, 1844, Jackson received a check from the treasurer of the United States for $2,732.90.

From Jackson's point of view, the episode had a fitting and satisfying conclusion. Besides claiming long delayed vindication for his action in 1815, there was a matter of money. In terms of financial renumeration, he got back more than double what he had paid to the court almost thirty years before. From the vantage point of hindsight in the area of American civilian-military policy, however, the results are less satisfying.

In the first place, the real issue—was Jackson justified in detaining Judge Hall and disobeying the writ—received no definitive resolution. To be sure, Hall himself must bear much responsibility for this fact. He refused to hear Jackson's explanation; a step difficult to justify if only because hearing the statement would in no way have limited his future course of action from the bench. On the other hand, his conduct indicated that he never assumed that Jackson could be immune from a federal writ or that a citizen could be denied due process by a general any more than by another government official. Jackson declined to appeal the decision, thus depriving a federal appellate tribunal of a great opportunity to explore this important question. Moreover, the ever present involvement of partisan interests in policy issues meant that the ultimate solution, remitting the fine with no mention of justification or assessment of responsibility, would be a political resolution in the context of Jacksonian politics.

Thus, it can be said that Jackson imprisoned a judge, defied a writ, and many years later was rewarded for it. Lincoln, who seems to have been much more sensitive to the nuances of military authority than Jackson, nevertheless followed his lead in 1861, when he ignored a writ issued by Chief Justice Roger B. Taney. While there is no way of assessing whether or not Jackson's actions had any specific effect on other judges, there is no doubt that in future cases involving questions of civilian-military jurisdiction, for the most part the bench was very careful not to contribute to a remake of this very unusual case.

2

Military and Civilian "Review" to 1900

By the mid–nineteenth century, American military justice had become a routinized procedure, thus far at least separate from its civilian counterpart. This separation, however, was not a result of any articulated congressional intention or of any statute. Rather, it was due to the exigencies and logic of the military environment. The Articles of War provided for a self-contained system. But they were less than clear on the extent of civilian review in general and civilian judicial review in particular, and there was *no* provision for any sort of appellate procedure.

Nor does much public attention seem to have been paid to these issues. Indeed, prior to the era of the Civil War, only two incidents involving military justice appear to have provoked any great public interest. The Jackson-Hall episode has already been discussed, and echoes of it were heard during the Civil War. The other occurrence, the execution of Philip Spencer in December 1842, caused a sustained public debate concerning military justice within the United States Navy. Moreover, it led to at least one proposal for creation of an appellate tribunal to review important cases within the armed services.

The court-martial and execution at sea of three crew members on board the U.S. Navy brig *Somers* might never have come to public attention at all had it not been for the fact that one of the accused, Philip Spencer, happened to be the son of the secretary of war. When the *Somers* arrived in New York fifteen days after the executions, Captain Alexander S. Mackenzie reported concerning Spencer's fate. Outraged, Spencer urged the navy to convene a court of inquiry. This proceeding concluded that Mackenzie had not acted improperly. In an effort to quiet the resulting controversy, Captain Mackenzie requested that a court-martial be held. Conducted on board a ship in New York Harbor from February to April 1843, this trial also resulted in an acquittal.

Officially, the verdict ended the incident. Yet, during 1843–1844, the

13

episode received wide publicity, and there had been extensive commentary both private and public, especially from writers, as the proceedings took place. Like many such observers, James Fenimore Cooper's initial reaction upon hearing that Mackenzie had put down a threatened mutiny by swift execution of the "culprits" was favorable. But after reading Mackenzie's lengthy report, the first account of what supposedly took place, and studying the statements of the witnesses, his view changed.

In 1843, Cooper's favorable reputation as a writer of Native American fiction was widespread, especially in Europe. In his own country, however, Cooper's criticism of contemporary American society had resulted in a lengthy and bitter feud with leading Whig editors and politicians. The son of a judge, he did not hesitate to sue his many critics for libel, and he seems to have won most if not all of his numerous court battles. One critic, for example, called the creator of Natty Bumpo "a base minded caitiff who has traduced his country for filthy lucre," a "slanderer [and] a traitor to national pride," the "viper so long nourished in our bosom." The *Somers* incident furnished another opportunity for the type of bitter public feud that Cooper apparently relished. Much of what he contributed to the debate focused on proper legal procedure within the navy, hence its relevance here.

SPENCER AND SCANDAL ON THE *SOMERS*

Never before in American naval history had a captain returned from a voyage with the news that he had executed three members of his crew, and this for a mutiny that never occurred. An early article published on December 20, 1842, and signed only with the letter "S" focused on certain disturbing elements of the case as revealed by Mackenzie himself. The writer noted that the three crew members were arrested on a charge of intended mutiny. In fact, no actual occurrence of a mutinous nature appeared to have taken place during the entire voyage. Nevertheless, Captain Mackenzie convened a court of officers, who in turn recommended that the three be executed. At no time did the court hear from the accused; the prisoners were not allowed to confront any witnesses or "to procure any testimony in their own behalf," or, indeed, were they even informed that a "trial" was in progress. The writer emphasized that "the laws of Congress prescribing the navy regulations, forbid the taking of human life, even by the sentence of a court martial, before which all parties are heard, without the sanction of the president . . . or, if without the United States, of the commander of the fleet or squadron."

Distinguished legal scholars such as Supreme Court Justice Joseph Story were quick to support Mackenzie. As the Court of Inquiry proceeded, Story's young assistant, Charles Sumner—later to succeed Daniel Webster as a member of the United States Senate—wrote that Story "had not the least doubt that

Mackenzie was justified in the alternative he took. . . . The law does not compel a person to stand still till he actually sees the blow descending which is to take his life. He may anticipate it; and the justification will be found in the circumstances which created a reasonable ground of fear for his life." Story probably based his conclusions on Mackenzie's account of the episode, a widely reprinted document written after the fact, full of self-justification and pious self-rightcousness. Cooper, writing to his wife one day after Sumner's comments about Story, dismissed Mackenzie's report as a "medley of folly, conceit, illegality, feebleness and fanaticism."

The Court of Inquiry lasted one month, concluding on January 28, 1843. It became clear that, fearing some sort of mutiny, Mackenzie had determined to hang the three prisoners as an example to the rest of the crew. Only *after* he had so decided did he convene a council of officers, all of whom were younger than he and obviously subject to his command. Moreover, whatever Spencer had conjured up in his mind, if anything at all, never reached actuality. Somehow, according to the *New York Herald,* Spencer's love of secret ritual and his list of various crew members written in Greek all combined to presage what Mackenzie saw as a mutiny. "It is probably the greatest farce, ending in an awful tragedy, that ever was enacted since the creation."

But Mackenzie appeared to be guilty of far more than an urge to execute three sailors as quickly as possible. The "trial" was held in secret, with none of the defendants present at any time. This meant that any direct testimony from the people with the most to lose or the exercise of other essential due process procedures was impossible. Moreover, when the officers reported that they were unable to reach a verdict, the captain made it clear that he wished the accused to be convicted and sentenced to death. Thus, the convening authority, the only practical source for any sort of trial review, and the perpetrator for the worst sort of "command influence" were all one and the same individual. On February 24, the *New York Herald* concluded that, far from demonstrating a mutiny, the *Somers* incident "discloses a tissue of barbarity, insolence, cowardice, farce and folly, that seems unparalleled in the history of human nature."

The role of the navy in its conduct of the two proceedings was also improper. In the first place, during both the Court of Inquiry and the court-martial, it permitted Mackenzie to remain in command of his crew. Thus, all witnesses to the events on board—including, of course, all those who were to testify—were under his control. Moreover, while Mackenzie was given the right to cross-examine every witness, he chose not to testify himself, thus escaping the burden of cross-examination. Instead, according to Frederic F. Van de Water, the navy permitted him "to present written explanations of the points raised by the timid, fusty little prosecutor." A quiet acquittal "became inevitable." The entire episode, depending on one's viewpoint, demonstrated the best and the worst of the military justice system. It had provided Mackenzie, on board a small ship at sea, with a swift but flexible method of discipline. On the other hand, the treatment accorded the three accused was disgraceful, as was the apparent inability of the navy to find anything improper with Mackenzie's conduct.

Cooper avoided public commentary until after the court-martial adjourned, but in private, he expressed outrage at the proceedings. Mackenzie, he fumed to one correspondent, "reverses the maxim of the Common Law, which says that if there be a doubt of guilt, the prisoner is to have its benefits; he reasons, if there be a doubt of his innocence, hang him." Moreover, where was the supposed threat of mutiny? Not from the crew who indeed "were so obedient as to hang men contrary to law." Cooper believed that "it is a stain on the American character that a transaction of this nature should be treated as this has been. Three lives were taken without legal process in any form, or manner." Anything, he insisted, was "better than hanging men without trial."

By December 1843, Cooper had finished reviewing the entire transcripts of the case. With his discovery that Mackenzie had first decided to execute the prisoners and had then convened a council, Cooper concluded that "a serious mutiny now became necessary to escape ridicule." Nothing, he wrote, "is plainer to me than the fact that the testimony was got up as it was wanted." In 1844, his eighty-page analysis of the entire case appeared as part of the published transcript.

Cooper's motives for agreeing to write the lengthy analysis are unclear. Perhaps he felt a sympathy for Spencer, whose background was in some instances similar to his own. Like Spencer, Cooper had been forced to leave college; like him also, he had gone to sea, and like him he too possessed an active imagination. On the other hand, Cooper had definite views on the role of law and governmental power in Jacksonian America. It may well have seemed to him that the *Somers* affair was a dramatic abuse of both. Whatever the motivation, the final result was impressive, and it was accurately described by Cooper's biographer as "a masterpiece of quiet sanity."

Cooper believed that Mackenzie's conduct, and that of the navy in refusing to punish him, represented a serious challenge to the American legal system: "Here is an officer . . . who has used his authority . . . to take the lives of three of his subordinates without a trial—by his own account of the matter, without a hearing—without any overt act of mutiny, violence, or resistance even in the gasp of death." If "the name of an American citizen cannot be a warranty that life will not be taken without the accusation, hearing and condemnation, required by the law, of what use are our boasted rights?" If an American, in this case a member of the crew, "is not assured of this privilege on board an American ship-of-war, which exists only to defend those sacred rights on the ocean, where can he be assured of its exercise at all?" As for the council of junior officers convened by the captain *after* he had decided upon executions, "were it not for the fearful consequences, they could meet with nothing but pity and contempt from every legal mind on earth."

Cooper was also outraged by the fact that Mackenzie had not conceived of any alternatives to immediate execution, even though a number of options were readily available. These ranged from keeping the three prisoners in irons until the return to the United States to stopping at a nearby port and requesting assistance. For Cooper, the incident reflected more upon the weaknesses in command leadership than on mutinous elements within the crew. Cooper also had some trenchant comments on the relationship between discipline and military justice. "Discipline," he wrote, "is the result of the authority exercised, in the name of the state, by the few over the many. Its entire virtue exists in its legality, without which it can have no salutary or permanent existence. . . . The essence of all discipline in this country, is strict legality." In short, military discipline and military justice were two sides of the same coin; if the latter was flawed, so too would be the former—to the extent of the imperfection.

Cooper found no justification for Mackenzie's flagrant abuse of due process. If there was such an urgent need for action, why did he permit seven officers to deliberate all day instead of remaining at their stations? Furthermore, Mackenzie had an obligation to "ascertain not the guilt merely, but the guilt or innocence of the men executed. This . . . could not be done, without giving the party implicated a hearing. In our view of the matter, the violation of justice connected with a departure from this sacred principle, is of more importance to the country, than the preservation of a dozen brigs."

Cooper hoped that "one good effect, at least, will result from this affair. The trial of cases like this, should at once be put exclusively, except in those beyond the reach of the tribunals, into the hands of the civil courts." Military men, he added, "are not qualified, as a rule, for such investigation. . . . The result of this very case shows how professional men can differ, leaving the strong probability that professional prejudices had more to do with some of their votes, than professional knowledge."

Finally, Cooper noted Mackenzie's insistence that he sought merely to save the ship, his own life, and those of his associates. Perhaps, "but the mental obliquity, so very obvious throughout the whole affair, renders any ordinary analysis of human motives exceedingly precarious. God alone can say how far any selfish feeling was mixed up with the mistakes of this terrible transaction. The act was, unquestionably, one of high moral courage, one of the basest cowardice, one of deep guilt, or one of lamentable deficiency of judgment."

There seemed to be four essential conclusions to Cooper's exhaustive critique: that civil tribunals were more knowledgeable and, hence, preferable to military courts; that in certain military cases (Cooper did not define the criteria but clearly felt this case to be appropriate), there should be a role for a civil court; that the command influence exercised by Mackenzie violated fundamental law; and that navy officials were culpable for not acting responsibly in the subsequent proceedings. Thus Cooper saw no incompatibility between civilian appellate review for military justice. He also believed that the better the quality of military justice, the better would be the quality of the soldiers and sailors subject to it.

MILITARY JUSTICE, 1858–1864

In theory, of course, executive and legislative branches of our government control the military establishment. Civilian control was a well-established and accepted doctrine by the mid–nineteenth century. But did it apply to civilian legal review of military justice decisions? To put it another way, did a civil appellate court have jurisdiction over military courts? This issue seems not to have been formally litigated until 1858. While there appeared to be no reason to doubt that in theory federal courts, and the United States Supreme Court in particular, could exercise such authority, the Constitution was silent on the question, and Congress, beyond its adoption of the Articles of War and the Act to Govern the Navy, had not clarified the issue. Moreover, while the special mission of the military pointed toward an independent system of military justice, incidents such as the *Somers* case made it clear that some sort of appellate review was necessary.

In 1858, the U.S. Supreme Court decided the case of *Dynes v. Hoover* (20 How. 65). It may well have been the first case before the Court that involved an actual member of the armed forces as opposed to a civilian in trouble with military authorities. As such, it offered the justices a good opportunity to clarify the parameters of military and civilian judicial jurisdiction.

In 1854, the Plaintiff was charged with desertion from the navy. A court-martial found him guilty of "attempting to desert" instead of the original charge. Sentenced to imprisonment, he filed suit on the grounds that the navy court-martial had no jurisdiction to try him for this offense. His counsel argued that the guilty verdict was for an offense for which Dynes had not been originally charged. Furthermore, the rules to govern the navy did not list "attempting to desert" as "an offense within the cognizance of a naval court martial." Since the court was without authority, the resulting verdict and sentence were null and void.

On behalf of the government, Attorney General Caleb Cushing conceded that "attempting to desert" was not included among the specific offenses forbidden by the statute. But the point was irrelevant. Section 32 provided that "all crimes committed by persons belonging to the navy which are not specified in the foregoing articles, shall be punished according to the laws and customs in such cases at sea." Without any citation of legal authority, Cushing insisted that the decisions of a court-martial, when within its jurisdiction—as was clearly the case here—could not be reviewed by the Supreme Court.

The U.S. Supreme Court heard the case on January 8, 1858, and handed down its decision on February 1. By a vote of 8 to 1, with no formal dissent submitted, the justices upheld contentions put forward by the federal government. Justice James Wayne readily conceded that lack of jurisdiction voided a court's action, including a military court. But in this case, there was no evidence that the navy had not followed proper procedure; moreover, the verdict had been confirmed by the secretary of the navy. Thus, there could be no doubt here about appropriate jurisdiction. A court-martial verdict "when confirmed . . . is altogether beyond the jurisdiction or inquiry of any civil tribunal whatever."

Hence, "with the sentences of courts-martial which have been convened regularly, and have proceeded legally, and by which punishments are directed, not forbidden by law, or which are according to the laws and customs of the sea, civil courts have nothing to do, nor are they in any way alterable by them." Wayne was equally emphatic as to the vague language of article 32: "Not withstanding the apparent indeterminateness of such a provision, it is not liable to abuse; for what those crimes are, and how they are to be punished, is well known by practical men in the navy and army, and by those who have studied the law of courts-martial." To a modern day observer, this statement verges on the preposterous. Indeed, there can be little doubt that even in 1858 the justices were well aware that abuses of discretionary authority by military officials did occur. How then can Wayne's statement—of both fact and law—that "it is not liable to abuse" be explained?

In part the answer may lie in the fact that pre–Civil War jurisprudence took a much narrower view of "due process" than would be true today, especially for the military. Also, historical practice, as previous discussion has indicated, resulted in a military justice system isolated from civil influence. Whether this was intentional or not, and there is virtually no evidence that it was, becomes irrelevant. To find for the plaintiff in this case would make the civil courts "virtually administer the Rules and Articles of War, irrespective of those to whom that duty and obligation has been confided by the laws of the United States, from whose decisions no appeal or jurisdiction of any kind has been given to the civil magistrate or civil courts."

The decision was almost unanimous, and the view that his brethren readily accepted Wayne's conclusions is strengthened by the fact that the Court handed down its opinion less than a month after oral argument. One can accept the claim that in adopting statutes such as the Articles of War, Congress intended to create a military justice system apart from civil interaction. But it by no means follows from this premise that there was to be absolutely no civilian appellate review of any sort within the military. Nevertheless, *Dynes v. Hoover* remains a landmark holding in American military jurisprudence.

The decision appeared to bar any civilian judicial intervention in a court-martial involving a member of the armed forces. But what if the accused was a civilian who had no military connection whatsoever? This question arose five years later in 1863. Involving action by President Lincoln as well as an appeal to the Supreme Court, the case of *Ex Parte Vallandigham* (1 Wall. 243) is an apt illustration of the American tendency for constitutional law sometimes to reflect an intriguing amalgam of principles and expediency.

The case began in May 1863 when Clement Vallandigham, an Ohio anti-war politician and former congressman running for the Democratic gubernatorial nomination, spoke at a political rally. He declared among other things that the war "was wicked, cruel, and unnecessary," that it was being fought for the "freedom of the blacks and the enslavement of the whites" for the "purpose of crushing out liberty and to erect a despotism." Promptly arrested by army authorities upon the order of General Ambrose Burnside, Vallandigham was tried, convicted, and sentenced to prison by a military commission. Very concerned about the effect that the case might have at a critical point in the war and assuming that Vallandigham's next move would be to seek intervention in federal court, Lincoln seriously considered issuing a special suspension of habeas corpus. However, after receiving assurances from Salmon Chase, his secretary of the treasury who also was extremely well versed in Ohio politics, that Vallandigham's efforts to seek a writ of habeas corpus would probably fail, as indeed they did, Lincoln took a different course. He ordered that instead of being imprisoned for the remainder of the war, as had been the sentence of the military commission, Vallandigham should be transported behind enemy lines and released from custody.

The case aroused much interest in the North, especially among conservative Democrats who supported the Union but not the inevitable expansion of federal authority engendered by the war effort. Thus, on May 16, a group of Albany Democrats led by a local manufacturer, Erastus Corning, forwarded a number of resolutions to Lincoln. They denounced "the recent assumption of a military commander to seize and try a citizen of Ohio . . . for no other reason than words addressed to a public meeting, in criticism of the course of the Administration." The signers expected Lincoln "to be true to the Constitution, and [to] maintain the rights of the States and the liberties of the Union." Lincoln assured the group that he would "give the resolutions the consideration you ask."

In the meantime, possibly with unintentional understatement, Burnside telegraphed Lincoln that he had heard that "my action here has been a source of embarrassment to you," and that it "was not approved by a single member of your Cabinet." Lincoln, possibly with intentional understatement, responded .that "all the cabinet regretted the necessity for arresting, for instance, Vallandigham, some perhaps, doubting, that there was a real necessity for it—but being done, all were for seeing you through with it."

On June 12, Lincoln replied to the Corning resolutions. He reminded the Albany malcontents that Vallandigham had been trying "to prevent the raising of troops, to encourage desertions from the army, and to leave the rebellion [Union] without an adequate military force to suppress it." Well aware of the realities of war, he insisted that the prisoner had been arrested not for "damaging the political prospects" of Lincoln's administration, but "because he was damaging the army, upon the existence, and vigor of which, the life of the nation depends. He was warring upon the military; and this gave the military jurisdiction to lay hands upon him." Long experience, he added, has shown that "armies cannot be maintained unless desertion shall be punished by the severe penalty of death. . . . Must I shoot a simple-minded soldier boy who deserts, while I must not touch a hair of a wily agitator who induces him to desert?"

Lincoln then summarized the Jackson-Hall controversy of 1815. He noted, "first, that we had the same constitution then, as now. Secondly, that we then had a case of invasion, and that now we have a case of rebellion, and thirdly, that the permanent right of the people to public discussion, the liberty of speech and the press, the trial by jury, the law of evidence, and the habeas corpus, suffered no detriment whatever by that conduct of Gen. Jackson." Lincoln added that quite possibly he might not have arrested Vallandigham, but that as a general rule, "the commander in the field is the better judge of the necessity in any particular case. Of course I must practice a general directory and revisory power in the matter." (Indeed, Lincoln reviewed more military justice cases than any of his predecessors.) As to this prisoner, "I have to say it gave me pain when I learned that [he] had been arrested,—that is, I was pained that there should have seemed to be a necessity for arresting him."

Although he had been placed behind enemy lines in accord with Lincoln's instructions, and although the Ohio federal district court denied him relief, Vallandigham sought a writ of certiorari from the U.S. Supreme Court as the first step toward his real goal, the writ of habeas corpus. He was represented by the same attorney who had unsuccessfully argued Dynes's case in 1858. There were, however, two important differences between the earlier litigation and Vallandigham's suit. First, he was a civilian with no connection to the military, and second, he had been tried not by court-martial but rather by military commission.

The military commission was a quasi-judicial military tribunal that differed from a court-martial in that it could deal with civilians accused of criminal acts in time of war. A court-martial, on the other hand, was restricted to dealing with members of the military "and to specific offenses defined in a written code," such as the Articles of War. Both, however, were composed solely of military officers. It was not clear in 1864 to what extent, if at all, a military commission had jurisdiction over a civilian, especially in the absence of a declaration of martial law. Vallandigham's case thus offered the Court a good opportunity to clarify an extremely important issue in civilian-military jurisprudence.

It would have been reasonable for the Court to make allowance for the commission's conduct, pointing to the claim that survival of the national government was at stake, and to the fact that the incident took place during the bloodiest war thus far fought in American history. Or the justices could have attempted some sort of balancing test, trying as Lincoln often did to reconcile the needs of the war with individual liberty. Instead, Justice Wayne reiterated essentially what he had rationalized in *Dynes,* this time for a unanimous bench.

He concluded that a military commission was *not* in fact a court; therefore, it was not one of those inferior tribunals over which the Constitution gave the Supreme Court appellate review. Thus, no writ could issue because the Court had no jurisdiction over a military commission. Wayne even admitted that a military commission was exactly like a court in that it had a "discretion to examine, to decide and sentence." Nonetheless, it exercised a "special authority" not reviewable by civilian courts.

It is possible to view the Vallandigham case as more an exercise in judicial avoidance than sound jurisprudence. Yet, one can understand why the Supreme Court would choose not to confront the United States Army in 1864 over treatment of a notorious Ohio malcontent, all the more as Lincoln had already taken final action in the case. On the other hand, by using lack of jurisdiction as the basis for his decision, Wayne avoided the much more difficult question of a military commission's applicability to a civilian accused of a nonmilitary offense. He also reinforced a key assumption of *Dynes*—that military tribunals were totally separate from civil courts. Still, the underlying issues raised in the case may well have troubled lawyers in a society where the military had never been dominant. Two years after *Vallandigham,* the Court decided a similar dispute, this time with what appeared to be very different results.

MURDER AND *MILLIGAN,* 1865–1866

Law, and thus legal history, tends to be a responsive rather than an innovative mechanism. It normally reacts to external forces and stimuli such as legislation or public opinion. The famous maxim that "the Supreme Court follows the election returns" may not be phrased in elegant, scholarly prose, yet it remains accurate. The 1866 decision about military commissions can be considered as an excellent example of its validity. From April to August 1865, there seems to have been a good deal of public comment on military commissions and authority over civilians. The cause for such interest was the treatment given the eight individuals accused of conspiracy in the assassination of Abraham Lincoln.

In mid-April 1865, the civil courts in Washington were open and functioning; there could be no doubt that, for the Southeast, the war had ended. Moreover, newspaper commentary reflected a basic mistrust of military commissions. They tended, as one writer put it, to be composed "of officers too worthless for field service, ordered to try, and organized to convict." Navy Secretary Gideon Welles believed that Attorney General James Speed had originally favored a civilian trial for the eight prisoners, but that Secretary of War Edwin Stanton had "persuaded" him otherwise. Welles also strongly objected to a secret trial, and indeed, after only a few days of closed sessions, public pressure ultimately forced the authorities to make the proceedings public.

What legal advice Speed offered Johnson was not made public until *after* the proceedings were over and four of the accused had been executed. The trial of the "conspirators" was controversial at best. In one instance, the commission accepted testimony from a witness whom the prosecutors knew had perjured himself. Moreover, the defendants were not allowed to testify in their own defense, and while this was still common policy in state civilian criminal cases, it was not usual practice in courts-martial. Most important for this book, however, was the argument presented by defense counsel Reverdy Johnson against the jurisdiction of a military commission.

Johnson took it for granted that the Constitution empowered only Congress to enact rules for governing the armed forces. He cited no less an authority than the late Supreme Court Justice Joseph Story, who had written that "since otherwise, summary and severe punishments might be inflicted as the mere will of the Executive." Furthermore, "citizens not belonging to the army or navy were not made liable to military law, or under any circumstances to be deprived of any of the guaranties of personal liberty provided by the Constitution." Since there was no proof at all that any of the accused were members of the armed forces, he questioned the authority of military commissions to try civilians. Finally, he denied that martial law provided any justification for such a trial. This condition, he argued, was not in effect in Washington. "It has never been declared by any *competent* authority, and the civil courts we know are in the full and undisturbed exercise of all their functions."

Johnson's argument was submitted to the commission in June 1865, after the prosecution had concluded its case. A lawyer for Dr. Samuel Mudd, the physician who had tended to Booth's broken ankle, also argued against military jurisdiction. Thomas Ewing Jr. reiterated many of Johnson's points. And with some courage, given the atmosphere surrounding the trial, he urged that the commission be cautious: "If you believe you possess the power of life and death over the citizens of the United States . . . where the regular tribunals can be safely appealed to, still, for the sake of our common country . . . do not press that power too far. Our judicial tribunals, at some future date . . . will be again in the full exercise of their constituted powers, and may think, as a large proportion of the legal profession think now, that your jurisdiction in these cases is an ununwarranted assumption." Despite the efforts of Johnson and Ewing, the commission found all the accused guilty and sentenced four of them— including Mary Surratt—to be executed. The sentences were carried out on July 7, 1865.

There is no way of knowing to what extent, if any, the arguments of Johnson and Ewing influenced public opinion. They were published after the case was over—although the issue of a military trial was widely debated in the newspapers all during the course of the trial itself. In the meantime, however, the case of another civilian involving a trial by military commission was pending before the U.S. Supreme Court.

The case of Lambdin B. Milligan was almost a carbon copy of *Vallandigham* in two areas. Milligan was also militantly antiwar and anti-Lincoln. A civilian resident of Indiana, he had been arrested, tried, convicted, and sentenced by a military commission. At this point, however, the similarity ended. Unlike Vallandigham, the commission had sentenced Milligan to death. Without actually approving the sentence, Lincoln had ordered the record returned for certain "errors." But before this could be done, he was murdered. President Andrew Johnson approved the death sentence and, indeed, even set a date for execution, May 19, 1865, whereupon Milligan's lawyers sought intervention from the federal circuit court, sitting in Indianapolis.

Before the Court took up the case, an unusual development occurred. The two judges presiding over the circuit, one of whom was a Lincoln appointment to the Supreme Court (David Davis), addressed a confidential letter to President Johnson. They urged that the execution be put off. Milligan had been sentenced by "a new tribunal unknown to the Common Law." Many lawyers "doubt its jurisdiction over citizens unconnected with the military." The judges declined to express their opinion on this point but added that "it is not clear of difficulty." If Milligan was executed, and the courts should then "deny the jurisdiction under which [he] was tried, the government would be justly chargeable with lawless oppression." Indeed, "a stain on the national character would be the consequence."

Five days later, Johnson commuted Milligan's sentence to life imprisonment at hard labor. But this action did not address the underlying issue raised by the judges—that the question of lawful jurisdiction be resolved *before* a sentence was executed. The case thus went forward in the circuit court. The two judges disagreed on the issues of federal jurisdiction concerning an appeal from a military commission as well as the authority of the military commission in general over civilians. It was because of this resulting split that they referred the case to the Supreme Court.

Counsel for Milligan repeated many of the arguments that Vallandigham had raised in vain. Also, there could be no doubt that civilian courts were opening and functioning in Indiana. Indeed, he noted that they had never ceased to function. Indiana had not been an active theater of war since the conflict had begun. Given Milligan's notoriety as a "gadfly" irritant to the Union cause, his lawyers refused to discuss his guilt or innocence. Instead, they focused primarily on the "competency of the tribunal by which he was judged" (*Ex Parte Milligan,* 4 Wall. 2 [1886]). Not only did they insist that Milligan's trial had been illegal, but they also denied the power of either the president or Congress to establish military commissions for civilian trials under *any* conditions.

Although the Court heard and decided the case in March–April 1886, the formal opinions were not filed until December. The justices agreed unanimously that the particular commission involved in this case had exceeded its authority. Its abuse of power was all the more flagrant because civil courts and grand juries had been functioning undisturbed throughout the state during the entire war. But to find that one military commission had acted ultra vires in a specific instance was far from saying that under *no* conditions could Congress establish such tribunals with authority over civilians. This contention carried by a bare majority, with the justices split 5 to 4.

David Davis, whose disagreement with his circuit colleague had sent the case to Washington in the first place, spoke for the majority. Early in his opinion, he hinted at the reason for the lengthy delay between decision and delivery. "During the late wicked Rebellion," Davis wrote, "the temper of the times did not allow that calmness in deliberation and discussion so necessary to a correct conclusion to a purely judicial question." Now that "public safety is assured, this question . . . can be discussed and decided without passion or the admixture of any element not required to form a legal judgment." In other words, with the end of hostilities, there was enough judicial confidence in military obedience to the Court's mandate to justify a ruling contrary to the military viewpoint.

Davis denied that a military commission using the "rules of war" could ever try a civilian where civil courts were in operation and governmental control unchallenged, as was the case in Indiana: "No usage of war could sanction a military trial there for any offense whatever of a citizen in civil life, in nowise connected with the military service." Neither the president nor Congress could authorize such a tribunal under these conditions. Certainly the appropriate authorities could indeed proclaim martial law, but not from "a threatened invasion. The necessity must be actual and present; the invasion real, such as effectively closes the courts and deposes the civil administration." Obviously none of these conditions applied in this case, nor presumably to the earlier litigation involving Vallandigham. Martial rule, concluded Davis, "can never exist where the courts are open, and in the proper and unobstructed exercise of their jurisdiction."

The *Milligan* case has been regarded as a landmark decision that protects a basic civil right of the American people. It should, however, be understood in its context. The decision did not ban imposition of martial law. Moreover, it appeared to apply only to states where civil courts and public administration were in full operation. The finding made no definitive pronouncement, in other words, about the federal government's military authority within the defeated southern states. Also, the case concerned a civilian. By emphasizing this fact, as he repeatedly did, Davis reiterated the point made in earlier cases: that military commanders when dealing with *military* personnel were beyond the reach of civil federal courts. Hence, as far as the control of military jurisdiction over the armed forces by civilian courts was concerned, the *Milligan* case established nothing.

Yet in one area, the case has real significance for this book. It indicated that when the Supreme Court wished to do so, it could and would intervene in a matter concerning military justice. To be sure, a trial by military commission was *not* a court-martial. Logically, however, all the self-imposed restraints against intervention in the latter should apply in the former, as appeared to be true in the *Vallandigham* case. Thus, *Milligan* can be interpreted as a message that institutional and political military constraints are not necessarily permanent bars to civilian judicial supervision over a military justice proceeding.

END OF AN ERA

Other than occasional commentary concerning the *Milligan* decision, military justice was not an issue of prime concern in the late nineteenth century. In 1889, however, James Fry, a retired army colonel, published a book of assorted essays accurately called *Military Miscellanies*. One of them dealt with a topic central to this book, a proposed establishment of a military court of appeals. Written during the transformation of American legal education, amid growing acceptance of European ideas concerning research and scholarship, Fry based his essay on the idea that "the science of military law is progressive" as is "the science of civil law in a greater degree." Progress in the civil field, "in principles or modes of procedure which are essential to the ascertainment of truth," cannot "be at variance with the objects of the military code, and they ought to be applied to it."

Fry then stated, correctly, that "all available means of ascertaining truth are not invariably resorted to by Courts-martial." Since Congress and the president were the only sources of appeal in such cases, the result was that many "cases are reopened which were supposed to be closed, and are retried by tribunals without legal power and without judicial modes of procedure." He argued that such practices resulted from too great an emphasis on prompt punishment. Less promptness and more "unquestionable judicial proceedings" were necessary. It has been held by high authority, Fry added, "that the findings of Courts-martial are final. The sounder view, it seems to me, is that they are final only in the sense that there is no appointed tribunal to which it is expressly provided an appeal can be taken."

Would it not be well "for the law to transfer the confirming power to a Supreme Court-martial, and leave the President to exercise, in these cases, merely the *constitutional pardoning power*?" It is true, he stated, "that the power of Congress and the President's pardoning power would exist with a Military Court of Appeal, just as they do without it, but the temptation and opportunity to exercise these powers would be materially reduced." After all, neither the president nor Congress "can proceed judicially in ascertaining the truth." Fry concluded his essay with the comment that under present conditions, Congress and the president "merely grope for justice, which such a tribunal as that under consideration might make so clear as to prevent their interference, or at least so probable as to give them good grounds for declining to interfere."

One suspects after a close examination of Fry's essay that he was less concerned about the quality of military justice than with the opportunities for civilian interference by Congress or the president. It should be emphasized that his solution was a military court of appeals, *not* a court of military appeals. This distinction is extremely important because a military court of appeals would be *within* the military justice system, whereas a court of military appeals would be outside and hence presumably more independent in its judgments. Given this bias, Fry still found it necessary to remind his readers that "it is the purpose of this paper merely to present a subject for consideration—not to advocate it."

As the late nineteenth century came and went, there were no innovations or even important changes in the exercise of American military justice. A military society tends to be conservative, and a small peacetime army with very limited federal funding probably more so. If there was to be a dramatic shift in its judicial procedures, it could only come if some major military conflict threatened to bring to public attention the peculiar nuances of the military justice system. In the late nineteenth century, this did not happen. What followed after 1900, however, was a very different matter.

3

The Ansell-Crowder Controversy, 1917–1918: Round I

Like so much of American society, the military justice system was unprepared for the rapid expansion of our armed forces between 1917 and 1918. With nostalgia if not total accuracy, William Rigby—a member of the Judge Advocate General (JAG) Corps—wrote after the war that in 1912, "the country was, and for many years had been, in the enjoyment of profound peace. The army was small and compact, and for the most part removed from centers of population. There was but little public interest, either in the army itself or in military affairs." American entry into the European theaters of war permanently altered this perception. In April 1917, the JAG Corps consisted of 17 officers; by December 1918, its commissioned strength had reached 426 officers. Again, Rigby recalled the "strain" caused by "the sudden multiplication of the army and the inclusion of tens of thousands of new officers, unschooled in Army traditions, unacquainted with each other and the men under them, and unaccustomed to command."

> These new officers, not sitting easily in the saddle, and feeling unsure of themselves (1) are prone as commanding officers to resort too readily to courts-martial, and (2) as court martial judges they display ignorance of military law and traditions, uncertainty of themselves, undue fear of showing leniency lest they be thought weak or unmilitary, and a tendency to avoid responsibility by giving severe . . . sentences, accompanied with recommendations to clemency, attempting thereby to shoulder onto higher authority the responsibility for determining the proper quantum of punishment; a responsibility which our system contemplates shall be assumed and discharged by the court martial judges themselves.

Here, Rigby accurately described the context in which arose a conflict between the judge advocate general and his senior assistant. Beginning in 1917 originally as an internal matter, by 1919 it had expanded into an issue of national interest, a controversy replete with political overtones, extensive newspaper coverage, and lengthy congressional hearings. Before its reverberations had ceased, one participant, Samuel Ansell, had been forced to resign from the JAG Corps and had become the bitter enemy of the judge advocate general himself, Enoch Crowder, a man who originally had taken much pride in Ansell's earlier successes as his chief subordinate. Personality conflicts, claims of integrity, counterclaims of disloyalty, and lasting enmity all beclouded the original dispute. But in 1917, there was no doubt whatsoever about the basic disagreement between Ansell and Crowder. It involved nothing less than the nature of military justice and the role of the JAG Corps in its administration.

ANSELL AND CROWDER PRIOR TO 1917

Enoch H. Crowder served as judge advocate general of the army from 1911 to 1923. A career officer, he graduated from West Point in 1881, studied law, and gained admission to the Texas bar in 1884. He also served as a professor of military science at the University of Missouri, where he had received a law degree in 1886. Crowder participated in the final Indian campaigns and by 1891 had been transferred to the JAG Corps. In 1901, he became deputy judge advocate general and a decade later received appointment as *the* judge advocate general (TJAG) from President William Howard Taft. As TJAG, Crowder labored for four years to revise the Articles of War; in 1916 Congress finally approved his revisions. Crowder's version provided for the establishment of a third level of court-martial, the "special," located in terms of authority between the summary and the general. It did not, however, make any substantial changes in court-martial procedure and offered nothing in the nature of an appellate process applicable to military justice.

From his letters, Crowder appears to have been a somewhat self-righteous and colorless individual, although he does seem to have had a sense of humor, at least at the unconscious level. In 1918, he wrote to former president William Howard Taft concerning numerous requests from lawyers—often with physical disabilities—for assignment to the JAG Corps: "If I do not stop in my tracks, I shall be commanding a Corps of invalids and will have to bring into the department a Corps of trained nurses to take care of my commissioned officers. Every one-armed, one-eyed lawyer and, of course, all the tuberculars, want to serve in my department." Crowder added that one general had even succeeded in getting a position for his cousin, "who appears on the firing line with an ear trumpet." Indeed, "if the Field Headquarters should mobilize, there would have to be a squad to take care of an immobile Judge Advocate Corps."

But Crowder's letters to Taft, his benefactor and political confidant, also reflect a deep-seated bitterness about his stature within the military. He very much desired to cap his career with a line field command, something Taft had assumed would be offered Crowder if only because of his very able administration of the draft during 1917–1918. "Nothing," wrote Crowder, "is further from the Secretary's mind. He does not regard such work as I have done during my life as calling for any reward and such too appears to be the service opinion." He noted "a propaganda of organized vindictiveness of line versus staff" that had been going on for almost twenty years. The worst offender was none other than General Tasker Bliss, the senior military aide to Secretary of War Newton Baker. "Bliss leads the movement. If he applied to himself the rule he applies to others, he would today be buying pork and beans for the army instead of being the trusted advisor" to Baker. Crowder reminded Taft that Bliss had moved to the rank of brigadier general from within the commissary department, "with less line service than any man ever promoted" to that rank. "Having gotten away with the alleged stolen goods in 1902, he has been crying stop thief ever since."

Samuel Ansell also graduated from West Point in 1899. Five years later, he received a law degree from the University of North Carolina. After teaching military law and history at West Point, he worked for the War Department and represented the governments of both the Philippines and Puerto Rico before American federal courts. Assigned to the JAG Corps, Ansell impressed Crowder with his legal ability and enthusiasm. Promotions came rapidly: major in 1913 and brigadier general in 1917. When Crowder became provost marshal general in 1917, Ansell, his senior assistant, took over as acting JAG.

Ansell appears in many ways to have been an opposite to his chief, a point that may help to explain the permanent and bitter rupture to their professional relationship within the corps. Crowder was reflective, somewhat hesitant in manner, and comfortable in a bureaucratic environment. Many years of administrative experience gained from dealing with several secretaries of war had convinced him that military reforms best came from within the army. He might pour out his anguish to Taft and former Secretary of War Henry Stimson in private letters, but he would not be inclined to go public in his criticism of either the system in general or specific officers in particular. Nor would he openly confront senior line officers over disputes concerning military justice.

Ansell was much more aggressive in manner. Articulate and impatient to get results, his statements reveal an intense individual who believed very deeply in his causes. He appears to have been a man to whom a cause could become a crusade, more important than a previously established friendship. Thus, one can understand his role in the JAG controversy and the ultimate severing of his ties to Crowder, the person who not only brought him to the department in the first place but also facilitated his advance within its ranks.

There is no doubt that between 1914 and late 1917, Ansell and Crowder were very close. Acknowledging some highly favorable comments from Crowder, Ansell wrote that "such praise . . . works in me a new and vigorous inspiration to do all that a limited capacity will permit. Praise from a Discriminating Superior is always gratifying, and it is especially so where . . . it is the expression of a disinterested and appreciative soul." He wrote "to express a sentiment which I could not express orally without embarrassment, and which a sense of gratitude will not permit me to leave unspoken."

ANSELL AS "ACTING" JAG

In August 1917, Ansell became assistant to Crowder, actually serving as *the* JAG in Crowder's absence. He did not wait very long before submitting a four-page, single-spaced memorandum to the chief of staff, proposing an organization and expansion of the entire office. As of August 24, 1917, he had already determined that this agency was obliged by statute to revise court-martial "proceedings resulting in punishment of a serious character," and that the conclusions drawn from such revisions be "reported for the information of the President, the mitigating and pardoning power." Where did Ansell find the source for this revisory jurisdiction? It came from a law originally enacted during the Civil War and retained in 1917 as section 1199 of the revised statutes. Like many controversial enactments, its brevity contrasts sharply with the controversy it later engendered. "The Judge Advocate General shall receive, revise, and cause to be recorded the proceedings of all courts-martial, courts of inquiry, and military commissions." By implication, Ansell would later make his point explicit—he claimed that this section authorized some sort of appellate review.

Today, there is virtual certainty concerning the nature of appellate review in general, whether civilian or military. Professor Daniel Meador has described such action as "to place a case before the reviewing judges in a way that permits them to focus meaningful thought on the contested issues which survive the trial court judgment and to reach a conclusion as to whether, under law, the trial court result should be upheld. Human judgment is the essence of the process. . . . Judgment must be informed, and it cannot be hurried. By its nature it is deliberative." Meador's use of the phrase "under law" should be noted. Historically, American appellate procedure seems to have focused not so much on a review of the case as of the record accompanying it. The question, according to Roscoe Pound, was "not whether the accused was guilty or innocent, but whether the rules of the game had been followed in convicting him."

The question immediately arises as to the extent that military justice had any procedures similar to those described above. The steps outlined by Meador required time; military justice required promptness. Meador's model assumed adversary appeal proceedings replete with counsel, but in 1917 the military had no facilities for appellate counsel, let alone a formal appellate process. Nevertheless, for many years the JAG Corps had as part of its statutory authority the section cited by Ansell. Indeed, by 1917 it had developed a uniform procedure for what officers within the corps believed to be the type of "revision" mandated by the statute.

When a court-martial record came on for review, it was examined to see if there were any "jurisdictional defects appearing in the record" or "irregularities occurring upon trial to the prejudice of the substantial rights of the accused." If errors were detected, "it was the practice to write a review and opinion" expressing the findings of the judge advocate general and to "transmit the record to the Secretary of War through the Adjutant General with the recommendation that the sentence be adjudged null and void and set aside"; *if* the secretary concurred, the appropriate order was issued. The essential characteristic of this procedure was that it was advisory only. It was with this approach in mind that the JAG Corps first considered the Texas mutiny cases of October 1917.

According to Colonel E. G. Davis, one of Ansell's colleagues in his department, these cases arose at Fort Sam Houston when a group of noncommissioned officers were court-martialed on charges of mutiny. It appeared that while under arrest for minor infractions of various regulations, they had refused to attend drill, claiming that one such regulation provided that a noncommissioned officer under arrest did not have to do so. The young commanding officer persisted; so did the defendants—with the result that they were convicted and sentenced to dishonorable discharges as well as various terms of imprisonment. After the cases came on for review, Davis prepared a recommendation that the sentences be set aside. When he submitted the draft for approval, Ansell followed a very different path to a similar goal. Davis proposed that the JAG recommend reversal; on October 30, Ansell himself reversed the verdicts.

To senior military officers, Ansell's actions must have seemed like a coup de theatre. It was inconceivable to them that by simple fiat a member of the JAG Corps could rescind an action ordered by a commander. They feared that "the destruction of a division commander's initiative in regard to the discipline of his command might lead to more disastrous results than an actual miscarriage of justice." Indeed, according to one member of the general staff, "as the action of the Judge Advocate General, if permitted to stand, establishes a precedent which may be far reaching in its bearing on the discipline of the Army, I recommend his action be disapproved." For his part, Ansell fully realized that his policy would be debated if not disregarded. He prepared to prove the validity of his claim. But just before submitting his arguments to Secretary of War Baker, he tried to solve a different problem; one that focused on his role in the JAG Corps.

ANSELL AS ADVOCATE

Since Crowder had become provost marshal general in charge of the draft system, Ansell as his senior assistant had assumed responsibility for the daily operations of the JAG office. The distinction between what he actually did and his title appears to have troubled him. On November 3, 1917, Ansell informed his chief that "I am at times considerably embarrassed . . . by the fact that it is not known to the service at large that you are not conducting the affairs of this office as well as those of the Provost Marshal General; the public conception being that you are, as you legally are, the head of both offices, as in fact you are not." The solution was to have the actual administrator of the JAG Corps "charged with the full responsibility for its policies and for its general administration. That is not the situation now, nor do I believe it can ever be the situation as long as you perform the duties of Provost Marshal General." In other words, "I ought to be designated in orders by the Secretary of War as Acting Judge Advocate General during your practical detachment from this office." Urging that Crowder join in a statement to Baker asking that this be done, Ansell concluded that "I defer to you in this matter absolutely, as I properly should, but at the same time frankly saying to you that I am entirely assured of the correctness of my views."

One day later, Crowder responded that "it would be entirely agreeable to me to have you take up directly and in your own way with the Secretary of War, the subject matter of your letter of yesterday." He also added that since becoming provost marshal general, he did not recall being "consulted by outsiders in a single instance respecting any matter pertaining to the Judge Advocate General's Department, except in respect of appointment to the Reserve Corps, except as you yourself have consulted me." Later in 1919, as the Ansell-Crowder feud gathered strength, much controversy resulted from this exchange of letters.

What Crowder presumably meant by his first sentence is that while he did not intend to discuss the matter with Baker, he would not object to Ansell raising the point on his own. Ansell may well have assumed that Crowder would agree to be associated with the proposed change in JAG command. Nevertheless, absence of opposition to a move is not necessarily the same as supporting it. Had he been a little more attuned not so much to what Crowder wrote and the words he used as to what he did not write, Ansell might have realized that at best Crowder was uneasy with his proposal. On the other hand, it seems that Crowder was unwilling to articulate his feelings directly on the issue. The ambivalence reflected in his last sentence may also have led Ansell to conclude that he could take action on his own. At any rate, he did. Two days later, on November 6, Ansell sent a memorandum to the chief of staff enclosing a suggested order and concluded that "I am authorized to say that General Crowder himself is entirely agreeable to my calling this matter to your attention." Having set the formal army machinery in motion, or so he thought, Ansell returned to the issue of JAG authority to revise records of courts-martial. He submitted a formal brief on his position to Baker.

"You, Mr. Secretary," he wrote, "can never appreciate, I think, the full extent of the injustice that has been done our men through" the inability of the JAG to do nothing about mistakes and abuses of courts-martial except to "point out the error and recommend Executive clemency." With a tone of urgency that seems to have characterized so much of Ansell's writing, he added that "such a situation commands me to say with all the emphasis in my power, that it must be changed without delay." The basic point of Ansell's brief was built on this premise, buttressed by the fact that the needed change was only one of policy, not law. Here of course, he cited section 1199. He showed, correctly, that the word "revise" had been applied to the statute since the 1860s. Through copious citations, he further sought to establish the essential legal meaning of the phrase "to revise." For him, revise was equivalent to review, and review could only mean the ability to reexamine, to reconsider and correct if necessary, a previous legal decision.

Ansell insisted that "revise" in the context of the JAG statute meant more than "a perfunctory scrutiny" of court-martial records, and "that it in fact vested this office with power to make any correction of errors of law found to be necessary in the administration of justice." He then noted without citing any evidence or examples that "Judge Holt, the Judge Advocate General [during the Civil War] did revise proceedings in the sense here indicated." Ansell also discussed the reviewing authority common to courts-martial and claimed that until it had been exercised, the sentence meted out at the trial level "is incomplete." He was correct in that the reviewing authority could indeed affect the ultimate decision in a court-martial. But it was far from certain whether or not the JAG Corps was the appropriate reviewing authority.

On the other hand, there was no doubt that in the past, verdicts of general courts-martial had been set aside, upon *recommendation* of the JAG Corps, due to "a want of jurisdiction." Without confronting the difficult issue of requiring as opposed to recommending, Ansell argued that "some functionary must sit in an appellate capacity for which there must be some statutory or common law authority." And, he concluded, "no statutory or other authority can be found for the exercise of the power to declare a trial [void] for want of jurisdiction unless it can be found in that provision of section 1199, which confers a general revisory power upon the Judge Advocate General."

CROWDER AS RESPONDENT

Ansell's brief was addressed to Baker. But before it was referred to Crowder, the provost marshal general's attention was called to the matter, still pending, of Ansell's request for formal designation as acting JAG. In due course, the order that Ansell had drafted had gone up the chain of command until it reached Newton Baker. There is no record of what conversation, if any, transpired between them on this subject, but since it appears certain that Crowder had not alerted his chief to Ansell's proposed change, news of it apparently came as a somewhat unwelcome surprise to Baker. On November 17, he wrote to Crowder acknowledging his awareness that "you would necessarily be withdrawn for a substantial part of your time from the active guidance of the Judge Advocate General's office, where I have learned so confidently to rely upon you." Baker praised Crowder's work concerning the selective service law but added that "I shall be happy when that work is so far advanced as to be more nearly automatic, and leave you free to return to your task here."

Crowder wasted no time replying to Baker, informing him on the next day that "I can resume my active supervision of the work of the Judge Advocate General's Department at once to the extent of giving at least half of my time to that office and continue at the same time an efficient adequate supervision of this office." For his part, Baker also responded very promptly. Crowder's letter was dated November 18. On November 19, the order drafted by Ansell was summarily canceled.

The timing of these actions, coming even as Ansell had submitted his brief to Baker, was extremely unfortunate. Crowder surely knew that sooner or later Baker would learn of Ansell's request. Ansell, on the other hand, might have assumed that the proper way to go was to move through regular channels, all the more so since Crowder had declined to join Ansell in a direct communication to Baker. The judge advocate general also had indicated that he had no objection to Ansell taking up the matter directly with Baker, in his own way. He probably did not expect his associate to request a series of endorsements culminating in a sort of automatic approval by the secretary. Baker's action ended the incident with Ansell right back where he had been before. But it may well have troubled Crowder and engendered an atmosphere of suspicion, if not distrust, that certainly did not provide an ideal setting in which he could consider Ansell's arguments for revisionary jurisdiction.

According to Crowder, Baker handed him Ansell's brief and asked, "How does it happen that you never advised me that we had here in the War Department a court of appeals that could reverse, modify or affirm sentences of court-martial?" Crowder responded that "we have no such court of appeal," and that if a power of revision "had been discovered in [section] 1199 of the Revised Statute[s] it was an original discovery." Four days later, he produced his reply to Ansell.

At the outset, Crowder responded to Ansell's reliance on the word "revise," noting with some accuracy that "indiscriminate definitions of the words 'revise' and 'review' are quoted throughout the brief." He suggested that revise did not mean the same thing as review, in that revise "imports a purpose of suggesting or making amendments." Surely, if the legislature had intended for a "statutory grant of power so wide as that contended for we should expect, by all the analogies of grants of appellate power, to find something more than authority to 'look over,' or 'to examine.' " Crowder added that he could not point to a

single instance where the "power to modify or reverse the judgment of inferior courts is deduced from the words 'review' or 'revise,' without the addition
of apt words specifically conferring the power to reverse or modify."

Crowder next turned to the matter of General Holt, JAG during the Civil
War. Ansell had claimed without any evidence that Holt had reversed courts-
martial in the manner endorsed in his brief. But Crowder could not find a "single instance" where Holt on his own authority reversed a court-martial. On
the contrary, he found several that contradicted Ansell's contention and cited
one case where Holt noted "fatal irregularities" that render the proceedings
and sentence invalid, "and it is recommended that it be so declared by the
President."

Finally, Crowder countered Ansell's insistence that "the power here contended for [has not] been questioned by the civil courts or other civil authority." In this context, he cited *Mason's Case,* decided by a New York federal
circuit court in 1882. Mason had been court-martialed, convicted, and sentenced for attempting to kill Charles Guiteau, the man who had assassinated
President Garfield in 1881. The judge advocate general had concluded that the
military court did not have jurisdiction and recommended that the sentence be
nullified, a conclusion and recommendation that the secretary of war rejected.
Whereupon Mason's attorney sought out a writ of habeas corpus and cited
among other things section 1199, arguing that under it, the JAG's action had
been tantamount to an exercise of appellate authority and by implication barred
any reversal by the secretary.

A unanimous Court denied that "because the statute makes it the duty of
[the JAG] to receive, revise and cause to be recorded the proceedings of all
courts-martial, the power to reverse is implied. It is not reasonable to suppose
that the exercise of such an important power would be conferred in vague and
doubtful terms, or that it lurks behind the word 'revise.' " Indeed, "had it been
intended by the statute to introduce such a marked innovation into the preex-
isting functions of [the JAG], and to convert a staff officer or the head of a
bureau into a judicial officer having the ultimate decision in all cases of military offenses[,] the power to affirm, reverse, or modify the proceedings . . .
would have been lodged in plain and explicit language."

Having found a case on all fours with his position, Crowder considered
ending his statement at this point. Instead, he informed Baker that he would
try to ascertain "whether this power of appellate review cannot be found in the
President himself, as the constitutional Commander in Chief; so that, instead
of issuing a simple order of restoration, you may by direction of the President,
modify or disapprove the findings and sentence." Crowder's statement is important because it indicates that he was not nearly as uncomfortable with the idea
of some sort of military appellate review as with Ansell's claim that it ought
to be exercised by *his* department. On the other hand, because Crowder, like
Winthrop, conceived of a court-martial as strictly an attribute of command, it

was logical to vest such review with the highest ranking commander of all—the president.

Crowder's rebuttal to Ansell is dated November 27, 1917. Within twenty-four hours, Newton Baker responded. Himself a lawyer of somewhat conservative inclination, he could not help but be influenced by the very unfavorable reaction within the military command to Ansell's move. Moreover, when the two briefs were compared to each other, it seems that Crowder's reply was more convincing. Ansell argued for a power that he could not prove existed in law, nor could he cite relevant examples where it had even been exercised. On the contrary, Crowder could point to almost half a century of consistent practice within the JAG Corps, to say nothing of a federal civil case that specifically rejected what Ansell had recited. It is not surprising, therefore, that Baker decided in favor of his JAG. "Ordinarily," he wrote, "the extraction of new and large grants of power by reinterpreting familiar statutes with settled practical construction is unwise."

ANSELL ARTICULATES ANEW

According to traditional military procedure, Baker's decision should have ended the incident. Crowder, a military superior, had advised; the secretary had acted; Ansell should acquiesce. If anything, however, Ansell seems not to have been a traditional military man. As he later recalled, "I was brought up with a good degree of freedom and independence; maybe too much. I was not used to military discipline. I came to it not easily." Within two weeks, he prepared a lengthy reply brief, which he submitted to Crowder with a request that it be placed before Baker. The subject, he wrote, "is one of tremendous importance," and if the JAG Corps could change its view of the law, the results would be "to the great benefit of the administration of military justice." If Crowder and Baker persisted in their views that legislation was necessary, Ansell hoped that "its exercise will not be subjected to General Staff supervision, [which] it seems to me, would necessarily destroy the judicial character of the power."

Ansell's second brief is a remarkable document. On a personal level, it reiterated intensely held convictions. But as an advocate, this time he went further, focusing on the nature of military justice, the status of courts-martial, and the difference between army legal practice and civil legal procedure. Furthermore, unlike his first effort, this brief reflected Ansell's growing frustration and personal bitterness toward those army elements he saw as blocking necessary reforms. To the military establishment in 1917, his views seemed pointless; to an observer of modern military justice, they seem prophetic.

Ansell's basic premise remained unchanged: the judge advocate general possessed statutory authority to revise. "If the revision is worth the name, it should be a revision for gross and prejudicial errors of law that make a [court-martial] conviction bad, as well as for those that make the judgement void." Moreover, both Baker and Crowder were wrong in their assertion that the traditional way of dealing with such cases, to quote Baker, was "a convenient mode of doing justice." The secretary "has failed to [distinguish] between executive action in the nature of a partial pardon and judicial action which goes to the erroneous judgment of conviction itself and modifies it, reverses it, or sets it aside." Restoration cannot undo an unlawful conviction. "The man who seeks a pardon does so upon an express or implied admission of guilt. The pardon itself conclusively implies guilt. A pardon is no remedy for wrong done [to] the innocent."

Ansell devoted the second part of the brief to an attack on the argument, consistently maintained by the army, that a court-martial essentially was an instrument of command more concerned with "the support of power rather than . . . the human individual rights offended by an abuse of it." Claiming that the views of officials such as the assistant chief of staff and the inspector general "savor of absolutism," Ansell added that "I poignantly regret the concurrence of the Judge Advocate General, who habitually and constitutionally entertains far more progressive views." It is difficult to maintain, he added, that a court-martial, "the crudest of all courts, exercising such an extent of jurisdiction, is entitled to greater deference than those of the civil tribunals, the review of which, to insure correction, is fundamental in our law." Nor did Ansell have any doubt as to who was to blame for this mistaken conclusion. It was none other than the leading writer on military law, William Winthrop.

In his treatise, which by 1917 had been recognized as a standard reference work for American military justice, Winthrop concluded that "not belonging to the judicial branch of the Government, it follows that courts-martial must pertain to the executive department; and they are in fact simply *instrumentalities of the executive power.*" For Ansell, this was an absolute and obvious "non sequitur," and "we have all been steeped in the teachings that follow upon that illogical and fallacious syllogism." The primary source of courts-martial authority could only be Congress. "Courts-martial are authorized by Congress. The powers that bring them into being are designated and authorized . . . by Congress. The offenses which they may try and the law which they apply are prescribed and enacted by Congress. Their procedure is regulated under the law of Congress. Their sentences and judgments must be in accordance with the law of Congress."

Ansell cited a number of Supreme Court decisions that, he claimed, established beyond any doubt that courts-martial were like other federal courts in that they were created by statute and were "inherently and exclusively" judicial in nature. As such, they could not be subject to military command. To be sure, a decision by a commander was required to bring them into existence, but once convened—Ansell implied—they took on a life of their own. On the other hand,

Winthrop concluded that while courts-martial were tribunals and "their legal sanction is no less than the federal courts, being equally with those authorized by the Constitution," they still were not courts "in the full sense of the term." This was because of the executive authority exercised by the president as commander in chief.

Ansell strongly denied that "court martials are subject to his control." When "Congress does speak out of its power, the President may not speak within the same field. He may not array himself in opposition to the legislative rules governing the administration of military justice." In fact, "Congress has designated what commanders subordinate to the President may convene courts-martial, but when convened they will be subject to all the law of Congress; he cannot, by reason of that power, control courts-martial convened by others."

Thus Ansell based his argument on two fundamental propositions: that courts-martial were judicial in character, and that they were a product of congressional statutory authority, not executive fiat. *If* one agreed with these dual premises, Ansell's conclusions were not unreasonable. Accepting the claim that courts-martial were judicial, "the power of revision, if it exists, is also judicial and therefore not subject to the power of command." Since the source of courts-martial authority was Congress, "only by Congress alone, or by some authority appointed by Congress, can a court martial be controlled." Hence, "judicial revision is not subject . . . to the usual General Staff supervision."

Crowder forwarded Ansell's brief to Baker on December 17, 1917, along with a brief memorandum summarizing the disputed issues. Citing the Texas "mutiny" cases, Ansell "says, I think justly, that there are other cases . . . which demand the exercise of such corrective power; and down to this point I follow him with substantial concurrence without, however, being able to concur with him that this power has been granted to the Judge Advocate General." Crowder had no doubt that Ansell's argument "presents, about as strongly as it could be presented, the necessity for an appellate power." His analysis, however, failed to convince the JAG that a change of the character advocated by Ansell was necessary.

The lawyer's mind, according to Crowder, "is not particularly shocked by the fact that there exists in military jurisprudence no court of appeal." Indeed, "there is no constitutional or necessary right of appeal." While Ansell had argued to the contrary, there remained "substantial reasons of expedience and good administration why [current court-martial jurisdiction] should not be disturbed. War is an emergency condition requiring a far more arbitrary control than peace, [and] . . . court martial procedure if it attain[s] its p[r]imary end, discipline, must be simple, informal, and prompt." The "embarrassments" cited by Ansell and conceded by Crowder could be corrected without resort to a strained interpretation of 1199.

Baker responded to Crowder on December 28 that "it is impossible not to admire the earnestness and eloquence with which Gen. Ansell presents his view." His arguments, however, pointed to "the necessity of the power rather than to its existence," although "it may very well be that this power should exist, either in the Judge Advocate General or in the Secretary of War, advised by the Judge Advocate General." In any event, Baker had no doubt that congressional action was required if Ansell's suggestions were to be implemented.

This tripartite colloquy between Ansell, Baker, and Crowder took place even as a major incident in American military justice also occurred, an event that none of the three participants knew had even happened until after it was over. A second Texas mutiny case involved a number of black soldiers who on August 23 had rioted in downtown Houston apparently as a result of jeers and insults from white civilians. The result had been a rampage that ended with a number of civilian deaths. Sixty-three soldiers were court-martialed on charges of mutiny and murder. Of this number a few were acquitted; all the rest were found guilty, with four facing short prison terms, forty-one being sentenced to life imprisonment, and thirteen sentenced to death by hanging. The death sentences were carried out the next day in what Wiener called "the first mass execution under American military law since . . . the Mexican War." He added that "until the news of the multiple hangings reached the Washington papers, no one in the War Department had even known of the trial," and there it landed, according to JAG Officer Rigby, "with a dull thud." By the time the record reached the JAG Corps, as one of Ansell's associates—probably with unintentional understatement—later recalled, "if . . . errors of law had been committed or that injustice had been done[,] it would not help the men any to find this state of facts in the record after the man had actually been executed."

In fact, under existing rules what had happened was perfectly legal. Yet the incident received national attention in part because of what appeared to be the undue haste with which the military had executed the black soldiers. If the army later found the Houston trial record to be "legally sufficient," it also quietly relieved the commander involved in the case of his command and reduced him in rank. Baker's response to Crowder was dated December 28. One day later, the War Department ordered that no death sentences could be executed "until the record of trial has been reviewed in [the JAG office] and the reviewing authority has been informed . . . that such review has been made and that there is no legal objection to carrying the sentence into execution." Within three weeks, the JAG Corps rescinded this regulation and promulgated a revised and expanded version known as general order no. 7.

As drafted by a JAG officer, E. G. Davis, the new order barred execution of a death sentence until the court-martial record "has been reviewed" by the JAG office and "its legality there determined," and "jurisdiction is retained to take any additional or corrective action that may be found necessary." If there were problems with the record, it "will be returned to the reviewing authority with a clear statement of the error, omission, or defect." If this "admits of correction, the reviewing authority will be advised to reconvene the court . . . ;

otherwise he will be advised of the action proper for him to take," such as approval or disapproval, remission in whole or in part, retrial, "or such other action as may be appropriate." In addition, a JAG Corps branch office in France was established for the American Expeditionary Force. The head of this branch was to review the records of all courts-martial involving sentences of death, dismissal, or dishonorable discharge, as well as all verdicts reached by military commissions, and "to return to the proper commanding officer for correction such as are incomplete, and to report to the proper officer any defect or irregularity which renders the findings or sentence invalid or void, in whole or in part, to the end that any such sentence . . . shall not be carried into effect."

Ansell described Davis's rule of procedure as "a weak and uncertain step in the right direction," but one "fundamentally wrong as a matter of law." Davis would have the reviewing authority "approve the judgement but suspend its execution until he can be advised of" its correctness, "and if advised of its incorrectness, then to revise it himself." Ansell viewed this as little improvement over what already existed. For him, the sine qua non was a reviewing authority independent of and binding upon the convening authority. He could find no such mandate in Davis's order.

"If the reviewing authority does not take final action, there is nothing for this department to revise. If he does take final action, then the judgment passes beyond his power to revise. . . . Viewed from whatever angle, it is perfectly apparent that the source of the [reviewing] authority is in this department and must be exercised by this department, if exercised at all. No system can be devised whereby the convening authority revises his own judgment at the mere suggestion of this department." In this sentence, Ansell encapsulated the crux of the controversy, one that would not finally be resolved until the adoption of the Uniform Code of Military Justice in 1950. "What reason can there be," he asked, "to require this office to review for errors of law and then be denied the power of correction?"

Ansell later described general order no. 7 as "a partial and ineffectual exercise of revisory power . . . simply an administrative makeshift, intended to head off a more thorough and drastic reform." To support this contention, he cited a letter from Crowder to one of the JAG officers assigned to Pershing's American Expeditionary Force. Crowder wrote that prior to the issuance of order no. 7, the inexperience of many officers with courts-martial resulted in "a large number of proceedings . . . which exhibited fatal defects. A congressional investigation was threatened and there was talk of the establishment of courts of appeal. The remedy for the situation was immediate executive action which would make it clearly apparent that an accused did get some kind of revision of his court martial proceedings." However one may applaud Crowder's candor, his letter strongly supports Ansell's point about the less than enthusiastic desire on the part of the army "establishment" for genuine reform concerning military justice.

Ansell's letter to Crowder can be seen as the end of the first phase of their controversy. Thus far, it does not seem to have been personal in tone as much as a strictly internal debate between two lawyers over an issue more of statutory interpretation than military policy. But problems of personality simmered just below the surface. Ansell's efforts to have himself named acting JAG clearly troubled Crowder just as his mentor's inability to move away from the status quo irritated Ansell. On the other hand, during 1918, Ansell continued as the senior assistant, and he found several opportunities to continue his drive for a substantial appellate review within military justice. As the United States approached the first anniversary of its entrance into the Great War, the Ansell-Crowder disagreement remained buried within the military. When the arena for the dispute became a public forum rather than the inner offices of the War Department, involving both the press and political figures, what had been discourse over issues became diatribes on individuals. Taking place during much of 1919, these developments were unfortunate for all concerned, but especially detrimental to the goal of reforming military justice.

4

The Ansell-Crowder Controversy, 1918–1919: Round II

Although clearly committed to established procedures, Enoch Crowder was too able a lawyer not to sense some validity in Ansell's strictures concerning military justice. He seems to have spent considerable time during December 1917 trying to draft a proposal for Baker that would remedy the objections while remaining within the existing structure of military command. On December 6, he submitted a lengthy memorandum to the secretary. Based on previously articulated assumptions to which Crowder still adhered, it led to his "firm conclusion that no additional legislation is necessary, but that an ample grant of statutory power already exists for the immediate establishment of a system of military procedure, the practical results of which will be to obviate the objections which have heretofore been made." Ansell had also argued that no additional legislation was required, finding justification for his views within the existing language of section 1199. Although sharing this premise, the types of review the two officers envisaged were very different.

CROWDER'S CAUTION

Crowder's analysis of military appellate jurisdiction was based on a simple syllogism: (a) the president as commander in chief was the supreme military authority, and (b) although judicial in character, courts-martial remained "instrumentalities of the executive power." Since presidential power therefore extended to all aspects of military justice, then (c) "the President has ample authority . . . through the office of the Judge Advocate General, to make any revision of the proceedings of courts-martial which may be necessary to accomplish the correct and orderly administration of justice." Furthermore, Crowder cited the thirty-eighth article of war, which authorized the president to issue regulations "which he may modify from time to time, [to] prescribe the procedure, including modes of proof, in cases before court martials." The JAG found the term "procedure" broad enough to encompass the establishment of "a system of revision and correction."

Unlike Ansell who equated the word revise with review and thus found section 1199 sufficient for his purposes, Crowder insisted that this section plus several other articles of war "relate to the same subject matter" and, according to established rules of construction, "must be construed together." Hence, *only* the president could breathe life into the provisions of section 1199. On the other hand, however, Crowder readily conceded that this section provided for some kind of "a statutory appeal." Crowder's conclusion followed inevitably from his premises: "Provision may be made by regulations to be established by the President to bring before the Judge Advocate General for revision such cases . . . as the Commander in Chief should deem it expedient [to] be so revised." In addition to his memorandum, Crowder also submitted to Baker a proposed revision of section 1199 that provided for this type of executive power.

Drafted by two JAG officers, E. G. Davis and Alfred Clark, the proposal reaffirmed that the judge advocate general "shall receive, revise and cause to be recorded the proceedings of all courts-martial." In addition, the JAG shall "report thereon to the President who shall have sole power to disapprove, vacate or set aside any finding, in whole or in part, to modify, vacate or set aside any sentence, in whole or in part, and to direct the execution of such part only of any sentence as has not been vacated or set aside." In a separate memorandum to Crowder, Clark emphasized that the presidential power just described "finds its analogy in the civil courts, in the appellate power lodged in the Supreme Court." Under existing practice, once a court-martial sentence had been reviewed and approved by the appropriate commander, it became final "and could not be revoked, modified or set aside by the President. . . . All that could be done was to mitigate or remit the sentence . . . and this left the conviction untouched."

Davis and Clark did more than provide an analysis justifying the revisions for 1199. They also drafted a letter for Baker's signature, addressed to the appropriate congressional committee chairmen. In it, the secretary strongly supported the proposed change and claimed that the president "bears to the Military Establishment and to the administration of military justice a relation analogous to that occupied by the Supreme Court in the structure of a civil judiciary." In actual fact, this statement is something of an exaggeration. In 1918, there was no established appellate review of any consequence within the military. Moreover, it is difficult to equate what the president actually did under existing practice, or even what was proposed in the revision, with traditional appellate process. No lawyers were heard on appeal to the president; no official briefs were filed; with his other responsibilities, one wonders how much reflection and time could be allotted to any presidential review of court-martial records, let alone the judicial deliberation described by Professor Meador in the previous chapter.

Even more striking was the apparent open-ended discretion vested in the president. Unlike many appellate procedures, the proposed revision could be interpreted so as to permit him to increase penalties as well as reduce them; he could even set aside a not guilty finding by a court-martial. Few are the civil appellate judges who can reverse an acquittal in a criminal case. On the other hand, General Crowder insisted that the words "disapprove, vacate, or set aside any finding" as well as the words "to modify, vacate or set aside any sentence" did not mean that the president could increase a penalty. "Is there anything said here about the power to substitute a finding of guilty for a larger offense for a finding of a smaller or included offense?" He conceded that the president might set aside a verdict of not guilty, but even that official could not "substitute a conviction for the disapproved verdict of acquittal."

Moreover, Crowder claimed that "modify," especially when used in a penal statute, meant if anything to reduce rather than expand. In terms of practice, he may have been right. In terms of the actual words used in the draft, however, it would seem that presidential discretion to disapprove, vacate, modify, or set aside in whole or in part any sentence or finding of necessity embraced any and every finding that a court-martial might hand down. To be sure, under the new changes the president had flexibility and many more options available to him. But in retrospect, the proposed change may well have resembled more an executive discretionary authority than an opportunity for real appellate review. Whatever its intent, the proposed measure died in the Senate Committee on Military Affairs.

ANSELL PERSISTS

By 1918, Ansell appears to have become somewhat obsessed with his ideas on appellate review. Although Baker had refused to accept his interpretation of section 1199, Crowder, on the other hand, strongly supported order no. 7 as well as the proposed "official" revision of section 1199—both considered by his associate as ineffectual if not inappropriate. With Crowder heavily involved as administrator of the national draft, Ansell—still listed as his senior assistant—spent much of 1918 trying to establish on paper at least a system of military review, although he conceded frankly that it could only be advisory to the commander. While his formal break with Crowder was more than a year away, the professional gulf between them deepened in 1918, possibly because of the zeal with which Ansell espoused his beliefs.

Even before order no. 7 had been formally promulgated, Ansell informed the chief of the JAG Military Justice Division "of certain views of mine which . . . must be observed generally in the establishment, if that administration [of military justice] is to be what justice requires it to be and what thoughtful public opinion would like it to be." He wanted to make sure that his views "may not be misunderstood and that they may . . . constitute your authority for action in which you and others may not personally concur." If Crowder advocated the proposition that courts-martial were essentially executive attributes of command, Ansell argued the proposal that they were "*courts,* tribunals for the doing of justice, as much so as any tribunals in the land." Their fairness was to be tested not only by the Articles of War, "but by those principles . . . which are designed to secure a fair and impartial trial and which are applicable to all hearings of a judicial character." Such in part was what Ansell described as the "legal view, now judicially established."

He went on to criticize court-martial penalties levied during the current war "for their undue and inexplicable severity. Frequently they are such as to shock the conscience." Not only do they violate justice, but "they invite and merit public reproach." As to the oft repeated official response that "nobody expects such punishments to be served," Ansell responded correctly that the truth of this claim was itself an "admission of the injustice of the punishments and is bound to bring courts-martial into disrepute. My sense of applied law and justice," he concluded, "requires me to enunciate these views clearly and unmistakably and ask you to be governed by them until they may be superceded."

Ansell later repeated and expanded on these points in a lengthy letter to Secretary Baker. He strongly objected to several courts-martial penalties recently referred to his office because of the courts' failure "to appreciate the high character of their judicial functions." To be sure, he had "advised" the commanders that the penalties levied were "so disproportionate to the offense as to shock the conscience." But this was not sufficient enough "to achieve and establish military justice." To support his contention that courts-martial were judicial in character, Ansell cited two Supreme Court Decisions that, he claimed, established this point in law.

The first case, *Runkle v. United States* (122 U.S. 543), was decided in 1887. The Court unanimously held that when it appeared that a president had approved a court-martial sentence, the sentence will not be binding "unless it is authenticated in a way to show otherwise than argumentatively that it is the result of the judgment of the president himself, and that it is not a mere departmental order which might or might not have attracted his personal attention." When approving a sentence, the president acted in a judicial rather than administrative capacity. What Ansell saw as important was less the actual decision than a description of a court-martial written in 1864 by Lincoln's attorney general, Edward Bates, and quoted by Chief Justice Waite during the course of his opinion: "The whole proceeding, from its inception, is judicial. The trial, finding, and sentence are the solemn acts of a court organized and conducted under the authority of and according to the prescribed forms of law. It sits to pass upon the most sacred questions of human rights that are ever placed on trial in a court of justice, rights which, in the very nature of things, can neither be exposed to danger, nor subjected to the uncontrolled will of any man, but which must be judged *according to law.*"

Ansell's second decision was another unanimous holding, handed down in 1907, *Grafton v. United States* (206 U.S. 333). It involved an American soldier court-martialed in the Philippines on a charge of murder and acquitted. Whereupon a local court proceeded to retry him for the same offense, resulting in a guilty verdict and a prison sentence of twelve years and one day. When the Supreme Court of the Philippines affirmed the verdict, Grafton turned to the U.S. Supreme Court, his principal constitutional arguments being that of the Fifth Amendment bar against double jeopardy and also a congressional statute enacted in 1902 that established civil government in the Philippines, providing that "no person, for the same offense, shall be twice put in jeopardy of punishment."

The Court unanimously reversed the second conviction. Justice John Harlan, echoing the 1859 case of *Dynes v. Hoover,* held that "civil tribunals cannot disregard the judgments of a general court-martial . . . if such court had jurisdiction to try the offense." The prohibition of double jeopardy, whether it came from the Constitution or Congress, meant that a civil court even if under federal jurisdiction "cannot withhold from an officer or soldier of the Army the full benefit of that guaranty, after he has been once tried in a military court."

Ansell made no effort to explain the significance of these cases either in his second brief or his letter to Baker. Not until August 1919, in the midst of his testimony before the Senate Subcommittee in Military Affairs, did he discuss them. He seems to have been much less than convincing, although in retrospect it becomes quite understandable why he relied so heavily on these two cases. They were important because the crux of his battles within the JAG Corps focused on what attributes of "judiciousness" attached to courts-martial. If a court-martial was inherently judicial, as indicated in *Runkle,* then it could be subject to judicial appellate review like any other criminal trial, whether it be under civilian or military jurisdiction.

Ansell's use of *Grafton,* on the other hand, is much less satisfactory. When as a civilian, he discussed this case before the Senate Subcommittee in August 1919, he stated that it involved "an issue in which I was then and still am deeply interested, . . . the very character of these courts-martial, and how far those principles of the Bill of Rights . . . are applicable to them. I say this was the issue involved." The trouble with his comment is that nowhere in his opinion for the Court did Justice Harlan mention any relationship of the Bill of Rights to courts-martial. Furthermore, while he held that the double jeopardy provision applied in this case, he failed—perhaps intentionally—to choose between the constitutional provision or the act of Congress as grounds for reversal.

Had this been the extent of Ansell's reliance on *Grafton,* his interpretation might have withstood some scrutiny. It could be argued that, just in mentioning the constitutional provision, by implication Harlan recognized its applicability to courts-martial. Perhaps this is what Ansell assumed. However, he proceeded to quote the following "excerpt" from the opinion to the subcommittee: "We base our decision not upon the fact that this clause of the Constitution . . . has been carried to the Philippines by congressional enactment; we do not base this decision upon the fact that Congress has enacted in the old fortieth article of war, an inhibition against double jeopardy. We base it upon the fact that the Constitution . . . applies, regardless of legislation."

Grafton apparently was not discussed again until Crowder's appearance before the subcommittee in October 1919. He indicated that he could find no such excerpt in the Court's opinion (nor it should be added, can this writer). Crowder's reference to Ansell's earlier testimony is accurate. Nevertheless, he specifically declined to "charge Gen. Ansell with having attributed language to the Supreme Court which it did not utter." Where the quotation came from remains unclear. The point, although admittedly intriguing, is not as important as the fact that Ansell apparently could not cite much convincing case law to support his claim that ample precedent existed for his views concerning the judicial nature of courts-martial.

Ansell's reliance on *Grafton* was not challenged until 1919. In the meantime, during the remainder of 1918, on at least three occasions Ansell sought to integrate JAG practices with traditional appellate procedures. He created within the JAG Corps a board of review. Presumably, he intended it to be the vehicle for the "revisions" mandated by law as well as those required by order no. 7. "The duties of such Board will be in the nature of those of an appellate tribunal, and shall be performed with due regard for their character as such." One cannot help but notice how much Ansell modeled his board along the lines of traditional appellate procedure.

Thus, once a JAG officer had examined the court-martial record, it would be transmitted to the board "and thereupon the members of said Board will proceed to consider the preliminary review . . . in the manner similar to that employed by appellate tribunals on reaching and expressing their decisions." Although this type of board outwardly resembled an appellate tribunal, it differed from the actual in the most important aspect possible—exercise of judicial power. Senator George Chamberlain aptly described the realities of Ansell's review boards: "In theory, that was a review without power to afford a remedy, without power to reverse, without power to modify, without any other power, where the court [martial] had jurisdiction and the proceedings were regular, than the power to advise the commanding officer."

Ansell had no choice but to accept the limitations of order no. 7. He persisted, however, in his efforts to broaden review authority; whether it actually existed in military practice, let alone law, seems not to have troubled him unduly. Thus, on October 25, 1918, he submitted another memorandum to the head of the JAG Military Justice Division, rejecting its position that authority to review courts-martial was "strictly limited . . . to the question of the legality of the proceedings." Employing an unusual interpretation of the regulation, Ansell argued that order no. 7 "was never intended to operate as a limitation upon the duties of this office." To the contrary, it had been adopted in order to carry out the obligations and responsibilities mandated in section 1199. Hence, the regulation had to be seen as a grant of, not a limitation on, JAG authority. This office, then, "must be assumed to have the duty, by reason of its powers . . . to speak beyond the strict question of legality authorized by said order."

Obviously undaunted by the earlier refusals of Crowder and Baker to find existing authority in section 1199, Ansell had no doubt as to how the military justice division ought to proceed now that he had provided the rationale: "There could be no present accomplishment that would operate to the greater good of the Army or meet with greater approbation of those of our people who are interested in the administration of military justice than the establishment in this office of an administrative procedure that would result in rendering the punishments in the military Establishment more nearly uniform, more scientific and intelligent, and better related to justice to the individual upon the one hand and military discipline in general upon the other." Finally, he instructed the department "to make such recommendations in all cases" reviewed under authority of order no. 7 that "will tend toward the achievement of this result, and [you] will no longer in such cases consider yourselves limited to the sole question of legality of procedure."

In November 1918 Ansell issued yet another internal memorandum on the procedures to be followed by the JAG Corps in its review of reports and proceedings of boards convened for administrative purposes other than examination of court-martial records. Because the "finding is made below and not here[,] accordingly the principles governing appellate review should apply." Hence, it will be the policy of this office to sustain a finding "whenever it is thought that an appellate tribunal, under general modern practice, would uphold a similar judgment by a lower court upon a similar issue."

Thus, as 1918 drew to a close, Ansell had persevered in his efforts to integrate military justice with civil procedure, apparently with minimal opposition or cooperation from the "establishment." Outwardly there was no dispute between Ansell and Crowder. The arguments over revisionary authority—what with Baker's decision supporting Crowder, implementation of order no. 7, and the short-lived submission to Congress of a revised version of section 1199— all had been settled and seemingly consigned to oblivion. Indeed, Crowder even recommended that Ansell receive a distinguished service medal. He paid tribute to his assistant's "exceptionally meritorious service[,] . . . his legal ability . . . personality, energy . . . and vigorous administration." Among "his leading opinions" enunciating "many great principles of law fundamental to military administration," Crowder specifically cited Ansell's insistence that the "Articles of War be construed with more and more regard to the Constitutional principles governing criminal prosecutions."

Even as Crowder prepared the nomination for submission to Baker, a new factor changed the nature of the controversy within the JAG Corps. Ironically enough, it had been anticipated by Ansell as early as August 1917, when, it will be recalled, he proposed sweeping changes in JAG administration. At that time, he had urged that the process of "revision" be thorough, if only "to provide against the time which will almost inevitably come when the conduct of the War Department will be the subject of Congressional investigation, without which no war has ever been conducted in the history of the United States." Of course, Congress had been concerned with the conduct of the war long before December 1918. But not until December 30 was its attention called specifically to problems with the administration of military justice. The speaker was George Chamberlain, Democrat from Oregon, chairman of the Senate Committee on Military Affairs, and a vocal critic both of Wilson's war leadership and Baker's administration of the War Department. Prior to his wide-ranging remarks, only part of which concerned military justice, resolution of the Ansell-Crowder dispute had been improbable; after Chamberlain's speech it became impossible.

GOING PUBLIC

Chamberlain's comments set the tone for the final phase of the Ansell-Crowder controversy, although he discussed neither the issues nor the participants. He criticized the role of the commander in the court-martial: "What use of a court if a commanding officer is to practically control its actions?" Next, Chamberlain turned to military justice in general. Courts-martial conducted during the recent war "show that we have no military law or system of administering military justice which is worthy of the name of law or justice." If, he stated, "we are to have a democratic Army, military justice ought to be administered . . . by courts which are constituted, whose procedure is determined, and whose action is controlled by law. Courts-martial should be required to accept the interpretation of the law by a responsible law officer in the same manner that a jury in a civil criminal court accepts the interpretation of the law by the judge of the court." Congress ought to "enact a code that would fix the boundaries of these courts, and which would define their jurisdiction and duties." Further, "the sure cure for it all is to have some sort of tribunal, appellate or supervisory, that shall have the power to formulate rules and equalize these unjust sentences."

This writer has been unable to find any direct evidence that Ansell and Chamberlain "collaborated" on these remarks. However, his words resemble many of Ansell's strictures so closely that the senator's familiarity with them may be assumed. Furthermore, by publicly mentioning the problems with military justice, Chamberlain removed it from within the War Department to the outside world. It was one thing to agitate privately for change within the establishment; it was quite another for a senator and chairman of the Committee on Military Affairs publicly to call for reforms. This new component of publicity invariably caused the military establishment to act defensively, seeking to retain and not to innovate. The fact that Chamberlain became the leading supporter of Ansell's proposed reforms is of great importance. Aside from genuine disagreement within the army as to their merits, the bitter antagonism between the senator and Wilson's administration, especially Baker and the War Department, made a hostile reception to what he favored a virtual certainty. Indeed, in November 1920, Wilson went so far as to issue a personal appeal to Oregon voters to defeat Chamberlain's bid for reelection. They did.

With comments on military justice now spread over the pages of the *Congressional Record,* the next step was for national press publicity. This possibility became reality on January 19, 1919. With an American president in Europe for the first time in history, with national attention focused on the preparations for the Versailles peace conference, the readers of the *New York World* (in general a proadministration paper) found the entire first page of the editorial section devoted to "the thing that is called military justice— concrete official evidence which establishes that the United States military courts-martial indorse [*sic*] and approve of oppression and arbitrarily impose gross injustice." The lengthy article was written by Rowland Thomas, who apparently had secured permission from Newton Baker to examine various court-martial records. Besides detailing much of the same material previously discussed by Chamberlain (indeed the senator was quoted in the article), Thomas went a step further. Unlike Chamberlain, he specifically mentioned the Ansell-Crowder disagreement, although he did not identify Ansell by name.

With Chamberlain's speech past history, Thomas reiterated the point that "in the United States Army at present[,] judicial power is only a concomitant and incident of military power." He added that within the JAG Department, "there is an irreconcilable difference of opinion about the proper answer" to Chamberlain's question "whether . . . we shall have . . . a system of administering military justice worthy of the name of law and justice, or whether we shall have simply a method of giving effect by courts-martial to the more or less arbitrary discretion of commanding officers." According to Thomas, Crowder believed in the theory that "courts-martial are mere instrumentalities of military command." Such "is not the view held by the officer who, throughout the war, has been Acting [JAG] . . . nor by most of the officers of the department."

The author noted Ansell's earlier attempts to enlarge the power of revision and Crowder's negative response to his efforts. He described Ansell as "an officer of the highest personal repute in the Army and a lawyer whose learning and ability are fully recognized at the bar." He even quoted a lengthy internal memorandum written to Crowder by his assistant and detailed specific examples of extreme penalties meted out by courts-martial. Thomas concluded that "the so called military justice of these United States of ours, besides being blundering and senseless, is archaic."

Chamberlain's speech represented congressional criticism; Thomas's "exposé" symbolized emerging popular criticism. Ansell probably had been involved behind the scenes with preparation of both pieces, although the extent to which he "assisted" remains uncertain. Shortly after the *World* article appeared, he decided also to "go public." He may have concluded that with both media and political pressure coming from outside, it was now time for evidence from a third source—one representing opposition from within the army itself to the administration of military justice.

On January 25, 1919, the *Chicago Daily News* reported about a luncheon address by Ansell to the Chicago Real Estate Board with the headline "Judge Advocate Hits Army Court System." According to the writer, he spoke "frankly of the weaknesses of the court martial system." Furthermore, the administration of military justice "is now the subject of popular criticism." Noting that as acting JAG during most of the war, he had in effect been in charge of the very system he now attacked, Ansell found it prudent to add that "I do not regard the criticism as personal or as directed at human agencies charged with the administration of the system, but as aimed at the system itself," one that "is in many respects patently defective and in need of immediate revision at the hands of Congress."

For the first time, Ansell articulated publicly what he had advocated privately to Baker and Crowder for almost two years. Courts-martial were first and foremost *courts*. Yet such a tribunal is the only court "in all our land that, holding in jeopardy the life and liberty of our citizen soldiery, under existing law, has to proceed to execute that sacred trust without the aid, guidance or control of any person in the least qualified in the law." Shocking as it might be, "the whole system of court-martial under existing law proceeds on the theory that it is to be administered by men who know not one word of law." The *Chicago Tribune* briefly mentioned Ansell's other speech, to the Chicago Bar Association, apparently very similar to the first in content. He "attacked the system of military courts-martial as unjust to the solider, and demanded that radical changes be introduced to the end that more exact justice might be meted out to the men in service."

A few comments need to be made concerning Ansell's public debut as an advocate for reforming military justice. In the first place, it seems clear that he tried to keep the attention on issues, not personalities. There is no indication from the press coverage that he mentioned any names of senior army officials at all, let alone in a critical manner. On the other hand, in calling for congressional changes to the military justice system, Ansell publicly pointed to the inability of the army to reform itself. By so doing, he committed an act probably resented more by the "military establishment" than all his various legal propositions: he did not keep his disagreements within the corps. With a move that is either a tribute to his resolve or testimony to his recklessness, in one fell swoop he proposed to challenge the army bureaucracy, the leadership of his own department, and the secretary of war; and he undertook this admittedly daunting challenge with his strongest source of support coming from a maverick senator, increasingly isolated within his own party.

CROWDER'S CONCERNS

From his perspective, Crowder saw these several pronouncements about military justice as part of a pre-conceived scheme—first Chamberlain's speech, followed by publication of Thomas's article, and a few days later the news accounts of Ansell's comments in Chicago. By late January, military justice had become a "hot item" for the American press, and it continued to be of popular interest for the next several months. Crowder had reason to be concerned less about the debate itself than its effect on his reappointment to a final term as JAG. Because of a quirk in military personnel procedures, he stood to become a civilian, with a corresponding loss of seniority and other benefits unless reappointed and confirmed by February 14, 1919. With Wilson out of the country, the document had to be sent abroad and returned with his signature. It did not arrive in New York until February 12 and barely reached the Senate in time for favorable consideration on the thirteenth.

On February 4, Crowder wrote his old friend and former secretary of war Henry Stimson that "a conspiracy, hatching out in my own office, is responsible for the arraignment . . . of military justice, their purpose being—not to reform the code in aspects where it might be reformed, but to prevent my reappointment. They were working in the interest of another man." As he had done in other instances, Crowder refused to make any specific accusations, but he obviously meant Ansell. Another of Stimson's correspondents, Felix Frankfurter, was a little more candid. Three days later he informed his former chief that Crowder's renomination was on the way: "I think the opposition will . . . peter out, but undoubtedly there is a strong undercurrent. I am sorry to say that I cannot, from the available evidence, acquit Ansell."

For his part, Ansell presumably realized that, by his actions if not his attitude, he was creating an impossible situation concerning his future in the JAG Corps. It may well be that by February 1919 this meant little to him. Even as Frankfurter was writing to Stimson, Ansell responded to a letter from a judge, the father of a draftee, concerning military treatment of his son. "Frankly," wrote Ansell, "our military system is absolutely Prussian. I have been very much interested in the subject of military justice, or rather, the system of military injustice. I have striven to establish in it even a little justice. My efforts have been largely in vain. . . . The thing is searing my soul, Judge. I have fought against it. I have fought a good fight; I have kept the faith in the eternal verities of right and truth and justice, the faith which came to me from my forbears and out of my own conscience."

In his December 1918 address to the Senate, Chamberlain had called on Congress to establish the boundaries of courts-martial, define their jurisdiction and their duties. Also, he wanted "some sort of tribunal, appellate or supervisory, that shall have the power to formulate rules and equalize these unjust sentences." On February 13, 1919, he opened hearings to consider Senate Bill 5320, "a Bill to promote the administration of military justice." At this stage of his inquiry, Chamberlain did not propose a formal appellate court; rather he sought to enlarge by statute the existing powers of the judge advocate general, much as Ansell had tried to enhance them by implication. Several provisions of his proposed revision should be noted.

A JAG was to be appointed for every general or special court-martial. He "shall not be a member of the court, but shall sit with it at all times in open session and shall fairly, impartially, and in a judicial manner . . . rule on all questions of law properly arising in the proceedings. . . . His rulings and advice, given in the performance of his duties and made of record, shall govern the court martial." Furthermore, a separate official was to prosecute the case, although it could be another JAG officer. In all court-martial proceedings, "the accused shall have the assistance of and be represented by counsel."

Also, the commanding officer was forbidden to refer any charge to a general court-martial unless the appropriate JAG officer "shall endorse in writing . . . that in his opinion an offense made punishable by the Articles of War is charged with legal sufficiency . . . and that it has been made to appear to him that there is prima facie proof that the accused is guilty." When the court found the defendant not guilty on all charges, "it shall not reconsider, nor shall the appointing authority direct it to reconsider its findings." Even today, with military justice at a sophisticated level and with appellate procedures long established, one is struck by the modernity of Chamberlain's suggestions. In many respects, what he called proposals are now called policies.

Ansell duly appeared as the first witness; indeed he spent the entire day testifying before the committee. He made public the actual documents generated during his debate with Crowder, including the responses of his chief and Secretary Baker. He discussed at some length the clash between the two opposing interpretations concerning the nature of courts-martial. "Prevention of injustice," he insisted, "is better than any attempted cure . . . after it has once been inflicted, and the way to avoid error is to put the case at the start in the hands of a man who knows what error is. In such a system as ours the errors accumu-

late from bottom to top, and at the top there is no authority for their correction." In his judgment, no legislation to establish revisory power would have
been needed during the war "if the existing statute [section 1199] had been
properly construed at the beginning of the war."

One senator correctly understood that when Ansell employed the term revision, he meant use of some appellate procedure and asked Ansell where such
power ought to be vested—in the judge advocate general or in the "President,
he to be advised" by the JAG? Ansell replied that "inasmuch as it is inherently
a judicial power, it ought not to be confused with or located by any considerations of military command." As a matter of fact, "it does not shock me to say
that there shall be some judicial authority, some independent law officer, some
skilled man, some man who has been designated by Congress and appointed
by the President for this purpose, to determine whether or not, in the subjection of this individual to this system of penalties, the law of the land was complied with, even to the point of restraining any power, however high, if it is
simply executive power or the power of military command."

Although he did not actually propose a court of military appeals for several months, the similarity between what Ansell described and what exists
today is noteworthy. Further, Ansell continued to insist that lawyers play a
major role in any appellate review: "The trouble is we have got to examine
the record as lawyers. Lawyers must examine the record. . . . We have got to
get down to the record as judges and lawyers and see what that record
reflects." Today, in the United States Court of Appeals for the Armed Forces,
the first step for a case after it has been received and assigned a docket number is to refer it for examination by a staff attorney.

CROWDER'S CONVICTIONS

Even as Ansell appeared before the Senate committee, Crowder had prepared
a detailed and lengthy rebuttal to Chamberlain that duly appeared in the *Congressional Record*. It took the form of a letter to Baker, dated February 13, 1919,
the very day of Ansell's testimony. Unlike Ansell, Crowder seems to have felt
it inappropriate as the JAG to make public speeches concerning a now public
dispute within his own office. On at least two occasions, lengthy letters to Baker,
which generally found their way into print, served to make his views known. In
addition to testifying before congressional committees, Crowder also did not
hesitate to make use of his private correspondence, which was extensive, to justify his views. He also encouraged his old acquaintants to write "public letters" to various newspapers on his behalf. Former secretary of war Stimson and
former president William Howard Taft were among several who did so.

Although he considered many aspects of the senator's speech, two points
were important for the debate over the reviewing authority. First, far from

receiving no real review, in military justice proceedings the accused, according to Crowder, received "an automatic double appellate review," initially from the JAG officer who examined the record and next from a board of review. Crowder even went so far as to say of this "thorough scrutiny," one that also included a third inspection of the record by the JAG himself, that it was superior to civilian justice. In the second place, while it was true that the judgment expressed by the JAG "in his appellate capacity is customarily phrased in terms of a recommendation to the commander," such suggestions "are given practical effect in the same manner as the trial courts in civil justice give effect to the mandate of the supreme court of the state." In other words, the commanders were under no statutory compulsion to accept the JAG's findings, but invariably they did. Crowder's description may be contrasted with Ansell, who said "we created some boards of review, consisting of very eminent lawyers, and made these reviews very formal and impressive, and they must have impressed everybody who read them. But again, they were only advice, carrying no authority, and I do not mind saying that when you are hedged in by limitations of that sort, you are bound to go at things rather timidly."

Chamberlain's committee recessed for more than a week and did not reconvene until February 26, 1919. In the meantime, the *Washington Post* noted that Ansell "may get out," and that his disclosures were said "to be deeply resented." Indeed, such revelations have created a situation that "will force his retirement." When it reconvened, the Senate committee first heard from Alfred Clark, one of the JAG officers who, although originally supportive, ultimately was unpersuaded by Ansell's claim of revisionary authority within section 1199. But Clark had a more fundamental problem with Ansell's approach, and it concerned the relationship of the JAG office to the power of revision. From 1917 to the spring of 1919, Ansell had argued that revisionary or review authority was inherent within the JAG Corps. He assumed that Congress "could provide for a court which would have just as much power over the complete proceedings as the trial court itself has." But he also assumed, thus far at least, that the logical place for such a body was within his own ranks. Perhaps this was a bit egotistical; Ansell probably had no doubts that with officers like himself reviewing cases, military justice would indeed be well served.

Clark, although he fully agreed that "there should be a military judicial appellate tribunal," denied that it should be either the judge advocate general or officers under his jurisdiction. He observed that the JAG was "the head of the whole prosecuting organization of the Army." It would be inappropriate to have such an officer in charge of appeals, just it would be unacceptable that the "Attorney General . . . should finally review all cases tried in all the Federal Courts . . . by his assistants. The proposition is entirely inconsistent with the conception of an impartial appellate tribunal." Such a judicial body "ought to be . . . constituted by Congress, which should provide for the appointment of the members thereof in the usual manner by the President and confirmation by the Senate, leaving to the President, the discretion as to selection—whether he shall select distinguished lawyers from the Army, or distinguished lawyers from civil life, or distinguished lawyers in part from the Army and part from civil life—and constitute the personnel so appointed to a judicial body subject to no military control."

Clark believed his proposal to be "the only way you will get an appellate tribunal that would function impartially as such." Under Ansell's interpretation of section 1199, "the Judge Advocate General was the Supreme Court of the Army; he could reverse, revise, and modify, or make such disposition as he saw fit of any case when it came up to him." When Ansell had an opportunity to draft a major revision to the Articles of War, he tried to act on Clark's comments. In retrospect, Clark rather than Ansell may have better anticipated the future direction that military appellate jurisprudence would take.

The final witness before the committee was Enoch Crowder. Since his dispute with Ansell about section 1199 was well documented, with himself clearly the winner, Crowder focused on a more fundamental flaw with Chamberlain's revision, the new role for the JAG. Part of the draft held that the ruling and advice given by the JAG during a trial "shall govern the court-martial." The authority of the court was thus reduced, and Crowder thought "that is rather a weighty matter to consider, whether you want to do it or not." The proposal would ultimately place the JAG "in a position to administer the discipline of the Army." Clearly, Crowder was troubled by a potential clash between congressional authority to adopt rules for the army and presidential authority as commander in chief.

It could be avoided, he insisted, by lodging an appellate power within the executive: "I deprecate very much [a] departure from so fundamental a theory as would be presented if you lodged in a staff officer outside of the hierarchy of command the authority to control the President . . . in his action upon any court-martial proceedings." With Chamberlain's proposed statute, Crowder emphasized that "the President is absolutely concluded by the opinion of his Judge Advocate General." He believed that under such a law, if in 1865 the JAG had found the proceedings under which the Lincoln conspirators were tried to be irregular, he could have "recorded his decision to that effect, and concluded Andrew Johnson from the execution of any one of them. That is the power you are conferring in this statute. Do you want to do it?"

Military judicial authority, concluded Crowder, "should be vested in the constitutional commander in chief[,] and . . . all appellate procedure should be in his name." Under these conditions, he was "in favor of an appellate power in the President[, and] I have been in favor of it always." When asked by one senator if such power should be exercised "by some officer of your department," or possibly to have an independent appellate tribunal, Crowder responded, "I do not think so." By 1919, Crowder readily conceded that there should be an appellate procedure within the army; the issue on which he and

Ansell differed was *where* it should be located. Crowder's inability to separate the existence of a military appellate system from the general grant of presidential power seems to have resembled a straw man, worth more in theory than actual results in American history. He agonized over the potential for conflict, perhaps not realizing that historically the two disparate grants of constitutional authority have complemented rather than collided with each other.

Crowder's convoluted interpretation of Chamberlain's draft did more than "conclude the President" vis-à-vis JAG authority. It apparently precluded him from conceptualizing any appellate procedure except one coming from the president. It seemed that Congress could not create such a tribunal, presumably because it would interfere with the constitutional mandate of the commander in chief. Thus, Crowder "concluded" himself into a corner somewhat analogous to a catch-22 situation. One sought an appellate tribunal independent of military command, but the only possible way to have it was through the highest ranking military commander of all. Moreover, if the president wished to create such a judicial body, how could it be free of military influence when, in reality, it would be administered by lower ranking military functionaries?

As Congress rushed toward adjournment during the last week of February, Chamberlain's bill disappeared. One is tempted to dismiss Crowder's objections as anachronistic, unrealistic, and trite, if not trivial. And in the light of the UCMJ, such temptation is hard to resist. Yet it would be a very serious error to underestimate the depth of his conviction concerning the proper constitutional location of military appellate jurisdiction. In 1919, other high-ranking officials, civilian as well as military, agreed with him, and his views were very influential in shaping the changes in the Articles of War that ultimately were adopted in 1920.

The Senate Committee on Military Affairs did not return to the topic of military justice until August 1919. With Congress out of session, between February and July the Ansell-Crowder battle resumed in the press and the corridors of the War Department. Ansell lost the battle, but whether Crowder would win the war was far from certain as Congress adjourned.

5

The Ansell-Crowder Controversy, 1919–1920: The Outcome

The public part of the Ansell-Crowder controversy began with the January 19, 1919, article in the *World* and accelerated with testimony before the Senate committee in February. From this point on, what had been a private discussion became a public debate—and usually in more contentious tones. By February 21, the *Washington Post* predicted that Ansell's "courage" would cause serious difficulties with Baker and Crowder. Clearly aware of the unfavorable reaction to his chosen course but possibly unaware of the depths of resentment it had caused within the "establishment," on March 1 Ansell addressed a personal, handwritten letter to Baker.

CROWDER'S COUNTERATTACKS

"It is the gossip of the Street . . . as well as of my own office," he wrote, "that you are to demote me." Noting that Crowder had been detailed to special assignment in Cuba to work with the Cuban government on political reforms, Ansell had heard that Baker would name a different officer as acting JAG, "and I be made to suffer the humiliation of serving in subordination." He informed the secretary that "I myself can suffer such humiliation . . . and shall not complain. But it seems to me that in matters affecting military justice you are being impelled by forces beyond you to do wrong—wrong to yourself, the Army, the Country; above all, wrong to justice." He believed that Baker "wanted to be helpful" in obtaining a system of court-martial procedures "that assure justice." If such was the case, "let me plead with you to help now; to lend your great influence on behalf of legislation to liberalize the unjust system." Ansell urged the secretary "to forget me, all men, and look at measures. The Congress wants to do something. The people want you to do something." "Could you not find

59

time," he concluded, "to let me present you with my views of the requisite remedial legislation?"

There is no indication that Baker even acknowledged this note. On the same day, however, he signed a letter to Crowder drafted by John Henry Wigmore that indicated outright opposition to Ansell's position. One of Crowder's staunchest supporters within the JAG Corps, in civilian life Wigmore served as dean of Northwestern University Law School and had already become a distinguished legal scholar on the law of evidence. Baker emphasized that the "recent outburst of criticism and complaint" upon our system of military justice "has been to me a matter of surprise and sorrow." More important, however, was his conviction that in spite of the "highly colored press reports of certain extreme statements" the system remained "essentially sound." Yet officials of the War Department "have not been in a position to make any public defense or explanation and have refrained from doing so." In other words, it was now appropriate to rebut Ansell's comments in public. Thus, Crowder should "draft a concise survey of the entire field and . . . furnish the main facts in a form which will permit ready perusal by the intelligent men and women who are so deeply interested in this subject."

Crowder's response to Baker's request, dated March 8 and apparently also written by Wigmore, was promptly published in the JAG *Bulletin*. Crowder fully agreed with Ansell that under existing procedure, "there is no further appellate body or officer who can review the appointing officer's review and modify, affirm, or reverse his action." He reminded Baker that more than one year ago, he had proposed a revision to section 1199 as a remedy for this admitted defect. The secretary not only had strongly endorsed the change but also had accepted without question Crowder's narrow interpretation of the revisionary power granted to the JAG Corps. "Countenance of a plan to play ducks and drakes with a statute of the United States, you refused." The dispute was not over the *existence* of an appellate power, but its *location*. Ansell claimed that it should be vested in the judge advocate general, and that "a complete judicial system with faithful analogies to the organization and procedure of civil courts should be substituted for the present simple and direct system of Army discipline." His own department maintained that "the power should be vested in the President. . . . These are the real issues and the only ones."

Crowder further noted that purposes of the military and civil codes are diametrically opposed. One "is designed to encourage, permit and protect the very widest limit of individual action consistent with the minimum necessities of organized government." The other "is designed to operate on men hurriedly drawn from the liberal operation of the civil code, and to concentrate their strength, their thought, their individual action on one common purpose, the purpose of victory." In time of war, an army in the field cannot function with "two commanders—one in charge of the discipline and one in charge of its strategical and tactical maneuver." Such a structure is "nothing less than ridiculous."

Crowder next turned to Ansell's conduct "as one of the most promising and trusted officers in my office." Why, he asked, had Ansell never advanced the changes he now supported during 1916 and 1917, when the Articles of War were revised, a project on which Crowder had worked diligently since 1912? Furthermore, he recounted Ansell's attempt to be named acting JAG. This episode plus the quality of the brief submitted on expanding the revisory authority in section 1199 led to one result: "From that time forth the feeling of trust and confidence that I had in Gen. Ansell was shaken."

Finally, Crowder mentioned the organized campaign of printed criticism concerning military justice. It was "too consistently connected and too instinctively based on distorted accounts of matter on record in the [JAG] office to allay the thought that a bitterly partisan propaganda rooted in this office was being conducted." As had been his public position all along, Crowder declined to accuse Ansell by name. "But I do say with the utmost confidence that . . . the propaganda was being fed into the hands of the press by those seeking not a reformation of the code, but the accomplishment of ulterior motives."

Thus, Crowder again alluded to the apparently intentional series of attacks against him and his department, beginning with the Chamberlain speech in December 1918. By March 1919, it may well have been Ansell's turn to feel the effect of an organized response, this time, against him. First, there was Baker's letter of March 1, followed by Crowder's reply of March 8, wherein for the first time he publicly mentioned his loss of confidence in his senior assistant. On the same day, Wigmore delivered a public address to the New York County Lawyers Bar Association. He offered a vigorous defense of military justice and excoriated its critics. Two days later, what Ansell had predicted, Baker now promulgated—Ansell was reduced to his "permanent" rank, that of lieutenant colonel in the JAG Corps. From the viewpoint of his cause, worse was yet to come. It may not be unreasonable to conclude that if Ansell had sown, Crowder had reaped.

ANSELL, BAKER, AND CROWDER

In his speech to the New York lawyers, Wigmore had listed fourteen current criticisms against military justice. Among the most serious were: "1. Arbitrary discretion of military commander. 2. Archaic criminal code. 5. Court martial ignorant of military law. 6. Prosecutor and judicial advisor the same man. 7. Second lieutenants defend serious cases. 9. Commanding Generals directing reconsideration of acquittals. 14. Judge Advocate General's action ineffective." The coincidence of these fourteen points, noted Wigmore, "with another celebrated fourteen is fortuitous, but . . . I am sure that military justice will win out on at least as many and perhaps more than the United States will secure of the other fourteen points." The charges "are nothing short of reckless defamation."

Most were totally groundless, while a few with slight basis in fact were cited in support of "grossly false inferences."

Wigmore reiterated Crowder's insistence that "there is an automatic appeal from every court martial." Nor was it true that courts-martial were conducted by men not acquainted with military law. "Every officer who graduates from West Point [or from training camp] is required to study and pass an examination based upon the system of military law as embodied in the Manual." Wigmore's glib assertion about the legal training received at West Point in no way rebutted Ansell's claim that as legal proceedings, defendants before a court-martial were entitled to a trained lawyer, not someone who had passed an exam on customary practices of military justice.

As Crowder had stated (and since Wigmore had drafted both pieces the similarity is not surprising), Wigmore noted that the defamatory charges against military justice "are repeated with such frequency as to give the impression that there is somewhere a deliberate effort to discredit all those who have been concerned in the administration of military justice. What the motive is, and who has organized that effort," he declined to hypothesize. But he predicted that "when all the ramifications of intrigue are permitted to be disclosed, our system of military justice will be amply vindicated." Moreover, such vindication would include Enoch Crowder, "whose reputation as a wise organizer and a sympathetic administrator has once [and] for all been established in the hearts of the legal profession."

Ansell reacted to the release of the Baker-Crowder exchange with a seventeen-page letter to the secretary dated March 11, 1919—one day after he had been reduced in rank. He probably was responding to the incidents just described. Unlike his earlier letter of March 1, written more in a poignant than polemical tone, this document reflects indignation, frustration, and anger. He accused Baker of giving the public "a bitter attack upon me" and stated that the secretary's opinion of military justice was "based upon inadequate evidence, very limited observation, and the statements of biased witnesses." Ansell demanded that he be given an opportunity through Baker's office to reply to "the same intelligent men and women" who had been given the Baker-Crowder version. The reality was that the system "does not do justice. It does injustice—gross, terrible, spirit-crushing injustice. Evidence of it is on every hand to those who will but see. The records of this office reek with it."

Ansell distilled the essence of his differences with Crowder into one sentence: "The issue is whether the convening authority, the court and the officer ordering the execution shall be a law unto themselves, or whether they shall be restrained by and required to keep within the limits prescribed by established principles of law; whether military justice shall be governed by the power of military command or whether it shall be the result of legal principles." He further accused Crowder (accurately, as it turned out) of describing order no. 7 as a mere adminstrative palliative, designed to head off a threatened congressional investigation replete with talk about a proposed system of military appeals. Moreover, Ansell insisted that Crowder had not only known about the proposed reinterpretation of section 1199 from the beginning but also had actually supported Ansell in his attempt "to put it over." Later, the JAG opposed his assistant "out of a mistaken notion of the necessity of self-protection and a desire to soothe his wounded pride." Ansell also strongly denied any surreptitious action on his part to displace his chief.

If there was any maladministration of military justice, primary responsibility for it "must be located first upon the Secretary of War." After all, it was he who had assigned Crowder to "more duties . . . that were in no sense related, than a man of greater capacity than General Crowder could carry. This was bad administration; operated to the great injury of this department. It proved an insuperable obstacle."

On March 27, Baker wrote to Crowder in Cuba that "I have now had an opportunity to read the Ansell letter, and have determined that because of its obviously improper character I shall return it to General Ansell without other comment." He addressed a curt note to that combative officer. The letter of March 11 "herewith returned is not only obviously useless and improper for publication, but in its present form improper to be received by the Secretary of War officially." Personal conflicts "between Colonel Ansell and other officers cannot be properly discussed, or at least determined by newspaper publicity." On the other hand, Baker "will welcome" any observations that Ansell desires to make "either through ordinary military channels or directly, looking to amendments or modification of legislation or procedure affecting military justice."

What Baker probably did not welcome was more public comment from Ansell. Before that officer responded to the secretary's invitation, he delivered a public address to the North Carolina Society. Not surprisingly, he focused on military justice. But he also had some comments on military discipline that indicated the depth of the split between his views and those of the army. "Discipline," Ansell stated, "is a quality that is but little controlled by law. [It] is not the result of the application of legal power." On the contrary, "it is founded upon respect for self, a respect for others, a respect for duty, a respect for obligation."

Of course, obedience to orders was absolutely essential. But "if legal restraint must be imposed to prevent delinquency upon the part of the soldier, like restraint must be imposed to prevent the capricious and oppressive use of power upon the part of the officer. There can be no discipline in our army without justice." Ansell reiterated his belief that the current system "does not lead to justice." The fault "is a fault of the system, and of no particular person." Probably with himself in mind, Ansell concluded that the only way to assure justice under the status quo is through "the interposition of strong personalities intent upon justice and intent upon extorting justice out of the system."

Baker had invited some sort of response from Ansell that presumably would be in a more "appropriate" format than his rejected letter of March 11. On April 2, 1919, Baker received a four-page memorandum listing a number of key requirements for an effective system of American military justice. They were all based upon Ansell's now familiar claim that courts-martial were essentially courts and thus inherently judicial in character. Ansell used this premise as the foundation on which to propose dramatic if not drastic changes. Even today, they remain a valuable guide by which to measure the transformation that has taken place in military justice since 1919.

ANSELL'S ACTIONS

Before Baker could respond, the complete text of Ansell's March 11 letter that the secretary had refused to receive was published in the *New York Times,* on April 3, 1919. Referring to it as "the suppressed letter," the anonymous writer specifically mentioned that it had not been given out by Ansell. But no information that might reveal the source of the leak appeared in the article. Two days later, Baker replied, through the adjutant general, to Ansell's memorandum.

His suggestions "merit earnest consideration, which they shall receive." Indeed, Baker heartily concurred with many of them "if, in fact, existing statute law is defective in the particulars suggested by the proposed changes." Furthermore, he ordered Ansell "at the earliest possible date" to prepare and submit a draft of a bill that would "carry into effect" the ideas expressed in his various suggestions. But Baker would have nothing to do with the letter of March 11, now published. "There is . . . no point in seeking to use the Secretary of War as a medium of publicity." He reminded Ansell that "the resort to personal comment . . . was not begun by General Crowder." It "plainly would have been more fitting and appropriate if never begun by anybody. It has certainly been carried far enough by everybody."

In this swipe at Ansell and his supporters, perhaps Baker was a little unfair. If Crowder had not been the first to resort to personal comments, he displayed great ease with the practice—but usually in private correspondence. On April 24, for example, he wrote that "Ansell is of an unstable mentality, brilliant in the extreme but without any poise; he is essentially destructive in character, personally inordinately ambitious, and utilized his incumbency of the office of Judge Advocate General to gather around him a bunch of snakes whom he allowed to warm at that very hearth-stone plotting every minute of the time how they could defeat my reappointment and put Ansell in charge."

Ansell immediately set to work and, as will be seen shortly, with impressive results. In the meantime, public discussion about military justice continued during the spring and summer of 1919, but at an increasingly desultory level. There were occasional indications, however, that some disputants still felt strongly about the issues. Thus, John Wigmore—commenting on the military justice experience of some pro-Ansell JAG officers—noted that they had been in the corps only a few months, assigned to the "War Risk Insurance Section, which has no more to do with military justice than kalsomine [sic] has to do with the stability of a sky scraper." As for Senator Chamberlain's claim that a court-martial system represented a system neither of law nor justice, Wigmore concluded that "if a man, after any rational inquiry whatever, holds to that view, he is hopeless."

On the other hand, Edmund Morgan, JAG officer and strong supporter of Ansell, and soon to join the faculty of Yale University Law School, stated on April 3 that defendants in courts-martial are often prosecuted by "officers of low rank who wouldn't know a law book from a bale of hay, and as frequently are defended by a chaplain who is hardly able to distinguish between a rule of evidence and the Apostle's Creed." Crowder was furious at Morgan's comments. Still fuming more than six months later, he cited Morgan's statement to a correspondent. Morgan must, Crowder added, "have some mental aptitude[,] but he is primarily a school man with no practical sense. I have no hesitation in saying that he is the smallest man from the standpoint of character that I have ever come into contact with[,] and three minutes [of] conversation with him shows this littleness of his soul."

Wigmore and Morgan, both law professors and scholars on the law of evidence, debated military justice once again in June 1919 when they appeared together at the Maryland State Bar Association meeting. For his part, Wigmore assumed that "the prime object of military organization is victory, not justice. . . . If it can do justice to its men, well and good. But justice is always secondary and victory is always primary." Next, Wigmore expanded on a point that Crowder had also raised in earlier statements. Rather than defend military justice, Wigmore attacked civilian criminal procedure as inferior in certain instances to the military version. Military justice, he insisted, was far ahead of its civilian counterpart in at least five areas, three of which warrant mention: centralized supervision of all criminal courts; verbatim record of trial—something, Wigmore observed, that was common practice in general courts-martial; and automatic appellate scrutiny for every accused's case.

Here, Wigmore glorified the "review" system practiced in the military, claiming that "every record of every case goes up to at least one higher authority." Wigmore failed to note, however, that this review was rarely if ever carried out by a superior legal officer or indeed by a military officer with adequate legal training. Records in general courts-martial "go up two stages, to the Judge Advocate General or the President." Every convicted man, he wrote, "thus obtains an appellate scrutiny without any cost. . . . This is an idea of which civilian justice has been dreaming ever since Magna Charta. Complete justice to the poor man is still a dream in our civilian courts. In the military courts it costs not a cent."

Unlike the dean of Northwestern Law School who spoke in generalities, Morgan offered numerous specific examples of incredible sentences meted out by military courts. He denounced the system that Wigmore "seems to consider well-nigh perfect." In fact, it was a system designed for professional soldiers serving an empire for hire but applied to an army of civilians, temporary soldiers, "protecting the republic." Military justice actually was governed by the whim of a commander rather than the rule of law. Moreover, all too often the military court, the prosecutor, and the defender were "all untrained and incompetent," thus making a "fair and impartial trial almost impossible." Morgan argued, contrary to Wigmore, that in actual fact there was no judicial supervision of a military justice proceeding "at any stage." As for the so-called "automatic appeal" that according to Wigmore "costs the accused nothing[,] in the vast majority of cases it is worth to the accused exactly what it costs." Morgan's observation that, in responding to Ansell's criticisms, defenders of the status quo would "predict bolshevism" is of interest when one notes Wigmore's response to Morgan's presentation: "As I listened to his speech, I thought I was listening to the kind of speech which must have been delivered somewhere before a Russian Soviet just before the Russian Army went to pieces."

By April 12, the press reported that Ansell had completed his draft of revisions to the Articles of War. If the dates on the various pieces of correspondence and press accounts are accurate, Ansell produced his draft in less than two weeks. One reporter stated that Ansell's proposed changes "are so drastic that it is difficult to predict what their reception will be [either] at the War Department or on Capitol Hill." The draft, however, "will be submitted to Congress whether it meets with [Secretary Baker's] approval or not."

When exactly Baker received Ansell's revisions is not clear, but on May 14 he established a three-member board of officers to "consider all recommendations looking to the improvement of the present system of military justice, and recommend . . . any changes which they believe necessary." Drawn from the regular army and chaired by Major General Francis Kernan, an officer well known for his devotion to the existing forms of military discipline, Baker's board reflected his reaction to Ansell's proposed reforms—many of which were aimed at lessening the influence of officers typified by those now assigned to evaluate them. Also, the secretary's response can be seen as an effort to undercut congressional initiative. From the army viewpoint, Kernan's report as the basis for legislative inquiry would probably be much more desirable than Ansell's bill. Crowder, of course, well understood the motivation behind Baker's decision and wrote to him the next day that the announcement of the Kernan board had brought "me the greatest satisfaction." Given Crowder's enthusiasm, Ansell's response was predictable. After his resignation from the army, he commented that "if [Baker] had gone out designedly to appoint the most reactionary set of men in the United States he could not have improved upon his selection."

A few days after appointment of the Kernan board, the *New York Times* reported that Chamberlain would introduce Ansell's bill "to establish military justice and cure defects in the existing army court martial system." An examination of the text shows, not surprisingly, that it incorporated the basic principles previously discussed in this chapter. But Ansell went beyond the issues of appellate jurisdiction and proposed additional changes in the Articles of War. As will be seen, many were doomed to failure in 1919–1920. Even today, in a more progressive era of military justice, some of his proposals have yet to receive military and congressional sanction.

Ansell suggested that military justice procedures be called courts rather than courts-martial, with three levels of tribunals—summary, special, and general. A general court was to have eight members; if the defendant was a private or noncommissioned officer, three members were to be of this rank. In the special court, which included only three members, one had to be drawn from the rank of the accused. His bill also established limitations on penalties that traditionally had been at the discretion of the military court. Thus, disrespect toward the president, Congress, and other public officials carried a maximum prison term of one year, while disrespect toward a superior officer was punishable by confinement "for not more than six months." He restricted the famous "catchall" article penalty to the same period of time. But Ansell went beyond just limiting punishments that could be meted out by the military. He provided that officers who failed to make required pretrial investigations were themselves subject to imprisonment.

Finally, Ansell specified operation of the revisory authority that he considered so vital to military justice. It was in the form of a proposed court of military appeals (*not,* it should be noted, a military court of appeals), "which for convenience of administration only shall be located" in the JAG Corps. The tribunal would be composed of three judges, "each of whom shall be learned in the law," appointed by the president, and approved by the Senate, and each would serve during good behavior with the salary "and emoluments including the privilege of resignation and retirement upon pay" of a U.S. circuit judge.

Given the later history of the U.S. Court of Appeals for the Armed Forces, it is noteworthy that Ansell saw no constitutional impediment to Congress creating such a court and providing life tenure for the judges without reference to their political affiliation. In his proposal, the issue of an Article 1 court contrasted with an Article 3 tribunal was conspicuous by its absence. He did not even discuss the possible clash between congressional and presidential authority that troubled Crowder. Unless clearly not desired by the accused, the new tribunal would review the record of every general court or military commission wherein a sentence of death, dismissal, dishonorable discharge, or confinement for more than six months had been rendered.

Crowder had already indicated his fundamental difficulty with any revisory authority unless in the name of the president. He opposed Ansell's "court" because, as he wrote privately to Baker, it would "divorce the President from his disciplinary relations to the Army by erecting between him and [it] a Court of Appeal with power to conclude him upon every question of discipline arising in [the] Army. I deny the Constitutionality of such legislation, and I also doubt its expedience." As for the rest of Ansell's reforms embodied in the Chamberlain bill, "some of them are silly, some ridiculous, but none vicious. We can stand for all of them."

At this point, Crowder added a sentence that reflected his belief that the JAG Corps was not on the level of a line command: "Although I should, out of deference to my military training, deprecate any provision which would undertake to say to General Pershing—You may try Division Commanders in France only when your Judge Advocate approves." Unfortunately beyond the scope of this volume, the relationship of the military command to the JAG Corps, particularly since 1919, is worthy of study. Ansell's aggressiveness about JAG authority and Crowder's ambivalence in a sense represent the two poles of a controversy that may be incapable of total solution. Recent cases in military justice indicate that Ansell's view may be closer to the mark than Crowder's.

ASSAULTED BY THE ARMY

Although submitted by Chamberlain to the Senate early in May, Ansell's bill was not discussed in committee until August. In the meantime, the Kernan board published its report to Baker on July 17, 1919, a few days before Ansell resigned from the army. It had been assigned to evaluate various proposals to reform military justice and also to submit its own recommendations for change. While the report claimed to be an objective assessment of current commentary on military justice, in reality it represented the response of senior officers and the military establishment to Ansell's suggestions; and it becomes quite clear why Crowder—weeks before he even read the report—could write to Baker of his "greatest satisfaction" in the board's composition.

The report, based upon comments and suggestions solicited from about 225 officers, opened with the observation that officers "who served with fighting units and had brought home to them the overwhelming importance of discipline in a command when it was subjected to the supreme test of battle" favored the present regulations and procedures. On the other hand those officers, typified by Ansell, "whose duties kept them remote from the scene of battle, and perhaps entirely disassociated from actual service with troops view the system with a more critical eye," comparing it with "criminal practice in the civil community to the advantage of the latter."

This view was widely shared in the regular army, where critical reaction to Ansell's draft had been evident even before Kernan's board was created. On May 10, for example, Major General David Shanks had expressed opinions to the adjutant general that were probably typical:

Courts-martial should be free from wrangling of lawyers and hair-splitting technicalities. . . . While I have great respect for lawyers[,] I have recently noted on the part of some of them such a lack of discipline and loyalty, considering the opportunities that they have had, that it is not only remarkable but it is absolutely astounding. . . . Nothing can be more discouraging to the seasoned officer who knows the difficulties connected with the control and management of soldiers than to find that all of his experience which has taken him a lifetime to acquire is set aside to the whim of some lawyer who has a hobby to ride. . . . When the sentence is reached[,] it should be imposed by men who know the soldier and not by a bookworm who knows a little law.

The Kernan report next turned to "the fundamental doctrine that the constitutional authority of the President as Commander in Chief can not be abridged by Congress in the exercise of its power to make rules for the government of our armies." The board argued that, in fact, his authority to appoint such courts predated the Constitution itself. Ansell would create "a new functionary with powers so extensive . . . as to constitute him the administrator of discipline, though he is not himself of the hierarchy of command." Is it not possible that such a proposition that takes away presidential authority from the court-martial "may be unconstitutional"? Is it not "in effect an attempt to withdraw from command an essential part of that which belongs to it historically and in sound reason? Is it not open to be questioned as an attempt by law to emasculate the legitimate and heretofore undisputed authority of the President?" Indeed, "in the opinion of this board the unwisdom of this new departure, assuming it to be legally competent, is startlingly apparent." Implicit in Kernan's report was a subtle emphasis that military justice be judged not in the abstract but in practical terms consonant with reality. It "is carried out at times under great urgency and stress, where the nice deliberation and finish of the civil procedure is utterly impossible."

Having come out in total opposition to the proposed court of military appeals, the Kernan report next considered other specific reforms suggested by Ansell. There was no need to change the name of "court-martial" to "court." The former title "is an old term, well understood, and indicates by its name that it is a military or martial court." Whatever abuses there were would not be corrected by a mere name change. The proposal that men of the same rank as the accused sit on the court "is out of harmony with the American conception of democracy. . . . The change would seem to be more in harmony with that form of discipline which in Europe recently resulted in the establishment of soldiers' and workmen's councils."

Ansell's proposal that federal rules of procedure be followed in courts-martial received predictable rejection. His plan "would require continued study on the part of officers." The idea "illustrates vividly the impracticability of suggestions made by officers and others who have had little or no experi-ence in the field, men whose military experience has been largely limited to permanent offices elaborately equipped with libraries and with abundant leisure to pursue the niceties of legal subtleties."

In place of the proposed court of military appeals, Kernan's board came up with a synthesis involving expanded power for the convening authority and the major provisions in the old (1918) bill to vest appellate review in the pres-ident. When the confirming authority believed that the rights of the accused had been injuriously affected, he could order a retrial before a new court, but only upon those charges of which the defendant was found guilty. And this new trial could not result in any greater penalty than the original sentence. In addi-tion to all the review powers given to the president, he also could "set aside the entire proceedings in any case," grant a new trial, or "restore the accused to all rights as if no such trial had ever been held."

THE LINGERING CONFLICT

Crowder was delighted with the Kernan report, understandably if not un-necessarily seeing in it personal vindication. "I get my greatest comfort," he wrote, "out of the report of the Kernan . . . Board. . . . I think that it is the last word in the argument. It is the voice of the Army in France speaking through its most experienced officers." Crowder anticipated strong support from General Pershing and had "no doubt that I shall be sustained on every question of fun-damental difference." He was correct, except that by August 1919, when the Senate subcommittee began hearings on the Ansell-Chamberlain bill, popular and political interest in military justice had waned. Crowder had already won.

Conducted before a subcommittee consisting of two and occasionally three senators, the hearings began early in August and continued on a very irregular basis through November 8, 1919. The focus was supposed to be on the Cham-berlain-Ansell bill, but in fact the testimony ranged far and wide and became a rehash of the entire controversy. Ansell testified for five days, even as Baker announced his endorsement of the Kernan report. Now free from whatever military constraints he may have previously felt (and by the spring of 1919, they could not have been many), Ansell lashed out at his critics. In retrospect, his performance can be seen as a furious epilogue to a futile exercise.

Yet there is ample evidence that, personalities aside, the question of mili-tary appellate jurisdiction had become an issue that by the fall of 1919 aroused more ambivalence than antagonism, as becomes clear upon examination of the testimony offered by Crowder and Baker. By the time they appeared (the for-mer late in October, the latter in early November), the subcommittee had re-ceived Ansell's original proposal (as embodied in the bill), the Kernan report, and commentary from numerous military officers, much of it repetitive. Unlike

Kernan, Crowder no longer wished to argue the issue of whether a civilian court for the military would be an unconstitutional interference with executive power as the commander in chief. "I am not," he stated, "predisposed to question the constitutionality of laws: and I am more in the attitude of assuming, and I am at present in the attitude of conceding, that Congress, in the exercise of its power to make rules and regulations for the government" of the armed forces, "may establish a court of appeals."

The judge advocate general still believed, however, that Ansell's bill would "take away from military men the discipline of the Army and transfer it to civilians." Such a policy "offends my sense of what is right much more than it would if the proposition were to turn over to civilian control common law and statutory felonies committed by persons within the Military Establishment." Moreover, under the Ansell proposal, if the president himself convened a court-martial, his authority would be severely circumscribed by the JAG's power. When one added to this an exclusively military court of appeals functioning independently of the president, the result "is wholly untenable from my point of view."

Crowder emphasized that since he was able to appoint extremely well-qualified officers to the various boards of review, and since they could scrutinize records for errors of both law and fact and present to the secretary and the president any possible grounds for reversal, there was no need to change the system. Wisconsin senator Irvine Lenroot observed that while such a board might indeed be exercising a supervisory authority, in fact "you have no jurisdiction to do so." In reality, these boards (and Chamberlain had made the same point earlier in the February hearings) exercised supervisory power in an advisory capacity. Crowder agreed and added that in practice the president relied on the advice of his civilian lawyer, his secretary of war. Indeed, Crowder went even further and claimed that the president is not "qualified to exercise command independently[;] he acts upon the advice of experts." And "I assume that the [JAG] and the Secretary . . . his legal experts, will advise him in the exercise of this appellate authority. . . . and that he will follow their advice." This point may have been what interested Lenroot. On the one hand, numerous witnesses had voiced concern about possible interference with the executive command authority, but in reality "you are creating an appellate tribunal in name that you do not expect will independently exercise the powers that are given [it]."

Although the Wisconsin senator was attempting to get Crowder to see this inconsistency, his point may have been too subtle for Crowder, who reiterated that the president would exercise appellate authority "upon a legal review" prepared by the judge advocate general. "I believe it would be 100 percent effective." It was more the possibility that an appellate court might "interfere with discipline if such a court is superior to the President" than the probability that the chief executive might choose not to exercise appellate review directly that troubled him. In addition, although he declined to oppose an independent appellate court on constitutional grounds, Crowder predicted that if such a tribunal emerged from Congress, "I have no doubt that in time of some great crisis, the constitutional question will arise." Such a prospect failed to daunt Lenroot: "I see no more reason why, upon questions of law, [the president] should not be governed by a military tribunal as Commander in Chief; he certainly is, just as a civil officer is, by the very men he appoints to the bench, and they control his action and find [it] invalid in a given case." Crowder could only fall back on an old theme: "I am afraid that this question of military relations is *sui generis*[,] and that it does not aid you much to invoke the analogies of our civil jurisprudence."

Newton Baker also had to confront Lenroot's questions, and his answers were even more contradictory than Crowder's—so much so that he felt it necessary to write an explanatory note before the transcribed hearings were published. The secretary readily conceded that, in spite of all authority flowing to the commander in chief, the president remained unable to "quash a trial and order a new trial de novo." There ought to be an opportunity "for reversal on either the facts or the law." But such appellate jurisdiction should remain within the military establishment, "supervised by the civilian authority, which is the President, and the Secretary of War for him." He cited three reasons why an independent appellate court was unacceptable. First is the constitutional command that "discipline shall flow through the President to the Army." Second, 88 percent of the cases tried by court-martial are military rather than civil offenses, and "military men are better able to judge the facts and circumstances." Finally, the military justice system should work in an emergency as well as in peacetime, and "any necessity for an appellate tribunal remote from the field of action, with the consequent delay, is not adopted to the emergencies of actual, active field operations."

Baker insisted that if Congress gave the president power to reverse, modify, or affirm court-martial decisions, there would be no need for an appellate court. But this jurisdictional might did not reach the ability to order a trial de novo. With Baker, just as he had done with Crowder, Lenroot tried to explore the perimeters of authority in a court that could supplement rather than supplant the president. If, he asked, an appeal from a court-martial could be taken to a tribunal whose jurisdiction was limited to questions of law, its duty being either in the face of error to transmit the record back to the convening authority for a new trial or otherwise for further action, "could there be any possible objection from the standpoint of controlling superior authority?" Baker replied, "None, and in time of peace, it would be a most desirable arrangement."

Adding that in actual fact most of the civilians in the JAG Corps were "a very high type of lawyers," the secretary agreed with Lenroot that such men would be logical candidates for such a court; and because they would devote themselves only to military cases for a term of years, they would become especially qualified. Moving to his main point, Lenroot asked if this court would be "much better qualified to pass upon these questions than . . . for instance, the convening authority?" Baker answered that "I think such a court . . . would undoubtedly bring to bear upon a record a higher degree of skill than can be looked for from convening authorities acting upon the record." Lenroot pushed ahead: "You would say . . . that unless pressing necessity exists for reposing authority in the President, or somebody who may not be qualified to pass upon the law, or who, because of his other duties, finds it physically impossible for him to give his consideration to the cases individually, it would be very much better to place that authority in the hands of qualified persons, who would give that attention to it?"

Baker agreed. And, added Lenroot, if a court did not interfere with the discretion of the reviewing or confirming authorities, "but to confine it solely to passing upon questions of law, you would see no objection to such a court?" Baker answered, "None whatever." What if such a tribunal could be established in the field of operations during war, "would there be any objection then?" For a third time Baker responded affirmatively, "None that I can see."

Before the transcript of the hearings was published, Baker had the opportunity to review his testimony. He found himself "perplexed at the inconsistency between my answers" to the questions of Chamberlain and Lenroot "with regard to the creation of an appellate power," so much in fact that he felt it necessary to add an explanatory memorandum to the printed record. Again, he feared that "any extraneous and independent appellate power" would "inevitably weaken and might conceivably gravely imperil" the authority of the president. Although the idea of an appellate power "is wise, and our experience in this war shows its propriety," there should be no case of army discipline "beyond the reach of the [President] for correction."

The Senate subcommittee finished its hearings in early November 1919, but seemed in no hurry to act on reforming military justice. In all fairness to Lenroot and Warren, their time was taken up by other issues (especially the battle over the League of Nations) that if not of more political import were certainly of greater public interest than military judicial procedure. The Senate voted on a heavily revised version of Chamberlain's bill in April 1920. After further changes in the House, the revised Articles of War were finally signed into law on June 4, 1920. Debate persists about how significant the changes were. Edward Sherman, a distinguished military-legal scholar, concluded that they "can hardly be considered an important reform of military justice." On the other hand, Frederick Bernays Wiener, a noted military-legal historian, described them as "genuinely enlightened." Whether of minor or major consequence, there is no doubt that the revisions provided for a new military review procedure; but it was far from what Ansell had proposed.

Article 50 1/2 established within the JAG Corps a board of review consisting only of officers. They would review records of all cases that normally had to be approved by the president, but they were not an appellate court in any real sense. Counsel did not appear before them; briefs were not presented. Indeed, the article did not even employ the word "court." Moreover, far from being independent of the military, the board was truly a subordinate body. Appointed by the JAG, the members served at his pleasure and in an advisory capacity. Only if he agreed with their recommendations for reversal was the record returned to the convening authority for dismissal or retrial. If the JAG did not concur with the board, or if he agreed with a recommendation for affirmance, the case was referred to the secretary of war for action by the president. While the chief executive had numerous options, unlike the wording in the Kernan report the final version of the article did not give him the power to order a new trial.

Many of Ansell's other suggestions were similarly emasculated. A pretrial investigation was now required before a general court-martial could proceed, but resulting recommendations were not binding upon the convening authority. Defense counsel was indeed provided, but there appears to have been no requirement that he be an attorney. A law member could now sit with the court, and he did have to be a lawyer from the JAG Corps, but with the sole exception of ruling on admissibility of evidence, his instructions or findings were not binding upon the court.

Thirty years later, in 1951, a staff member in the office of the secretary of defense informed an assistant to Senator Estes Kefauver that "there is nobody that I can find around the Department of Defense who has a clear recollection of the facts of the famous Ansell-Crowder controversy." This indication of slight interest in a significant controversy is unfortunate. Actually, the episode was highly important to the future of American military justice. It may indeed have had, as Wiener put it, a "seamy side," but it also has great relevance in several areas for this book.

For the first time, the army, and to some extent the American polity, debated the issue of a military appellate procedure. Prior to Ansell's agitations, according to Crowder, "There was no such thing as appellate review." To be sure, Ansell raised many questions that he failed to answer. Yet he forced the military establishment to consider the complex relationship between command structure and an independent source of trial review; at the same time, the lengthy hearings revealed a perceived incompatibility between the totality of command and civilian norms of appellate jurisprudence. Definitive answers were not forthcoming in 1919, but the first step was taken.

The episode also offered another example of the important role that politics plays in the formulation of military policy. Political figures such as Senator George Chamberlain, though their concerns for the American soldier may indeed have been genuine, saw the issue through partisan eyes. Chamberlain's antagonism toward Wilson and his harsh criticism of Baker as secretary of war, when matched with his equally vigorous support for Ansell, made it highly improbable that the reforms could have been considered in nonpartisan terms.

Moreover, Ansell's complex relationship with Crowder, together with his own conduct and the resulting split within the JAG Corps, had more to do with their ultimate rejection than did reasoned discourse on their validity. His plan for an appellate court was unacceptable both to civilian leaders of the military establishment, such as Baker, and to the army hierarchy. Finally, in 1919–1920, public interest in military justice proved to be fleeting. Independent of each other, these factors might not have been important, but taken together they were dispositive.

The characters in the controversy went their separate ways, and military justice continued to operate as provided in the 1920 amendments. After he retired from the army, Crowder served a term as ambassador to Cuba; he died in 1932. Wigmore and Morgan returned to teaching law. In 1925, Morgan became professor of law at Harvard, where he stayed for the next twenty-five years, until his retirement. Ansell resigned from the army in 1919 to establish a law practice in Washington. He was still alive in 1949, when he received a copy of a proposed new military code, drafted by a committee chaired by none other than his old supporter Edmund Morgan. Contained in that new proposal was provision for a court of military appeals, and in Morgan's last evidence class before he retired from Harvard Law School was a future chief judge of that court, although neither knew it at the time.

Americans have a proclivity to reargue old conflicts in new contexts. In 1919, reform of military justice became a political issue that split the military. In 1949, reform of military justice was proposed by the secretary of defense on behalf of the armed services. In 1919, a dissident JAG officer drafted a reform bill. In 1949, a committee dominated by civilians but working closely with the JAG Corps drafted a bill. Only when the civilians were satisfied with the measure was it submitted to Congress. In 1919, the proposed reforms largely came from the military; in 1949, they came for the military.

History, observed Mark Twain, does not repeat itself, but it does sometimes rhyme. When Morgan resigned from the JAG Corps in 1919, he believed that he would not see major changes in military justice during his lifetime. But, in fact, both Morgan and Ansell lived to see the Court of Military Appeals in actual operation. How these changes came about, and what factors led to failure in 1919 but success in 1949–1950 are discussed in the following chapters.

6

Renewed Calls for Reforming Military Justice, 1943–1948

In 1922, Ansell published a short article in the *Yale Law Journal* commenting on "Some Reforms in Our System of Military Justice." Written apparently to note the enactment of the 1920 "revisions" concerning the Articles of War, the piece also reflected ambivalence about the extent to which the new enactments represented real reforms. Ansell observed the American allegiance "in our first war, as in our latest, and in all the years of our national existence between" to the "Arkansas Traveller philosophy: when war was on we could not change the Articles [of War] and when it was over we no longer needed [to change] them." The American articles, "at utter variance" with our political ideals, had been adopted "as an incident of emergent circumstance rather than the result of free intelligent consideration." Ansell recalled that "those who saw the daily grist of injustice" pointed out from time to time, in official memoranda and otherwise, vices that they aptly characterized as "destructive of every assurance of justice." These efforts had culminated in the submission to Congress of the Chamberlain bill in 1919 "to establish Military Justice."

Ansell recognized that many of his key proposals, including establishment of a real appellate court within the military, had been cut from the bill—which in fact he, rather than Chamberlain, had authored. Nevertheless, he still believed that if "properly administered" the revisions would "establish military justice." This was because the new version "accepts the general principles and for the most part the specific revisions" in the original draft as submitted by Chamberlain. On the other hand, Ansell conceded that administration of the new provisions "by reason either of uncontrollable circumstances or a lack of sympathy—apparently the latter—has not been in accord with the letter, spirit or purpose of this highly remedial legislation." His comments were probably as accurate between 1943 and 1948 as when they were written in 1922.

REFORM SEEMS THE NORM

As Robert White noted in 1961, the essence of the complaints raised by critics about military justice in World War I can be distilled down to six key abuses: there were an extremely high number of convictions, about 88 percent; the penalties meted out by courts-martial were excessive, resulting in later reductions by review boards of at least 75 percent of the noted cases; there were incredibly wide discrepancies in punishments for the same offenses (inappropriate language merited a prison term of three months imposed by U.S. Army Court in England but up to twenty-five years from a similar tribunal in France, while punishments for "common absence offenses" could range from a few months to a ninety-nine-year term of confinement); rights of the accused were not protected during a court-martial proceeding; defense counsel was often incompetent; and sentences as rendered by the court could be increased before the court-martial was formally ended. If these problems were troublesome during the relatively brief period of actual American conflict in World War I, how much greater was the potential for complaint during the three and a half years of fighting in World War II?

Ill-prepared to cope with what was considered in 1917–1918 to be a major increase in American armed forces, the military justice system was in a much worse position to meet the dramatic needs engendered by the Second World War. The army expanded from 1,460,000 personnel to more than 8,000,000. By 1945, the navy's ranks had doubled in size to over 4,500,000. In all, at least 12,000,000 people were subject to military justice, and at the height of the war, approximately 600,000 courts-martial were convened per year. Over 1,700,000 trials were held, more than 100 executions were carried out, and at the end of the war in 1945, some 45,000 members of the armed forces were in prison. Given these numbers, plus much greater public awareness of the war through advances in communication (e.g., radio and motion pictures), it is not surprising that severe criticism of the military justice system resulted. The dimensions of American involvement exacerbated weaknesses that, as the last three chapters have demonstrated, were repeatedly raised but not resolved more than a generation before.

While there may not have been a modern version of the famous *New York World* exposé of military justice during World War I, nevertheless, as was true in 1918–1919, during the aftermath of World War II the popular press featured numerous articles critical of military justice. Many of them mentioned the 1919 controversy and recalled Ansell's role. Moreover, members of Congress publicly criticized military justice after the war had ended. Following his late predecessor, George Chamberlain, Oregon senator Wayne Morse stated, for example, that military courts "have been guilty of the grossest types of miscarriage of justice." His colleague William Jenner accused the army of "stacking the courts against defendants in courts-martial," and Representative Charles Elston believed that "under present law[,] command has an abnormal and unj[u]stified influence over military justice." While disputes over military justice tended to be less partisan than other controversies, in this case all three speakers were Republicans.

Unlike the Ansell-Crowder era, which focused attention primarily on the army, during the period from 1943 to 1948, it was the navy's turn to receive extensive critical scrutiny. In view of the not unreasonable conclusion that without changes similar to the 1920 reforms the navy court-martial system "was even more inadequate than that of the Army," the success of the navy in avoiding extended external inquiry during the earlier controversy is noteworthy. Nor, indeed, had the contrast between public treatment of the two branches been lost on Enoch Crowder. Why, he wondered in 1919, "has not the storm broken out against the Navy? The answer is, I imagine, because the Judge Advocate General of the Navy was more alert in instructions and admonitions given courts than ourselves."

Unlike World War I, American entrance into the 1941 conflict was precipitated by a dramatic navy and air attack. Indeed, much of the war—especially in the early period—was primarily fought at sea. Understandably, therefore, beginning with the attack on Pearl Harbor public attention focused on the navy, and interest in or complaints about the quality of its military justice were to be expected. Judging from the fact that seven different reports, some from within the navy, others from externally appointed commissions, on the subject of naval military justice were submitted to the service within a four-year period (1943–1947), the navy was not unaware of the problem. Why it took such an effort, with the inevitable resulting duplication of findings and recommendations, is unclear. One explanation might be based upon the navy's desire for thoroughness before determining to change its judicial procedures. A less charitable but more accurate analysis could focus on the dilatory tactics of a bureaucracy encrusted with tradition. Not without reason was the cumbersome volume *Naval Courts and Boards* (the navy's version of the Army Manual for Courts-Martial) generically known as "Rocks and Shoals." It is not surprising to discover that in 1943 and thereafter, comments about naval military justice were similar to those made about the army's system twenty-five years earlier.

Between 1946 and 1950, when the Uniform Code of Military Justice was signed into law, along with the inevitable political issues such as the presidential election of 1948, Congress also had to deal with such difficult questions as the unification of the armed services, the establishment of the Department of Defense as well as the administrative machinery to run it, and the Berlin blockade and airlift, to list only a few. As was clearly demonstrated in 1919, military justice thirty years later also was not high on the congressional list of priorities. Nevertheless, out of such a plethora of proposals came a revised code that included a real appellate court. The initial bills reforming military justice focused on either the army or the navy. But once the services were better coordinated (perhaps "unified" is too strong a term), improving army and navy justice through separate revisions of their already complex legal systems made less and less sense, while the need for a single uniform system became readily apparent, even as specific congressional proposals were pending. The role of the armed services in the ultimate enactment of a unified code, however, would be very different in 1949 than thirty years earlier.

In 1943, the navy received the first of a number of reports that examined naval judicial procedures. A board headed by former undersecretary of the treasury Arthur Ballantine concluded that "nowhere do we find a requirement of law that any member of a general court martial shall be skilled in the law." Indeed, the report pointed (not unreasonably) to the connection between the quality of naval justice and the qualifications of its administrators. They should, it emphasized, be trained in law, and while experience can substitute for training "to a degree," legal work in the navy was generally performed either on temporary assignment or on intermittent tours of duty, neither of which "is hardly conducive to the accumulation of experience." Even worse was the committee's finding that "competence in law does not appear to be a factor of particular importance contributing to a successful career in the Navy." Nor should it be expected "when it is neither influenced by instruction, nor developed by experience, nor rewarded when acquired by independent effort."

The recommendations made in the Ballantine report were in the form of polite suggestions, a tactic that may have undercut its impact. In November 1945, another committee presented its version, and the contrast between the two documents is striking. The panel, headed by Federal District Court Judge Matthew F. McGuire, introduced its written evaluation with the comment, "It may be said categorically that the present system of military justice is not only antiquated, but outmoded." Based on the needs of a navy "where bread and water was routine, and flogging not an unusual occurrence," current navy judicial procedure is unable "to meet the demands of a modern" service. According to McGuire, "Certain basic rights vital in our viewpoint as a people, and by virtue of that fact inherent in, and essentially a part of any system, naval or otherwise that purports to do justice, must be accepted and safeguarded." Here also, "the present system fails."

McGuire reiterated a point made in the earlier Ballantine report about the incompatible duality in the judge advocate general's office. The trial judge advocate was "to inform the Court as to the law," but "he is told in the same breath that he *must* never forget he is the prosecutor—two positions diametrically opposed and mutually exclusive." Moreover, the navy mandated no provision for the most rudimentary procedures in criminal trials. Nor was this blatant omission remedied by requiring the judge advocate "to advise the Court in all matters of form and law." In fact, "it is advice with no sanction—it is not binding—and coming from one whose primary function is so completely diverse emphasizes the necessity for change. Humanity simply does not admit of such perfection."

Recognizing that grave miscarriages of justice can result when basic requirements of due process are not followed, McGuire was well aware of the standard military response to such criticism. "Nor can it be argued with any degree of persuasion or cogency that provision for such instruction interferes in any way with the function of command, and the maintenance of discipline. It *simply means* that if there are to be trials for violation of naval law, the rights of the individual accused are to be scrupulously respected and safeguarded—as they ought to be—which is emphatically not done under the present system of naval justice." Neither was the cause of justice aided by verdicts in a large number of cases that "strangely comports to what is felt is the desire of the convening authority." Finally, McGuire described *Naval Courts and Boards* (the navy equivalent to the army Manual for Courts-Martial) as "unprepossessing in format" and suffering from the "same lack of modernity as the Articles on which it is based." This volume is "hopelessly inutile, and apart from decided defects of prolixity, unfortunate choice and sequence of subject matter . . . is more confusing and harmful than helpful."

CONGRESS CONSIDERS

In retrospect, these multiple investigations into American military justice during World War II represented an unfortunate though understandable waste of resources. Had there been some mechanism for coordination of such activities between the army and navy, much duplication might have been avoided. Moreover, neither the Ballantine nor McGuire reports appear to have considered the lengthy materials that had accumulated during the army hearings in 1919. Not until 1947 did the navy receive a comprehensive, comparative analysis of military justice—one that not only compared other military systems but also drew heavily on the earlier army experiences. In the meantime, Congress as well as the army prepared their own proposals for change.

Between 1945 and 1946, the House Committee on Military Affairs conducted an extended examination of "the National War Effort" and spent more than a year studying both the court-martial procedure as well as the entire judicial system of the army. On August 1, 1946, it presented a number of recommendations to the House. Seen in the light of the Chamberlain bill in 1919 and the 1920 revisions of the Articles of War, the proposals reflected a desire to consolidate what existed rather than to construct new procedures. Thus, rather than create an appellate court, the committee urged that the judge advocate general be vested with appellate powers. Although similar to what Ansell had envisaged, the 1946 recommendations would have given the JAG even more authority than he had proposed.

The committee suggested that the JAG "be empowered to consider appeals from general court-martials both as to law and fact," and that he be able "to retry any case de novo, [or] order any case retried de novo [from the beginning]." In addition, he should have the power "to void any original proceeding, or to alter any sentence, or to issue an honorable discharge . . . or to take other action as may be required to correct any injustice and so far as possible to make whole the part or parties injured." Moreover, enlisted men, when tried by special or general court-martial, would have the right for a number of their peers to sit on the court, to the maximum of one-third of the total membership. "Failure to comply with this provision shall be a jurisdictional error."

The committee further proposed the requirement that the law member as well as the trial judge advocate and the defense counsel were either to be officers of the JAG Corps or officers who were members of the bar of a federal court or of the highest court of a state. The law member would not vote either on the findings or any resulting sentence. The convening authority would be forbidden to "censure, reprimand or admonish any member of a court-martial . . . with respect to the findings or sentences adjudged by such court."

Even as the committee sent these recommendations to the House, the army had selected its own advisory committee—nominated by the American Bar Association—to study military justice. Appointed on March 25, 1946, it consisted of nine civilians with Arthur Vanderbilt, dean of New York University Law School and soon to become chief justice of the New Jersey Supreme Court, as chair. On paper, the committee's investigation appeared impressive. It held regional hearings in nine cities throughout the country, accumulated more than twenty-five hundred pages of testimony, and received several hundred answers drawn from all ranks of the army to a questionnaire dealing with military justice.

There is little doubt that this panel received an accurate picture concerning many of the flaws in military justice. Indeed, earlier investigations and hearings had already exposed them. Thus, in retrospect the findings of the Vanderbilt Committee were to be expected, and their recommendations were not very innovative. Had the army, to say nothing of Congress, not already undertaken inquiries of similar import based upon similar complaints in 1919, they might have been more impressive. In actuality, however, they indicated the tenacity of tradition, and the fact that in 1946 the military establishment seemed unwilling to make changes first recommended more than twenty-five years earlier. For the reader familiar with the Ansell and Crowder controversy, a sense of déjà vu rather than doctrinal initiative hung over the Vanderbilt report.

It found, for example, that "the command frequently dominated the [military] courts in the rendition of their judgment"; that "defense counsel were often ineffective because of (a) lack of experience and knowledge, or (b) lack of a vigorous defense attitude"; that sentences "were frequently excessively severe and sometimes fantastically so"; that military justice afforded to enlisted men and officers differed "as to the bringing of charges[,] . . . convictions and sentences"; and that the pretrial investigations called for in article 70 (a result of the 1920 amendments) "were frequently inefficient or inadequate." As Ansell had repeatedly noted during 1918–1919, the committee also emphasized the need for the soldier to know that "if he is charged with an offense, his case will not rest entirely in the hands of his accuser, but that he will be able to present his evidence to an impartial tribunal with the assistance of competent counsel and receive a fair and intelligent review."

Moreover, the convening authority should be forbidden to reprimand members of the court in any way. Enlisted men should be able to serve as members of a court-martial. Both the defense counsel and law member should be trained lawyers; the ruling of the latter on legal questions should be binding on the court, "except as to the sufficiency of evidence." This exception had some justification. As the committee noted, "an adverse ruling . . . on the sufficiency of the evidence would result in an acquittal[,] and this question should therefore be left to the whole court." Although the navy was by far the worst offender, both services had failed to recognize "law as a profession in the same sense in which they recognized medicine." One committee member, Federal District Judge Alexander Holtzoff, later recalled that a retired army colonel testified "that the law member of a general court-martial did not have to be a lawyer, since he was given a manual which he could study and which would guide him in making his rulings." Holtzoff, who happened to be presiding at this particular session, asked the witness "whether he would be willing to designate a layman as a regimental doctor, if the latter would study a brief pamphlet on medicine. Naturally, the witness had no answer to make."

The Vanderbilt report was delivered to the War Department on December 13, 1946. Within about two months, Secretary of War Robert Patterson announced through the public relations division of the department that he "had approved the principal recommendations" of the committee. And indeed, to a much greater extent than Newton Baker in 1919, he did endorse various changes. These included the enlargement of the JAG Corps, the prohibition against any sort of reprimand to members of the court from the convening authority, the requirement of legal training for the law member, as well as the expanded appellate authority within the JAG office. From this list, as well as the title of the release itself, one could easily get the impression that substantial reforms were now inevitable.

On the other hand, the last three pages of the release contained information on what the secretary, presumably after discussions with his military advisers including Undersecretary of War Kenneth C. Royall, had declined to approve. These included the suggestions that the judge advocate general (presumably from Washington) be empowered to appoint members of a court instead of the convening authority; that the JAG, rather than army commanders, be responsible for evaluating members of his department; and that there be a separate promotion list for the JAG Corps. Also, the Vanderbilt recommendation that defense counsel should always be lawyers received short shrift. Not only was it impractical because there were not enough lawyers available, but also "in many simple military cases line officers are equally effective as counsel as are lawyers."

One month after the press release, the War Department submitted a bill to Congress that amended the Articles of War along the lines noted above. It was assigned to the Committee on Armed Services, which held hearings on the measure. Unlike the proceedings of an earlier era, in 1947 the most controversial issue did not deal with appellate jurisdiction. The War Department proposed that a three-member board of review be established within the JAG Corps. Called a "judicial council," it was to consist of three officers. Neither the proposed version nor the committee's amended draft that ultimately became law made any reference to civilian membership on the council. Moreover, neither version envisaged any formal rules of appellate pleading. The council did, however, have some expanded jurisdiction over the existing review boards.

With commendable understatement, the committee noted that "any system of judicial review is complicated, technical, and difficult to understand." Indeed, the military establishment apparently found the old article 50 1/2 so difficult to comprehend that they replaced it. With what success, however, is not clear. One student of military justice wrote in 1970 of the 1947 revised article that it "is nearly incomprehensible," while Frederick B. Wiener later stated that the creation of the judicial council added "an extra layer of further examination over the existing boards of review. The details of this expanded reviewing process were fully as complex as the wiring diagram of a large automobile's dashboard."

The committee made two additional changes, including one that disturbed the military establishment much more than the creation of a judicial council, which remained under the control of the JAG Corps at all times. Kenneth Royall had heralded the proposed change to permit enlisted men to serve on courts-martial "at the option of the appointing authority." To the committee, such an option undercut the force of the proposed change. The choice of whether or not to have enlisted men on the court should be "at the option of the defendant," not the commander. The other change involved the decision to establish a separate JAG Corps with a promotion list independent of line command—a step strongly opposed by the army on the grounds that it "would hurt discipline by reducing the power of the line commander."

THE KEEFFE-LARKIN PANEL

In 1947, James Forrestal received the report of the General Court-Martial Review Board, dealing with naval military justice. Originally convened in 1946, this board was charged with reviewing some five thousand prison sentences. It consisted of six officers and two civilians, one of whom was Arthur J. Keeffe, professor of law at Cornell University, who served as chair. Much of the actual direction for the board, however, came largely from its vice chair, Felix Larkin, a young lawyer who had previously assisted a municipal judge in New York City. A thoughtful analysis of almost four hundred pages, replete with scholarly citations, appendices, and references to the other reports submitted since 1943, it so impressed Forrestal that he invited Larkin to join his staff. Because Larkin later played such an important role in the drafting of the UCMJ as well as the specific proposal for an appellate tribunal, some of the particular comments and recommendations made in the report should be noted.

At the outset, the report strongly endorsed an earlier conclusion that "it can no longer be expected that [naval] legal affairs can be handled competently except by qualified, full time experts." While it specifically eschewed "considerations relating to possible unification of the armed services" (something that although imminent had not yet happened), most of its proposals "can be readily coordinated with any proposals for reform of the Army court-martial system." Both systems had retained the automatic review of court-martial findings and sentences by the convening authority. But Larkin's committee insisted that such a procedure be seen exactly for what it was.

It was not an appeal "in the true sense, and the analogy, if pressed too far, is misleading." In fact, such review "is a condition precedent" to the implementation of the court's "findings and sentence. It is a procedure peculiar to our military and naval law, deriving directly from the concept that the court is the arm or agency of the commander, and it has no real counterpart in Anglo-American civil law." Moreover, dispassionate analysis revealed major weaknesses with the practice, however it was labeled.

In the first place, "the reviewing authority is usually the same officer who convened the court and referred the case to trial." It is "humanly impossible for a person, no matter how high his purpose, to dissociate himself from his prior actions and opinions . . . and to view it later as though he were seeing it for the first time." Furthermore, as indicated earlier, the review actually undertaken was "not really analogous to an appeal." Technically speaking, defense counsel could submit briefs, but "he does not often do so, and rarely, if ever, resorts to oral presentation of the case to the convening authority." Even while conceding that—in theory—objections raised concerning evidence and rulings were weighed as though on appeal and that the record could be carefully scrutinized for jurisdictional errors, "it is difficult, [with] such a procedure, to detect all the errors which may exist, sometimes serious ones."

The "practical result" of these proceedings was "that the reviewing authority rather than the court" fixed the sentences; and while he could extend clemency, all too often such action consisted "merely [of] reducing the sentence to something approaching what it should have been in the first place." Such a practice inevitably gave the reviewing authority "a large measure of indirect control over the court and its actions." Members of the court, usually of inferior rank to that of the reviewing authority, would be less than human if they were not aware of his preferences concerning penalties.

Larkin's committee further concluded that the solution lay in strengthening the initial court-martial proceeding, not in relying "on subsequent [internal] reviews to correct deficiencies therein." The best ways to accomplish this goal were to separate the reviewing officer from the one ordering the case to trial and "abolish the intitial review altogether . . . making the court's sentence self executory, subject however to being set aside by a Board of Review or other higher authority." To be sure, a step that eliminated control of a convening authority over the sentence "might be destructive of discipline." To their credit, the report's authors did not flinch from the implications of these recommendations. Once a case has been referred to trial, "it ceases to be a mere disciplinary matter, and from that time on the process of law should be paramount, and command control should cease."

Moreover, the form of review beyond the convening authority in many instances was less than satisfactory. In fact, the secretary of the navy might receive a case from the judge advocate general's office or from the Bureau of Naval Personnel. For the most part unable to examine these cases personally, he would refer them to other officers—with the possibility of receiving several distinct and varying recommendations. Thus, the final action taken by the secretary frequently might be a "compromise of half a dozen views. Administratively, and from the standpoint of justice, such a result is deplorable." Also, the secretary was ill-equipped to distinguish between the need for "legal review, for legal sufficiency of the proceedings, findings, and sentence; and sentence review, for appropriateness of the sentence, clemency factors, and the like."

Building on similar suggestions put forth by the Ballantine and McGuire reports, Keeffe's committee recommended that a board of legal review be established by statute, and that it be housed in the office of the secretary rather than in the JAG Corps. Although there seemed to be general agreement on a three-member board, "five would be equally satisfactory." At least one member should be a civilian. But possibly more important was that all members "be highly qualified for their important duties and that they be appointed on a long term, semi-permanent basis." The civilian member should have a term of at least six years and should be "a well qualified civilian lawyer or judge of long experience. He should not be a naval officer or civilian official who has been retired for age." He should "be appointed by the President, as the Commander in Chief of the Navy, on the recommendation of the Secretary." In terms of salary, "there is no reason why he should receive less than a federal District or Circuit Judge." In short, "the goal should be the establishment of a Board of Legal Review occupying the same place in the scheme of naval justice as the Circuit Court of Appeals does in the system of federal courts, and having the same dignity, standing and importance."

Finally, the committee turned to the relationship between the findings of its proposed board of legal review and civilian appellate courts. As earlier chapters have noted, collateral attack—often on jurisdictional grounds—remained an acceptable route to civilian judicial review of court-martial decisions. This approach, however, while viable, was also cumbersome. The committee suggested in appropriate cases "authorizing a petitition for review of the findings and decisions of the [proposed] Board of Legal Review to be filed directly with the United States Supreme Court." Granted that the high court, already burdened with a heavy calendar of cases, might not welcome such a change, its adoption "might improve and strengthen the system of naval justice." Although they would not occur until more than thirty years after the UCMJ had been enacted, the two proposals for a five-member court as well as a limited appeal to the U.S. Supreme Court ultimately became law.

Indeed, "from the standpoint of full justice, it is important that this ultimate right of appeal be granted to every accused," especially "in cases involving constitutional privileges and due process." Just as the highest civilian state courts were not infallible, "it is not to be expected that the Naval Board of Legal Review would be entirely free from error." The report noted how promptly the cases of Nazi saboteurs and Japanese generals had received review before the Supreme Court. "The granting of such an extraordinary privilege of appeal to a nation's enemies has been applauded, and properly so." Their "defense counsel secured for the accused . . . every right and privilege known to our law." However, "we should be no less ready to grant similar privileges to our own military and naval personnel, when substantial questions of jurisdiction and due process arise in court-martial proceedings." If this can be done for our enemies, "provision should be made to insure that it is done for our military and naval personnel, not merely as a matter of theoretical right, but as a matter of deed and fact."

THE NAVY BECALMED

The navy's "official" reaction to the plethora of proposals for change took the form of a congressional bill. Presented at the request of the service about five months after receipt of the Keeffe Committee's report, the bill "to amend the Articles for the Government of the Navy[and] to improve the administration of Naval justice" was introduced in the Senate on May 26, 1947, and in the House on June 2. There is no doubt that the navy "brass" seriously considered some of the suggestions for change previously put forward. But on the whole, the generalization that tradition dies hard in the military, and hardest in the navy, received little challenge from this suggested legislation. All commanders were still required to "show in themselves a good example of virtue, honor, patriotism, and subordination." Unspecified penalties could still be meted out by courts-martial for more than fifty-five specified offenses. These included "profane swearing, falsehood, or gambling" as well as the act of "send[ing] or accept[ing] a challenge to fight a duel or act[ing] as a second in a duel."

Navy officials did recommend some changes. The Keeffe report had urged that "qualified officers who are lawyers should be provided to act as prosecuting lawyers and defense counsel for every general court-martial." The proposed bill stated that the convening authority shall appoint "a prosecutor and a defense counsel who shall be persons qualified to perform such duties." Did this language mean that the prosecutor and defense counsel had to be lawyers?

In an article published only a few months after the bill had been submitted to Congress, Larkin and Robert Pasley Jr., a staff member of Keeffe's committee, so concluded. The actual language of the navy version, however, does not seem to support this interpretation. The word "lawyer" has a definite meaning to it, especially in terms of qualifications to practice. Had the navy wished to require that its prosecutors and defense counsel be lawyers, it could have employed the specific term (as did the Keeffe report) instead of the language used.

The report had also suggested that the convening authority be required to appoint as judge advocate an officer so certified by the navy judge advocate general. This individual would be responsible *not* to the convenor but to TJAG. The navy bill accepted both these proposals, but with a change that reflected the service's traditional concern with command.

The committee had favored a trial procedure where the ruling of the judge advocate on matters of evidence and interlocutory questions was to be binding upon members of the court. The navy supported this recommendation so far as the judge advocate should indeed advise the court on this and other matters as well, but added that he "may be overruled by a majority vote of the court in which the reasons therefore shall be spread upon the record." Larkin and Pasley explained that "the Navy's reasons for [this proviso] are understood to be based upon the feeling that an anomalous situation would be created if the judge advocate, who might be a junior officer, could impose his judgement on the rest of the court, who might all be senior to him. The Navy believes as a practical matter, the judge advocate will rarely be overruled, because of the requirement that in any case where he is overruled, the reasons therefor[e] be spread upon the record."

The Keeffe committee had desired that the traditional post–court-martial review be undertaken by an authority other than the convenor–who presumably had brought the case to trial in the first place. The navy declined to accept the change, probably concluding that it repudiated "the importance of the command function." On the other hand, it proposed restriction of the convenor's authority "to a clemency function solely." Finally, the navy draft made no mention whatsoever of the proposed board of legal review. Instead, it included a provision that "under such regulations as may be prescribed by the Secretary . . . the proceedings, findings, and sentence of a court martial shall, upon good cause shown, if requested by the person convicted, within one year after such person has been informed that the review of his case has been completed, again be reviewed." The draft was unclear as to who would review, the extent of such a procedure, and the composition of its members.

Pasley and Larkin prepared their article during the summer of 1947. When Keeffe saw the draft, apparently he was less than enchanted with its treatment of the navy response to his committee's report. "It gives me great pause," he wrote to Larkin. "I think it is dull as dish water and picked clean of any conviction. If we [presumably Keeffe was referring here to the *Cornell Law Quarterly*] publish it, I think I will precede it with 10 hot pages as to what is really wrong with the Navy bill. Want to join me?" Larkin promptly replied from Washington, where he had recently become a full-time member of Forrestal's staff.

He reminded Keeffe that the aim of the article, undertaken "at a great sacrifice of time and effort," was to take "an approach quite different from the critical approach we took when we examined the Navy system and, hence, called for no propaganda." He was "considerably disturbed by your idea of writing a ten page blast. I think the time for that kind of thing is past, and I have neither the inclination nor opportunity to join you on any such fiery project." Somehow Larkin had assumed that the committee, including Keeffe, was "one on our criticisms of the Navy system and that we all agreed that the Navy Bill incorporated 98 percent of our recommendations." What "has changed your mind about the Navy Bill . . . ? Maybe you have been eating too much red meat."

The perturbed professor's response, if indeed he wrote one, has not been located, and the Pasley-Larkin piece was duly published in the *Cornell University Law Quarterly* without any prefatory comments from Keeffe. In correspondence Larkin admitted that the article "isn't very spicy reading." Quoting Keeffe's unflattering description of it, Larkin added that "Keeffe's objection, of course, stems from the fact that we refrained from stirring up every controversial issue and we did not break a lance for all his pet theories." Nor was Larkin surprised that the ten-page diatribe "never materialized. I was confident that it wouldn't because that would mean that Keeffe would have to sit down and write something."

With the submission of the navy bill, even as the Armed Services Committee had voted to report major reforms in military justice, Congress now had two separate plans to consider as 1947 drew to a close. But it had recently enacted legislation that "unified" the armed services and established the office of the secretary of defense. Indeed, although Larkin may not have realized it, by the time he sent out reprints of his article, the time for changes applicable to a single service had passed. To the greatest extent thus far in our military history, unification was now a fact, and a uniform approach to military justice seemed to make very good sense. In the spring of 1948, both the chairman of the Senate Armed Services Committee as well as James Forrestal were ready to move in this direction.

7

Forrestal Creates Two Committees, 1948

As amended by its Committee on the Armed Services on January 15, 1948, the House passed the bill to revise the Articles of War. Later known as the Elston Act (named for its sponsor, Charles Elston of Ohio), it languished in the Senate from January to June 1948. The chairman of the Senate Armed Services Committee, J. Chandler "Chan" Gurney, had been deeply involved in the congressional drive toward unification. With that goal accomplished, he preferred to wait on the House measure, seeking a broader military justice revision that would be applicable to all the services, not just the army. Moreover, it seemed that the chair, if not the full Senate Armed Services Committee, was not nearly as enthusiastic about a separate Judge Advocate General Corps as the House had been. Thus Gurney had at least a two-part justification for not moving forward quickly. Whatever his reasons, this lengthy delay for Senate consideration of Elston's bill irritated not only numerous members of Congress who had labored over its provisions, but also segments of the legal community who saw it as an important move toward court-martial reform, albeit only a first step.

Gurney's dual dissatisfaction with the House enactment may have convinced him to propose a shift in the stage for court-martial reform to, as it were, another theater. On May 3, 1948, he wrote to James Forrestal concerning both the Elston bill and the naval counterpart. Because these pending proposals "do not provide a uniform system of military justice applicable alike to all three services, I think it would be well to have an over-all study made, and defense establishment proposals ready for the convening of the 81st Congress." Gurney assured Forrestal that "this letter is a personal one from me and gives only my thoughts in the matter. It does not in any way reflect any action that has been taken by the Senate Armed Services Committee."

Three days later Forrestal replied to Gurney's letter and indicated that internal discussions within his office had already been held "concerning the feasibility of such an approach." After congressional adjournment, the three services "could profitably look into the matter." He added that "I offer the foregoing as my personal and interim comment." The question arises why both men were so careful to hedge their comments.

In actuality, Gurney was suggesting to Forrestal a radical departure from previous practice. His innocuous words concealed a proposal that Forrestal's office (the "defense establishment") prepare some sort of legislative draft that *it* would present to Congress on behalf of *all* the armed services. The army and navy had traditionally been treated separately by Congress. As the Ansell-Crowder episode well demonstrated, the army had not hesitated to involve itself in the legislative process. Similarly, the army and navy had each taken the lead in preparing their drafts of the legislation under consideration in 1947–1948. Gurney's idea that a civilian official undertake to speak for the armed services also reflected his awareness that unification was now a political reality. He possibly believed that his suggestion to Forrestal would undercut the need for Senate consideration of the pending House measure.

Forrestal's next step, on May 11, was to meet with the secretaries of the several services. They agreed to establish an ad hoc committee, consisting of a representative from Forrestal's office as chairman and one civilian undersecretary from each service—Gordon Gray, W. James Kenney, and Eugene M. Zuckert—representing respectively the army, navy, and the recently created air force. The task of this committee would be "preparing a uniform code of military justice which would be applicable alike to all three Services, and which could be submitted to the 81st Congress as the recommendation of the National Military establishment." At this date, the chairman had not yet been selected, nor had the drafting of the "final terms of reference" (the instructions for the committee) been completed.

The appointment of this committee was followed promptly by the creation of a second panel, known as "the Working Group." It consisted of at least one military representative selected by each member of the main panel plus a number of lawyers and civilian researchers within Forrestal's office. Felix Larkin, then a full-time member of Forrestal's staff, was named chairman of this group as well as executive secretary of the first committee. It would be the responsibility of this panel to cull through all the reports and investigations that had been prepared; to compare and contrast the present army and navy rules and procedures; and finally to produce a working draft of each article in a proposed new uniform code of military justice, applicable to all the services. Each article would be submitted to the ad hoc committee, as yet without a chair, for modification, rejection, or ultimate final approval.

SENATORS AND SELECTIVE SERVICE

By May 22, it was clear to members of the House Armed Services Committee that Senator Gurney was not about to move on the Elston bill. Forrestal received a phone call from its chair, Congressman Walter Andrews, who informed him that "they are upset that Gurney never did anything on the bill, and they realize now he's never going to do anything on the bill." Elston accepted this fact, and therefore—according to Andrews—"he will cooperate and welcome anything that's done over in your department[,] trying to bring them together." Andrew's phone call is important in that it established from the very beginning the preference that the code project would be linked to the congressional Armed Services Committees—as indeed turned out to be the case. This meant that when it came to implementing some provisions of the new code, such as appointment of judges to the Court of Military Appeals, approval of their nomination would come from the Armed Services Committee, *not* the Judiciary Committee. As will be seen in later chapters, this fact has had great significance for the Court's subsequent history. Having already received Gurney's encouragement, Forrestal was thus assured that—although for very disparate reasons—both Houses of Congress would be inclined to support the idea of a complete code being submitted to them by the "defense establishment" for consideration.

For his part, however, Gurney may have underestimated his colleagues' desire to reform military justice. When, early in June 1948, the Selective Service Act came up for Senate action, James Kem, a first-term senator from Missouri, moved to attach Elston's bill as a rider to the measure establishing the first postwar draft in American history. Indeed, according to a member of Larkin's staff who had also worked on the Keeffe committee's report, some members of the Senate refused to provide crucial votes for the Selective Service bill unless it was accompanied by immediate reform of the court-martial system.

Gurney was uncomfortable with Kem's motion. To adopt the Elston bill, applicable only to the army, "would amount to piece-meal legislation, and would not accomplish the true purpose envisioned by the Congress when it passed the unification legislation." Furthermore, the question of "fundamental control of the Military Establishment is of such consequence that it cannot be lightly considered by the Congress." It certainly should not "be hastily tacked onto a bill of such importance" as the draft. Gurney told his colleagues about Forrestal's new committee and read into the record the various communications between himself and the secretary dealing with it. The Senate should wait for "careful and complete consideration of the entire problem" rather than rush to "enact a piece of legislation which will be repealed by other legislation—soon, I hope."

Kem was not impressed. Why, he wondered, had Gurney's committee been unable to hold even one hearing on the House measure, a proposal that had been unanimously approved by that chamber? Kem further noted the lengthy hearings that had been held by Elston's committee and the wide public support the resulting legislation had received. Gurney responded that the House bill was in fact a composite proposal that "might be better and it might be worse. [His] committee has a right to change the language of a House passed bill." Gurney's colleague on the Armed Services Committee, Massachusetts senator Leverett Saltonstall, added that it should not be "attached blindfold" to the Selective Service bill.

Kem insisted that if Congress had time to reinstate the draft, it had time to revise the Articles of War. By a margin of only five votes (44 to 39), the Senate agreed. According to the *New York Times,* its action was "by a generally unexpected vote." With minimal discussion, the House accepted the amendment. No further hearings were held, and when President Truman signed the Selective Service Act of 1948, the provisions dealing with courts-martial became law— to go into effect nine months later. As far as Forrestal was concerned, this fact made it all the more important that a uniform code be drafted within this period of time.

With the ad hoc committee selected and the working group ready to construct an outline for a systematic revision of army and navy rules into a single code, the need to select a chair for Forrestal's committee had to be addressed. Between the middle of June and July 17, 1948, Forrestal's general counsel, Marx Leva, considered several possibilities. After graduating from Harvard Law School in 1940, Leva had clerked for Supreme Court Justice Hugo Black. He served in the navy during World War II and later filled several legal positions including counsel to Secretary of the Navy Forrestal. When Forrestal was appointed to the new position of secretary of defense, Leva went along as the first general counsel and also as one of the first assistant secretaries of defense.

There were a number of distinguished lawyers and scholars who had been very active in the drive since 1943 to reform military justice. Several had authored one or more of the numerous reports now available. Ballantine and Vanderbilt, to say nothing of Arthur Keeffe, were among this group. And, as will be seen shortly, Keeffe certainly was considered, at least in his own opinion, as an appropriate candidate.

Yet Larkin believed, and so ultimately did Leva, that the chair should "be one who had not previously engaged in a study of any one service." Since each service viewpoint would "be represented through the individual [under or assistant] secretary," it was all the more important that the chair be unconnected with the recent spate of investigations and reports. "On this basis," as Larkin tactfully wrote Keeffe, "which I am sure you will agree is logical, such stalwarts as Vanderbilt . . . and yourself were disqualified." In addition, Owen J. Roberts—a former justice of the Supreme Court and recently named dean of Pennsylvania Law School—was at least mentioned, if not seriously considered as a candidate.

There seems to be no doubt that Leva first proposed Edmund Morgan as a possible chair for the committee. He had been a student of Morgan's at Harvard Law School in 1939. Another of Forrestal's assistants, John Ohly, also had been a Morgan student, as had John Kenney, who was to represent the navy on the code committee. Fully aware of Morgan's interest in military justice during World War I and his strong support for Ansell in 1918–1919, Leva believed that, far from being a handicap, these factors were positive justification for Morgan's candidacy.

Moreover, it is very clear that Forrestal and other defense officials were well informed of Morgan's past activities involving military justice. Thus, Leva told Larkin on July 13 that "he had talked to [army secretary] Royall about Morgan for Chairman of the [new committee], and Royall thought he would be good." Because Forrestal agreed with Leva that an outside figure (a sort—as Leva put it—of "a stormy petrel") would be most suitable as a strong chair of the committee, by the middle of July he was ready to talk with Morgan. There is no indication that Forrestal or Leva somehow sought to ensure that Ansell's ideas would be incorporated into the new code through Morgan's appointment. On the contrary, he would be only one of a four-member committee, with three of the four well able to speak on behalf of a particular service. Like most strong committees, give-and-take and ultimate compromise rather than domination by the chair characterized the workings of this Committee on Military Justice.

Morgan, at that time seventy years old and soon to be retired (not by choice) from Harvard Law School, had been at that institution for almost a quarter of a century, including two stints as acting dean. During World War II he served as chairman for one of the war shipping panels with the War Labor Board. This diminutive academician (barely five feet tall) seemed to resemble something of a pixie rather than an intimidating professor. Yet he was known for the demands he made upon his students, and opinion concerning his skills as a teacher of law—aside from his undoubted distinction as a legal scholar—was far from unanimous.

Among Morgan's papers is a five-page, handwritten letter from one of his students in civil procedure during 1936. At the outset, the writer (identified only as "J.R.D.") informed Morgan that "you are the world's worst expounder of the law." If he was teaching torts, "we would not mind so much since there are abundant sources of clear exposition, we could ignore everything you said." If "you are really trying to make things reasonably clear (this may be an enormous assumption), the only fair thing for you to do would be [to] go back to practice." Morgan should realize that he is "a terrible instructor." Perhaps, added the student, "you do not care whether your students respect you or not—but whether you do or not it is clear that they don't. [We all] like you as a man, but a lot of us still think you are the world's worst expounder of the law."

Conversations with several of Morgan's former students as well as interviews with both his children indicate that he was indeed regarded as a very "tough" instructor. According to the *Harvard Law Bulletin,* "his kindness and deference mitigate in part the medieval horrors to which he subjects his students." Morgan's son, the distinguished historian Edmund S. Morgan, recalled that after his father had flunked several students in his evidence class, they arranged to retake the course in the summer at the University of Denver Law School. Unknown to them, however, Morgan had agreed to teach that evidence course at Denver—and the reaction of the students upon walking into the classroom and learning the identity of their "new" instructor can only be imagined.

Such was the man to whom Forrestal wrote on July 17, 1948: "I sincerely hope that your personal affairs will permit you to accept the Chairmanship which I now offer to you on behalf of myself as Secretary of Defense, and on behalf of the Secretaries of the Army, Navy and Air Force." Even before seeking approval from his dean, Morgan informed Forrestal about his support for Ansell and his opposition to Crowder during 1918–1919. Pending Forrestal's response, Morgan contacted Erwin Griswold, then on the threshold of what would turn out to be a very distinguished tenure as dean of Harvard Law School. Although Griswold was troubled about the proclivity for some of his faculty to spend a lot of time in Washington, he also realized that Morgan soon would have to retire from Harvard. Moreover, "you are old enough to know what you want to do, and I feel very clear that the School should be happy to have you take the leading position in this task." It "is an important one, and you are surely well qualified to deal with it. I think it is an honor for you, and an honor for the School."

Meanwhile, Forrestal reassured Morgan that "I was already familiar with your service during World War I, but it was very thoughtful of you to mention it in your letter. The part which you played in connection with the necessity for reforms in the military justice system at that time should be an asset rather than a liability." Duly appointed on July 29, 1948, as an "expert advisor on the military justice study being undertaken by OSD [office of the secretary of defense]," Morgan was to be paid fifty dollars a day.

MORGAN AND LARKIN

Before Morgan had accepted the appointment as chair and the instructions (the precept, or terms of reference) had been drafted, Larkin proposed a new approach to committee deliberation and decision-making that turned out to be of great importance. Because of his work on the Keeffe report, he had necessarily become familiar with the voluminous prior reports, hearings, and investigations concerning military justice. He also knew of their usual fate, one not unique to many studies of the government by committees. Upon completion, they had to be returned to the originating department for review and reaction. Frequently, the reports never appeared again. They were, in reality, almost always exercises in futility. The last thing Larkin wanted was to spend a lot of time on a comparative study and then have the judge advocates from the three services "review it, and have it interminably debated and nothing ever happen."

He pointed out to Forrestal that the services were well represented on both the working group panel and the committee of the three under secretaries—each of whom could draw on whatever legal or military expertise he felt appropriate from within his own service. Once this committee had agreed among itself, Larkin urged that the resulting decision not be reviewed again by any of the services or even by the office of the secretary of defense, but that it be *final*. In those instances where the committee could not reach consensus, he suggested that Forrestal himself have the last word. The secretary accepted Larkin's proposals with the result that in more than three-fourths of the articles, approval by the committee would be the last step prior to the process of submission to Congress. In those few areas where the committee could not agree, Forrestal's decision would also be final. Unlike the Ansell-Chamberlain proposals in 1919, the military in 1948 could discuss and even debate—but they could not derail.

Larkin submitted a draft of the precept and terms of reference for the Committee on a Uniform Code of Military Justice (hereinafter called the CUCMJ) to Forrestal on August 12, 1948. As he saw it, three objectives could be met by drafting a uniform code in time for submission to the 81st Congress: (1) The proposed code should integrate three military justice systems into one, "on as uniform a basis as possible." (2) Modernization of substantive and procedural aspects of military justice should be undertaken with a view both to protect "the rights of those subject to the code" and to increase "public confidence in the military justice system." (3) The language and draftmanship of both the army and navy military justice procedures should be improved, and matters of jurisdiction or substance should be organized "in a logical and orderly manner." The CUCMJ should "take advantage of the studies, reports, articles, recommendations and proposed legislation which exists in the field of military justice."

Forrestal accepted most of Larkin's draft but added a provision that "the Committee shall . . . invite the views of such individuals and organizations from outside the National Military Establishment as it may desire." Forrestal, possibly on advice from Marx Leva, may have concluded that, given the very limited time in which to draft the code as well as the vast amount of prepared material already available, it would not be necessary for the committee to hear witnesses as much as to ensure that interested parties could submit their views in writing. This, it did.

With the first meeting of Morgan's committee scheduled for August 18, Larkin submitted a progress report to Forrestal. He informed the secretary that the working group had already been meeting since June. Representatives from

the Armed Services Committees of both the House and Senate would participate. Again, he saw three major aspects to drafting a uniform code between
August 1948 and January 1949: (1) To recodify "in a logical, sensible form,
new articles applicable to the three [services]." At present, he added, "the Articles of War and the corresponding Articles for the Government of the Navy are
so mixed up [that] it is difficult to find anything in them." Indeed, a recodifi-
cation "without change would be a major contribution in itself." (2) The differences between the three services had to be addressed. (3) There also was the
need to consider the wishes of Congress as indicated in the Elston Act, to say
nothing of "other criticisms which have been made over the years." In conclusion, Larkin reminded Forrestal that Morgan's committee "will require a maximum amount of delegation of authority from you and the three departmental
secretaries, because I am certain that time will not permit a restudy by the
Departments of the uniform code."

Morgan presided over the first meeting of his committee on August 18,
1948. It agreed that the proposals prepared by the working group "are to serve
as a basis for the Committee's deliberations." Moreover, "the members of the
Committee will reflect to the extent they desire the viewpoint of their respective departments [services], and have authority to bind them." Zuckert of the
air force noted that "it might be helpful to have the views of key representatives of the services on certain controversial issues. It was [decided] that they
would be invited to appear personally before the Committee in that event." As
to the code to be drafted, it should "be uniform in substance . . . in interpretation and application."

In response to the press announcement concerning the formation of Morgan's committee and his request to various interested parties for comments
and suggestions about military justice reforms, numerous letters were received
at Larkin's office during the fall of 1948. They, together with the copies of
documents and reports previously given to him by Larkin, represented a valuable introduction to the Harvard professor's new role. A committee from the
New York County Lawyers' Association reminded Morgan that, for all its supposed reforms, the Elston Act—to go into effect in February 1949—still
vested review power strictly within the military. Prosecutors and defense counsel were to be members of the JAG Corps or otherwise qualified lawyers only
"if available—a qualification which realistically leaves the situation in status
quo." So far as the basic "fundamental matters at which the movement for
court martial reform has been aimed, little is accomplished by the Elston Act."
The "torturous" system of review it set up "is completely at odds with American concepts of justice."

The collection of comments contained one letter from William Hastie, at
that time governor of the Virgin Islands and soon to be named by President
Truman to the U.S. Court of Appeals. Hastie urged that military trial judges
"should be persons of the temperament and professional training considered

essential for judges of civil courts. Moreover, through tenure and freedom from responsibility to field commanders, military judges should be relieved of pressures which now affect their work."

A different view came from a 1932 graduate of Harvard Law School. Allen Miller wrote to Morgan that "we have noted the resolutions of the Vanderbilt Committee, and the suggestions of other lawyers' committees composed of lawyers, many of whom never spent a day in the Army, much less a day involved in military matters, and we are quite concerned lest overemphasis of the individual's rights as an approach to military justice undermine the paramount purpose, that is, administrative control in a war organization as the chief mission of a disciplinary code."

The disparity of viewpoints illustrated by these excerpts represented only one of several challenges confronting the CUCMJ. In addition to the difficulty of constructing a code that could ensure due process for the military and at the same time not impede the armed services in their functions, both Morgan's panel and the working group in particular had to consider the political preferences already demonstrated by Congress as well as differences between the services—primarily the army and navy—in their military justice procedures. A third problem lay in the larger context within which the new code would be drafted.

At an early stage in its work, Larkin told the working group that since 1947, there had been a dramatic increase in habeas corpus petitions filed on behalf of federal prisoners, many of whom had been convicted by courts-martial. Both the implication and impact of this trend were clear. Larkin emphasized the desirability of "keeping [these cases] out of the federal courts. This could only happen if military justice in fact represented "a system which would perhaps bend over a little backwards to fulfill" basic requirements of due process. If the military establishment was unable to draft such a procedure that worked, one would ultimately be created for it. Indeed, it can be argued that the decision to establish dual committees, both dominated by civilians, to construct a uniform code was recognition that the military had been unable to impose on itself the type of military justice reforms sought by the external legal order.

Although the committee achieved a surprising extent of unanimity on most of the provisions of the uniform code (there were ultimately over 140 of them), consensus broke down concerning three issues. Linked to the problem of both appearance and reality of fairness in military justice procedure, they also clearly reflected the challenges just described. The three areas of difficulty concerned the questions of enlisted men serving on courts-martial, the role of the law member as a judge, and the nature of the review and appellate process.

It will be recalled that the Elston Act had provided enlisted soldiers with the right to have a limited number of their peers as members of a court-martial. Larkin accurately characterized the army viewpoint as "we don't like it, perhaps, too much, but actually we don't object." He further suggested that the committee take the same position vis-à-vis the other services: "I don't think it would cause any great harm and I am frank to say I am quite sure it won't do a heck of a lot of good." The navy representative opposed expanding this policy to his service. The congressional decision to adopt it for the army underlined the fact, in his opinion, that "we should not yield to expediency here. . . . We are not a political branch of the government. . . . Congress is, and if they properly feel they must do it as a matter of expediency, I do not feel it is up to us to anticipate that and to do something." Larkin reminded his working group that Congress had already spoken on this subject, and "they are going to expect and we are going to try to come up with something uniform."

A second example where consensus failed was the question concerning the law member of the court-martial and whether or not he should function strictly as a judge or retire to deliberate with the other members of the court and actually vote on the case. The army and the newly independent air force supported the latter option, in part because they apparently lacked the personnel to support a panel of judges who did nothing else but preside at trials. Moreover, according to Stewart Maxey of the air force, if the law member had to give instructions in open court, they would have to be drafted to withstand legal challenges. This would lead to numerous errors for other courts to review. If, on the contrary, he retired with the other members, he could explain the law in simple layman's terms that could be clearly understood—thus increasing the chances for a legally acceptable verdict. This time, Larkin found himself supporting the navy.

What Maxey was actually saying, Larkin argued, was that there were many errors in informal layman's language that the law member uses, "and if they were to be spread on the record [in open court], they would have to be disclosed . . . and as I see it, we don't want to catch those errors because it slows up the system." Maxey responded that errors are not committed by the law member. Numerous questions are asked, "which he answers, and we don't have the errors in law. Actually, there are few errors." Larkin replied, "Of course we don't know, do we?" In fact, "what he [the law member] tells them in layman's language is not preserved. We know nothing of what he tells them." In turn, Maxey pointed to the outcome of the trials as evidence that the great majority of verdicts were properly determined.

> *Larkin:* "But you don't know what he told them, what is the law on the basis of which they found the facts and applied them."
> *Maxey:* "I won't concede that there is any error being committed now."
> *Larkin:* "I don't charge that there is because I don't know. I don't think anybody else knows because they never see what he does say."

The army representative emphasized that "the glory of the court-martial system has been its freedom from technicalities. . . . we are apprehensive that this proposal . . . will give rise not to justice, but to innumerable injustices from the government's point of view by affording loopholes and technicalities on which men clearly guilty will escape." Larkin ended the discussion by noting that this issue would have to be solved by Morgan's committee. He could not see any compromise between the two positions: "I'd be delighted to recommend one but I can't see one. There isn't any. I dislike sending up something that is split, but I . . . think it is inevitable that we'll have to do this at times."

When Morgan's committee considered the question of the law member, it reflected the same split apparent in the working group. Larkin and Kenney supported the idea of the law member acting as a judge: "Any errors he may make in charging the jury will be reviewable if placed on the record[,] and since instructions on the law to the jury are a source of a great number of reversible errors [they] should be subject to review." Moreover, "if the judge does not vote with the jury, his position as a judicial officer is more clearly established." Morgan agreed, but Gray and Zuckert remained unconvinced. As with the issue of enlisted men serving on courts-martial, so here with the question of the judicial role of the law member—Forrestal would have to make the ultimate decision.

The problem of what sort of appellate review should be implemented for all the armed services represented the most difficult challenge for the CUCMJ, if only because of the disparity between the two existing models, army and navy. The Elston Act, for example, had rescinded the old article of war 50 1/2 and replaced it with a confusing system that included the establishment of "judicial councils." Whatever the functions of these new tribunals, one characteristic of the army policy remained unchanged: the entire review process stayed within its purview. All boards of review were to be composed of JAG officers, with the judicial councils to include three "general officers" from the same department.

The navy proposals for appellate review had been embodied in a bill that never passed Congress, and since the Elston Act applied only to the army, no changes were imminent. Thus, important differences remained between the two services. The navy board of review, for example, was only advisory to the judge advocate general, while the functions of the army judicial councils were specifically defined by the statute, which gave them at least some measure of judicial independence. Unlike his army counterpart, however, the secretary of the navy had full power concerning both clemency as well as other legal aspects of a court-martial. He alone among the three service secretaries, for example, had authority to convene a court-martial.

When the working group first took up the issue of a uniform appellate procedure, Larkin acknowledged that "the review should be as expertly done as possible from the legal standpoint and from the disciplinary standpoint" as well. Thinking possibly from a view of practicality, he indicated that perhaps reviews of legal issues as well as the severity of sentence should be undertaken by the same tribunal. But the real challenge was less overcoming technical difficulties than obviating interservice parochialism. His language might have been awkward, but Larkin's meaning was very clear: "I think your own mind is based on all you see of merit in your own system, and now if you would see if you can see any merit in the opposite system . . . for instance in the Army [and] Navy . . . and see if you can't work out a relatively uniform system for everybody and not think of your difficulties as a representative of your own Department but as a justice of defense, maybe we can come up with something workable."

The normal procedure was for the working group to present both suggestions and actual drafts of proposed articles to Morgan's committee. However, it was evident that the working group was far from any sort of agreement, and Morgan's panel was "impressed by the complexity of the review procedures." Larkin's minutes indicated that a change in approach was coming. This time, Morgan would not wait for the working group. "He had given considerable thought to this very important problem, and, after additional thought, will reduce his ideas to writing for distribution to the members of the Committee."

It is difficult to assess the extent to which Morgan influenced his committee, even though all of its other members were both much younger than he and law school graduates as well. Larkin recalled that in the give-and-take of drafting, Morgan "lost the argument in many cases and had to recede from some of his pet ideas." However, Larkin also stated on another occasion that Morgan "was a most dynamic factor in our deliberations. His erudition carried most arguments." What Morgan proposed to his committee concerning a uniform appellate review system, and whether Larkin's generalization was accurate concerning it, is discussed in the next chapter.

8

The Committee, the Code, and the Court, 1948–1949

By early October, Edmund Morgan was ready with his proposal for a uniform system of appellate review. On October 5, he sent a copy of it to Felix Larkin for distribution to the committee. "Enclosed," Morgan wrote, "please find a copy of the bombshell which I threatened to let go concerning the plan for appellate procure." Morgan assumed from the outset that his proposals would be controversial. He was absolutely correct.

MORGAN'S BOMBSHELL

Because he was concerned with a uniform code applicable to all the services, Morgan proposed a uniform review system of similar scope. His first level of review was by the convening authority who would receive "the entire record, including findings and sentences of every trial by general court martial." This officer "shall have the record examined by his staff judge advocate or legal officer." After that advice had been received, he had four options:

1. to "set aside any proceeding, finding or sentence or part thereof, as he finds legally insufficient, with the power to return the case for a rehearing";
2. to "remit or mitigate, but not commute, all or any part of a sentence, if he deems such action for the best interests of the service";
3. to combine "two or more" of these two options; or
4. to "approve the findings or sentence."

If the commander chose not to set aside the entire sentence or to return the case for a rehearing, Morgan's second stage called for submission to a board of review that would be established in the judge advocate general's office. Here, too, Morgan appeared to be echoing army procedure that had been in effect since the 1920 amendments to the Articles of War. Examination of the section indicates, however, that he would have gone much further in allocating powers to this board than existing practice dictated. Under his proposal:

> The Board of Review shall examine the whole record to ascertain whether the court has committed any error which has injuriously affected the substantial rights of the accused; it shall have the authority to weigh the evidence, judge the credibility of witnesses and determine controverted questions of fact, bearing in mind that the court saw and heard the witnesses who testified before it, and the Board shall determine whether the findings or sentence or both insofar as heretofore approved by the convening authority shall be set aside in whole or in part or affirmed in whole or in part, or modified, and whether the charges shall be dismissed or the case reheard.

Morgan did not spell out the implications of this second level, but they must have troubled senior officers comfortable with the existing procedures. Could the board of review supercede the judgment of a commander? Was the commander compelled to obey the mandate of the panel? My reading of Morgan's draft indicates an affirmative answer to both these questions.

Morgan's third level of review was the most radical of all, although, as with the other two parts of his plan, he described it in traditional terminology—in this instance as a "judicial council," the exact term that had been employed in the Elston Act. But his council was a very different tribunal from that envisaged in the legislation:

> The Secretary of Defense shall constitute in his office a Judicial Council composed of not less than three members, each of whom shall be a member of the bar admitted to practice before the Supreme Court of the United States (and of at least ten years' experience in the practice of the profession of law). Each member shall be nominated by the Secretary of Defense and be appointed by the President and shall receive a salary equal to that of a United States Circuit Judge. . . . The term of a regular member would be long, probably for life.

Morgan specified that in three types of cases, "the entire record, including findings, sentence, action by the convening authority and the opinion of the Board of Review, shall be forwarded to the Judicial Council for further review":

1. All cases in which the sentence affects a general officer, or in which the sentence is death;
2. All cases which the Judge Advocate General orders forwarded to the Judicial Council for review;

3. All cases in which a petition for review by the Council is filed by or on behalf of the accused and in which after considering the petition the Council determines that the petitioner has shown that there is a reasonable ground to believe injustice has been done to the accused[;] or that the determination of the Board of Review is in conflict with that of a Board of Review of another service; or that the best interests of the service will for some other reason be furthered by a review.

In its review, according to Morgan, the council "shall have authority to weigh evidence, judge the credibility of witnesses, determine controverted questions of fact and to order such disposition of the case as the demands of justice and the best interests of the service require."

In several instances, Morgan's three-part appeal plan represented a radical departure from existing practice in 1948. Besides the basic change to one uniform appellate system applicable to all the services, Morgan gave each level an unusual degree of independence. Possibly because he himself was uncertain, it was unclear from his first draft what relationship the board of review and the judicial council would have to the judge advocate general. In the Elston Act, they apparently had been intended to function more in an advisory capacity. Morgan's plan clearly put the judicial findings of both panels beyond the purview of the judge advocate general to approve or alter them. Moreover, Morgan took the judicial council out of the JAG office entirely and opened its membership to civilian lawyers with life tenure. Finally, he gave that panel broad discretionary jurisdiction over what cases it could hear. Compared to existing military appellate practice in 1948, Morgan's proposal could well be described as a "bombshell."

From Morgan's choice of words in this first draft, it is not certain that he originally intended to preclude members of the military from serving on the judicial council. There were numerous officers in the JAG Corps who met the criteria he listed. On the other hand, Larkin and members of the working group assumed from the outset that the judicial council would be dominated by, if not consist totally of, civilians. Furthermore, the fact that the council would be appointed by the secretary of defense, himself a civilian, lends credence to the view that Morgan wanted a civilian board. Subsequently, as the committee considered the ultimate form of the council, Morgan made it very clear that he had intended a court *only* of civilians. Thus, later drafts—including the one ultimately enacted—employed the term "from civilian life."

MILITARY REACTION

The working group met again on October 11, and the army representative emphasized that "we are opposed . . . very strongly [to] cutting the Judge Advocate or our Secretary out of the picture." The army also opposed Morgan's plan for a judicial council, calling instead for what had already been enacted under the Elston Act. The air force representative added that "military justice is a service function and action should be final in the service concerned." A judicial council for all the services might go too far in the direction of enforced uniformity. "We wish to approach uniformity as closely as possible but absolute flat uniformity is not a judicial matter at all." Moreover, the air force, like the army, did not support a judicial council in the secretary of defense's office. Larkin concluded that his working group opposed "a supreme court in the office of the Secretary of Defense, whether it be civilian or general officers or anybody else."

These viewpoints reflected an important distinction that troubled several service representatives to the working group. They were concerned less with some sort of advisory council than with the fact that it would be housed in Forrestal's office. At this time, unification was not even one year old. The relationship between the new secretary of defense and the three under secretaries was still in a very amorphous state. What new authority Forrestal possessed and what powers the three service secretaries still retained was not yet clear. The services could envision their respective secretaries with some role in the military justice appeal system. But Morgan's plan housed his council in Forrestal's office and apparently left the three undersecretaries virtually out of the picture. Thus, the various adjustments and changes to the proposed code that are discussed below must be seen in the context of an emerging Department of Defense with centralizing authority that appeared to diminish the traditional roles of the three service secretaries.

Although there appears to be no surviving transcript of the October 14 meeting of the CUCMJ, Larkin's minutes make it clear that Morgan's original proposal received major alterations. It should also be noted that Gordon Gray was absent from the meeting, and the consensus reached by those present was "subject to an expression of Mr. Gray's views and a draft of the [revised] proposal." It would seem, therefore, that whatever changes were made caused the air force and navy to drop their opposition.

The first major change involved the composition of the judicial council. No less than three "qualified civilians" would be appointed by the secretaries of the three services (instead of the secretary of defense), each secretary to appoint one-third of the council. Although the members were to be paid a salary comparable to that of federal circuit court judge, each would serve at the will of the secretary by whom he had been appointed rather than for the long terms that Morgan had originally suggested.

A second modification dramatically curtailed the authority of the council. Now it would be limited to a legal review in only four categories of cases: death sentences, dismissal from service, appeals by the accused, and referrals by the JAGs. The council would be without authority to weigh evidence, judge the credibility of witnesses, or determine controversial questions of fact. Instead, these functions were to be vested in the boards of review, appointed—it will be recalled—by the judge advocate general of each service. The final change restored a good deal of authority to the respective secretaries, including residual clemency powers.

A comparison of Morgan's original draft and the changes just noted reveals how much the Harvard law professor had to compromise. He had sought a council of civilians, appointed by the secretary of defense for extended terms. Instead, each secretary would appoint one-third of the tribunal. Since council members would hold office at the pleasure of that official, and since service secretaries were political appointments (rarely serving more than four years and often less), the outlook was for a frequent turnover of council members, something Morgan had wanted to avoid. Moreover, he had vested the council with very broad powers, including authority to decide matters of both fact and law as well as extensive jurisdiction in the area of rehearing. Instead, his council would be limited to a legal review only. On the other hand, the categories of cases that the council might hear remained essentially unchanged. And all these alterations had yet to receive endorsement from the army through Gordon Gray. Nevertheless, Larkin and one of his assistants agreed to redraft Morgan's plan into separate articles that embodied these changes and to have them available for further discussion at the next meetings of both the working group and the CUCMJ.

Morgan had originally proposed a tripartite review system. During the last part of October, Larkin, assisted by Cornell law professor Robert Pasley (who had worked so well with him on the Keeffe report), revised Morgan's suggestions into a series of separate articles. Although they "tightened up" some of Morgan's prose, Larkin and Pasley left his first two levels of review— i.e., by the convening authority and the board of review—essentially as he drafted them.

Article 56 redrew the new judicial council along the lines agreed upon at the October 14 meeting, with one key difference. Larkin's minutes for that meeting indicated that the council members were to serve at the pleasure of each secretary who had nominated them. Somehow, that provision was dropped from the Larkin and Pasley revision. Indeed, no term limitation of any sort whatsoever appears in the new wording. It may well be that Morgan's committee decided to leave the decision as to the length of years up to Congress. In any event, as will be seen, the final decision was not what Morgan had envisaged, and it seems reasonable to conclude that he acquiesced in this deletion.

MORGAN'S "READJUSTMENTS"

Although Morgan, Kenney, and Zuckert had tentatively endorsed what Larkin called "the Morgan plan as amended in many respects," they had also agreed to discuss the appellate process again at the meeting of October 28, 1948, when Gray would be present. On the morning of October 28, however, the judge advocate general of the air force wrote to Zuckert opposing a judicial council "composed of civilian lawyers." Major General Reginald Harmon reminded Zuckert that

> the administration of military justice is a function of the Military Establishment and not of the Federal Judiciary. There should be no division of authority between the military and civilian branches of government. . . . It is questionable . . . whether a civilian lawyer, unfamiliar with military justice and the customs of the service, will be more competent to discharge the functions of appellate review than will those lawyers [in] the Judge Advocate General's Department. In my opinion, the judicial counsel should be composed of officers from each service.

Harmon failed to convince Zuckert, who remained committed to the Morgan plan as amended.

Later, when Harmon testified before the Senate subcommittee considering the UCMJ, he endorsed Morgan's proposed court, possibly as a result of "instructions" from Zuckert. Nevertheless, Harmon—who served three consecutive terms as air force JAG—believed he had been consistent in his opposition to an appellate court. In 1987 he recalled that "I had some strong feelings about that development and still do. I don't think we needed it, and I don't think we need it now." As to the UCMJ, "I was not for the Uniform Code of Military Justice, and I'm not for it now."

When Morgan convened the meeting, Gray "regretfully but firmly" dissented from "the agreement you all agreed to." In the first place, he argued that the plan was contrary to the National Security Act of 1947. Reflecting the tension discussed earlier, Gray emphasized the statutory provision that the army, navy, and air force "shall be administered as individual executive departments by their respective secretaries." He held that until such time as Congress might decide to merge the three services into one, an unlikely eventuality, the secretary of the army "has and must have independent responsibility as to all matters pertaining to the Army, including courts-martial." He "strongly objected" to Morgan's "radical change" because it deprives "the Secretary of the Army of judicial authority, and lodges ultimate judicial authority in a tribunal composed of members without military experience and without responsibility for results."

Morgan replied that the judicial council "carries out both the letter and the spirit of the National Security Act. I'd be prepared to argue that before any court in the land." It seems too clear for argument, he added, that "in establishing a general program and exercising general authority and control . . . the Secretary . . . may set up a uniform system of military justice, and establish as the instrument for exercising his control a tribunal of civilians for the uniform construction and application of . . . a code of military justice." Morgan conceived of his judicial council as "the final interpreter of the law for the National Military Establishment" as embodied in a new uniform code. Functioning like a circuit court of appeals, "it would be like a court of last resort over a group of states, applying a uniform statute governing matters as to which their separate state courts had theretofore not been in harmony."

However, Gray's objections went beyond his belief that Morgan's judicial council violated federal statute. The proposal was bad enough as Morgan had drafted it. But John Kenney's revision, accepted by Zuckert and Morgan in Gray's absence, was even worse. The change would have the three secretaries each name one member of the council—to serve at their pleasure. If, according to Gray, "it was done on the basis that . . . the secretaries retain some sort of control[, you] cannot in theory have an independent Judicial Council. If they are removable at the will of the appointing secretary for what he might consider bad judgement or conduct that doesn't agree with his point of view, then you are really in trouble."

It seemed to Gray that Morgan's judicial council "seeks to serve two purposes—uniformity of application and civilian participation in review of cases." If this was so, he proposed a two-part alternative plan that would accomplish these goals but in a way that would not involve an independent civilian tribunal. On the contrary, it would involve only a change in the existing boards of review as set forth in the recently enacted Elston Act. He suggested that these tribunals be reconstituted to consist of three senior JAG officers, or two officers and one senior line officer, plus three "especially qualified civilian lawyers, who would be well paid." If the judge advocate general disagreed with a board's finding, he could take the matter to the service secretary.

Similarly, if the board split 3 to 3, the JAG could then present the record to the secretary. Gray saw several virtues in this proposal that were all absent from Morgan's plan. First, it involved civilian judges but *only within* a military appellate procedure. Second, these judges could contribute important input, but by themselves they could never obtain a majority. Third, the secretary of the army would be kept in this appellate review system. Gray failed to convince his three colleagues that his alternative was preferable to Morgan's plan as amended. They agreed, therefore, to disagree—and left it to James Forrestal to decide the ultimate form of the appellate process.

But before turning to other articles, Gray asked Morgan if he would consider substituting judges from the circuit court of appeals for his judicial council. Morgan's answer is of interest, especially in the light of the history of the U.S. Court of Appeals for the Armed Forces (USCAAF) since 1951. Although the Harvard law professor strongly favored civilian judges as the basic part of a court-martial appeals system, he drew a sharp distinction between an external civilian court and his proposed civilian court to be established under the auspices of a military code. Morgan had noted "an increasing tendency, particularly in the District Courts, to interfere with the court-martial on the grounds that their proceedings were too far off. I think if you had a council like [the one he proposed] at the head, you'd find a tendency to trust that council. Say, if it had gone through them and you had the opportunity to have certiorari there[,] the judges would be much more likely to keep their hands off."

Morgan's answer was prophetic. As will be discussed later, from its first sessions in 1951 to the present term, the USCAAF has been notably free of interference from other courts. Not until 1984 did Congress provide for appeal from certain of its decisions direct to the U.S. Supreme Court, and that tribunal has been very selective in accepting such petitions. Indeed, it could be that in one sense Morgan's plan may have worked too well. Surveillance of military justice by a civilian appellate court is not as extensive or effective as it could and—arguably—should be.

The CUCMJ had already restricted the judicial council to ruling on matters of law. Possibly to ensure continued support from Zuckert and Kenney, Morgan agreed to even narrower wording in the latest revisions, language that further diminished what little discretionary authority the council still retained. The new section provided that

> in any case reviewed by it, the Judicial Council shall act only with respect to the findings and sentence as approved by the convening authority and as affirmed or set aside as incorrect in law by the Board of Review. In a case which the Judge Advocate General orders forwarded to the Judicial Council, such action need be taken only with respect to the issues raised by him. In a case reviewed upon petition of the accused, such action need be taken only with respect to issues specified in the grant of review. The Judicial Council shall take action only with respect to matters of law.

There may be several factors that explain why Morgan acquiesced in restricting his proposed court only to matters of law. Like any good lawyer, he was fully aware that such a limitation rarely restrained a resourceful appellate court from intervening in a case it wished to hear. Further, he had prevailed in his insistence that the council would have the right to review "all cases in which, upon petition of the accused and good cause shown, the Judicial Council has granted a review." This very broad discretionary jurisdiction could well mitigate against the narrow restriction to matters of law. Finally, Morgan may have concluded that by insisting on what he had originally proposed, he might split his committee on this issue even more than it already was.

Morgan also had to accept the fact that the boards of review, the second level in his tripartite review system, had emerged with the broad authority to review matters of fact and law that he would have placed in his judicial council. To be sure, under Morgan's plan, these boards had greater independence than had been provided to them in the Elston Act; nevertheless, they were selected by each judge advocate general to serve at his pleasure. Moreover, although the November revision provided that such tribunals were to be "composed of not less than three officers or civilians," the JAG could, and in fact usually does, appoint only officers to serve on them. Whatever Morgan's true feelings may have been on the extent to which he had to compromise, he seems to have understood better than many of his fellow attorneys the realities of a military establishment and its requisite command structure. The Morgan who with marked indignation defended Ansell to William Howard Taft in 1919 was not the same Morgan who in 1948–1949 worked in apparent harmony with his committee to fashion the UCMJ.

GORDON GRAY'S GRIEVANCE

Even as Morgan's committee moved steadily toward an understanding, if not total agreement, concerning the form of the review system, the topic remained controversial. At the meeting on December 9, Gordon Gray raised a point "inherent in some of the problems of this Committee." Apparently troubled by his inability to persuade his colleagues to abandon a civilian appellate court for the military, he asked what would happen to a split vote within the committee. Suppose "Professor Morgan makes the recommendation to the Secretary of Defense[, who] adopts a point of view that the Chairman . . . has proposed." Could the other service or services in the minority "not have the privilege of going up before the Congress and opposing it?" Whether Morgan conferred with Forrestal is not clear, but on December 22, "Professor Morgan expressed his understanding that Mr. Forrestal had announced his decision that after [his?] approval of the UCMJ none of the armed services would be permitted to oppose or criticize it. He [Morgan] stated that this ban would also apply to himself."

Within two weeks of these CUCMJ meetings and after talking with Secretary of the Army Kenneth Royall, Gray contacted two well-known public figures in civilian-military administration, Henry Stimson and Robert Patterson. Stimson, secretary of war under Presidents William Howard Taft and Franklin D. Roosevelt, was living in retirement at the close of a career in public service that had lasted more than half a century. Robert Patterson served as secretary of war after Stimson and held office during the period when the Elston Act was under consideration in Congress. Both men were highly respected in the military establishment and well acquainted with James Forrestal. It may have been this fact that led Gray to seek them out.

From the outset, the Morgan committee had agreed that they would not make any provisions of the new code public until after the entire document had been approved by Forrestal and submitted to Congress. Nevertheless, on December 21, after he had set up a meeting with Stimson for December 29, Gray sent the former secretary a copy of Morgan's proposed judicial council, a description of its functions, and Gray's counterproposal. Knowing that his actions were in direct violation of committee policy, Gray asked both men to consider the enclosures classified, "as I am not at liberty to make public the deliberations or findings of the committee in advance of our report to Secretary Forrestal and his decision."

One can only speculate as to why Gray took this highly unusual action. There is no doubt that he strongly believed Morgan's judicial council to be inappropriate, if not illegal. He probably hoped that a few private words from such luminaries as Stimson and Patterson might influence Forrestal to a greater degree than if the current secretary of the army, Kenneth Royall, attempted to do so.

Gray informed Stimson and Patterson of his belief that Morgan's plan "would divest the Judge Advocate General of all power now exercised by him on appellate review . . . , [and] would divest the Secretary of the Army of his present power to determine the legality of court-martial convictions. . . . This plan, if adopted, would effect a radical change in Army appellate review procedure. . . . It would remove final authority from the Judge Advocate General and the Secretary of the Army and lodge such authority in a body of civilians who would have no responsibility for the successful operation of the . . . Army."

Unfortunately, because neither Gray's nor Forrestal's papers contain any response from either Stimson or Patterson, it is unclear what actions—if any—resulted from Gray's efforts. But Gray did more. Besides writing to Stimson and Patterson, the assistant secretary of the army also sent the same material to Army Chief of Staff Omar Bradley. Bradley responded with a short letter to Gray that remained classified until 1988. Acknowledging that mistakes in military justice had indeed taken place during World War II, Bradley expressed agreement with Gray's "objections and remarks." He was concerned that in attempting to correct these mistakes, "we will go so far as to make what I consider two great errors. First, the people responsible for results will have most of their powers to discipline and their authority over trials taken from them. Second, we will end up with a maximum emphasis on legality and minimum attention to justice. . . . Not only must we give the accused justice, but in so doing we must not go so far as to disregard the rights of his comrades and of his country."

It is doubtful if Morgan ever knew about Gray's actions. There is no doubt, however, that Felix Larkin was unaware of what Gray had done, and he reacted with a sort of amused surprise when this author informed him about it early in 1989. As will be seen, however, Gray's efforts came to naught. Within two weeks of the letters to Stimson and Patterson, Forrestal made his decisions concerning the disputed provisions of the new code. But even after this action, the army continued to resist.

Toward the end of his life, Gray recalled his experiences as a member of Morgan's committee. Not surprisingly, of course, he made no mention of his "extra curricular" letter writing. In a 1966 oral history memoir, Gray remembered Morgan as "a very able man." He added that "I was a strong dissenter as to various points in that report, the only dissenter, I think, and I'm still of the opinion that I was right in my dissents. But in any event, the majority prevailed, and I guess it [is] working reasonably well."

The various "adjustments" to Morgan's original proposal for appellate review in response to service objections resulted from Forrestal's decision that a particular provision once agreed upon by the panel or decided upon by him would not be subject to further change. The inevitable concomitant of such a policy was a great deal of interaction among the working group and the various services, especially when a controversial article was at issue. Forrestal and Morgan understood very well that the new code had to have at least the silent acquiescence of the military, if not outright approbation. This meant numerous compromises that would not have been acceptable had the code been drafted by a committee of civilian lawyers. One example, of course, was the appellate procedure. Another concerned the problem of command influence.

As work on the code moved toward conclusion, Morgan found it impractical to remove the convening authority from the early stages of a military justice proceeding—even though he had been strongly advised to do so by a group of lawyers. They insisted that "command, which controls the prosecution, should not also appoint and control the court and defense counsel. That morale may be maintained without interference with the proper functions of command, requires the appointment of the court and defense counsel by an independent judicial arm of the service."

Of course this argument was not new, and largely as a result of similar comments in 1946–1947, the Elston Act included an amended article of war that dealt with "unlawfully influencing action of court." It provided that

> no authority appointing a . . . court-martial nor any other commanding officer shall censure, reprimand, or admonish such court, or any member thereof, with respect to the findings or sentence adjudged by the court, or with respect to any other exercise . . . of its or his judicial responsibility. No person subject to military law shall attempt to coerce or unlawfully influence the action of a court-martial or any military court or commission . . . in reaching the findings or sentence in any case, or the action of an appointing or reviewing or confirming authority with respect to his judicial acts.

From Morgan's viewpoint, it was necessary to include this provision in the new code and thus make it applicable to all branches of the military. The navy, however, disagreed. Its representative informed Larkin that there was no objection to ensuring that "the freedom of courts-martial to function must be preserved unhampered by improper influence from command or any other sources." This principle, however, "should not preclude a statement from responsible authority when a sentence is so palpably inadequate as to being a mockery of justice." Ultimately, Morgan's committee retained and indeed expanded the language and scope of the Elston amendment while rejecting Curry's proposed revision. Further, his panel—not satisfied with mere prohibition—voted to make violation of this article subject to punishment. When it came time for Forrestal to resolve the several issues that had eluded settlement, this article was not among them. It may be assumed, therefore, that the CUCMJ handled it internally, probably through compromise and flexibility.

Each service, as well as Morgan himself, had certain priorities concerning the UCMJ considered so essential that compromise could not be possible. It is not surprising that such issues had to be settled by Forrestal. What is remarkable, however, is that he had to deal with so few. Nevertheless the secretary had to resolve at least three of them: the appellate process, the question of enlisted men serving on courts-martial, and the role of the law officer. As 1948 drew to a close, and with the UCMJ almost ready for submission to Congress, Larkin undertook to bring Forrestal back into the picture to decide these points.

9

Congress, the Code, and the Court, 1948–1949

By December 1948, the essential parts of the Uniform Code of Military Justice were in place. Although Forrestal had yet to meet with Morgan and the committee in order to settle several issues, Larkin was confident that the new code could be submitted to Congress early in 1949. On December 29, he so informed John Adams, a staff member of the Senate Armed Services Committee. Both congressional committees dealing with the armed services had been represented at the working group meetings on a regular basis since October. Larkin hoped that such continuous involvement would lessen any political maneuvering that might occur concerning introduction of the proposed statute. So much for Larkin's hopes.

FORRESTAL FORMULATES

In Washington, politicians come and go, but politics remains a permanent institution. By November 1948, President Truman had been reelected, and control of Congress had switched back again to the Democrats. This meant that Senator Gurney, who with some justification may well have considered himself a titular "godfather" to the UCMJ, would no longer be chairman of the Senate Armed Services Committee. Adams, however, told Larkin that "the code should have the color of being Gurney's bill." Further, he thought that "Gurney wants to introduce it in the Senate a few days before it is introduced in the House." Larkin, who had been working closely with Robert Smart from the House committee, responded that "it would be very bad practice for us to deliver it to the Senate before it goes to the House." He proposed instead that copies be delivered simultaneously to the appropriate officials in both Houses. Adams agreed, and in due course Larkin's plan was followed.

Both Larkin and Morgan assumed from the outset that the finished code would be guided through Congress under the aegis of the Armed Services Committees. It was for this reason that staff members from these panels had sat in on working group sessions. Although Morgan believed that the "center-piece" of the entire code would be the new judicial council, in reality this provision was only one part of a lengthy compilation of statues dealing with military law. However, even before the UCMJ had been formally submitted, Adams further informed Larkin that Senator Patrick McCarran—chairman of the Senate Judiciary Committee—was interested in holding hearings on the proposed UCMJ. He advised Larkin to discuss the matter with Millard Tydings, the incoming chair of the Senate Armed Services Committee.

Larkin did so, and although McCarran strongly pushed for his commit-tee's jurisdiction—as will be seen—he lost. Having conceived of the code in nonpartisan terms, Larkin was anxious to get it through Congress as quickly as possible. Internal Senate bickering over committee assignment—with the UCMJ as a potential hostage—was not desirable. Furthermore, he had kept the Armed Services Committees informed on a continuing basis as the code was drafted. From Larkin's point of view, in terms of overall planning it made good sense to keep the proposed statute within their purview. On the other hand, he probably did not appreciate the implications of such a step in terms of later selecting and confirming judges for the new council. Whatever strengths the Congressional Armed Services Committees may have, a means for careful and thorough evaluation of judicial candidates has not been one of them. As will be seen later, this fact would have important implications for the history of the U.S. Court of Appeals for the Armed Forces.

On January 5, 1949, Larkin informed Forrestal about the remaining points of difference between Morgan and his own committee. In no instance, he observed, "is Morgan in single dissent. He is either on the side of the majority in the three to one votes, or is supported by one of the Services on the split vote." This was very important, because Larkin knew that "inasmuch as you indicated that you plan to look to Professor Morgan for guidance in resolving the differ-ences, we have gone forward and are drafting the disputed provisions based on the side taken by [him.]" Had Morgan ever stood isolated 3 to 1, with all the services against him concerning a disputed section of the code, it is uncertain what action Forrestal might have taken. One suspects that Morgan was fully cognizant of this and it probably contributed to the skillful merging of adjust-ment and compromise by which he ensured that such a situation never arose.

Larkin further reported to the secretary that he had already discussed the new code in detail with the staff of the Budget Bureau "in an effort to prevent delay in clearing the bill." According to him, "they are extremely enthusiastic about [it, and] think it is one of the best examples of unification to date, and a progressive and modern penal law" as well. The bureau objected, however, "to the proposal that the civilians on the Judicial Council be appointed by the three [under] Secretaries. They believe that the appointment should be by the President. In addition . . . , all regulations to be promulgated by the three Secretaries should be subject to the approval of the Secretary of Defense." The insistence on these changes by officials of the Budget Bureau is yet another example of the tension between the old civilian secretaries of the services and the new civilian secretary of defense, a tension reflected in Larkin's report and about which Forrestal was only too well aware—that the three services had yet to accept fully the conclusion that in terms of initiating policy, by 1949 they were all subordinate to the secretary of defense.

Turning to Morgan's plan for appellate review, Larkin reminded Forrestal that the army had a "complex" system with separate reviews by the convening authority, the judge advocate general, a board of review, and a judicial council as set forth in the Elston Act. This council, however, was in reality a "further agency of review which would be staffed by three General Officers" within the JAG Corps. The navy procedure was "less complicated than the Army . . . , but very much more informal, with the ultimate authority for decision, both as to law and fact, residing in the Secretary of the Navy." Neither the army nor the navy "likes each other's system," and it was the inability to reach a compromise that had led to Morgan's "bombshell."

In terms of procedure, Morgan's plan would have made the various services' lower levels of review virtually identical. He eliminated the army judicial council of three officers and proposed instead a "Judicial Council in the National Military Establishment, which will act as a Supreme Court *on law only* for the three services." Gray "dissents from the whole plan, although in essence the dissent centers around the single Judicial Council staffed by civilians." Along with his report to Forrestal, Larkin also included a copy of Gray's earlier memorandum to the committee.

On January 7, Forrestal and his key advisers (including Leva and Larkin) met with Morgan and his committee. The secretary heard all the dissents on the disputed articles and indicated that he would make a final determination shortly. In the meantime, another member of Forrestal's staff wrote to Leva that Morgan's judicial council would be an important element in establishing a *uniform* code. Robert Wood observed that without such a body, under the new law "the possibility of varying interpretations by the three [services] is enhanced. With it, [they] have an excellent means of passing upstairs problems which, by attempting to resolve themselves, might well present odious comparisons with similar decisions by their sister services and the consequent unfavorable public reaction." Wood added that "Mr. Gray's arguments are, undoubtedly, based on sincere convictions but I feel they do not hold water when looked at from the standpoint of the overall good of the National Military Establishment."

On January 17, 1949, Forrestal informed Morgan that his positions on the three essential areas of dispute are "accepted and should be incorporated into the Code." With that decision reached, all that remained were some corrections and minor clarifications. The provisions of the UCMJ were grouped into coherent sections, such as those dealing with punitive articles or trial procedures or review of courts-martial. And another change was incorporated into article 67, dealing with Morgan's judicial council. A new sentence was added to the end of the article. It stated that "the Judicial Council and the Judge Advocates General of the armed forces shall meet annually to make a comprehensive survey of the operation of this Code and report to the Secretary of Defense and the Secretaries of the Departments any recommendations relating to uniformity of sentence policies, amendments to this Code, and any other matters deemed appropriate."

This sentence appears to have been an after-thought. It set up the members of the council (or Court, as it soon would be called) and the three JAGs as equals on an advisory committee. However, as will be seen later, the relationship between the court and the JAGs by its very nature is sometimes an adversarial one. In retrospect, this provision has been less than significant in the Court's history. Nevertheless, provision for an expanded committee remains in the latest version of the UCMJ, a statutory compulsion, as it were, that the two parties communicate with each other.

Larkin then prepared a summary of the code's provisions for submission to Forrestal along with the text of the entire document. He listed eight provisions that were "designed to prevent interference with the due administration of justice":

1. The convening authority could not refer charges for trial until "they are found legally sufficient" by the staff JAG.
2. The staff JAG could communicate directly with the judge advocate general without having to go through the commander.
3. All counsel at general courts-martial had to be lawyers and certified by the JAG "as qualified to perform their legal duties."
4. The law officer was to be "a competent lawyer" who would rule on most legal questions.
5. The convening authority could not act on a finding or sentence "without first obtaining the advice of his staff judge advocate or legal officer."
6. The boards of review were to be established in the JAG office and thus "removed from the convening authority," to be composed of lawyers empowered to review a trial record for errors in both law and fact.
7. A civilian judicial council would pass finally on all questions of law.
8. Defendants appearing before either the board of review or the judicial council must be represented by qualified lawyers.

Finally, Larkin noted that "censure by a commanding officer of a court martial or any member or officer thereof because of any judicial action of the court or any member or officer is forbidden[,] and any attempt improperly to influence official action in any aspect of a trial or its review is prohibited."

Inexplicably, Larkin failed to include the fact that the new code not only forbade such conduct but made it punishable as well. This provision has remained in the UCMJ down to the present day, but this author has been unable to locate *any* case wherein the U.S. Court of Appeals for the Armed Forces has dealt with any punishments levied upon a commander under this section.

As will be seen later, the Court has repeatedly denounced "command influence" but has limited its role to mitigating the abuse rather than moving against the alleged perpetrator. Moreover, diligent research has turned up only one instance where military authorities have prosecuted a commander under article 98. In his exhaustive treatise on military justice, Homer Moyer Jr. cites the case of a Marine Corps officer convicted in 1953 under article 98. He was sentenced to forfeit $350 a month for one year as well as an unfavorable change of position on the service seniority list. Moyer notes that the assistant secretary of the navy later reduced the fine. Concerning article 98 he concludes, I think correctly, that "as a sanction against unlawful influence, it is a dead letter."

Larkin also noted at least three areas where command function remained undisturbed: commanding officers refer the charges in courts-martial and convene them; they appoint the members of such courts, including the law officer and counsel for the trial; and they retain full power to set aside findings of guilty and to modify or change the sentence. On the other hand, they could neither interfere with a not guilty verdict nor increase the severity of a sentence duly imposed.

Historical hindsight can blind as well as illumine, and what Larkin saw as major procedural innovations in the new code should not be minimized—especially in the light of developments in military justice since 1951, including several important changes in the UCMJ. Considering what had been in place before, Morgan's committee broke new ground. Furthermore, Larkin had presided over a project that produced the new code in a remarkably short period of time. The working group first met on July 9, 1948, and Morgan's own committee did not convene until August 18. By the end of December, most of the 140 articles had been completed, and Larkin had already discussed the UCMJ draft with the office of the Bureau of the Budget. Even Gordon Gray, who, as will be seen, still smarted from Forrestal's rejection of his proposal concerning appellate procedure, could write that "a monumental job had been done."

GRAY GRUMBLES

Prior to the formal submission of the UCMJ to Congress, protocol required Morgan's committee first to present it to Forrestal. Larkin assumed that such a step would be pro forma and prepared to draft a very short letter of transmittal. In it, however, he wanted to mention the consensus that had been attained in so much of the drafting process. Here, once again, Gordon Gray raised objections.

The incident well demonstrated that his disagreement with Morgan did not end with Forrestal's decision. Indeed, Gray's persistence reminds this writer of Ansell's determination to persevere in his cause even after Baker thought the issue had been finally resolved in Crowder's favor in 1918–1919. On January 31, in his absence, Gray's secretary informed Larkin that "mention should be made in the letter of transmittal to Forrestal that all the decisions on the Code were not unanimous."

Anxious to resolve the issue, if only so that Forrestal could at last officially receive the UCMJ, Larkin redrafted his letter of transmittal. He retained the sentence just quoted but added two sentences at the end: "The provisions of the proposed Code were unanimously adopted by members of the Committee with the exception of the provisions submitted to you on January 7, 1949. These provisions, on which the members . . . were divided, have been drafted in accordance with your decisions." Back in Cambridge, Morgan's reaction to the controversy over what probably appeared to him as an extremely simple matter can be gauged from his phone conversation with Larkin on February 1. Morgan "said he is not willing to spell out the points which were not unanimous. . . . If the members of the Committee do not approve the second draft of the letter, Morgan said he will send the first letter and they can write Forrestal anything they please."

The question arises why Gray was so antisemantic on what appears to be such a minor question of wording. In part, the answer may rest in the fact that the issue of the appellate process was very important to Gray—so important that he had willingly violated his agreement concerning confidentiality of committee decisions. Even more vital from his viewpoint was the extent of Forrestal's authority over his three secretaries. In early 1949, the National Military Establishment (not yet named the Defense Department) was more a confederation than a unified agency. The three services "were still largely autonomous organizations with nearly full control over their internal affairs." Moreover, powers not specifically "conferred upon the Secretary of Defense became part of the authority [belonging to] each respective departmental secretary." Finally, any of these three individuals could appeal the secretary's decision on a matter relevant to his service directly to either the president or the Bureau of the Budget. Gray's insistence that the letter of transmittal be accurate may well have been a part of positioning in order for his chief, Kenneth Royall, to have grounds for such an appeal.

Larkin received Gray's "amendment," apparently drafted on February 3. He had added a sentence that "these areas of disagreement and the members of the Committee involved in the dissents are referred to in an attached paper." There then followed a statement that Gray "records a dissent to the appellate system as provided in the proposed articles, particularly with reference to the Judicial Council." Both Gray and Zuckert "record dissents from the proposed article which would prohibit the law member from participating as a full member of a general court." Finally, Kenney changed his mind and decided to record his dissent "to the proposed article which would provide enlisted men on general and special courts-martial."

Larkin and Morgan consulted concerning Gray's "revisions" on February 4. The Harvard law professor told Larkin that "he didn't like it and thought it highly improper and thinks Gray is being unreasonable." Larkin may have commented to Morgan about the realities concerning relations between Forrestal and the three services, because Morgan "did agree to do it that way if Gray insists. He said he would rather have it that way than to have Gray not sign the letter." So Larkin sent Gray's draft to the other members of the committee. "I have spoken with Professor Morgan about it," Larkin wrote, "and, although he feels that this kind of letter is unnecessary and unwise, he is willing to sign it in the interest of completing the job." The fact that Morgan did not insist on Larkin's original letter may be taken as further evidence of his awareness that the relationship between the secretary of defense and the under secretaries of the three services had not yet clarified. In view of the still tenuous nature of this relationship, one can readily understand why neither Larkin nor Leva felt it appropriate simply to order the under secretaries to sign the letter and be done with it. With probable relief, on February 7 Larkin noted that he visited the three under secretaries "to secure their signatures on the letter of transmittal to Forrestal."

The next day, Larkin personally delivered copies of the code to the appropriate congressional leaders, along with a covering letter signed by Forrestal but drafted by Larkin. Forrestal concluded "his" letter by emphasizing that "in my opinion, the proposed bill is well-designed to protect the rights of those subject to it, will increase public confidence in military justice, and will not impair the performance of military functions. Accordingly, I strongly urge its passage by Congress." Thus, at the end of the drafting process, Forrestal again mentioned the same three points he had raised in his initial instructions to Morgan's committee during the summer of 1948.

To Morgan, Forrestal (through Larkin) acknowledged "your great contribution." Your "leadership and your personal contributions to the subject are, in large measure, responsible for the accomplishments of the Committee." To the three under secretaries (each addressed by first name), Forrestal "was very gratified by the amount of agreement achieved by the Committee, and I attribute it to the generous cooperation of your fellow members and yourself." Such "teamwork could have been motivated only by a sincere desire to foster the interests of the National Military Establishment."

Morgan responded with a letter to Forrestal. "I am grateful to you," he wrote, "for giving me the opportunity to contribute to a project which I had not dared to hope would receive official support in my life-time." Moreover, the reason why the committee had successfully completed its work "is to be found primarily in the exceptionally thorough and efficient work of Mr. Felix E.

Larkin." Finally, Morgan noted of his three service colleagues that they were "men of fine personality, great ability and tact with the capacity to see and appreciate conflicting points of view."

Whether Morgan would have been as effusive had he known about Gray's efforts to torpedo the new appellate procedure remains a matter for conjecture. On the same day he wrote to Forrestal, Morgan also drafted letters to his three associates, each note revealing something of the way Morgan had worked with them. To Gray he implied that if Gray had not been a product of Yale Law School, things might have been different. "I am sorry that I was unable to persuade you of the merits of the proposed appellate system; but I think I appreciate your point of view, even though I attribute it, not to heredity, but to unfortunate environment." To Zuckert he wrote that "even though you are a dyed-in-the-wool Yale man, I have to thank you for the splendid support which you gave my views in a number of important features . . . as well as for your arguments which made me change my mind on a number of others." To Kenney he "reported" that "rumor hath it that you and I were in agreement on so many debatable points regarding the proposed code because you had been corrupted in your youth by my course in Procedure."

MIXED REACTIONS .

The official press release heralding the submission of the UCMJ to Congress was distributed to the wire services on February 8, 1949, directly after the statute had been presented to Congress. Reaction from the various lawyers' groups was prompt. George Spiegelberg, chairman of the American Bar Association's (ABA) military justice committee, complained that the "proposed Forrestal Code, so far as I can see, hasn't changed command control a bit. We strongly advocated the necessity of checking the influence of command over courts-martial[,] and the new proposed code is totally lacking in this." From the New York County Lawyers Association, Richard Wels was even more blunt. The new proposal was "a pretty facade[, one that] is good as far as it goes, but it doesn't go far enough. . . . It doesn't touch the jugular vein where most of the military injustices are hidden."

Both Larkin and Morgan had already talked at some length with Spiegelberg and Wels about the new code and apparently were unprepared for Wels's dismissal of so much hard work as "a petty facade." Morgan informed Spiegelberg that "Mr. Larkin and I did our utmost to meet your recommendations; and we were both greatly disappointed at the blast which was directed against the Code on its first release." Morgan had also received a copy of the ABA resolutions and at Forrestal's request responded to them. His letter is of interest because it shows Morgan's realization that a military commander could not be totally isolated from the operation of military justice.

The ABA had long insisted that the judge advocate generals and *not* the commanders should have the exclusive right to appoint members of courts-martial. Morgan wrote to the ABA secretary that "it would be entirely imprac-tical to have such appointments made by the [JAG] without the closest cooperation with the commanding officers concerned. . . . It is unthinkable that he could be permitted to dictate to the commanding officer the assignment of duties of officers" under his authority. Morgan's unequivocal position appears to be very different from what he held in 1919, when he had been a staunch supporter of Ansell. Certainly he had matured in years and experience. But per-haps the most telling reason for the change is apparent from his next sentence: "This view of the [Committee] members . . . was founded in large part on in-formed opinions expressed by representatives of the Judge Advocate General's Departments of the several services."

In their final form, legislative enactments often tend to be an intriguing amalgam of desired principles that become softened in a context of compro-mise. Morgan may well have believed that he could gain support for an inde-pendent civilian appellate court only if he was "flexible" concerning command control. Such a choice may have disturbed Wels and Spiegelberg. Apparently it did not trouble the Harvard law professor.

Morgan and Larkin realized that representatives from the various lawyers' associations would make their views known to Congress in due time. Had they but known, Gordon Gray also was thinking about testifying before Congress. He wrote to Henry Stimson on February 23, 1949, that "I regret to say, not for publication of course, that I lost the battle on the two main points I was inter-ested in, the appellate system and the function of the law member. . . . I have no doubt that hearings will soon begin. Officially, of course, I am bound by the National Military Establishment's position. Whether I shall be called upon to express my personal views, I have no idea." Gray apparently did not testify—either on his own behalf or that of the army—concerning the UCMJ.

In the meantime, a nationally televised debate on military justice aired on February 14, 1949. The specific issue "on trial" was command influence. Should military lawyers and judges "be independent of the officer who is responsible for bringing the charges?" Apparently organized with the support of the various lawyers' groups interested in military justice and deliberately timed to air just before Congress took up the new code, the moderator (or pre-siding "judge") was none other than Samuel Ansell. Ansell was extremely care-ful to be absolutely neutral in his role as judge. If not familiar with the earlier battles against Crowder, a viewer probably would never have sensed his prior involvement. Among the other participants as "plaintiffs" were George Spiegel-berg of the ABA and Ernest Gibson, a former JAG officer and at the time gov-ernor of the state of Vermont. Colonel Frederick B. Wiener, a graduate of Harvard Law School and also a former member of the JAG Corps, represented the traditional military viewpoint.

Spiegelberg again urged that the judge advocate general should appoint members of a military court. Wiener responded by insisting that the proposal to separate military courts from military command was "utterly impractical because it fails to take into account the basic difference between an army and a civilian society." An army, he added, is supposed "to win wars[,] not just fight them, but win them. They don't pay off on price in a war. And therefore an army has to be so organized that it will lead men obediently against the enemy to their deaths if necessary." In response to a question by Governor Gibson, Wiener conceded that commanders could abuse their court-martial authority. However, "all power can be abused if placed in unworthy hands[;] that does not mean, sir, that the powers should not be placed in some hands." Gibson reiterated his point that the commander's power over military justice procedure was in reality "pure dictatorship." Wiener's argument of necessity to the contrary, the current practice "is inhuman. It is un-American and it is dangerous."

CONGRESS CONTEMPLATES CONSIDERATION

In accordance with usual practice, the chair of the Senate Armed Services Committee selected a subcommittee of three to consider the proposed UCMJ. After this panel's first meeting on February 16, one of its members—Massachusetts senator Leverett Saltonstall—informed his good friend Judge Raymond Wilkins of the Massachusetts Supreme Judicial Court that "the Committee in the House will [hold] full hearings[,] and presumably the Senate will wait until this is done." He hoped that Wilkins "will give the bill a going over and make any comments that you care to when you have had an opportunity to study it." Given the multiple demands on a senator's time, it was not at all unusual for Saltonstall to have a lawyer he trusted, such as Wilkins, examine a complex and lengthy statute such as the UCMJ. As will be seen, Wilkins's comments on parts of the new statute would influence Saltonstall to support a key change in the bill, one of vital importance to the later history of USCAAF. Wilkins apparently had already discussed parts of the code with Saltonstall's assistant, who in turn had drafted a sheet of notes for Saltonstall's use during the first subcommittee meeting—to which Larkin had also been invited to attend. In general, stated one note, the code was a "big improvement." As to the proposed judicial council, "this may be a good idea but would want to know a lot more about [it]. . . . It looks too much like giving three people a job without thinking how it would work out in relation to present authority."

Once the decision to have a House subcommittee hold hearings on the proposed code, now listed as H.R. 2498, had been reached, Larkin held several meetings with Robert Smart, a lawyer attached to the House Armed Services Committee and an unofficial participant in a number of Larkin's working group sessions. In notes from a meeting on February 23, 1949, Smart asked Larkin,

"Why should the Judicial Council not weigh evidence, credibility, etc?" The council "should not usurp military functions. Although [it] would do no more than [a] Circuit Court would do, [the judicial council] would specialize in [a] peculiar type of law. One tribunal [is] needed for purposes of uniformity." Why, in other words, should the council not do exactly what Morgan had first proposed that it do? One day later, Smart sent Larkin a more detailed set of questions along with a candid letter explaining why they were important.

"I realize," Smart wrote, "that both you and I already know the answers to most of these questions, however, I am including them in order to insure a proper legislative history." Yet, he was a little troubled.

> While you and I know that there is nothing at all sinister in my furnishing you with a copy of these questions, I think it would be advisable to keep this matter confined to those agencies and individuals who are directly involved with the legislation. I would also suggest that departmental witnesses refrain, insofar as possible, from answering these questions in their opening statements. To do so would deprive Mr. [Overton] Brooks [Democrat from Louisiana and chairman of the House subcommittee] of much of his participation in the hearings. If that should occur, it might prove most embarrassing to me.

Again, Smart called attention to the fact that, as drafted, the UCMJ denied the judicial council authority that the lower boards of review would retain. "What reasons have motivated this change?" Moreover, the omission of any mention as to the terms of council members did not escape Smart's notice: "What term does the Secretary of Defense recommend—for life, a fixed term or staggered terms?" Also, "is it considered desirable that such civilian appointees have some military experience in addition to their legal qualifications?" On the basis of current caseload in each service, could Larkin estimate "how many cases per month would be reviewable by the Council?" If too heavy a burden, does the code "authorize . . . one or two additional members, rather than another Council of three . . . ? [H]ave you considered the possibility of providing one or more commissioners to assist the Council rather than new . . . members?" Since the members of Morgan's council would "perform substantially the same duties as judge[s] of the United States Courts of Appeal, have you considered the advisability of granting the reviewing authority . . . to the Federal Courts of Appeal?"

Larkin instructed representatives from both the army and air force to submit answers to Smart's queries in written form suitable for his use in testimony before the House committee. Stewart Maxey, the air force member of Larkin's original working group, focused on the decision to limit the judicial council to matters of law. Because it "will be composed of civilians unfamiliar with military procedure and the military service in general, it should not be extended the powers which a court has in weighing evidence taken before them, judging the credibility of witnesses appearing before them[,] and determining the truth from the testimony of such witnesses." Moreover, he believed that "the lack of knowledge of military matters . . . will be a severe handicap to the proper performance of their duties and the interests of the government."

Finally, Maxey estimated that approximately 247 cases per month from the air force alone would be reviewable by the council. Because it would cost the accused nothing, "I anticipate practically every man convicted by general . . . or special court-martial whose case is legally reviewable by the Judicial Council will petition for such review." (The first report of USCAAF, submitted for the period May 31, 1951, to March 1, 1952, listed 39 cases docketed from the air force; for the calendar year 1953, 273 air force cases were docketed.)

On behalf of the army, another former member of the working group, John Dinsmore, repeatedly emphasized Gordon Gray's dissent to the entire appellate procedure as endorsed by Morgan's committee. He agreed with Maxey that members of the council should have military experience. Dinsmore also noted that while Gray had suggested that appeals from courts-martial be authorized to a federal circuit court "in lieu of the creation of a Judicial Council, . . . no action on this suggestion was taken by the Committee." Dinsmore predicted that in peacetime the number of army cases reviewable by the council would be "about 1,100 per month, and in wartime about 2,600 per month." (For the same periods, through March 1952, 372 cases from the army had been docketed; in 1953, 1,638 army cases were submitted.)

One day after Larkin received the questions from Smart, Judge Matthew McGuire—the jurist who had been so critical of navy justice during World War II—informed Larkin that Congressman Brooks had asked him to testify on the UCMJ. McGuire could not do it but wrote a letter instead, a copy of which he sent to Larkin. Larkin "suggested that it would be helpful to us if he would not phrase his letter in such a negative manner, and he agreed that he did not want to scuttle the bill because he actually thought it was very good." Upon examination, it becomes very clear why Larkin urged the jurist to "revise" the text.

McGuire complained to Brooks that the new UCMJ "still labors under the basic defects of the older systems which have been so critically and bitterly inveighed against." As to Morgan's judicial council, "what shall they do in time of peace? And . . . why should they be paid more than the United States District Court judges [such as McGuire] who sit on constitutional courts? Are they to be confirmed by the Senate?" Although McGuire believed that Morgan's committee "should be congratulated for a job well done," his final sentences reiterated potential weaknesses in the UCMJ of which Morgan and Larkin could have been only too aware. "My strictures are levelled against what I consider fundamentals, the absence of which in any system that purports to do justice according to our concepts is fatal. I have no doubt that the Committee agrees—and the end result in this respect being perhaps the result of compromise—where agreement was impossible. But no matter how far reaching are reforms, unless the old vices referred to are completely eradicated, even handed administration of military and naval justice will still remain as elusive as ever, the more so because of the fact that the vicious defects of the old systems still remain—dressed up in new garb it is true, but still as unregenerate as ever."

With hearings on the UCMJ scheduled to begin on March 7, 1949, before the House Armed Services Committee, Larkin sent two memoranda to Forrestal and also drafted a statement for him to read before the committee as the first witness. He did not "believe that you will be asked any questions, and I think you can refer [any] questions addressed to you to Professor Morgan or to me." Larkin was especially concerned about "the problem of coordinating any testimony that might be given by the members of the committee—that is, Mr. Gray, Mr. Kenney and Mr. Zuckert. . . . I feel very strongly that the Military Establishment should present a united front on this bill and that explanations of dissents should not be phrased in such a way that our witnesses will become engaged in a debate before the Committee." He warned Forrestal that "while I feel that the bill is a very good one and strikes a very fair balance between military command and a system of justice, we have to expect that various items will be criticized by different groups."

Two days later, Larkin sent a more detailed explanation of Forrestal's resolution concerning several disputed items on the new code, chief among them being the civilian judicial council. In a uniform system, he told the secretary, it is absolutely necessary "to have a final court on the law. Otherwise, the system would be uniform in name only, since lawyers differ on the construction of law and statutes[,] and the Services would undoubtedly construe the provisions of the uniform system in different ways." He explained further that the "civilian aspect of the . . . Council is entirely consistent with the concept of civilian control of the armed forces, . . . and since it would rule on law only, it would not interfere with the discipline and morale factors."

Finally, Larkin stated that Morgan's judicial council was "part of an effort by the Committee to restrict command control," which, "to the extent that the commanding officer still appoints the court and reviews the case, is retained in the Code." This fact made it all the more necessary "that there should be other measures which would keep such control confined to its proper function." Again, Larkin warned Forrestal that the decision to retain "the commander will be criticized in the hearings by Bar Associations, etc. If you are asked questions on this subject, I think the answer should be that we have left the command with functions which we think appropriate and have added provisions—namely the Judicial Council, law officer, etc.—to keep that control properly circumscribed." As he had done for Forrestal, Larkin also drafted an introductory statement for Morgan. "As I contemplate your role," he wrote to the Harvard law professor, "I think it should be a combination of explaining the broad outline of the bill and a bit of statesmanship." Ultimately, Morgan's "performance" more than satisfied Larkin's criteria.

10

Congress, the Code, and the Court, 1949

Like his boss Forrestal, Larkin conceived the work on the UCMJ as nonpolitical, although probably he would have strongly agreed with Forrestal's observation that you can no more divorce government from politics than you can separate sex from creation. He had employed a variety of techniques to keep the proposed code from becoming a vehicle for legislative partisanship, ranging from inviting representatives of the congressional Armed Services Committees to sit in as participating (but nonvoting) observers of the working group meetings to cooperating with Robert Smart with answers prepared in advance for key questions to be asked by the House committee leadership. But Larkin aimed at more than eliminating opportunity for partisan bickering. Both he and Morgan conceived of the new code as a finished entity, one that could benefit from some stylistic corrections or additions, but not from congressional tinkering with its main provisions. Thus, in advance of the hearings, each member of the Armed Services Committee received a booklet of more than 160 pages, which not only listed each article but also provided the sources from which it was drawn and explanatory analysis on the way it would work. This *Text, References, and Commentary* reflected the complex challenge of shaping various disparate military justice provisions into a uniform single entity. But it also encouraged the perception that the UCMJ had to be "analyzed as an integrated whole," an approach strongly recommended by Forrestal when he testified before the House committee on March 7, 1949, as the first witness on behalf of the new code.

CONGRESS CONSULTS

Forrestal's brief appearance on Capitol Hill to launch the campaign for swift congressional approval of the UCMJ was one of his last as secretary of defense. His resignation had already been accepted by President Truman, to take effect on March 31, 1949. Initially drafted for him by Larkin, Forrestal's short remarks strongly endorsed the proposed legislation. He emphasized that every participant in the UCMJ project "partially compromised his views on a number of points," and they all, himself included, "support the many individual provisions with varying shades of enthusiasm." In reality, "the point of proper accommodation between the meting out of justice and the performance of military operations—which involve[s] not only the fighting but also the winning of wars—is one which no one has discovered." But the finished document represented a remarkable consensus. Indeed, he added, "we are striving for maximum military performance and maximum justice. I believe the proposed code is the nearest approach to these ideals."

By prearrangement, Morgan immediately followed Forrestal's remarks with some additional introductory comments, originally drafted for him by Larkin. He summarized the main provisions of the UCMJ, including that for a judicial council. "It is apparent," he noted, "that such a tribunal is necessary to insure uniformity of interpretation throughout the armed services." Moreover, it is consistent with the principle of civilian control of the armed forces that a court of final appeal "should be composed of civilians."

Morgan concluded his presentation with some observations concerning certain general assumptions that his committee had kept in mind as it fashioned the UCMJ. The members recognized from the beginning "that a system of military justice which was only an instrumentality of the commander was as abhorrent as a system entirely administered by a civilian criminal court was impractical." Obviously, the new code "cannot ignore the military circumstances under which it must operate[,] but we were equally determined that it must be designated to administer justice." The code provided "functions for command and appropriate procedures for the administration of justice." Echoing Forrestal, Morgan admitted that the draft before the committee "is not exactly what any one of us would have drawn had he been alone and starting without precedent." He also offered his view concerning the term of membership on the judicial council, noting "we felt that Congress would have to determine the term. . . . Certainly it is my opinion that these men should be appointed in exactly the same way that the circuit court of appeals judges are appointed. . . . During good behavior, by the President, with the consent of the Senate."

This issue also interested Senator Saltonstall. Although the Senate agreed to delay consideration of the UCMJ until after the House committee had acted, he continued to receive feedback from his adviser, Judge Wilkins, even as the House began its hearings. Wilkins was "not convinced that [the judicial council] is a necessary thing, although I don't know that I would vote against it." He visualized the tribunal "as a body—most likely composed of politicians— which would be overwhelmed in war time and, once precedents shall have been established, would have a very soft job at other times, except perhaps on a very few occasions." From what he had seen thus far, Wilkins doubted "that we need any such permanent outfit as this bids fair to be." He realized, however, "that it is pretty hard to talk against the establishment of an attractive job." Saltonstall replied to Wilkins that "the Judicial Council rather appealed to me. I agree with you that it should not be a full-time job except in war time."

Larkin and Robert Smart may have expected that after the UCMJ had been introduced by Forrestal and Morgan, the House committee would begin its consideration immediately, section by section—with Smart reading each article of the code to the committee, followed by discussion based on the questions for which Larkin had previously been prepared. Instead the committee chose to hear from a large number of witnesses—including spokesmen for several lawyers' groups such as George Spiegelberg and Richard Wels—with whose views Morgan's committee was well acquainted. While the speakers praised the UCMJ as a positive advance in general, there were many specific criticisms offered, some of which applied to the proposed appellate process.

For the New York County Lawyers' Association, Richard Wels insisted that "there is no question that this bill retains command control in all its ugly aspects." On behalf of the War Veterans Bar Association, Arthur Farmer stated that in the proposed UCMJ, "the elimination of command control from the courts is conspicuously missing." Franklin Riter, a former JAG officer representing the American Legion, was not impressed with the safeguards against command influence that Morgan's committee had written into the UCMJ. Making such conduct an offense under article 98 "means nothing." As for the other section that prohibited interference with the court (article 37), "I want you to write into it a jail and fine provision enforceable in the United States district court and indictable under the civil law."

If Riter seemed a bit excessive in his suggested remedy for command influence, his comments on article 67 (establishing the judicial council) were equally vigorous. He strongly supported the idea of such a tribunal, but "that section is badly drafted. I cannot imagine how the draftsmen let that by. The section as it is is ambiguous." (Riter was referring to the failure to specify a term for the council members.) More important, "I want the name changed. I want that called [the] military court of appeals. I do not want it called [the] judicial council because that carries the idea that [it] is another administrative body set up within the confines of the War Department. . . . Let us give it its right name and dignity. And it will have a tremendous influence on the public. Let us call it the military court of appeal—that is what it is—and give it its dignity. . . . I make a special plea that the name be changed."

A CHORUS OF CRITICS

On March 11, Larkin told Morgan that the "Committee hearings are going very slowly inasmuch as [its members appear] to be willing to listen at great length to every witness." He hastened to reassure "Eddie" that "in the meantime, I still think we are doing pretty well." More witnesses were expected, however, and although the panel began its section-by-section analysis one week later, Morgan did not reappear to testify until March 30. In the meantime, the proposed draft received more negative comments.

Frederick B. Wiener, a member of the Army JAG Reserve, testified on March 16 and 17. An experienced but opinionated observer of military justice, he informed the committee that Morgan's bill "in my judgment . . . is a distinct retrogression" and "a step backwards" from the Elston Act enacted some months earlier. This conclusion was predicated on three provisions in the new code, all of which had been strongly supported by Morgan. Wiener particularly objected to the proposal that the law member of a court-martial would not deliberate and vote with his colleagues. Such action "is the most retrograding step in this bill." In fact, "By taking him out you take out of the deliberations the one man who can make the most helpful contribution" to them. "I cannot help but think," added Wiener, that this provision "was not the product of anyone who ever sat on a court. . . . It was only ignorance."

Similarly, the requirement that trial and defense counsel had to be lawyers was "worse than unnecessary, it is impractical." Moreover, in time of peace such a requirement would be "utterly impossible" because "you won't get the lawyers." Congress would "have to appropriate an awful lot of money to supply the lawyers that will be necessary to [argue] the simple cases, desertions, and the small larcenies, and the disobedience cases, if this bill goes through."

Wiener reserved his harshest criticism for Morgan's cherished judicial council. "I don't think it is sound; I don't think it is necessary; and I think it is wholly self-defeating." In the first place—"and I think we should face it frankly—the appointments to the specialized courts of our judicial system haven't attracted the same sort of talent that the courts of general jurisdiction have attracted." (Wiener's point was prophetic and remains valid to this day, as will be discussed later in this book.) Furthermore, "I think it is terribly important to have some sort of provision which is not present here that the people on this judicial council have military experience." Wiener was troubled by what he saw as an attempt to "drive a wedge between civilians and military people." What was needed, he implied, were outstanding judges, and there was no justification for the implied conclusion that they were available only in civilian life. Why should we seek to interpose civilians "for decision matters that are basically military?"

On the other hand, taking sharp issue with numerous other lawyers who had already testified, Wiener insisted on the absolute necessity for keeping the power to convene a court-martial *within* the command. "We make a man a multi-starred commander. He is generally trained at public expense; he is sent to service schools at public expense; and we give him a command of several millions of men; and he gives the signal to go; and as a result of that signal, thousands of men lose their lives and thousands more are maimed or blinded. . . . Yet when it is proposed that [this] same general, with those incalculable powers of life and death over fellow citizens, be permitted to appoint a court for the trial of a soldier who has stolen a watch, oh no, we can't have that; we have to have a panel. Doesn't make sense, does it?"

Among the final witnesses to appear was a future president of the United States, Gerald Ford, at that time a Michigan congressman. He recalled hearing conversations among members of courts-martial during his several years in the navy "along this line: What does the Old Man [an old but still current navy term referring to the ships's commander] want us to do?" Ford concluded that all too often such individuals were concerned less with determining guilt or innocence than "with what the captain of a ship, or the commanding officer of a station, wants done with the man. . . . I also participated in various courts martial; and the whole system is fundamentally wrong; and I am particularly pleased to see something being done about it." (It might be noted that as president, upon recommendation by his staff, in 1975 Gerald Ford would appoint a judge with minimal military experience to the U.S. Court of Appeals for the Armed Forces; he was Albert Fletcher Jr., whose tenure would be among the most controversial in the Court's entire history. The episode is discussed at some length later in this book.)

It is not clear how closely Morgan followed the testimony offered between March 8 and March 30, 1949, when he returned to Washington. He was probably not surprised at the nature of the criticism. Indeed, Larkin had already warned Forrestal that the proposed UCMJ would be attacked both by those who felt it to be a needless intrusion upon a fundamentally good military justice system and observers who believed that in reality the code represented less than effective reform. If Wiener typified the former, Arthur John Keeffe well personified the latter. What united both witnesses was the certainty if not stridency of tone with which they articulated their opinions. Keeffe did not testify but sent a long statement that was the final "opinion" read into the committee records on March 18, the day the panel began detailed analysis of the UCMJ.

Referring to Morgan and Larkin as "the ablest of lawyers and the finest of fellows," Keeffe denounced the proposed code as "a sorry substitute" in place of the 1920 Chamberlain bill "for which Professor Morgan once fought so hard." He pointed to the mistake of not providing for an advisory council, an error compounded "by sending this code to the Congress without clearing it with the American Bar Association and other representative lawyer and veteran groups." He disliked the idea of having "three civilian judges buried in the Department of Defense." Also, there was "no advisory council created for the same reason that the drafting of this code was not done by such an advisory council. The armed services want a minimum of civilian control, preferably none. I don't blame them."

Keeffe next turned to the judicial council's authority, which he described as "badly limited." Everyone, regardless of rank "should have his case automatically heard before this top civilian judicial council. . . . I say expand the [council] to five judges and give review to every one alike." He labeled Morgan's provision for petition for cause as "a phony [, designed] for the wicked and well connected, not for GI Joe." Even worse was the failure to provide for a chief defense counsel. "Such an officer, and not the Judge Advocate General should have the responsibility of appealing cases to the top civilian court."

To top off all thcsc weaknesses, Keeffe pointed to the limited scope for the judicial council. Morgan's code "limits [it] to review of questions of law and chains the judicial council to the facts as found by command. This is not the kind of civilian review that we ought to have." The proposed code reflected an unpleasant fact: "The hope of those in the armed services who oppose reform is that those of us who are informed and interested will lose interest and tire out. It is a severe personal sacrifice for busy lawyers and busy men to take the time that is necessary to present thc civilian point of view on reform to the Congress."

One can dismiss Keeffe's anger in part because of his understandable frustration at being isolated from the process by which the code had been drafted. But there was more to his comments than mere personal pique. Morgan's panel had a number of policy choices it could have made concerning the appellate review system. Keeffe may or may not have known how badly the committee was divided over this issue, but his criticism of its final choices has considerable merit. For what they deemed good and sufficient reasons, Morgan's committee opted to limit judicial review. Keeffe's position as contrasted with his Harvard colleague's reflected a continuing tension between the presumed needs of military justice and the perceived requirements for civilian due process.

THE HOUSE AND THE CODE

On March 18, 1949, Robert Smart, the staff member to the House Armed Services Subcommittee, told the panel that "I think you have heard all the general statements you want. It is time to get down to business now." "Business" meant a reading of the entire code, article by article, allowing time for discussion, comments, and changes. By the time the group completed this procedure, Morgan had returned to testify again. However, the bulk of the analysis was provided by Larkin, whose comments on every article were often prompted by Smart's questions. Examination of the transcript makes it possible to consider the extent to which the subcommittee accepted the changes urged upon them by the witnesses, such as Wels, Wiener, and others.

Wiener had strongly criticized the proposal to make the law officer a nonvoting member of the military court. Larkin admitted that "it is a difficult problem. There's no question about it." Army officials "feel that the law member is of great assistance when retiring with the court and instructing them in closed session. They feel it is a protection for the accused, as a matter of fact." Having accurately restated Wiener's position, Larkin destroyed it with equal facility. "Inasmuch as no one knows what goes on, however, behind the closed doors[,] and the elements of the crime and the law of the case are not preserved for the record, it is impossible to tell whether erroneous law is given or not." With minimal discussion and no recorded dissent, the subcommittee approved the article as drafted.

Although it had heard consistently from several distinguished lawyers that the proposed UCMJ retained the undesirable potential for command influence, before taking any action the subcommittee waited to hear from Morgan, who returned to testify on March 30, 1949. He stated that the "panel idea is one that theoretically is very attractive. I think it will not work practically." In wartime, he added, "I suppose that it is absolutely impossible for a commander to know in advance what men he could spare for a panel." One of the basic goals of the code was that it be *uniform* in that it apply not only to *all* armed services but also that it apply at *all* times, during peace and war. Morgan explained again the various steps his committee had taken to contain command influence "as far as that is humanly possible." However, he added, "it is true whether you have the panel system or any other system, if the commanding officer is determined to beat it he can beat it." The panel accepted the CUCMJ's original proposal and left the commander with initial authority to select the court, authority which that officer still retains.

On April 4, 1949, the subcommittee held the last of its public hearings and took up article 67, dealing with the judicial council. It made no major changes in the scope of this proposed appellate court, thereby rejecting the various suggestions that its mandate be broadened to include matters of fact. Nor did the panel directly confront the implications of Wiener's perceptive comment about attracting outstanding judicial talent. The panel did, however, discuss some possible changes, and its members made sufficient remarks about the new tribunal to indicate how seriously they considered its role in military justice.

The subcommittee assumed that although the council was "not a constitutional court," the terms of its members should be "for life, subject only to good behavior." Representative Rivers further suggested that the "terms should be staggered so as to always have a man on [the] Judicial Council who knows about the makeup of the court." Congressman Brooks added that "I feel very strongly that the success or failure of the whole thing is going to lie in the Judicial Council, and it seems to me that you ought to have a strong court, whether you call it a Judicial Council or otherwise makes no difference." Moreover, there was consensus among the lawmakers that rather than be bipartisan, the judges ought to be "non political and non partisan." As Congressman Elston put it, "I want it certain that this court[,] which is going to be an exceedingly important court[,] is not filled by political appointments."

The panel also had some difficulty with understanding the term "from civilian life." Larkin noted that this clause "would exclude officers of the Regular components and retired Regulars. A retired Regular, I should say, would be eligible if he resigned. If he just retired, he wouldn't be." This statement is one of the very few from Larkin that may have confused rather than clarified, and he immediately added that "the notion specifically was to make this as civilian as possible, otherwise perhaps the court would consist of nothing but Regular officers who have resigned for the purpose of taking the job[,] and in effect you would have it more military than civilian." Morgan had intended that a judge on the court should be a civilian "as distinguished from a military officer who is either on Regular service now or is a retired Regular who is still, of course, an officer of the United States. But it would not exclude a Reserve on inactive duty, or would not exclude anybody who has military service, of course." Although the term "from civilian life" has remained in the UCMJ article to the present day, the difficulty in meaning that troubled Larkin also remains, but not so much with appointments to the bench as with appointments to the staff either of the Court in general or to a specific judge. The subject is briefly discussed in a later chapter.

As the subcommittee continued discussion on the appellate tribunal, it became clear that General Riter was not the only one who disliked the term "Judicial Council." Larkin explained that since the Elston Act had used this name, "we just picked it up and carried it along." Actually, "we have no pride of authorship at all." Robert Smart suggested that "you should adopt some judicial terminology and get away from this 'Council,' which suggests to me one of the usual basement operations here in Washington." Elston agreed: "That sounds too much like a city council." Larkin added that "it sounds like a round table, instead of a court." After minimal discussion, the subcommittee settled on "the Court of Military Appeals," now known as the U.S. Court of Appeals for the Armed Forces.

At first, Elston suggested the "Supreme Court of Military Appeals," because "if you say 'Court of Appeals,' it might imply that there is a supreme court above that." He withdrew his proposal because, "of course, there isn't." However, this issue was more complicated than Elston's statement implied, and it has become even more complicated today. As earlier chapters have indicated, from time to time—albeit rarely—the U.S. Supreme Court has involved itself in military justice. And in 1984, Congress amended the UCMJ to provide for direct appeal from USCAAF to the high court under specified conditions.

With the hearings completed, the subcommittee went into executive session on April 5. Smart informed Larkin that "they want me and only me to be present . . . to testify on the [UCMJ.]" Because no records have been located for the session, there is no way of knowing exactly what Larkin discussed. In his papers, however, there is a typed version of article 67, dated April 5, and because it incorporated the changes discussed during the open hearings, it seems reasonable to assume that this draft served as the basis for his comments concerning the judicial council now renamed the U.S. Court of Appeals for the Armed Forces.

Several changes had been approved. First, the revision provided for exactly three judges—the original draft had called for "not less than three"—appointed by the president from civilian life. Second, the appointments required Senate confirmation, and the term of each appointment was "during good behavior." These two stipulations were not found in the original article. Third, Morgan had proposed that each judge had to be "a member of the bar admitted to practice before the Supreme Court." During the hearings, this requirement had been transformed into "no person shall be eligible for appointment to [this court] who is not a member of the bar of a federal court or of the highest court of a state." Finally, the earlier draft provided compensation and allowances equal to those received by a federal appeals judge. The later version called for "compensation, allowances, perquisites and retirement benefits" of such a jurist.

The subcommittee had failed to resolve one final issue before its members unanimously reported the revised draft of the UCMJ (now called H.R. 4080) for favorable consideration to the full House Armed Services Committee. Representative Elston and others on the subcommittee had wanted appointments to the new court to be nonpolitical and nonpartisan. When the full committee met on April 27, Elston said that originally he had even intended to propose amending article 67 to include a section stating that "not more than two judges of such court shall be appointed from the same political party." The committee chairman, Carl Vinson, then endorsed this amendment. Because "this is a new military court of civilians, it is nothing but right and proper that it be a non partisan court."

It is, admittedly, difficult to follow the reasoning behind Elston's and Vinson's support for this change. There was no provision in existing law that federal courts be bipartisan, but Elston claimed that "this is a special court." Granting this premise, the question can be asked how it becomes nonpartisan in nature when two of its three judges can be from the same political party. Moreover, if the committee had truly desired to make the new court nonpartisan, it would have been just as easy to stipulate in article 67 that specific party affiliation should not be the basis for judicial appointment.

To put it another way, if this tribunal was to be like other federal appeals courts except in its scope of jurisdiction, why should it be necessary to provide such a stipulation here but not for these other judicial bodies? At any rate, on April 27, 1949, the committee unanimously approved the amendment, and with another unanimous vote sent the UCMJ to the full House. Under the House "rule" that cleared the bill for legislative action, only three hours of general debate were scheduled, clear evidence that the leadership assumed the entire code would be approved in one session. In what turned out to be an extremely impressive display of legislative choreography, the leadership proved to be correct.

LEGISLATIVE LOVE AT FIRST CITE

On May 5, 1949, almost three months to the day after James Forrestal and Edmund Morgan had addressed the Armed Services Committee, the House took up the UCMJ. Considering the importance of the proposed legislation, the debate was short, surprisingly superficial, and characterized more by excessive amounts of self-congratulations among the leadership of the committee than by any systematic exegesis of key provisions in the code. Allowing for the pages devoted to the reprinting of the revised bill, this first 1949 House debate on the UCMJ appears to fill less than thirteen pages in the *Congressional Record*. Prior to introducing Congressman Brooks, the Louisiana Democrat who had chaired the subcommittee, Vinson reminded his colleagues that the bill was based on five weeks of careful study by a subcommittee that unanimously supported the bill as did the full committee. Moreover, the bill was endorsed and recommended by the bureau of the budget, approved by the National Military Establishment, and supported by Truman's administration.

Carl Vinson told his colleagues that "I am sure you will all agree that the technical provisions of a bill of this character are about as difficult and uninteresting as the formula for atomic energy." Preparation of such a statute "has involved efforts that can best be characterized as plain drudgery" for the "eight lawyers and three laymen of the [House] subcommittee." Another member of that subcommittee, Representative Philbin, added that "this measure has been given exhaustive and most diligent and painstaking consideration." This subcommittee, he stated, "has among its membership some of the very best lawyers in the Congress." Its chair possessed "penetrating judgment, wisdom, patience and sagacity" as well as "a keen analytical, legal mind."

Philbin expounded enthusiastically to his colleagues about the merits of the new code: "It regulates and checks arbitrary, capricious, and whimsical action of commanding officers at every level and every point." (Members of the House who listened to Philbin might have wondered how he could make such a claim in light of Brooks's admission only a few minutes before that explained the decision *not* to remove the commander's authority to convene courts-martial and select their personnel as one resulting from a desire to "avoid the enactment of provisions which will unduly restrict those who are responsible for the conduct of our military operations.") Furthermore, "we have carefully combed every possible way by which the rights of the accused have been or could be violated and have closed up any gap which we have been able to discern by which any member of the armed forces might be denied equal and full justice under the law." A key link in this process was the proposed Court of Military Appeals.

It was to be a tribunal similar to the federal circuit courts of appeal. Forgetting that from the very beginning Morgan had assumed that the new court would be "in the National Military Establishment," Philbin emphasized its independence. "This court will be completely detached from the military in every way. It is entirely disconnected with the Department of Defense or any other military branch, completely removed from any outside influences. It can operate, therefore, as . . . a great, effective, impartial body sitting at the topmost rank of the structure of military justice and insuring as near as it can be insured by any human agency, absolutely fair and unbiased consideration for every accused." To this day, the Court claims total independence from the Pentagon except in matters of fiscal administration. But the Court functions under the very large shadow cast by the awesome size of the American military establishment. The subtle result of being inextricably connected to it can only affect the way the judges perceive their mission.

Aside from the House members who had participated in the hearings, only seven additional representatives joined in the debate on the UCMJ. Due possibly to the effective presentation by the committee leadership, which may well have discouraged many congressmen from raising questions about a complex code with more than 140 separate articles, interest in the legislation appears to have been so desultory that not all the time allotted for discussion was needed. All of the numerous technical amendments presented by the committee were approved by voice vote. On the other hand, Vinson reminded his colleagues that "the bill is highly technical, and we don't want to throw it out of balance."

Vinson's comment was further indication—seen also in the committee's repeated emphasis on the length of subcommittee time devoted to the bill and the number of experts involved—of the leadership's successful desire that the House make virtually no changes whatsoever in the UCMJ as reported to them by Vinson's committee. The practice of discouraging open debate on major legislation by pointing to its complexity and the number of competing interests that support it is, of course, nothing new. Nevertheless, the skill employed by Brooks, Philbin, and Vinson in using this technique remains impressive. Without even a roll call, the House passed the bill.

Even before this step, the Senate had turned to its consideration of the UCMJ. As in the House, the chair of the Senate Armed Services Committee appointed a subcommittee to examine the bill. Many of the same witnesses who had already presented their views at the earlier hearings now returned for a repeat performance. Although he had reason to be pleased with the UCMJ's progress through the House, Larkin assumed that the Senate would have its own agenda. He was right. More than another year was to go by before the UCMJ became law.

11

Creation of the Court, 1949–1950

Although there seems to have been an informal agreement that the Senate would defer consideration of the UCMJ until after the House had acted, the upper house actually began its proceedings before the House Armed Services Committee unanimously sent the revised bill to the floor. When compared with the earlier House subcommittee hearings, the Senate action revealed several differences. In the first place, the Senate spent much less time on the proposed code than its House counterpart. Brooks's panel had consumed at least twenty days in consideration of the UCMJ, with its sessions—as well as those of the full committee—spread out over more than five weeks. By contrast, the Senate subcommittee devoted only three days to public hearings, with a fourth and final session reserved for further discussion with Morgan, Larkin, and his assistant. The House panel included more than a dozen participants, while for most of its of public hearings the Senate subcommittee consisted of only two members, Kefauver and Saltonstall.

Moreover, the House subcommittee conducted its business at a leisurely pace. By comparison Kefauver, a newly elected Democrat from Tennessee, urged each speaker to limit himself to twenty minutes. He asked Wiener, for example, "to make your points fully, but try not to get into any extraneous matters." Finally, at the House hearings, in addition to Morgan, two of his colleagues—Kenney and Zuckert—also testified. None of the judge advocate generals came before the panel. The situation was reversed for the Senate subcommittee. Not one of the service undersecretaries testified, but the three JAGs were invited to speak, and all duly appeared.

Kefauver's decision to call the three senior military justice officers concerned Larkin, who was all too aware that, for the most part, the major modifications in the code had been accepted to accommodate their needs. He feared that the invitation might open the door to additional changes. "I do not know," he wrote to Leva, "what impels Senator Kefauver to call [the JAGs] at this time or who persuaded him to do so." Larkin urged Leva to discuss (army judge advocate general) Green's testimony with Gray. More important, "I think a decision should be made as to whether General Green will speak as the official army representative expressing the army views or whether he will give his own personal views."

With the exception of the judge advocate generals, most of the witnesses before Kefauver's panel were content to reiterate and indeed in some cases merely repeat verbatim earlier statements made to the House subcommittee. Not unreasonably, attention tended to focus on the articles that had generated controversy since they were first considered. Three of these were of special importance to military justice: the problem of command influence, the role of the law member, and the new appellate process. The committee's staff prepared a summary of the conflicting views on these points, including what had been said before both panels as well as action taken by the House. Before reporting the bill to the full Senate committee, Kefauver decided to bring Morgan and Larkin back for a final session to comment specifically on these several issues.

Kefauver received other information as well about opposition to some of the articles. Thus, an unsigned memorandum in his file on military justice concluded that the proposed UCMJ "is no improvement" over the recently enacted Elston Act. Like some other suggested changes, the proposed Court of Military Appeals will "simply add expense, without improving efficiency." The writer advised Kefauver to avoid "hasty enactment of legislation on such an important and far reaching subject." It would be better to see how the changes prescribed under the Elston Act (which went into effect in February 1949), worked out in practice.

One of the new witnesses who appeared before Kefauver's subcommittee was William Hughes Jr., president of the Judge Advocates Association. He testified that the proposed UCMJ "civilianizes a thing that is basically noncivilian in character, namely, the discipline of the Army. It does this by toning down and minimizing the military control and exaggerating the civilian control." The flaw with Morgan's proposed court was that "in serious cases the discipline of the Army is in the hands of civilians, and no longer in the hands of the Army." Hughes also presented a summary of answers to a questionnaire concerning the new code that he had submitted to the members of the association. Many responses opposed the principle of civilian control concerning military justice. "This is a code obviously drawn up by some fuddy-duddy who never saw a day in the field with troops and certainly no combat. . . . [It is] too technical to work." Another respondent observed:

> Military justice is a means instead of an end anyway. It's too bad we have to have it at all and if we ever have lasting world peace we can abolish it all. But until we reach that state of security let's keep our military establishments military. . . . Let's just admit that the military can't do as good

a job of justice as the civil authorities, but the military can do a better job of fighting and since military justice is a necessary part of the fighting machine we will have to keep it.

But the anonymous comments on the proposed uniform code were by no means uniform in their reactions to it. One response argued that "ultimate [judicial] recourse should be civilian, because the ultimate government and law of the land are civilian. Soldiers, as such, do not lose their citizenship. Citizenship is a civilian capacity and should not be impaired with ultimate civilian supervision." And at least one member of the association echoed Farmer, Wels, Spiegelberg, and Keeffe in their less than unrestrained enthusiasm for the new statute: "I am for the uniform code even though it is a single, faltering, inadequate step—yet it is a movement in the right direction."

GREEN'S GRIPES

Of the three judge advocate generals who testified seriatim on May 9, 1949, Army Major General Thomas Green was most critical of the proposed civilian appellate process. Military justice, he argued "is a field . . . which requires not only a thorough familiarity with criminal law, but also experience and training in military matters." The civilian high court proposed by Morgan should, according to Green, consist of "those military lawyers who are most highly experienced and trained both from a military and judicial viewpoint: both as soldiers and as judges." Echoing Wiener, Green insisted that these individuals were already available within the JAG Corps; there was no need to have civilians on such a tribunal.

Hence it followed that no real necessity for a *civilian* high court existed. In reality, this panel "would be at best an administrative board." A more desirable alternative would be the type of judicial council mandated in the Elston Act. It consisted of three general officers, appointed by Green himself, "each of whom has more than thirty years experience in the Army." Moreover, "this panel operates without the benefit of any civilian corps to supervise it."

Yet the army judge advocate general conceded the need for coordination among the services in both the administration and application of military justice. Thus, he too proposed a court of appeals, one that was far from what Morgan had in mind. It would consist not of judges drawn from civilian life but rather the three judge advocate generals themselves, joined by a senior official from the Treasury Department who would represent the Coast Guard—Green's sole concession for a civilian dimension to the Court and one that could always be outvoted by the majority.

Finally, Green—as had Keeffe—called for creation of an advisory council *within* the military establishment, to consist of not more than five lawyers. They were to be drawn from civilian life but would be appointed by the secretary of defense, not the president. Unlike Keeffe's council, however, this one would have no authority over military justice. Instead, it could provide for "a continuing study on the administration of military justice by a body of eminent jurists in conjunction with" the JAGs. Green submitted his suggestions in the form of specific amendments to the UCMJ as passed by the House. They provided for no civilian judicial supervision of any sort within the military justice system. Green even did away with the option of naming civilians to the boards of review. As to General Green's proposals, noted Morgan, "I can tell you confidentially that he was uncooperative from the beginning although he had a representative from his office sitting in at all sessions."

Although Admiral Russell also suggested some amendments, he voiced no complaint about Morgan's proposed court. Similarly, Air Force Major General Harmon not only supported the new tribunal but also saw "no particular objection to having civilians serve on the board of review if they are men of sufficient experience in the administration of military justice to act." Given Harmon's initial opposition to the UCMJ in 1948 as well as his somewhat negative comments in his interview almost forty years later, these statements to Kefauver's subcommittee probably did not reflect his own opinions. Yet Harmon also believed that Morgan's court should not be limited only to civilians: "I certainly think they should have military experience, whether they are military or civilian, on that court." The criterion "should turn on the question of qualifications. The test should be the qualifications of the man rather than the suit he happens to be wearing."

During the Senate subcommittee hearings on the UCMJ, Gray's lingering irritation with Forrestal's decision to support a civilian appellate court surfaced again. As with the earlier episode, it demonstrates anew the extent to which Gray was willing to go to win his point. On April 25, Army Secretary Royall wrote to Defense Secretary Louis Johnson. He reminded Johnson that Gray had "differed radically with the Committee report on one or two vital matters, including particularly the establishment of a civilian review board. My views were entirely in accord with those of Mr. Gray." Royall suggested "that you personally discuss this matter with Mr. Gray with a possible view to reconsideration of the position of the National Military Establishment. Even if your decision is not changed, I would like you to consider permitting Mr. Gray to express his personal views in this matter in the event he is called upon to testify before Congressional Committees." The impetus for Royall's letter came from Gray, who wrote upon the copy he had received from Royall that "this was written in response to a request from me."

Johnson turned Royall's letter over to Larkin, who submitted a memorandum to the new secretary explaining the background of the controversy. He also enclosed a draft of a suggested reply to Royall. In it, he emphasized the unanimous vote in favor of the UCMJ by the House Armed Services Committee as well as the endorsement received by the Bureau of the Budget, thus making the bill "an administration measure." Finally, Larkin recommended that the new secretary write the following: "I shall be glad to speak to Mr. Gray and would like Professor Morgan and the other available members of the Committee present when I do so." Johnson signed the letter, thus apparently ending Gray's final attempt to reverse support for Morgan's civilian court. There is no indication that either Royall or Gray ever accepted Johnson's invitation.

McCARRAN'S MACHINATIONS

As Kefauver's panel proceeded with the hearings, another Senator—Nevada Democrat Patrick McCarran—offered his views on military justice and the UCMJ. A colorful, conservative, and controversial political figure, in 1949 Senator Patrick McCarran was preparing to seek reelection to a fourth term. As chairman of the Senate Judiciary Committee, he claimed a sort of proprietary interest in any bill related to the judiciary. By the late 1940s, he had managed to broaden the scope of his committee to the extent that 40 percent of all national legislation came within its purview. His "views" took the form of a thirty-five-page letter to Kefauver, one that McCarran specifically requested be made a part of the subcommittee's record on the bill. He described his missive as an "intensive study" of the proposed code. McCarran probably had much more on his mind than merely an interest in military justice, and there may have been a number of reasons for this rambling if not confused analysis.

His letter, replete with numerous complaints and suggestions for changes in the code, perhaps was the first step in an effort to ensure that *his* committee rather than the armed services panel controlled the bill once it reached the Senate floor. As will be discussed later, this issue was resolved with McCarran as the loser. However, several of his comments about the proposed system of appellate review warrant brief discussion here.

McCarran implied at the outset that Morgan's committee had been dominated by the military, thus furnishing all the more reason for the Judiciary Committee to take jurisdiction of the bill. He went on to ask two questions about Morgan's appellate system: Is the judicial council "a court?" and, if so, Can it be set up within the military? McCarran argued that, "used in the general sense, this is a court; however it is not a court in the strict constitutional sense in that it does not derive its power from Article III of the Constitution" but rather from Article 1, which, among other things, grants plenary authority to Congress concerning enactment of "rules for the government and regulation of the land and naval forces."

Accepting McCarran's premise, two conclusions followed. First, Morgan's judicial council did not belong to the judicial branch but to the executive. Second, and more important, though it might have the trappings of an appellate court, in fact the council findings "are subject to executive or administrative action of the President or the Secretary of the [military] department." McCarran concluded that the "proposed tribunal is in the final analysis nothing more than an agency of the executive department."

These assertions were merely a reiteration of the traditional view put forth by Winthrop and debated at great length during the Ansell-Crowder controversy. McCarran believed, as had Crowder, that somehow the presidential authority as commander in chief affected judicial independence. Rather than confront this conviction, Morgan's approach had been simply to ignore it as irrelevant. He assumed that power to create military courts did indeed come from Congress, vis-à-vis Article 1. Such authority, however, included congressional discretion over both jurisdictional parameters and the terms of its judges. Nothing, in other words, except its own inclination prevented Congress from giving life tenure to the judges of a court created under Article 1.

For Morgan, the issue of presidential control over military courts had been a brick without straw. The president could always mitigate a sentence or pardon the defendant. Presumably, he could also pardon any criminal defendant in a federal court. As far as the functioning of the proposed military appeals court was concerned, it made no difference. Morgan believed—correctly as later history would reveal—that this tribunal would operate as did any other federal appellate court, subject to the specific limitations set forth in the proposed statute.

Maintaining that the proposed court would be "merely another administrative agency . . . rather than a military supreme court," McCarran recommended the use of existing federal courts as a final forum in which to resolve issues of military justice. These decisions would emanate from an Article 3 judicial panel and would be more creditable than findings handed down by a "military tribunal appellate in character." The same proposal had been made by other witnesses before the congressional panels considering the UCMJ. Besides rejecting the premise upon which McCarran based this suggestion, Larkin and Morgan had other objections. Given the size of the military justice system and the admitted need for uniformity, how could separate federal district courts operate efficiently in this area? Also, if one tribunal outside the military justice system—such as the Court of Appeals for the District of Columbia—was selected, how would it interact with the judge advocate generals and the judges of Morgan's proposed court, all of whom were required to confer together and make recommendations with respect to the military justice system? Finally, "the complex military matters involved in many of the offenses" required a specialized court.

MORGAN'S PENULTIMATE POINTS

Although Kefauver had declared the public hearings on the UCMJ concluded with the evidence offered by the three judge advocate generals on May 9, the subcommittee was unable to meet until May 27, when Morgan returned for a final appearance. He focused on all the controversial issues that had to be resolved by the panel. Three of them are of special interest here: command influence, the law member of the Court, and the military appellate process. Although the senators had listened sympathetically to those witnesses urging changes beyond the provisions enacted by the House, after meeting with Morgan the alterations they actually approved turned out to be very few—due in part, perhaps, to Morgan's powers of persuasion.

Virtually all of the witnesses, including Morgan, had conceded the undesirable potential for command influence when that official was permitted to select members of the court-martial. Emphasizing that the UCMJ had to be practical as well as practicable, Morgan reminded the senators of the specific safeguards against command influence that had been incorporated into the proposed draft—i.e., making such conduct an offense and providing for its punishment. He further noted that if a commander is determined to use "undue influence, . . . he can use it on men of his command who are selected by the JAG just as well as if he selected them himself." Kefauver and Saltonstall, the only two senators present for this final session, agreed to leave the matter of command control untouched but to "put the services on notice that . . . we are watching to see whether there is going to be undue influence."

Turning next to the question of the law officer voting with the other members of the Court, Morgan observed that the issue of having lawyers on military courts was not new. During World War I, commanders had not wanted attorneys as members of the Court because of their fear that lawyers "would bitch up the thing by telling them some law." Again, the senators agreed with Morgan that the law officer, who under the UCMJ now had to be a lawyer, should not participate in the deliberations of the Court.

Several witnesses had objected to the proposed power of a board of review to reduce sentences, arguing that it interfered with the authority of the judge advocate general. Morgan commented that the problem of excessive sentences "is one of the places where there has been . . . tremendous criticism of the [armed forces.]" He recalled that during World War I, "I happened to sit for 6 weeks as chairman of the clemency committee, and I know we remitted 18,000 years in 6 weeks. The sentences are just fantastic at times." Without further conversation, Saltonstall and Kefauver decided to make no change.

Kefauver opened discussion on the Court of Military Appeals (Morgan's old "judicial council") with the point that several witnesses, such as Wiener, had urged that previous military experience be required for the civilian judges. Morgan replied, "Well, I ask you, after you saw Colonel Wiener here, he is a civilian, would you like to have him on a court of military appeals?" One would like to know the response of the senators to Morgan's question. Unfortunately, right at this point there was "discussion off the record." Both senators, however, determined not to impose a requirement of prior military experience.

Saltonstall then turned to the one area where he proposed a real change in Morgan's court as it had been drafted by the House. (His prior thinking on the question of terms for the judges has already been discussed in his correspondence with Raymond Wilkins.) At this point, Saltonstall told Kefauver and Morgan that "my feeling would be to establish this civilian court, but not give them life tenure on good behavior, but make it for a period of years." Kefauver added that there should be initial terms of three, five, and seven years, with future terms for reappointed judges set at either seven or nine years. "We want," he said, "to see how this court is going to operate and what kind of personnel we are going to get."

Saltonstall had already noted that "we have got to gamble that the President is going to appoint good men. That is a gamble[,] and there will be some good and some bad." The Court's subsequent history seems to have vindicated his prediction. Later, Kefauver wrote that "I have no deep convictions about the length of time appointments should be for. The idea . . . was that if the original appointments were made for a shorter term than life, this would give us an opportunity of having another look at how the Court works."

Assuming, wrongly as it turned out, that the Court could begin operation in March 1950, Larkin noted that three-, five-, and seven-year terms "would scatter pretty well," missing presidential elections in each case. Morgan stated that "I have no objection to whatever term you fix, just so the thing is not made a football of politics. I am just as anxious as you are, Senator, that they shall not have a lot of lame ducks running around here." Perhaps with insights gained from actual experience as a politician, Kefauver immediately added, "Unless they are good lame ducks."

One can only speculate as to why Morgan was so quick to endorse this change, even though it represented a major shift away from the type of tribunal he had envisaged. Perhaps he was more concerned with getting the appellate court established, something that obviously required Senate support. For military justice, a court without tenure was certainly better than no court at all. He may also have been aware of Saltonstall's consistent inclinations against life tenure. Whatever the reason, the Senate decision to go with fixed-year terms was the most significant alteration made in the House version of the UCMJ. Inevitably, both congressional and presidential politics played a role in judicial appointments to the Court. Moreover, this action ensured a frequent turnover of judges, resulting in a future source of judicial instability during much of the Court's subsequent history—probably to its overall detriment.

With his labors on the new code now concluded, Morgan drafted letters of appreciation to Leva and Larkin. "My work on the Code is finished," he wrote to Larkin, adding with unintentional understatement that "you still have quite a job on your hands. . . . If I have deserved a Certificate of Merit [something Morgan received at the behest of Larkin], you ought to get two." In a letter to Leva written the same day, Morgan acknowledged his gratitude for securing "the opportunity to take part in this important project. It was especially welcome because of my experience in 1919–1920, when I supported General Ansell in his heroic losing battle with General Crowder." As for Larkin, "it has been a joy to work with him. He is proof positive that not all first-class lawyers and administrators come from the first string law schools."

Speaking for the Armed Services Committee, Kefauver favorably reported the UCMJ by a unanimous vote to the Senate on June 10. He emphasized that the appeals court "is established in the National Military Establishment for the purpose of administration only, and will not be subject to the authority, direction, or control of the Secretary of Defense." The panel had ultimately fixed on eight-year terms, and "the judges are to be highly qualified civilians." Under Senate rules, the bill would take its place on the consent calendar and when called up could pass without debate, provided there was no objection. If, however, senators objected, not only could the bill be subject to debate and amendment, but its place on the calendar also would depend on other business before the Senate.

SENATORIAL SWIPES

Even as Kefauver presented the proposed code to the Senate, he had already received a warning that its immediate and uneventful passage would be unlikely. New Hampshire Republican senator Charles Tobey informed him that if the House bill was reported substantially without changes by Kefauver's committee, which, as has been shown, is just what happened, "I shall consider it my duty to bring the facts to the attention of the Senate by introducing the bulk of the Amendments proposed by [the JAG] of the Army and discuss them thoroughly upon their merits." Since Green had suggested more than twenty-five of them, Kefauver's concern was understandable. He immediately asked Larkin "to have little talks prepared for him on the amendments."

Larkin received word from a staff member of the Armed Services Committee on June 21 that Oregon Republican Wayne Morse had objected to the UCMJ on the calendar call, and that other senators, including Joseph R. McCarthy, were also ready to object. Why the Wisconsin senator opposed it, "he doesn't know, but said no one pays any attention to him." Discussing Morse's action later that day with Morgan, Larkin echoed his committee source, Mark Galusha, about McCarthy: "I am unable to find out, as of this writing, what he has in mind, and, generally, would write him off as unimportant." (Given the national role that McCarthy shortly assumed, this observation is of some interest.) Morse, unfortunately, was another story. Apparently, he had decided to support the ABA proposal to solve command control by using a panel for the selection of court-martial members.

At the age of thirty-one, Wayne Morse had been appointed dean of the

University of Oregon–Eugene. Prior to this post, he taught "argumentation" at the University of Wisconsin. First elected to the Senate in 1944, he served four terms, two as a Republican, two as a Democrat. A well-known political maverick, Morse resigned as a Republican during the 1952 presidential campaign, charging that "reactionaries were running a captive general" (Eisenhower) as Republican candidate. Later, Morse broke with President Lyndon Johnson over the Vietnam conflict. He was defeated for reelection in 1968 but captured the democratic nomination again in 1974. His unfortunate death during the ensuing campaign deprived Oregon voters of the opportunity to return him for a fifth term.

Larkin assured Morgan that he would try to see Morse, but "I don't believe I will be able to convince him. . . . [I]t appears to me that he has now publicly committed himself in such a way that he would be reluctant to back down. It is vastly annoying to find that he is such a demagogue in those matters, particularly when it is perfectly obvious that he knows nothing about the bill, command control or the implications of the panel." Larkin may have been overly harsh in his criticism of Morse, who, when the bill finally came up for Senate debate, offered some very cogent criticisms of the UCMJ. At any rate, he asked Morgan to write to Morse directly: "A few choice words about the panel, the unwieldy labyrinth it provides and the fact that it will be no more effective in eliminating command control than present provisions—all might be helpful."

Upon receipt of Larkin's letter, Morgan wrote to Morse on June 24, expressing sorrow "that you were unable to be present at the meetings of the Sub-Committee of which you were a member." He explained again why the panel idea was impractical and pointed to the new provisions in the UCMJ as the best means to provide against command influence. "I trust," he concluded, "that you will give personal attention to this letter, and not be satisfied with a word from your personal secretary as to its content." Morse responded to "Dear Eddie" with a friendly but firm rejoinder. "I am sure," he wrote, "that I've given the matter as conscientious study as those members . . . who did attend the meetings." He objected to quick approval of the UCMJ in part because he had not completed "to my own satisfaction my study and analysis of the issue," and also "because I am satisfied that legislation as important as this should not be passed in the Senate of the United States by unanimous consent." Finally, "I am not going to vote for the proposal until I am thoroughly convinced on it."

As Larkin's office hastily prepared separate responses to each of Tobey's amendments, Millard Tydings—chairman of the Armed Services Committee—received a not unexpected letter from his colleague, Patrick McCarran. Aware that Kefauver's subcommittee had demonstrated little interest concerning the points raised in his lengthy "analysis" of the UCMJ, McCarran informed Tydings that "I intend to move that the bill . . . be taken from the Senate Calendar and referred to the Committee on the Judiciary." He cited several "compelling instances" that he felt should have the scrutiny of *his* committee.

The Nevada Democrat criticized in particular the provisions of article 76, which made decisions reached through the military justice system "final and binding upon all departments, courts, agencies and officers of the United States." Failing to cite the clearly stated exemption for presidential authority, McCarran attacked the validity of this section on constitutional grounds: "It is questionable whether an Act of Congress could rob the Supreme Court of appellate jurisdiction. I do not believe all civilian courts should be closed to anyone with respect to all matters which may have been tried before a military tribunal or administratively determined by the military. I question the wisdom of conferring absolute finality upon the decisions of an alleged 'court,' the members of which are subject to removal by an administrative officer."

McCarran failed to cite one very plausible justification for giving jurisdiction of the bill to his committee, and this was the fact that traditionally all federal judicial appointments were scrutinized first by the Senate Committee on the Judiciary. Morgan's committee had skirted the issue of whether or not the status of the proposed appellate judges under Article 1 blocked consideration of the appointments by the Judiciary Committee although Senate approval had been required in the House version and retained by the Senate. Nor did McCarran raise the point in a later rebuttal to Tydings. It may well be that McCarran saw the issue as one of turf jurisdiction rather than an important issue both in political and philosophical terms.

Larkin kept Morgan closely informed about the developments threatening prompt consideration of his code: "Morse is not going to be nearly so difficult as he otherwise would have been if it weren't for the fact that you are in the picture." As for McCarran and his claim of jurisdiction, "Kefauver is in favor of meeting the issue head-on and vigorously opposing McCarran. That, of course, is just the position I want. . . . I suspect that McCarran will change his mind, and if he doesn't, I feel confident that we can beat him with the Parliamentarian and on the Floor, if necessary." More worrisome was the fact that "the Senate is so far behind and there are so many important measures still to be taken up." These included time-consuming debate over changes in the National Labor Relations Act (the Taft-Hartley Law) and the newly created North Atlantic Treaty Organization (NATO).

McCarran responded with another letter to Tydings that demonstrated his not inconsiderable skill in appearing to concede points without retreating on the primary issue. He denied any challenge to the jurisdiction of the Armed Services Committee: "All I am doing is asserting that the bill includes subject matter clearly within the jurisdiction of the [Judiciary] Committee, and asking that now, after [Tydings's Committee] has had its say, the bill may be referred to the [Judiciary] Committee for consideration of those matters which do lie within [its] . . . jurisdiction." McCarran reminded Tydings that the Judiciary Committee retains jurisdiction over "judiciary proceedings, civil and criminal, generally, and over civil liberties. Where the rights and liberties of civilians are concerned, I believe that the jurisdiction of the [Judiciary] Committee should stand unquestioned; and there is no doubt that such rights are involved in the [proposed UCMJ.]" Finally, McCarran assured Tydings that "if the bill is referred . . . it will be considered most promptly, and most promptly reported back to the Senate."

As long as the UCMJ draft remained on the Senate calendar, McCarran could do nothing. But his efforts to take the bill from the Armed Services Committee represented only one in a series of obstacles that arose as spring 1949 turned into summer and fall. Besides McCarran's machinations, Morse had invited members of the ABA to prepare an amendment for him along the lines strenuously endorsed by George Spiegelberg, one that would set up a panel within the JAG Corps for appointment to courts-martial. Tobey had submitted more than two dozen amendments embodying the changes that had been proposed by Army JAG Thomas Green. And if all this was not sufficient, Missouri senator Kem proposed an expansion of what he had undertaken in 1948—to make the provisions of the Elston Act applicable to all the armed services, not just the army. As for the UCMJ, the senator saw no need for it at all.

In the Senate on July 29, 1949, Kem argued that "one of the main purposes of unification was simplification." Incredibly, he described the UCMJ as a code that would "abolish all existing rules and start with a completely new set . . . a complication that is entirely unnecessary." The "simple, direct and satisfactory way" to bring about uniform court-martial procedure would be to "make this improved system [now in effect for the Army] applicable to all three services. We will then have the unification desired." Larkin was less than impressed with Kem's proposal. As he wrote to Morgan, "The delay in bringing the UCMJ up for debate has created a few extra problems, because it has given some of the busybodies a little more time." Leading the list was Kem, "the latest nuisance, [who] now comes up with the wholly ridiculous idea that the best way to unify the court-martial system is to subject the Navy to the Articles of War. . . . This idea is so bad that I don't worry about it."

Morse's action, Kem's proposed amendment, McCarran's jurisdictional ploy—together with Senator Tobey's introduction of twenty-seven separate amendments—left Senate consideration of the UCMJ up in the air. Regretfully, Larkin informed Morgan on June 30 that "there is no fixed date for the debate on military justice." By September 16, he suspected that the bill "may go over to the 2nd session." One month later nothing had changed, and "the Uniform Code rests peacefully on the Senate Calendar." Although Larkin remained optimistic, in fact there would be no debate until the Eighty-first Congress convened for its second session beginning January 2, 1950.

Larkin so informed Morgan on November 23, 1949: "We are initiating plans to have it brought to the Floor . . . in the first few weeks of the 2nd Session, and I am sure that when we get it to the Floor we will secure its passage." Part of Senate failure to consider the UCMJ can be attributed to legislative logjam. But politics may have played a role as well. Tydings had entrusted the bill to the care of a freshman senator from Tennessee, Estes Kefauver who, for reasons irrelevant to this study, was regarded with marked hostility by the senior senator from his state, Kenneth McKellar, who had been in office since Wilson's administration and was a high-ranking member of the conservative southern clique that effectively ran the upper chamber. The consistent refusal of the Senate majority leader to bring the UCMJ to the floor may have been due in part to McKellar's preferences rather than Kefauver's priorities. McKellar's biographer wrote of him that "his bailiwick was the United States Senate, and he was its dean." McKellar, it might be noted, ultimately voted to refer the UCMJ to McCarran's committee.

Not until February 1, 1950, did the Senate turn to the UCMJ. Kefauver formally presented the bill with a section by section analysis that had, of course, been prepared for him by Larkin's office. Indeed, at Kefauver's request, the Senate permitted Larkin and his assistant Robert Haydock to sit with Kefauver on the Senate floor during debate on the code. When Kefauver took up the appellate process, he told his colleagues that "since the court represents a new concept in military law, it was advisable to provide the appointment of the judges for a term of years, rather than for life." Senator Kem questioned whether the "court would have enough to do . . . to keep three men busy throughout the year, in time of peace." Kefauver answered that "that was one of the questions which . . . caused the Senate committee to recommend that the terms of the three judges be not for life, but for a certain number of years."

The Senate spent February 2 on other issues, with only desultory comment on the UCMJ. Senator Wayne Morse noted, however, that on February 3, McCarran would propose that the bill be referred to the Judiciary Committee. Morse added that he would support McCarran's motion. "It is my opinion that the bill should never have been referred to the Armed Services Committee" at all. He could "see no reason why questions as to judicial right[s] on the part of men in the armed services should be considered by any committee other than" the Judiciary Committee. Morse sensed, correctly, an implication in the UCMJ that military justice differed in key essentials from its civilian counterpart. "I happen to be one," he concluded, "who believes we should not draw the type of curtain between civilian and military justice that is drawn by this bill."

When Saltonstall pointed to the heavy weight of precedents favoring the Armed Services Committee considering military justice, Morse responded that "I do not quarrel with the citation of precedents. I quarrel with the advisability of following those precedents. . . . It is high time—in fact it is long overdue—that we bring about a uniformity of principle in the administration of criminal justice, covering both civilians and military personnel." Here, Morse raised a fundamental, and possibly insolvable, issue. On the other hand, numerous witnesses had argued these questions before both congressional committees. The UCMJ had accepted the premise he rejected, a duality of the two justice systems. But Morgan's committee had taken several important steps to render military justice as close to its civilian counterpart as feasible. Also, it was very late in the legislative game for Morse to bring up these points, especially since the Senate majority leader had informed his colleagues that the vote would be taken the next day, February 3.

True to his promise, McCarran duly moved to have the bill referred to his committee. The ensuing debate essentially reiterated the points made in earlier correspondence between McCarran and Tydings. McCarran noted the less than rapid pace with which the bill had been considered by the Senate, and asked, "Why deny [his] committee jurisdiction? Are Senators afraid of the 13 men of whom the able Senator from Tennessee [Kefauver] is one?"

Kem added that it "is difficult for me to understand why any harm can be done to the public interest by having the subject deliberately considered by the Senate [Judiciary] Committee." McCarran further argued that, given the complaints received by his committee concerning military justice, "I say to the Senate that it cannot afford not to refer this bill to the Judiciary Committee." Military courts, he concluded, "are reeking with injustice, if we are to believe the charges which have been made." Finally, McCarran inquired, "Is it desired that Senators who, like myself, favor something of the kind designed by the bill shall vote against [it]? I certainly shall vote against it if it comes to a vote and my committee is denied the right of review."

When the vote was taken, the Senate defeated McCarran's motion, 33 in favor, 43 opposed, with 20 not voting. Among those supporting McCarran were Kem, McCarthy, Morse, and Michigan senator Homer Ferguson, for whom the future held both defeat for reelection in 1954 and appointment to the very court soon to be created by the UCMJ. Had Tobey been present, he also would have voted with McCarran. With this motion lost and with both Kem and Tobey making no effort to move on their proposed amendments, the only remaining obstacle appeared to be Wayne Morse, who immediately claimed the floor after the Senate returned to consideration of the bill.

Morse's lengthy speech in support of the ABA-Spiegelberg amendments to the UCMJ was noteworthy for his release of a letter from Arthur Farmer— another New York attorney—severely critical of Morgan's opposition to the panel idea. The Harvard law professor had been "sold a bill of goods by those who advocated retention of command control . . . made possible because he is not familiar with the practical workings of either military justice or the Army line of command." He shows "an extraordinary and lamentable failure" to understand the proposed plan. Because Morgan lacked "complete familiarity with the processes of military justice," he was "at a tremendous disadvantage when faced by the Judge Advocate General or others equally experienced."

Morse also had some comments about the Court of Military Appeals. Emphasizing that such a tribunal "must be free of the slightest imputation of political or military pressure," he argued that the Senate decision to reduce the terms from life or during good behavior to eight years was "inadvisable." Moreover, limiting tenure in this manner could well cause individuals with outstanding qualifications to decline appointment. Finally, and most important, Morse chided his own subcommittee for inconsistency. It wanted the new court to be on a par with U.S. Courts of Appeal, but it refused to give the judges that security and tenure common to their federal counterparts." He urged that the bill be put off for a week, so that the Senate could consider the ABA amendments. "I think they are entitled to a much more careful consideration than can possibly come to them in the short few minutes they will receive this afternoon if the Senate now rushes into a vote."

Although they had considerable merit, these comments were ineffectual, Even as Morse uttered them, Kefauver probably knew that the votes to pass the UCMJ were well in hand. He reiterated the point that the command influence issue had been discussed and debated many times over, always with the same results. Because Morse had to leave the floor to meet a prior appointment, Kefauver even agreed to move the amendments on his behalf. They were rejected without a roll call, and late in the afternoon of February 3, 1950, the Senate passed the bill, 62 in favor, 9 opposed, 25 not voting. True to his threat, McCarran voted against the measure, as did Morse and Tobey.

Although the Senate had added a number of amendments to the House bill, the only one of major importance was the change in terms for the judges on the new Court of Military Appeals. Larkin wrote to Morgan that since the bill cleared the Senate, the House Armed Services Committee had been holding hearings to determine if the Senate changes were acceptable. "I testified at three of those hearings, and was able to persuade them to take forty-four out of the forty-five amendments." One, however, was put off for a future hearing, "and, of course, they held it the day after I left town, and, contrary to my expectation, decided that they would not adopt it and, hence, the bill must go to Conference."

Larkin added that the committee had settled for a fifteen-year term rather than the eight as decided by the Senate. Because the lower chamber had accepted the principle of a finite term rather than life tenure, he saw "the whole thing as inconsequential" and more as a delaying maneuver on Vinson's (the chairman of the House Armed Services Committee) part than anything else. According to Larkin, this was because Vinson "wants to wait until April to pass the bill so that members of this Congress will be eligible for the Court," which could not come into formal existence until 1951—after Congress had adjourned. One week later, Robert Smart informed Larkin that Vinson now believed that the first terms should be on a staggered (five-, ten-, and fifteen-year) basis: "He said that Kilday [a Texas Democrat and member of the House committee] is Vinson's candidate and he wants him to get the fifteen-year term." In terms of prognostication, on this matter Vinson performed rather well. Congress ultimately accepted the staggered-term concept. Not in 1951 but rather in 1961, the first Democratic president since Truman—John F. Kennedy—did in fact appoint Paul Kilday to the Court.

Larkin may well have been correct in his implication that practical politics rather than philosophic principles lay behind the decision to send the bill to conference. The conferees agreed to the fifteen-year term, both Houses accepted their recommendations without a roll call, and on May 5, 1950, President Truman signed the Uniform Code of Military Justice into law. In urging his colleagues to accept the compromise, Representative Brooks stated that "it was my idea that this court would correspond as nearly as could be made to that of the Federal courts of appeal." To be sure, we have "to some extent fallen short of this goal; but the tenure agreed upon . . . is sufficiently long to insure a stability and a permanence to the court which will serve to inspire confidence in its vitality and integrity." Whether Brooks was as good at predicting the future as his friend Carl Vinson appeared to have been can be seen in the first three decades or so of the new Court's history, which the following chapters will examine.

The reform of military justice between 1919 and 1950 followed an intriguing course. As retired Army JAG George Prugh stated in 1975, the judge advocate generals "are not going to be the originators of ideas that are going to change the military justice system, at least not very often." One explanation for this fact may lie in the continuing tension between line and staff officers. Indeed, the history of attempted change in military justice during World War I and immediately thereafter demonstrates the validity of Prugh's insight. That a staff officer (such as Army JAG Enoch Crowder) avoided open confrontation with a line officer (such as General John Pershing) concerning military justice is very understandable.

The unusual conditions resulting in Ansell's failure to bring major reforms to military justice need not be reexamined here. As an insider, the severe criticism he applied to certain internal practices was unusual. In retrospect—given the personal antagonisms, political disputes, and genuine disagreement over both the appropriate place for military appellate review and by whom it should be exercised—the outcome of this episode is not surprising; and it is instructive to compare conditions in 1918–1922 with 1948–1950.

The magnitude of American involvement in World War II produced extensive interest and concern with the way military justice was administered. After the war ended, the armed services were unified, although not by choice and not without severe internal friction. Both the decision to unify and the concomitant step to promulgate a uniform code of military justice were inspired by civilians and mandated by Congress. Moreover, it was a civilian, James Forrestal, as secretary of defense who convened the Morgan committee, instructed the various services that ultimately they would be bound by its decisions, and decided the final form of proposed articles where Morgan's panel could not reach agreement. When the UCMJ was submitted to Congress, again it was civilians such as Forrestal and Morgan who spoke on behalf of the "Defense Establishment." Although the three JAGS appeared before Kefauver's subcommittee, they apparently could offer only their personal views. The difference in approach between Forrestal in 1949 and Newton Baker in 1919 is striking.

Twenty years after the UCMJ went into effect, retired Army JAG Kenneth Hodson recalled concerning creation of the code that "the military departments were pretty much out of the picture with respect to [the UCMJ]. . . . we were given several opportunities to comment on the draft . . . , but our comments were not always given much weight by . . . Mr. Larkin and Mr. Morgan and by the various congressional committees. Once in a while we would point out an absolute error, and they would make a change. But for the most part the whole concept, the philosophy of the Code, remained pretty much as it was when . . . drafted by Professor Morgan and Mr. Larkin. In other words, it was pretty much a civilian effort."

Actually, as has been shown, Morgan's committee made far greater allowance for military preferences than Hodson realized or at least remembered. The limitation on jurisdiction for the court, the expanded powers for the intermediate courts (which were to be appointed by the JAGs themselves), retention of basic command authority to convene courts-martial and to select their members—all are examples where UCMJ provisions were drafted or altered to meet objections raised by the military. Finally, the decision to limit the terms of the judges can be seen as a compromise between those who favored a court as much like a federal appeals tribunal as possible and those in the military who believed such a court to be unnecessary.

Important questions concerning the new court, some of which had already been raised in congressional testimony, could only be answered in the future. Would the court be truly independent of the military establishment? Would it receive the type of cooperation from the JAGs necessary for its operation? Would its presence inspire public confidence that command influence could not affect the quality of justice administered by our armed services?

These questions were more than important; they were troublesome. Never before had Congress created a civilian appellate court for the military. Nor had the new code provided a clear demarcation between the JAGs and the court concerning supervision of military justice. Thus article 6 of the UCMJ mandated the JAGs to make "frequent inspections in the field in supervision of the administration of military justice." Yet it was probable that an appellate tribunal, one that had already been labeled by various congressional speakers as "the supreme court of the military," would claim for itself ultimate supervision of military justice. The new code mandated cooperation between judges and JAGs but at the same time established a basis for inevitable friction.

Finally, the success of the court would depend largely upon the legal and, to a great extent, diplomatic skills of the new judges. However, compromise and political considerations affected the final form of the court. They would also affect selection of the judges to sit on its bench. In this context, it is appropriate to cite a letter from Donald Dawson, Truman's administrative assistant in charge of personnel. On August 29, 1949, he wrote to the chairman of the Democratic National Committee, reminding him that while the UCMJ had not yet passed the Senate, "it would be well for us to line up the judges to be appointed."

12

Journeys to the Judgeships, 1950–1951

Even before the bill creating the USCAAF reached President Truman, interest had begun to focus on selection of the first three judges. The House bill provided for life tenure, while the Senate opted for eight-year terms. The compromise ultimately established fifteen-year terms, with the first three judges only being named for fifteen, ten, and five years. Two names frequently mentioned were Felix Larkin and Edmund Morgan, although in fact neither man was a serious contender for appointment.

EARLY COURT CONTENDERS

On February 9, an old friend—New York attorney Richard Wels—wrote to Larkin. Alluding to the continuing and mostly unsuccessful efforts by the various lawyers'associations to change the new code, he nevertheless felt that it "is going to be able to accomplish the objectives that we all have had in mind—despite the carpings of us perfectionists up here." More important, he added, "I hope that someone is going to see that you are one of the three judges . . . because the success of the Code is going to depend upon having someone like you on that initial court." Larkin agreed that "a great deal will depend on the caliber of the three judges . . . [but] I am sure no one is thinking of me in those terms, nor have I given any thought to whether I would want such a job if anybody was serious about it."

It soon became clear that in spite of Wels's compliments to Larkin, the New York County Lawyers' Association—for which he spoke—continued to criticize the UCMJ. In a statement prepared for release on April 17, the day before the conference committee was to meet, the association accused Congress of abandoning "the heart of the proposed reform, the elimination of the

power of commanding officers to influence the decisions of court-martials."
Equally undesirable was the Senate's decision to provide the judges with eight-
year appointments: "We are of the view that the utmost support should be given
to the House in its efforts to resist this Senate change." Finally, the lawyers
were "disturbed that the court for administrative purposes should be placed in
the Department of Defense rather than in the administrative office of the United
States Courts."

The not unreasonable fear that the new court could somehow be dominated
by the military establishment led to lawyers' groups adopting a series of resolutions. The one drafted by Wels's colleagues was typical. The association was
authorized to consult with the president, the secretary of defense, and the attorney general; to appear before the Congress in order to ensure the nomination
and confirmation of persons deemed "to be competent and specially qualified";
and to oppose those candidates they "deem to be unfit or not sufficiently qualified." What the lawyers actually sought was less the opportunity to testify for
or against a candidate and more the ability to screen individuals in advance of
Senate consideration.

Thus, I. Howard Lehman, president of the New York County Lawyers
Association, wrote to President Truman that his group "is anxious to be of all
possible service in connection with the nomination and confirmation of such
persons as may be selected for this important court." Truman should consider
"our" special committee on military justice or the panel on the judiciary "at
your command in connection with any advices [*sic*] or suggestions with
respect to the selection of the Judges. . . . May we hope that, before definite
appointment is made, we be given an opportunity to be of possible assistance?" Although Lehman could not know it, more than a year would pass
before Truman sent his three choices to the Senate. Numerous letters similar
to Lehman's were sent to Truman, and the response through his secretary followed a predictable pattern. The offer of service "will be borne in mind, and
you may be sure that careful consideration will be given to any recommendations which you may care to make regarding the membership of the Court."
Conspicuous in the reply is the absence of any commitment to submit the
names of possible nominees to Lehman's committee in advance of formal
nomination.

In the meantime, Morgan wrote to Marx Leva, who had become assistant
secretary of defense: "It seems to me exceptionally important that the first court
should be composed of highly competent men and that no 'deserving' politician be appointed. The best assurance I could have that the Court would get
off to a good start would be to have Felix appointed for the 15-year term. Is
there any way that this could be accomplished or that I can help?"

Leva showed this letter to Larkin, who promptly replied to Morgan: "I
treasure that recommendation above any other I could ever get. While, naturally enough I have thought of the Court, I have not been a candidate. . . . [A]t

the present moment I wonder if I should, at my age, try to commit myself to what would probably be the last job I would ever do."

Leva also wrote Morgan, expanding on what Larkin had intimated: "My own reaction—and I think that Secretary Johnson feels about the same as I do on this score—is that everything you say about Felix is true—but that his appointment to the Court at this state of his legal career, while it would be extremely beneficial to the Department of Defense, might not be equally beneficial to Felix, himself. . . . I hope that I will have an opportunity to discuss this matter with you further before the names of the judges are finally decided upon."

If Larkin had doubts about his desire for judicial service, others had none about their own inclinations. As will be seen, it remains unclear exactly how many individuals were seriously considered for the first appointments. Two days after the bill creating the Court became law, one candidate—George Latimer—wrote to Truman's military aide, expressing real interest in the position. Shortly thereafter, another prospect—Paul Brosman—emerged with the support of the air force JAG, Reginald Harmon. Since both ultimately received appointments to the new Court, their early candidacy deserves some attention.

On May 8, 1950, Harry Vaughan received a letter from George Latimer. A native of Utah, Latimer had successfully combined a dual career as counsel and combatant. During World War II, as an officer in the Utah National Guard, he saw active duty in the Pacific, rising to the rank of full colonel. In 1947, after he returned to Utah and reestablished his law practice, Latimer was elected to the Utah Supreme Court. While in the guard, he had become acquainted with Harry Vaughan, who later became Truman's military aide.

In a draft of his unpublished memoirs written toward the end of his life, Latimer claimed that "I heard through the grapevine that my name had been suggested to President Truman as a possible appointee" to the new court. The "source of my recommendation," he added, "was and is unknown to me." Recollections recede as the years pass, and Latimer can be forgiven for his lapse of memory. It may well be that Vaughan brought Latimer's name to the attention of Truman. If he did, however, it was at the behest of Latimer himself.

Noting that the president had just signed the bill creating the new tribunal, in a letter to "my dear Harry," Latimer told Vaughan that "I am very much interested in being considered for one of these appointments but realize that being a member of the Republican Party makes it difficult to receive support from Democratic sources." He emphasized, however that "if the appointment is not to be partisan[,] I believe I can recruit in my behalf the out-standing members of the President's party in this state and both Democratic and Republican members of the bar." Latimer understood that the new court would not become effective until May 1951, "and it may be that efforts at this time are premature. However, I would rather be early than overlooked."

Vaughan was surprised to receive Latimer's letter: "I would imagine that a State Supreme Court Justice is a much more important legal job than this

Armed Forces Court Martials Appeals board; but maybe the latter is more interesting and exciting. I don't know about these things." Vaughan, known more
for his friendship with President Truman than for political insight or influence,
assured Latimer that "I will put your name on the list of those to be considered." Meanwhile, Latimer hastened to educate his friend. "To remove your
wonderment and justify my claims to sanity," the Utah jurist cited three reasons for his interest.

In the first place, "I have a very honorable, dignified and respected position, which suffers only from meager pay and emoluments." Moreover, the
Utah governor had just vetoed a nonpartisan judiciary bill. Thus, "if I remain
here, I shall be required to accomplish the almost impossible, namely, to convince the voters to elect a Republican Justice in a normally Democratic state."
Finally, "I am still ambitious and I would like to earn some kind of reputation
nationally. . . . It may be that I have over-estimated the importance of the proposed court, but I believe the opportunities there to formulate and build a system might be challenging."

But Latimer was not without an immediate rival, even at this very early
stage of the selection process. Not only was another Republican candidate,
Franklin Riter, also from Utah, but he too was an officer in the National Guard
and had previously testified before the House committee that passed on the
UCMJ. Writing to Utah senator Elbert Thomas (shortly to be defeated for
reelection), Riter reminded the senator that "improper influence upon Courts-
Martial by any person should constitute, not only a military offense, but [one]
indictable [and punishable in federal courts.] In other words, I would make it a
civil offense for an appointing authority to coerce the verdict of a Courts-
martial." Riter admitted, however, that both Morgan's committee and Congress
had rejected this suggestion.

Unlike Latimer and Riter who might draw on their National Guard contacts
for endorsement, Paul Brosman enjoyed the active support of Reginald Harmon, the judge advocate general of the air force. A graduate of the University
of Illinois Law School, Brosman was appointed to the faculty of Tulane University Law School in 1929. Four years later, he became its dean and retained
that title until 1951, although his tenure was interrupted by World War II, during
which he served in the army air corps. In 1950, at the request of the JAG of the
now independent air force, Brosman, with the approval of his university,
returned to active duty. Nine years later, Harmon—still air force judge advocate
general—recalled that Brosman had expressed interest in the new court during
the spring of 1950. According to Harmon, he and the prospective candidate
agreed that Harmon would gather support within the Defense Department, while
Brosman would enlist the backing of key legislators from Louisiana.

There seems no reason to doubt Harmon's recollections. By July 12, 1950,
Truman's assistant for personnel, Donald Dawson, had already requested a
"full field investigation" into Brosman's background from the FBI. Ten days

later, Dawson indicated that Brosman "has already been mentioned to us for such an appointment and we have background information concerning him in our files." Harmon later recalled receiving a phone call from Dawson: "I understand you're recommending a Paul Brosman for a court appointment." Harmon replied, "Yes, I am. He's a good officer, a scholar, and a fine gent." Dawson then asked, "What do you really think of him?"

MORGAN CONSIDERS

It is not clear to what extent Riter, Latimer, and Brosman actively pursued their candidacies during the remainder of 1950. The outbreak of the Korean War occupied both President Truman and his new secretary of defense, George Marshall. Morgan, now settled in at Vanderbilt Law School, received word from Larkin that "candidates continue to appear" for the new court, but "nothing more is being done, and I expect no decisions will be made until February. At this time, I have no idea of the preferences of Secretary Marshall. You, of course, remain my number 1 candidate, and I hope you will continue to consider the idea."

In September, Larkin informed Morgan that, under pressure from George Spiegelberg, the American Bar Association proposed that all potential nominees for the new court "be submitted to the [ABA] for ratings as to qualifications. Within very specified limits, I don't think it is too bad." However, Larkin added, if ABA standards included "adherence to their ideas, I didn't think their judgments would be too useful." He asked Morgan what he thought of the ABA rating the candidates for the new court.

Morgan promptly replied to Larkin's letter with some comments that indicated both a respect for the ABA evaluative procedure and a concern for the independence of the new court: "I think it would be well to have the candidates handled by the A.B.A. Committee. . . . But I think it would be unwise to have the matter in the hands of a committee of the J.A.G. Reserve Officers or any such bunch. They will think only of the Army and may have too many axes to grind." Morgan added another caveat: "If the A.B.A. has a committee which would not rate experience in the field too highly, its opinion ought to be well worth considering[,] but it ought not to be decisive. On the other hand, if the A.B.A. is not consulted, there will be some adverse publicity."

Apparently, the ABA did not wait to be consulted. On November 9, its president, Cody Fowler, sent identical letters to President Truman, Defense Secretary Marshall, Attorney General J. Howard McGrath, and the chairmen of the Senate Armed Services and Judiciary Committees. Fowler reminded Truman of a long-standing ABA goal: the requirement of "the effective elimination of command control of courts martial." Unfortunately, in its present form the UCMJ "does not insure the desired goal." It was all the more important, therefore, that selections for the Court should "in addition to the high character and qualifications" needed for judicial appointment also "possess a real interest in the possibility of improving the basic legislation under which they act."

Fowler detailed for Truman how closely his organization had worked in the past with the president, other administration officials, and the Senate Judiciary Committee in selecting federal judges. Truman replied that "should the Association care to submit a list of those it considers eminently qualified for appointment to the Court, I shall be glad to give consideration to its suggestions, along with the many others which are coming to me." Truman's letter was carefully worded. While willing to accept suggestions for the new appointments, apparently he declined to submit any names to the ABA in advance of nomination—something Fowler clearly desired. He had offered the president ABA assistance "in any manner in which it can be deemed to be of service, in the selection or screening of members for appointment to the newly created court."

As the year came to an end, its seems clear that several groups assumed that they would have significant input into Truman's appointments. The ABA and its committee, the Defense Department as well as its Office of General Counsel—a position to which Felix Larkin had been appointed—all prepared to offer their suggestions. The only problem was that the administration appears to have had little more than polite interest in what they had to offer. Several lists of nominations were ultimately submitted to the president through Donald Dawson. But Dawson apparently went about the process of narrowing the list of candidates for Truman's consideration much the way he did with other intermediate presidential appointments. In the meantime, barely five months before the new code was to go into effect, Truman had given no indication as to his preferences.

With the outbreak of the Korean War, Morgan wrote to Larkin that "if the situation gets really bad, I do not want to sit on the sidelines if I can help it." Of course, he added, "my age is against me." (Morgan was then seventy-two.) As for becoming a judge, "the possibility of appointment to the new Court is, in my opinion, definitely out." The recent congressional elections have "left too many prime candidates available—and some of them entirely competent." Yet Morgan hoped he might still be of some service, and with an understandable pride of parentage—despite the realities of chronology—service on the Court he had proposed continued to tempt him. Morgan revealed his true feelings to some of his former students rather than to Felix Larkin.

Writing to Van Tanner, Morgan acknowledged that John Kenney had urged his selection, but "I told them immediately that my age made such an appointment not only unwise but practically impossible." Morgan added that "the best man I know of is . . . Felix Larkin. He knows more about the Code and its background than any other living man." But it was to Marx Leva that Morgan most clearly indicated his ambivalence:

As to the Court of Military Appeals, I am in a fog in my own thinking, except as to one thing. I am absolutely certain that if I were in the position of Secretary Marshall, I should not nominate anyone of my age; and if I were in the President's position, I should not appoint such a person if nominated by the Secretary. . . . I certainly am not a candidate for the position, for I could not say to the Secretary or to the President that my appointment would be evidence of good judgment on his part. I am not too modest to think that I could do a reasonably good job in spite of my age; but I am convinced that there are among the applicants younger men who could do quite as well or better and (an important consideration) who would prove worthy of reappointment at the end of five years.

Later, Morgan reiterated these points for yet a third time in a letter to Larkin: "I could not tell the President that I believed it would be either wise or politic to appoint me." Again, he ruled out a flat rejection, "if it were offered to me, but I cannot help hoping that it will not be offered." One can understand and sympathize with Morgan's ambivalence. He had just left Harvard Law School, not voluntarily but because of age. On the other hand, Leva and Larkin had endorsed Morgan for the short, five-year term on the new court, a period of time that, given Morgan's excellent health, did not seem unreasonable. It is interesting to note that George Marshall had become Truman's secretary of defense at the age of seventy, while Henry Stimson was almost seventy-eight when he finally retired in 1945 as Truman's secretary of war. Ultimately, Morgan found himself caught between the forces of reality and desire.

In the meantime, Deputy Secretary of Defense Robert Lovett had received an angry letter from George Spiegelberg, still chairman of the ABA Special Committee on Military Justice. The committee had been informed that "the positions on the Court must be used to build politically for 1952," when presumably Truman would run for reelection. For Spiegelberg, "it would be a shocking thing politically to prostitute the Court, the last judicial forum for millions of young men and women of this country." He reminded Lovett that the UCMJ "leaves much to be desired." If the new court, obligated by statute to suggest reforms in military justice, "is made the depository of political hacks . . . essential needed reforms will never be proposed." Further, the Court, "if political, will be subject, because of its limited tenure, to baneful influences which will require independent and fearless men to combat." Lovett should "interest yourself actively in preventing what appears to be inevitable unless someone makes the good fight."

By February 16, two separate lists of possible nominees, one from Marshall and the other from Fowler, had been submitted for Truman's consideration. "It appears of the utmost importance," Marshall reminded the president, "that men of clearly outstanding ability be named to this newly created Court. Your initial appointees to this Court will set [its] tone . . . for many years to come." Even before their arrival, however, Donald Dawson had already received a set of suggested nominees from the chairman of the Democratic National Committee. It included a name conspicuous by its absence from Marshall's and Fowler's choices. This individual would ultimately be Truman's preference both as chief judge and the holder of the fifteen-year term: Robert Quinn. Since Quinn would serve on the new court longer than any other judge in its history—for almost twenty-four years—the absence of his name from so many of the supposedly "inside" lists deserves some attention.

THE QUINTESSENTIAL QUINN

In 1950, Robert E. Quinn was quietly serving on the Rhode Island Superior Court. A 1918 graduate of Harvard Law School, Quinn had been attracted to Rhode Island politics soon after World War I. In 1924, following a term in the state senate, he had unsuccessfully sought the Democratic nomination for lieutenant governor. If it is true that the smaller the state, the more labyrinthine its politics, Quinn's later career well illustrates the principle. He served another term in the state senate and in 1932 came to the attention of a wealthy Democratic political figure, Theodore Francis Green, a candidate for governor. The young Irish-Catholic lawyer with strong ties to urban democratic circles provided a valuable counterweight to Green. Nominated for lieutenant governor, Quinn and Green were elected in 1932 and reelected two years later.

Quinn presided over the state senate during an era for which the word "turbulent" may seem an understatement. On January 1, 1935, his appointment of a new senate committee to recount ballots in two disputed contests resulted in the first Democratic majority of the Rhode Island legislature in over one hundred years. Before the day ended, Quinn orchestrated votes for "initial reorganization of state administration, swept away the [entire] Supreme Court, and eliminated" various state office positions that had long been Republican power bases. In 1936, he succeeded Green as governor when Green won election to the United States Senate—where he would remain until 1960. Quinn served only one term as governor, and his tenure was characterized by intensive infighting that helped contribute to his defeat for reelection in 1938.

The most unusual episode in Quinn's term involved a feud with a fellow Rhode Island Democrat that rapidly escalated into a power struggle between the governor and yet another Democrat, who was also the owner of a Rhode Island horse racing track. Before it was all over, two state supreme court decisions had gone against Quinn. He responded by proclaiming martial law, calling out the National Guard, forcibly closing the race track, and filing charges of libel against its owner. The best account of the entire incident, which seems as bizarre today as when it took place, is Zechariah Chafee Jr., *State House Versus Pent House* (1937).

Two years later, the Democrats nominated as their gubernatorial candidate J. Patrick McGrath, a lawyer and state Democratic chairman with strong ties to the National Democratic Committee. Quinn actively sought the nomination yet did not force a vote during the state convention. It is interesting to note that one of McGrath's first acts as governor was to appoint Quinn to the superior court. "In political circles," according to the *Providence Daily Journal,* Quinn's acceptance of such a position "was interpreted as meaning his retirement from active politics." Well aware of this interpretation, the former governor had made no secret of his ambition to become a U.S. senator, "but observers believed that [McGrath] would not offer him the [judgeship] unless . . . Quinn would consider the appointment permanent." Quinn was barely confirmed by the Rhode Island state senate, the final vote being 22 to 21—with the lieutenant governor voting to break a tie. One Republican partisan hoped that Quinn "will make a good judge and uphold the Constitution on the bench better than he did as presiding officer of the Senate."

During World War II, Quinn requested and received legislative permission to take a leave of absence for service in the navy and returned to the bench just in time to encourage his supporters to launch an attempt to gain the senatorial nomination in 1946. Declining to play an active role in these efforts because of a fear of judicial impropriety, Quinn coyly stated that "he would run if the people want me." In the meantime, McGrath, completing three successful terms as governor, had resigned to become President Truman's solicitor general. For the second time (but not the last), the paths of Quinn and McGrath converged.

In 1972, Judge Quinn claimed that McGrath had promised him that he would not seek the Democratic senatorial nomination in 1946. Possibly McGrath attached the same importance to this "promise" as Quinn had to the assumption that his 1941 judicial appointment implied an end to what political aspirations he might still have. At any rate, McGrath resigned as solicitor general on June 7, 1946, to begin his campaign for the Senate seat, with the strong support of Theodore Green, himself ensconced in that chamber, as well as Governor (and future senator) John Pastore. Against such an effective alliance utilizing appeals to Catholic, Protestant, Irish, and Italian interests, Quinn's supporters had little chance. The convention rejected his candidacy by a vote of 145 to 52, although Quinn himself was not present. In November, McGrath was elected, but his tenure as senator would be very short.

Two years later, Quinn again seriously considered running in the Democratic primary for U.S. senator against the incumbent, Theodore Francis Green. But on July 30, 1948, the *Providence Daily Journal* reported that Quinn had removed himself as a candidate "in the interests of party harmony." In the meantime, McGrath resigned from the Senate to become attorney general, succeeding Tom Clark whom Truman had appointed to the U.S. Supreme Court. Again, Quinn found his way blocked to another chance at a Senate seat, this time by the plans of Governor Pastore to run himself, with the support of both

Green and McGrath. By 1950, it may well have been clear to the former governor that a seat in the Senate was not to be his. And while Green, McGrath, and Pastore realized the same thing, they were also well aware that Quinn's nickname, "Fighting Bob," had some basis in fact. Comfortable neither with Green's organization nor with McGrath's supporters, Quinn's continuing availability as a "dark horse" candidate might explain why all three politicians were so quick to urge his name upon Truman for appointment to the new court.

Indeed, Green had first written to Truman about "my interest in having Judge Quinn appointed to this position" on August 1, 1950, when the selection process had barely begun. He also reminded Truman that Quinn had been named to the superior court by "the Governor of Rhode Island, now Attorney General of the United States, our friend, J. Howard McGrath." "Both my colleague John Pastore and I," Green concluded, "wish to recommend Judge Quinn for this appointment and we trust, Mr. President, that he will receive your favorable consideration." Five days later, the chairman of the Democratic National Committee, William Boyle Jr., wrote to Dawson urging that President Truman give "serious consideration" to four individuals. The first name on Boyle's list was Robert E. Quinn.

By March 1951, Marshall was aware of Quinn's candidacy. On March 26, his aide informed a member of Truman's staff, presumably John Steelman, that the secretary wanted the Rhode Island judge listed for the new court. In turn, Steelman told Truman's assistant, Martin Friedman, that the former governor "has already been brought to our attention as a candidate for this Court, [and] you will no doubt want to show the Secretary's interest." Truman had very great respect for Marshall. Certainly his endorsement of Quinn may well have bolstered a candidacy already assured, as has been shown, of strong support by important Rhode Island political figures—not the least of whom was Truman's own attorney general and former chairman of the Democratic National Committee, J. Howard McGrath.

TRUMAN'S ULTIMATE CHOICES

Thus by spring 1951, Donald Dawson—the presidential assistant charged with maintaining files from which Truman made numerous appointments—knew that Brosman, Latimer, and Quinn all were important candidates for the new tribunal. Even as George Marshall endorsed Quinn, additional efforts were launched on behalf of Latimer, a Republican from Utah, by a Democratic congresswoman—Reva Beck Bosone, the first woman ever sent to Congress from that state. She served from 1949 to 1953, being defeated for reelection during the Eisenhower landslide of 1952. An attempt at recapturing her seat in 1954 failed, and she never again sat in Congress. A strong Truman loyalist during the 1948 campaign, in 1951 Bosone took aim at Frank Riter, the other Utah

Republican in the running for a seat on the Court. She advised both the White House staff and the president himself that "Riter is a vitriolic and venomous hater of the President, the Administration, [and] practically all Democrats, and she sincerely hopes that the President is not thinking of appointing him." Dawson was promptly informed of Bosone's comments.

Bosone was not the only Utah Democrat in favor of Latimer's appointment. Essentially uninterested in politics, the state supreme court justice enjoyed bipartisan support. His candidacy, for example, was strongly endorsed by the Utah secretary of state and the chief justice of its supreme court, both Democrats. Indeed, Chief Justice Wolfe emphasized to Truman that "in making this recommendation I have allowed nothing but my belief in Judge Latimer's fitness for the position to influence my recommendation."

Although it seems likely that Dawson had narrowed the list of candidates to about a dozen by April 1951, it is far from clear how many applicants were known to the White House. On July 3, 1950, Vaughan wrote that there were about "six thousand applications for the three positions," adding that "I can't see how the Department of Justice would have any influence in this choice as it is largely a military matter." Possibly unaware of the McGrath-Quinn connection, here Vaughan indicated yet again his failure to understand the nature of the politics involving presidential appointments. Three months later, he informed another correspondent that there had been thirty-five hundred applications, including "several members of Congress and two State Supreme Court Judges." By the end of January 1951, Vaughan observed that "there were almost four thousand applications for the three jobs and the amount of political pressure for some of the candidates is really remarkable." For his part, Truman stated on February 2, 1951, that "I have almost a thousand applications for these three jobs . . . and I am having a very difficult time in getting them sorted out." In April, Donald Dawson remarked that, "actually, it seems there are many people who feel qualified and want this particular appointment more than any other I have ever seen."

On May 15, Connecticut senator William Benton wrote to President Truman concerning segregation in the military. Evidence compiled by Thurgood Marshall, "special counsel for the NAACP . . . indicates a considerable degree of race prejudice in the administration of the court-martial machinery." The problem was worse in the army than in the other services. Benton knew that "race problems in the administration of military justice cannot be eliminated merely by a Presidential directive or by a blanket amendment [to the UCMJ.] Your appointment of a qualified Negro to the highest tribunal of military justice, however, would give dramatic emphasis to your policy and program of equality, and would have cumulative and incalculable effects on the administration . . . throughout the armed forces."

According to Truman's secretary, Benton's letter was not received at the White House until May 23, one day after the president had sent the names of his three choices up to the Senate. He assured Benton that Truman's appointments, all of whom were white, "will constitute a Court eminently qualified to take fair and impartial action in all cases which come to it for review." In fact, neither Presidents Truman, Eisenhower, Kennedy, nor Johnson appointed any blacks to the Court of Military Appeals. That precedent fell first to Richard Nixon, followed by Gerald Ford, as will be discussed in a later chapter.

Truman interviewed each of his ultimate choices before announcing their appointments. Although he left no written evidence as to why he specifically selected Brosman, Latimer, and Quinn for the Court—besides the political connotations that have already been discussed—the president may well have been aware of some, if not all, of the following factors.

Each service was represented on the new bench: Quinn from the navy, Latimer from the army, and Brosman from the air force. Each had worked in military justice, although only Latimer appears to have had actual combat participation. They came from disparate sections of the country, Quinn from New England, Brosman from Louisiana, and Latimer from Utah. In terms of religious preference, the new judges included a Catholic, a Mormon, and an Episcopalian. Two of the three had prior judicial experience, Quinn at the trial level as a Rhode Island superior court judge, Latimer at the appellate level as a member of the Utah Supreme Court. Although both Quinn and Latimer had long been away from the mainstream of major changes in legal education, Paul Brosman was currently dean of Tulane University Law School.

It is not unreasonable to conclude that Truman chose carefully. Unlike any of his successors, Truman took the time to interview all three men before making his final selections. Politics, of course, was a factor, but such considerations may not have dominated his thinking. Thus, he could have named the Republican, Latimer, to the short five-year term. Instead, Latimer received the ten-year appointment.

On the other hand, the president appears to have been party to an arrangement unique in the history of the Court. When he named Quinn as chief judge with a fifteen-year term, Truman agreed that Quinn could maintain his chambers in Providence, commuting to Washington only when the Court was in session or conference. There were probably two reasons for Quinn's preferring such a policy. He would not have to uproot his family, which included five children. Also, while remaining in Rhode Island he might be better able to capitalize on an opportunity, should it arise, to run for the Senate. It may well be that Quinn, who alone among the first three judges appears not to have solicited his appointment, insisted on such an arrangement as a condition to accepting the new post. Whatever the reason for it, Truman's acquiescence in this arrangement has not been followed by any other president in appointing future judges to this tribunal. While it may have benefited Quinn, on the whole this practice was highly detrimental for the Court as an institution. The arrangement frequently left Latimer acting as a quasi chief judge, with much of the responsibility but little authority. In a more subtle vein, Quinn's absence from the Court for weeks at a time inevitably meant a loss of collegiality.

With the three nominations pending before the Senate, George Spiegelberg wrote to his fellow members of the ABA Special Committee on Military Justice. He described Quinn as "almost surely a McGrath appointee," one who during his term as Rhode Island governor "gave as fine a demonstration of command control as has ever been seen." The episode, according to Spiegelberg, "does not augur well for the future of military justice." Latimer—while apparently well respected in Utah—"was a classmate of Gen. Harry H. Vaughan at one of the courses given by the Army, and there would seem to be little doubt as to the source of his backing." Brosman, on the other hand, "is universally respected." Spiegelberg concluded his letter with the accurate observation that "as you know, none of the [three] men were on the list sent the President by the [ABA] president."

Truman sent the three names to the Senate on May 22, 1951. But the Armed Services Committee, absorbed in the MacArthur removal controversy, did not take up the nominations until June 16 and then with an interest that was desultory at best. At an unusual Saturday morning hearing, the committee chairman, Georgia Democrat Senator Richard Russell, remarked that "this court is something new in anything I know of in the judicial system. . . . I personally had misgivings about the creation of this court." Conceding that there were cases within the military where individuals had not received even decent treatment, let alone justice, Russell still insisted that "any abuse of the powers of this court will be disastrous to this Nation." He further noted, "I am sure that you gentlemen will in your duties temper justice with that knowledge that this will indeed be a court of military justice and will not be an agency that will be damaging to the observance of discipline in the armed services."

From the Court's earliest history to the present, Russell's sentiments, insisting on the point that military justice was somehow subordinate to military discipline, have been reiterated in different forums. In fact, they should be seen as two sides of the same coin: without a meaningful system of military justice, military discipline—especially in the American context—becomes unworkable. Whether or not Russell's views cast a pall over the independence of the new tribunal is unclear. However, their continued emphasis has probably been detrimental to rigorous civilian-judicial scrutiny concerning military justice.

Nevertheless, Russell recalled that members of his committee "were so impressed by the qualifications of the nominees that they took the unusual step of voting unanimous approval, with the appointees present in the committee room." The full Senate concurred three days later. If the Armed Services Committee reflected little concern with the nominations, the Senate seemed even more disinterested, if possible. The three judges were not even approved by voice vote, but merely with the presiding officer stating of each appointment that "without objection, the nomination is confirmed." Senator Russell Long spoke briefly about Brosman, Utah senators Watkins and Bennett paid tribute to Latimer, and no senator commented about Quinn. On June 20, the new judges were sworn into office by District Judge Matthew McGuire, whose criticism of military justice during World War II had preceded creation of the code committee.

Its former chairman, Edmund Morgan, wrote to Felix Larkin that the columnist Drew Pearson had indicated "that I should have been named. This seems like high praise for the President's choice." According to Pearson, Robert Quinn "has some of the dictatorial brass hattedness that needs to be cured in the Army." Pearson's column, "The Washington Merry-Go-Round," also stated that Latimer owed his appointment to Harry Vaughan, who responded that the column was "in line with Pearson's usual inaccuracies." Moreover, "Pearson, as is characteristic of him, is more interested in writing an article that he considers will attract readers than he is in writing facts." According to Judge Latimer's son, George Latimer Jr., Pearson later acknowledged that he had been wrong in attributing Latimer's appointment to Vaughan's influence. The biographers of James Forrestal described Pearson as "a muckraking journalist of demonic dimensions . . . endowed through a perversion of his Quaker origins with an invincible self-righteousness. . . . [H]e was, in fact, moved by his own ingrained prejudices."

Morgan added that one reason he would probably have accepted the appointment, had it been offered, "was the chance to be where I could frequently see you and Marx (not Karl), and the chance to put our notions as to the Court in operation." Larkin responded with "a keen disappointment that you were not nominated . . . , but I recognize that you are well out of it. Having met and talked with the Judges at some length, I feel fairly encouraged, and I think we can look forward to some fairly good operations." The extent to which Larkin's optimism was justified is discussed in the following chapters.

13

Initial Court Organization and Operation, 1951–1955

The selection and confirmation of Judges Quinn, Latimer, and Brosman represented the culmination of Felix Larkin's official involvement with the new court, an association that began in 1948 with plans to enact a uniform code of military justice. Before 1951 ended, both Larkin and Marx Leva had left the Defense Department. But while still serving as general counsel, Larkin received the draft of tentative job descriptions for the various administrative positions within the USCAAF. Although not dated, the memorandum submitted to Larkin was probably prepared in the spring of 1951 and may well have served as the basis for the initial organizational meetings held among the three judges during June and July. The document provided descriptions for proposed staff positions—such as librarian, reporter, and marshal. Of special interest, however, were the descriptions for the "Law Assistant" and clerk of the Court. John Henderson, the member of Larkin's staff who signed—if not wrote—the memorandum, noted the unusual importance of the law assistant.

CONFIGURATION OF COMMISSIONERS AND CLERK

This law assistant should be a lawyer "of considerable maturity with experience in the field of military justice." His basic function "would be to provide continuity of legal assistance to the three judges." His responsibilities, in other words, were to be quite different from those of a law clerk to a specific judge. Here, Henderson could draw on the traditional law clerk responsibilities as developed in other appellate tribunals, functions that have remained remarkably constant over the years. The law clerk would summarize briefs, abstract cases, research points of law, develop a legal position on other issues that might not have been covered in submitted briefs or oral argument, and prepare rough drafts of opinions on pending cases for the judge. Henderson assumed, quite reasonably, that as with many appellate courts, the law clerk would be a recent law school graduate.

On the other hand, since the court was a specialized tribunal, "the recent . . . graduates who will be the law clerks will have a greater problem training themselves to the point where they can be useful to the judges than do law clerks for circuit court [jurists.]" Moreover, traditional appellate courts "operate in the broad spheres of constitutional, administrative and private law for which law school training is peculiarly apt." But "the substantive problems of military justice . . . will have been considered little if at all in law school curricula." Henderson assumed, therefore, that the law assistant "will help indoctrinate each new law clerk, and will, at least for the first part of a law clerk's tenure, review the written material the law clerk prepares for his judge." He "must [also] be an expert at researching with speed and accuracy all varieties of legal questions in the field of military justice. . . . It is to be expected that he will not only prepare legal memoranda for individual judges but that he will also do intensive research on questions propounded by the Court as a whole." The question arises why such a memo came from the general counsel's office in the Defense Department rather than from the judges themselves, and whether it indicated inappropriate intimacy between the military establishment and the new tribunal. As will be seen, Quinn and his brethren became much more sensitive to this issue.

There may well have been additional reasons, however, why this early draft for court structure called for a legal assistant or commissioner besides the factors just cited. Law clerks, often just beginning their legal careers, would understandably tend to reflect the nuances, style, and approach to issues demonstrated by the judge for whom they worked. The law assistant, and by implication the lawyers with whom he worked (now known as the central legal staff), would presumably have no such sense of juridical parochialism. Thus, at the outset the judges could receive an assessment of the case completely independent of chambers, and while their law clerks might later prepare their memorandum of the cases including recommendations, an additional independent opinion could be of great value. Moreover, there was an important element of practicality. Time constraints indicated that it would be impossible for three judges to read every page of every record of every case submitted to them for possible review. Initial scrutiny from an experienced legal staff could only make the mandate of the new tribunal easier to fulfill.

A final factor, though not articulated, was probably assumed. While all three appointees to the Court were familiar with the military, none had had that extensive experience in working with military justice possessed by full-time attorneys specializing in this field. The new tribunal needed a specialist with hands-on expertise. Such a position might be unusual in a federal appellate court, but for jurists interpreting a new code within a new court of specialized jurisdiction, it was necessary—and the judges knew it. The candidate they selected, Richard Tedrow, possessed such qualifications; and in August 1951, Judge Paul Brosman explained the rationale for this new appointment to the Court staff.

Although ultimately the judges would decide for themselves whether or not to hear a case, "it is essential that first consideration and analysis be afforded by others, and that we enjoy the detailed guidance of mature, able, and experienced lawyers." It was to be expected that a law clerk "will be a bright but inexperienced young law school graduate, and ordinarily . . . there will be a good deal of turnover in the position." Seeking, on the other hand, "maturity and experience, as well as continuity, the Court provided for a functionary . . . and arranged for him a position of relative dignity in the Government service, and a substantial compensation." Viewed from the bottom, according to Brosman, "he might be regarded as a super law clerk. However, considered from the top, he might almost be characterized as an assistant judge." This "functionary" was briefly known as a law assistant, general counsel, and by July 16, 1951, as the chief commissioner, a title that remained constant for the next twenty years. Only the judges received a higher salary than the chief commissioner.

As Brosman indicated, the usual expectation in most federal tribunals is that the judges stay for many years, while their subordinates change on a regular basis. The U. S. Court of Appeals for the Armed Forces has not followed this pattern. Less than half of its members remained on the bench long enough to complete their terms. Thus far in the Court's history, only five judges out of sixteen have served more than ten years. Of this number, Robert Quinn served for almost twenty-five years, a record thus far unmatched in USCAAF history. Homer Ferguson, who joined the Court in 1956, continued to sit as a senior judge after the expiration of his fifteen-year term. On the other hand, some lawyers originally described as law assistants or commissioners but now called the "central legal staff" have remained at the Court, while the judges have moved on. Even among counsel assigned to each judge's chambers, there has been a tendency for these lawyers to continue on the court staff, often working first for one judge and then for the replacement.

Richard Tedrow, the first chief commissioner, served in this capacity for eighteen years, during which period six judges sat on the USCAAF bench. There is no doubt that an appellate judge should be exposed to ongoing and changing developments in law, and new talent fresh out of law school can be very helpful in this sense. Nevertheless, it might be observed that lawyers who have worked for fifteen or twenty years on the staff of a specialized tribunal such as this one may well have developed expertise that an incoming judge will disregard, to his or her detriment as well as that of the overall quality of military justice. On the other hand, however, it should be noted that while Morgan intended the Court to be truly independent of the military, in fact its judges have tended to appoint career military lawyers to their staffs.

Typically, JAG officers who have served twenty or thirty years as prosecutors or military judges will retire from active duty, only to begin work immediately as commissioners to an USCAAF jurist. Their expertise in military law may be assumed, but whether they can offer their judges an open mind and a familiarity with emerging legal trends, needs, and scholarship is a much more difficult question to resolve. A partial solution, which USCAAF has followed in recent years, is for a judge to have at least one position within chambers arranged so that there can be regular turnover, but not at the expense of continuity.

It seems clear from Henderson's draft that the chief law "commissioner" (now known as the director of the central legal staff) was to receive a higher salary than the clerk of the Court, who had to combine a "good legal background with a highly trained administrative ability." The clerk was responsible "for the general administrative supervision of Court proceedings." Legal training and experience was required "so that the clerk can draft orders of Court in accordance with opinions, present emergency matters to the Court, answer inquiries regarding court procedure[,] and in general function as an expert on the rules of Court and on the Federal Rules." But from the early years of USCAAF history to the present, the Court clerk has had minimal involvement with the actual process of judging, such as examinations of petitions, assigning cases for review, decision preparation, and so on.

For the post of clerk, Quinn selected Alfred C. Proulx, a native of West Warwick, Rhode Island, the chief judge's hometown. As a young man, Proulx had played golf on Quinn's West Warwick Country Club, a course still operated by the Quinn family. A graduate of Holy Cross and Georgetown University Law School, by 1951 he was a captain in the Naval Reserve and working for the *Federal Register* in Washington. Possessed of an ability to organize administrative procedures, comfortable in office management, and knowledgeable in the somewhat unusual nuances of governmental life in Washington, Proulx apparently was Quinn's first and only choice for the job. In addition to his long acquaintance with the former governor, Proulx shared his love of golf, lifelong identification with the Democratic party, and branch of military service.

Like Proulx, Chief Commissioner Tedrow had also been in the navy and indeed had become acquainted with the new clerk during this period. But there the similarity between Tedrow and Proulx ended. Although he would work with Proulx and Chief Judge Quinn for almost twenty years, Tedrow seems never to have gained that close relationship that existed between the judge and the clerk of the Court. Intense in manner and easily agitated, Tedrow combined ability with irascibility. He also had a marked appreciation for his own considerable proficiency as an expert in military justice. Proulx, on the other hand, radiated charm blended with an easygoing efficiency, often disguised as informality.

Together with Richard Tedrow, the two men worked with Quinn for almost a generation, providing a link of continuity between the beginning and early maturation of the Court as an institution. The link was unbroken until 1969, when after 18 years of service Tedrow took early retirement on the grounds of ill health. Proulx would complete more than twenty years, not leaving until 1972, after Quinn had been summarily removed as chief judge by President Nixon. Quinn undoubtedly appreciated Tedrow's legal acumen, but the relationship between the two never attained the level of confidence and trust that Quinn placed in Proulx.

As the new court recruited its staff, apparently the judges considered political endorsements as well as legal and military experience. In June 1951, the administrative assistant to Senator Green informed Chief Judge Quinn that "Major David F. Condon, a personal friend of mine . . . is definitely interested in being considered for appointment as a member of your staff. Between you and me, Bob, he is a darn good Democrat, got plenty on the ball and a fellow that you would like to have working for you." Other candidates employed different kinds of political contacts.

When navy JAG officer Francis Tappaan applied for a job as commissioner, letters on his behalf came in from the chairman of the Atomic Energy Commission, Senators Richard Nixon and Harry Byrd, and Congressman Albert Gore (father of the former U.S. vice president). Chief Judge Quinn not only acknowledged all the endorsements but also later wrote another series of letters confirming that Tappaan had indeed been appointed. One individual, Charles Dickson—a former JAG officer—not only expressed interest in the new tribunal but also claimed to have been one of its creators. His almost proprietary concern for the Court was understandable, although ultimately unrewarding.

Dickson believed that USCAAF "has made a good start[,] but I am convinced that unless a few of us 'civilians' get together and give this infant court some real help," its machinery "may break down of its own weight." In 1953, he prepared a "Citizen's Petition" on the subject of military justice and, as he had done five years before, took care to see that it was widely distributed. Making due allowance for Dickson's myopia, his suggestion for changes in the Court remains a remarkable statement—especially in the light of future USCAAF history.

In his mimeographed petition, the sixty-five-year-old retired army officer called for an increase in the number of judges from three to seven. He urged that the Court be removed from administrative control of the Pentagon and that it "function as an independent unit of the Judicial System of the U.S.A." Moreover, he proposed that the limit of its authority to matters of law be removed; that all intermediate boards of review be abolished; that USCAAF appellate jurisdiction be expanded; that the Court, not the JAGs, appoint appellate defense counsel, drawn from its own bar; and finally that the "orders, judgements and decrees of [USCAAF] be enforceable by the Court's own process, with power to punish for contempt[,] for disobedience—as well as disorder in the Court's presence."

Although Dickson failed to articulate his point clearly, the implication of his proposals was that, as currently constituted, the Court was not a real court, clothed with the authority common to most federal appellate tribunals. As will be seen, the judges of the U.S. Court of Appeals for the Armed Forces felt the same way, and while the name of Charles Dickson is not mentioned in any of the numerous memoranda that would flow from the Court seeking such powers, they echoed his perceptions. Dickson concluded with a "statement which I am ready to prove to anyone who doubts its accuracy. If the suggestions I have made are adopted . . . the current cost to the Government of administering Military Justice will be cut to one half of the present amount, and the quality of Justice dispensed will be greatly improved to the benefit of both morale and discipline in our Armed Forces."

Fiscal considerations aside, Dickson (like Cassandra of ancient legend, doomed to tell the truth but be ignored) seems to have been more right than wrong—even as those who reviewed his petition probably dismissed it as the work of a retired crank. Apparently oblivious to the requirements for political and practical compromise that had guided Morgan's committee as well as Congress in enacting the UCMJ, Dickson nevertheless identified what USCAAF's judges also felt was a weakness in their court's mandate. The extent to which it has affected the tribunal's ability to operate and how the Court has acted to increase judicial authority where it is believed to be necessary remain matters for debate.

THE QUEST FOR QUARTERS

With three judges appointed and confirmed and with two senior administrative officers of the Court selected, the new tribunal was ready to begin receiving cases. But where would it hold court? Although attention had been given to this question even before the judges were nominated, the actual process by which the USCAAF came to its present home remains an intriguing if unlikely tale. Quinn, it turns out, was quite right to rely on Proulx, who in this matter, like so many others, demonstrated discretion together with an adroit sense of timing.

From the Court's early years to the present, its relationship with the Defense Department on occasion has been uneasy, although rarely hostile. As has been seen, there was no doubt that Morgan's committee intended the new tribunal to be judicially independent of the Pentagon. Yet, it is equally certain that the Court was to be administered by that branch of government. In retrospect, Defense Department officials have managed—for the most part—to respect this bifurcation, drawing a fine line between judicial interference and fiscal/administrative management. And indeed, while there have been instances where the line may have been obscured to some extent, it has yet to be obliterated. After a history of fifty years, all parties involved in appellate military justice pay homage to the concept of an independent civilian appellate court. Much more difficult to assess is the effect of its very close relationship to the Pentagon in administrative areas. This author feels that, rhetoric aside, the shadow of the Pentagon looms large over the Court; and while USCAAF can be described as a sort of "judicial menace," looking, as it were, over the shoulders of the services, the same might be said of the awesome defense establishment in relation to the Court itself.

Even as President Truman sent the names of his three choices for USCAAF to the Senate, Larkin's office was concerned about the possibility that the new tribunal might be assigned quarters outside of Washington due to the shortage of available space. On May 23, 1951, Robert Haydock, a member of Larkin's staff (and—like his boss—soon to leave the Defense Department), drafted a letter to the functionary charged with space allocation. The new court "is conceived on a level with the United States Court of Appeals. It is a tribunal to which a significant share of public confidence in the administration of military justice will be attributable. For this reason it is appropriate that the Court should be located at the seat of government."

Less than a month later, Deputy Secretary of Defense Robert Lovett addressed another letter to the administrator of the General Services Administration. Again, he emphasized that the "success or failure of the Code [UCMJ] and its acceptance by the public depends to a large extent upon the distinction and influence of this court." Anticipating the point that the new court could have taken space in the Pentagon, Lovett emphasized that "this has been rejected as contrary to the wishes of Congress and the judicial character of the Court. While the Department of Defense is charged with performing certain administrative functions for the Court, these must not interfere or in any way appear to interfere with the independence of the Court." Apparently the plan to have the Court housed in the Pentagon went no further, but there remained a question of its actual location.

In the meantime, Proulx and his boss had not been idle. Originally, Chief Judge Quinn sought to get the old Supreme Court chamber in the Capitol assigned as permanent quarters for the new U.S. Court of Appeals for the Armed Forces. He even spoke with the chairman of the Senate Rules Committee, only to learn that some senators were currently using adjoining rooms, and "he felt it would be impossible to move them." Through a few of his contacts, Proulx negotiated an agreement to use the courtroom of the U.S. Court of Customs and Patents Appeals, then located in the Internal Revenue Service's building, on a temporary basis. In use only several days each month, it was readily available, all the more convenient since the USCAAF planned—at least for the immediate future—to be in session for just two consecutive days each month.

At the same time, Quinn and his colleagues addressed a letter to Chief Judge Harold M. Stephens of the U.S. Circuit Court of Appeals for the District of Columbia. Knowing that this court would soon be moving into a large new building and that Stephens would "have control of allocating space" in it, Quinn asked his help in providing appropriate accommodations for USCAAF. The letter added that "during a recent conference with President Truman concerning the future of the court Judge Quinn raised the pressing problem of the court's quarters. The President expressed interest and concern and indicated that he would consult you on our behalf. We have thought best that you should be advised by us of this conference."

These sentences at first smack of candor. In reality, they were an excellent example of judicial disingenuousness. Quinn had indeed met with President Truman, and they had indeed talked about space. But there the accuracy of Quinn's account ended. The clerk had previously learned that Stephens had an informal agreement with the chief judge of the Court of Customs and Patents Appeals (CCPA) to move his tribunal into the building soon to be vacated by Stephens's court. This explained, according to Proulx, why the CCPA judges were so willing to let USCAAF share their courtroom. In consultation with Stephens, they had planned to move into the stately structure on E Street, perfectly suited for a small appellate court but now too cramped for the D.C. court of appeals, which had expanded in numbers and cases. In other words, they would invite USCAAF to share their facilities and would willingly let the new tribunal stay there once the CCPA moved over to the old appellate court building. But Quinn also coveted this judicial edifice.

Proulx discovered that upon becoming vacant the old court of appeals building was to be placed under the jurisdiction of the public buildings commissioner. He convinced Quinn to seek an appointment with President Truman in order to ask that he "write a chit out to the Public Buildings Commissioner that this is the building for [USCAAF]"; to get a statement, in other words, that it was presidential preference that Quinn's court move into the soon to be empty building. What Proulx, who probably drafted the judges' letter to Stephens, could not say was that Quinn had sought—successfully, it turned out—to undercut the earlier understanding through presidential intervention.

Apparently Proulx and the judges had their eyes on the old court of appeals building as early as July 1951. Proulx began his tenure as clerk on July 24. The week before, Quinn informed McGrath that "it would be best for us to exert every effort to obtain the Court of Appeals building. . . . I have an appointment with the President . . . and will request him to have this building set aside for us, and I will deeply appreciate anything you can do to help us along these lines." One month later, Brosman stated, "It is certain that we shall remain in Internal Revenue until the completion . . . of the new Federal Courts Building. . . . At that time we shall move to the new building, or to the present Court of Appeals Building . . . or to other adequate quarters—outside the Pentagon. If I were to guess at this time in the bosom of the family, I would suppose that we will end up in the present Court of Appeals Building."

It is unclear when Stephens was informed, if indeed he ever was, of the ultimate decision to give his old building to USCAAF. By November 27, Proulx had submitted space plans for the building to the space officer in the Pentagon, "who will immediately enter into formal negotiations with the [Public Buildings Service (PBS)] for the Circuit Court of Appeals Building." On the same day, Stephens notified Judges Latimer and Brosman that there would be no space available for their court in the new building, and that he would write PBS that the old building "will be declared surplus by him as soon as they move out." The way was thus open for USCAAF to get its chosen home.

Yet Proulx remained vigilant, fearing that some other governmental agency might covet the courthouse. In August 1952, a couple of months before the Court finally moved into the building, he wrote to Quinn that "in talking to a [newpaper] reporter . . . I mentioned to him that we had 50 employees on the staff[,] lest the actual number should give anyone the idea that the building would be too large for us." As for the judges of the court of customs and patents upon discovering the presidential letter to the public buildings commissioner and what it apparently had wrought, Proulx summed up the matter with characteristic candor—"They had a deal they were trying to work too, and in this town possession is 9/10ths of the law." Although USCAAF had planned to stay in the temporary quarters for only a few months, it was not until October 1952 that it finally moved into the old court of appeals building at Fifth and E Streets. It has been the home of the U.S. Court of Appeals for the Armed Forces ever since, and on more than one occasion, the judges have fought to keep their space from other hopeful federal occupants with a tenacity reminiscent of an earlier era.

A COURT IS A COURT IS A COURT? ROUND 1

Everyone interested in the new tribunal conceded that it had been created by Congress, acting upon its constitutional authority to makes rules and regulations for the governing of the armed services. In other words, USCAAF was an "Article 1 court" in that the enacting power for Congress came from the first article of the Constitution. Did it therefore follow that the Court was an agency of the executive branch of government rather than the judicial? Confusion and disagreement over this question and implications arising from the different ways it has been answered have dogged the Court since 1951. Supposedly settled, the issue remained unsettling.

A few months after USCAAF began to function, the Court—through the Defense Department—stated to the Civil Service Commission that the new tribunal should be located within the judicial branch rather than the executive. Thus, as with most federal courts, appointment of court personnel would not come under the purview of the Civil Service Commission, and the judiciary "could make appointments as it saw fit." If, however, USCAAF was in reality a sort of judicial and administrative hybrid rather than a real court, it would fall under the executive branch of government. Yet, language creating the Court "include[s] a mixture of the usual attributes of both courts and administrative agencies of a quasi-judicial nature. It is difficult to decide into which category the Court fits." This conclusion, part of an internal memorandum from Daniel Walker—a newly appointed Court commissioner—indicates that USCAAF judges were aware that questions concerning their status and powers might have had some basis in fact. The memorandum, written by a court employee— one sympathetic to the Court's purposes—warrants some attention.

Walker's statement was probably written during the fall of 1951. Its author, along with Tedrow and Condon, constituted the first group of commissioners appointed to the Court staff. Able, articulate, and ambitious, he later worked for Illinois governor Adlai Stevenson. Indeed, in September 1952, Walker wrote to Chief Judge Quinn that "Stevenson has really caught the imagination of a lot of people—which is more than can be said for Eisenhower." (Eisenhower, it might be observed, carried Illinois in both 1952 and 1956.) Walker's future would include two very disparate terms of his own—one as governor of Illinois, the other in prison as a convicted felon.

Walker assumed, as did most scholarly opinion on the subject, that Congress had created USCAAF by virtue of its legislative authority under Article 1 of the Constitution. Therefore, "even aside from the lack of life tenure by the judges, the Court may not be considered to be a constitutional court." He noted, correctly, that the Supreme Court "has held that tenure is a basic consideration in deciding whether a court is created by the virtue of power granted by Article III." Since Congress clearly denied life tenure to its newest court, his conclusion was understandable. On the other hand, what was to prevent Congress from creating a court, clothing it in the raiment of courts, but providing terms for its judges rather than life tenure? Was it, therefore, a legislative tribunal? The answer to this question was complicated by the fact that Congress could also "create administrative agencies as well as courts to handle quasi-judicial or even fully judicial functions. The attributes of the tribunal created must be examined in order to determine into which category it fits."

Walker found several factors to support the contention that USCAAF belonged in the judicial, not the executive, branch of government. Congress called its creation a court and provided for three full-time judges. The legislators had clearly intended the jurists—regardless of their terms—to be on a par with other federal appellate court judges. Indeed, their salaries were to be identical, and ultimately judges of the courts of appeal could be designated to fill temporary vacancies on the USCAAF bench. Moreover, the purpose and function of the tribunal was first and foremost that of judging. Hence it should be treated in the same manner as existing federal courts.

But Walker also found "several weighty factors" that in his judgment militated against USCAAF status as a member of the federal judiciary. Salary similarity aside, much more important were the differences between USCAAF judges and their federal counterparts. USCAAF judges had fixed terms and could be removed by the president, while federal district and appellate court judges served for life and could not be removed by the chief executive. Second was the placement of the Court within the Department of Defense. This fact, "while certainly not by itself determinative, indicates a close relation to the executive department, as opposed to the judiciary."

Most difficult for Walker was the fact that "review of military courts-martial has historically been entrusted by Congress to the Executive department, and the new code [the UCMJ] contains no clear intent to depart from that traditional procedure." Reviews of courts-martial from the convening authority up even to the boards of review established by the judge advocate general within his office all pointed to the executive branch, to say nothing of presidential review of certain sentences. Indirectly supporting Walker's contention, a Civil Service Commission (CSC) report had also focused on this point.

Its memorandum stated, correctly, that the president as commander in chief must approve certain court-martial verdicts. How then could USCAAF be located within the judicial branch of government? To so hold "would be to find that the decisions of a court in the judicial branch were subject to review by the Executive Department through the President. This would be an entirely new concept in the field of law," if only because the Constitution requires that the three branches of government operate "on a par with each other, the functions of one of which are not subject to control by the other two." Moreover, because the military was part of the executive branch and because courts-martial also came under the executive umbrella, "it does not appear that Congress intended to make any change in the basic concept that courts-martial are purely executive functions."

Although he did not cite it, an additional point could have added support to Walker's position. The CSC report observed that as early as 1939—more than ten years before USCAAF was created—Congress had established the Administrative Office of the United States Courts, to do just what its title implied. By any reasonable rule of statutory interpretation, the fact that in 1950 the lawmakers had specifically designated the Defense Department to administer the Court undercut its claim to parity with the other federal tribunals. USCAAF judges, when they retired, were to be covered by the Civil Service Retirement Act, while federal appellate jurists could retire with a different (and better) set of benefits. These points, although debatable, are tenable, and they may have been sufficient for the commission to decide against the Court, which it ultimately did.

Walker emphasized what to him were the clear implications in his report: "There is, at the least, considerable doubt as to the legal status of [USCAAF]." But while important, clarification of its status should yield to more pressing reasons for congressional action. "Substantial question[s] may be raised as to whether the Court has the attributes of judicial power necessary to the exercise of its appellate and supervisory responsibilities. If [USCAAF] is not a court in the true sense of the word, then it lacks several weapons of judicial action which may well . . . make the Court's jurisdiction advisable only." Here, Walker meant the power to issue injunctions and other orders, to hold parties in contempt, to exercise subpoena powers, and to issue prerogative writs, such as writs of mandamus. His solution was "simple Congressional action." The appropriate provision of the United States Code included among the tribunals properly called a "Court of the United States" any "court created by Act of Congress[,] the judges of which are entitled to hold office during good behavior." Giving USCAAF judges life tenure would therefore bring the Court to the status of a U.S. court and "would clearly make the Court a 'Court.' "

Walker's arguments, similar to those that convinced the Civil Service Commission to find that the new tribunal came within the executive branch rather than the judiciary, do not appear to be tenable. They reflect more closely the tenacity of outdated conceptions than a clear understanding of the transformation of military justice by 1951. Although Walker did not get into this point, it was far from accurate by this time to characterize courts-martial as "purely executive functions." As early as 1917–1918, the Ansell-Crowder controversy explored in some detail the conflicting claims that courts-martial were strictly within the presidential prerogative. Ansell himself had vigorously rebutted this viewpoint.

For the time being, however, the judges did not challenge the decision of the commission. Instead, the Court set out to gain life tenure, a quest that remains unrealized to this day. In the meantime, the Court proceeded to judge cases and—possibly with Walker's comments in mind—adopted an unspoken strategy. Absent a specific enactment by Congress or a definitive holding to the contrary by the U.S. Supreme Court, Judges Quinn, Latimer, and Brosman quietly assumed the applicability of all appropriate appellate judicial authority to their court and acted accordingly.

To some extent, subsequent USCAAF history has vindicated this assumption. From time to time, its judges have not hesitated to claim authority to issue certain writs and orders. Invariably in such litigation, one party would argue that the Court was without authority in the matter—a position consistently rejected by a majority of its jurists. On the other hand, the judges have been hesitant to apply their supposed authority in specific instances, contenting themselves with vigorous expressions of its existence, if not its implementation. But they remained dissatisfied with the commission's conclusions, in part because they had implications that went far beyond the original contention that, as part of the judiciary, the judges could hire and fire without regard to Civil Service Commission requirements. There was, for example, the question of the new court reports.

Barely one month after the CSC released its findings, Proulx and his deputy met with James Ryder, a representative from West Publishing Company, then as now the dominant source for publication and distribution of judicial reports, both state and federal. Realizing that the reputation of the new court would depend on how its opinions were received and eager for them to have as wide-spread a circulation as feasible, Proulx hoped that USCAAF decisions could be reported in the *West F.2d* (the second series of West's *Federal Reporter* and one that included decisions of the courts of appeal for the various circuits). But Ryder "informed us that the Judicial Conference decides what shall or shall not go into the F. 2d reports. West . . . does exactly what the Judicial Conference tells it in regard to said reports."

Ryder cautioned, however, that "inasmuch as USCAAF is not under the Administrative Office of the United States Courts for housekeeping purposes, but is dependent on the office of the Secretary of Defense for such purposes, it might be difficult for USCAAF to get its opinions reported in F. 2d." Ultimately, Chief Judge Quinn met with Chief Justice Fred Vinson, seeking to enlist his support for using *F.2d*. But the chief justice was noncommittal and asked Quinn to have his request "incorporated in a letter marked to his attention." Nothing favorable, however, came of it, and decisions of the U.S. Court of Appeals for the Armed Forces have never been part of *F.2d*.

While it is true that since 1975 West has published the *Military Justice Reporter,* replete with its own digest, efforts to achieve total USCAAF integration with a national state and federal appellate court system of digesting and citation have not been successful, and failure to attain it after more than half a century continues to disturb the Court. There is, after all, a very close relationship between the influence that an appellate court may have on other tribunals and the way in which its decisions are or are not digested and distributed.

JUDGES AT WORK: THE SETTING

During the summer of 1951, the three judges, Proulx, and Tedrow worked out basic procedures for the Court. The first set of rules of practice and procedure were promulgated on July 11, and two weeks later the judges held their first session in the Court of Customs and Patents Appeals courtroom on the seventh floor of the Internal Revenue Service building. A number of lawyers were admitted to its bar, including the judge advocate generals of the air force, army, and navy. Very quickly, the new court settled into the routine of receiving, hearing, and deciding the cases placed on its docket. The judges functioned well together, although they brought divergent experiences and philosophies to their work. On the other hand, operations of the Court—often without the presence of the chief judge—occasionally created tensions not only between the staff and other judges but also among the jurists themselves.

Quinn spent most of his time in Providence, usually coming to Washington only for the oral arguments and resulting judicial conferences, returning two or three days later. He maintained a prolific correspondence that included not only frequent letters from Proulx, who served as the main conduit between the chief and the Court, but also a wide variety of contemporary political figures. Moreover, his files contain an unusual variety of requests for assistance, most of them from Rhode Island residents who may well have remembered Quinn as "Governor Fighting Bob." The requests ranged from a patient in a state mental hospital, to anguished letters from parents concerning their children in the armed services, to people in trouble with the law, to commentary on local politics, to persons seeking advancement in government, education, or some other career. One anonymous correspondent wished "that you were still up in the County Court House so I could refresh my perspective a little every once in a while. This is a very unwholesome place politically. . . . They'd sell tickets to the Crucifixion!"

Quinn apparently acknowledged the great majority of these requests, usually referring the matter to Proulx with a notation, "Can we do anything to help?" The former governor had never abandoned his conviction that the first rule of politics was to help people who seek and need it. He had developed this patristic tendency during his tumultuous years in Rhode Island politics. By the time he came to the Court, he felt neither the inclination nor the obligation to change his practices, and his attentions to the needs of others, often strangers, persisted to the end of his two dozen years on the federal bench. One observer wrote of Quinn in 1970 that "every day, in some way, he does something for someone."

Quinn served as a USCAAF judge for almost twenty-five years, longer than any other jurist in its history. Until 1971, he was also chief judge. He seems to have had little difficulty in arriving at his decisions, sometimes relying on instinct rather than intellectual persuasion. One observer described Quinn as a "hell yes, hell no" kind of judge. Proulx later noted Quinn's occasionally "instinctual" jurisprudence, that he "never had second thoughts about decisions. In other words, when he decided a case and he made a decision, that case was closed as far as he was concerned. He didn't agonize about it. He went on to the next one." He sometimes found it difficult to accept the fact that it might take his commissioners longer to draft an opinion than he took in reaching the verdict.

Unlike Quinn and Brosman, George Latimer had commanded troops in combat. This fact, according to his son, gave him a different perspective from his brethren when it came to military justice. "My father fought at Guadalcanal. He commanded troops at Leyte. . . . So my father first of all was interested in the services doing justice in the broadest sense of that term. He was not so concerned with small details." For different reasons, Latimer shared with Quinn an ability to decide the given issue with little difficulty. However, he was in no hurry to release a decision until it had been refined and polished to his satisfaction.

The only one of the original judges to have had both prior experience as an appellate judge and involvement in actual military combat, Latimer was not comfortable with Quinn's prolonged absences. They resulted in what he saw as a vacuum in leadership, all the more annoying to Latimer because he could not fill it. Although he functioned as senior judge in Quinn's absence, in fact the commissioners and Proulx looked to Providence for guidance and ultimate decisions. Much more reserved in manner than the gregarious former governor, Latimer felt frustrated by the management style Quinn brought to the Court. He also had difficulties with the way the commissioner system was evolving within the new tribunal.

Alone among his brethren, Paul Brosman came from an academic background, and he seems to have experienced the most difficulty in the actual process of judging. If Quinn and Latimer brought some sort of outlook to their judging, whatever its origin might be, Brosman approached military justice with intellectual curiosity rather than institutional consistency. Courtly and quiet in manner (Quinn affectionately referred to Brosman as "his Lordship"), the former dean bought a home directly across the street from Latimer. Often they traveled to and from court together, and while they frequently disagreed as to results, each relished the opportunity to discuss and debate the legal issues presented by the cases. Proulx remembered that Brosman had a Packard Roadster, which he apparently did not like to drive—one reason why he may have driven so often with Judge Latimer. At any rate, added Proulx, Brosman used to say, "Fred, there are only two happy days for a man who owns a Packard Roadster: the day he buys it and the day he sells it."

With the judges, commissioners, clerks, and staff in place, all that was needed were the litigants. By June 1952, the Court had docketed almost one thousand cases, releasing ninety-seven written opinions. One year later, between June 1952 and June 1953, more than two thousand cases were docketed. What types of issues did they raise? How did the judges respond, and with what results?

14

The Court Commences, 1951–1955

Although the judges of the U.S. Court of Appeals for the Armed Forces faced the challenge of interpreting a new statute, in large measure the UCMJ itself was a synthesis of existing military law. Judges Quinn, Latimer, and Brosman assumed, not unreasonably, that Congress had not intended the Court to interpret military justice with a tabula rasa, with no regard for principles and policies articulated in an earlier era. On the other hand, they realized that the UCMJ mandated substantial improvements in military justice, especially in the area of due process. On one level, this did not appear to be a difficult challenge. A new code of military justice was on the books, and the armed services were expected to follow the new law in its administration. Military justice was not to be dispensed in the same old way. In a real sense, the early years of USCAAF history can be seen as a determination by its judges that the revolution wrought by the UCMJ would not fall victim to a sort of silent "counterrevolution," nurtured by efforts of the military to conduct business as usual. The clash between a guilty plea and a superficially simple doctrine of harmless error illustrates the point.

EARLY CONSENSUS ON THE COURT

Using several cases decided in the fall of 1951, the judges unanimously agreed that in certain instances a guilty plea by the defendant obviated the necessity for a military court to comply with provisions set forth in article 52 of the UCMJ. It specified procedures for the casting of votes by court members during the course of a court-martial, as well as listing the number of votes required for conviction. These findings may have reflected a desire not to disturb the trial practices of the military justice system without clear evidence that the alleged error itself had a substantial influence on the trial's outcome. When the record of trial presented such evidence, however, the outcome on appeal might be very different.

Less than three weeks after deciding this series of cases, the Court decided *United States v. Clay.* The case was the first landmark opinion issued by the new tribunal. It involved two separate pleas, one guilty, the other not guilty. Again, the trial court had not followed required procedures. Judge Latimer had no trouble excusing this error in the guilty plea, in accord with the earlier decisions just noted. The accused's plea of not guilty to the other charge, however, was a more serious matter.

Latimer stated that a not guilty plea automatically "placed the burden upon the government to prove beyond a reasonable doubt all the essential elements of the offense." Moreover, unlike a guilty plea, "it permitted the assumption of innocence to weigh in his favor and required that any reasonable doubt must be resolved against his guilt." Under these circumstances, to neglect instructing members of the court on issues such as the burden of proof and the presumption of innocence was unacceptable. Latimer could have ended the opinion at this point. Instead he went on to detail those rights for an accused that even, as he put it, "a cursory inspection" of the UCMJ would reveal:

> To be informed of the charges against him; to be confronted by witnesses testifying against him; to cross-examine witnesses for the government; to challenge members of the court for cause or peremptorily; to have a specific number of members compose general and special courts-martial; to be represented by counsel; not to be compelled to incriminate himself; to have involuntary confessions excluded from consideration; to have the court instructed on the elements of the offense, the presumption of innocence, and the burden of proof; to be found guilty of an offense only when a designated number of members concur in a finding to that effect; to be sentenced only when a certain number of members vote in the affirmative; and to have an appellate review.

In identifying the source of these rights beyond the text of the UCMJ, however, Latimer hedged: "In keeping with the principles of military justice . . . we do not bottom those rights and privileges on the Constitution. We base them on the laws as enacted by Congress." Later in the opinion, he added, "We need not concern ourselves with the constitutional concepts." If a civilian court could find that denial of these benefits resulted in a loss of due process, "it should be apparent to a casual reader that denial of a similar right granted by Congress to an accused in the military service [violates] military due process." One can only speculate why in 1951 USCAAF was unwilling to find a constitutional source for the due process safeguards it articulated so clearly—especially since Latimer discussed a number of federal cases affirming them. The era of the Warren Court was still in the future. Later USCAAF decisions reflected a preference to rest these rights on a constitutional basis rather than a statute.

The tribunal reiterated this concern with military due process in a different context. *United States v. DeCarlo* involved a soldier accused of unpremeditated murder in the shooting death of a young Korean boy. Shortly before the victim died, he stated that "it was an accident." Upon motion of the prosecution, this statement was stricken from the record, and DeCarlo was convicted. In an opinion by Chief Judge Quinn, the Court reversed. Drawing heavily upon civilian law precedents, he emphasized that the dying youth "would have no reason to tell an untruth. His testimony, although certainly not conclusive, should have been before the court to assist them in evaluating what was a difficult question of fact." Exclusion of the statement was prejudicial error.

On the other hand, the Court tried to maintain a balance between zealous concern for the rights of an accused and the realization that the administration of military justice had to be practical. *United States v. Monge* illustrates the difficulty of maintaining this balance. It involved an eighteen-year-old soldier, apparently with limited intellect, who had completed only the ninth grade in school. Suspecting him of burglary, at 4:00 A.M. two soldiers "pulled him from his bed, forced him to lie on the floor, held a bayonet at his back, and questioned him concerning the thefts." Shortly, the defendant admitted stealing some money. Later, he made a second confession but was not informed that "any prior involuntary confession could not be used against him." Had he known this fact, "he would not have made the second." Speaking through Chief Judge Quinn, the Court unanimously affirmed the conviction. After emphasizing that, especially in the military, a confession in the presence of superiors "gives cause for additional suspicion," nevertheless he declined "to conclude . . . that the effect of the prior abuse was so strong as to make unreasonable a conclusion that it did not dominate the mind to such an extent as to render the subsequent confessions involuntary." Critical reaction to *Monge* came from an unexpected source—none other than Edmund Morgan.

MORGAN AND BROSMAN—CONSTRUCTIVE COLLOQUIES

Monge was handed down on January 8, 1952. It took Morgan barely a week to react concerning "the perfectly outrageous conduct of the arresting officers, conduct which is rarely equalled in civilian cases." Even worse, he commented to Brosman, "When you take into account the inexperience and low grade intelligence of the accused . . . , the result, and particularly the failure of the Chief Judge to denounce the original coercive conduct, will shock most laymen, and it will cause the critics of the services to insist that the Court has pointed out a way in which coerced confessions can be obtained and their results used in all contest cases." Brosman tried to defend the Court's opinion—all the more so since he had joined it. But he had much more to discuss with Morgan than just this case. Morgan had alluded to some talk at a recent bar association meeting about "the inadequacies of the Code and the non-civilian character and attitude of the Court." His remark bothered Brosman.

"I earnestly invite," wrote the former law school dean, "any comment you may care to make at any time about the Court, any of our cases, or my own judicial conduct or ideas. As you know, I am rather new at this business and I am not too familiar with the amenities of my craft." Morgan could be only too aware "that appellate judicial administration is not without its compromises and that every member of this Court can be expected to make some mistakes." The Court has to "take into account the realities of the military situation on the one hand and the demands of an enlightened approach to civilian criminal law on the other." Hence, "it is sheer nonsense to apply the term 'noncivilian' to the character and attitude of any of us. . . . [I]t is just plain silly for anybody to think of me as 'service minded.' . . . We are doing our level best, I promise you, to call them as we see them."

In reply, Morgan emphasized that "I do not want any member of the Court to think that I imagine that my opinion will cut any more ice than that of any other lawyer." Of course he was anxious that the Court should stand "high with the Bar and be the instrument for deleting that much advertised command control and devious hidden exercise of it by camouflage in legal formulae." However, "the securing and use of confessions in the services has been a source of violent criticism; and when a situation such as appears in this record is dealt with by the Court, its attitude should be made so clear that he who runs may read. 'Not while this Court sits' has lost much of its force since Holmes died." "I may tell you confidentially," Morgan added, that the civilian court "was my chief personal contribution, the one feature that I was prepared to fight for even if the lid had to be blown off to accomplish it."

When writing to Brosman, Morgan had not hesitated to voice his critical reaction to a particular decision, be it Brosman's or another judge's. Brosman appreciated his candor: "A good job needs doing here and I want to do the very best I can. . . . I shall always be grateful for whatever criticism you are willing to pass on to me." He further informed Morgan of his desire to establish as broad a base as possible for USCAAF authority. After explaining his move toward this end in a series of cases dealing with prejudicial error, Brosman stated that "anything you can say about this whole business—including my nefarious motives—will be greatly appreciated."

In one of his letters to Morgan, Brosman included a copy of an interim report prepared by the judges summarizing USCAAF activity through March 1, 1952. Barely eight pages in length, the report came only from the judges. Although the UCMJ required a joint committee of JAGs and judges to report to Congress on an annual basis about the workings of the code and military justice, the JAGs refused to participate in this first effort. After less than six months of activity by the Court, the decision of the judge advocate generals not to join with the judges reflected a growing tension between them—one that warrants examination.

NOT SO CONSTRUCTIVE CRITICISM

An early sign of friction between practitioners and administrators of military justice came in a letter to Secretary of Defense Robert Lovett from Congressman Overton Brooks, one of the key members of the House Armed Services Committee and chairman of the subcommittee that had considered and supported the UCMJ. He had spent, Brooks reminded Lovett, "four months almost uninterruptedly working on [this measure] and entertained the high hope that it would be the solution of our military judicial problems and that it would work towards the elimination of the suspicion and mistrust which fills the mind of many in our civilian population regarding military justice." In recent months, however, "I am beginning to receive a good many complaints about the lack of proper administration of the act. . . . Perhaps it may be due in part to the failure of the Defense Department to immediately and energetically put into effect the provisions of the [UCMJ.]"

Lovett hastened to reply and reminded Brooks of the requirement that the judges and the JAGs "shall make a comprehensive survey of the operations of the Code every year," with submission of the same to Congress. He informed the congressman that "this report will be submitted shortly" and sent copies of his letter to all the JAGs as well as to the USCAAF judges. It was this report that the JAGs declined to join. The judges felt it important to inform Congress that the Court was functioning, even though, as Brosman wrote to Morgan, "we are only speaking for ourselves." However, he added, "between us girls, I am not sure how much joinder there can be between the JAGs and ourselves. Some fairly sharp differences are developing and—while they may be ironed out— it is entirely possible that no one of them will be willing to join fully in whatever report we send over later. Of course, these expressions must be strictly between ourselves. I certainly do not wish to prejudge the situation—but I have my fears."

The interim report identified key issues that had been confronted by the Court in the first six months of operation. Among them were its own jurisdiction, due process of military law, trial and appellate procedure, sufficiency of the evidence as a matter of law, improper representation, insufficiency and inadequacy of instructions, and legality of sentences. Unintentionally, this matter-of-fact list concealed the underlying causes for the friction between the judges and the JAGs. To better understand these causes, some comments about the historic relationship between the judge advocate generals and military justice may be appropriate.

As has been shown in earlier chapters, while the views of the JAGs were certainly considered during the drafting of the UCMJ, they were not controlling. In several instances, their preferences had been rejected. Moreover, although few would admit it, members of the JAG Corps may well have seen USCAAF as an institution that had been forced upon them by outsiders, not military officers. Such resentment, though unfortunate, is understandable. In point of fact, with incredibly few changes the "modern" American military justice system had prevailed for over 150 years, long enough—among other things—for American armed forces to win two world wars. And from first to last, the entire system revolved around the JAGs. In 1991, the judge advocate general of the army stated that "historically, securing the fairness of the justice system in the Army has been our principal reason for being."

Indeed, for military justice the JAGs were the sine qua non without which the military justice system could not operate. After World War I, a professor of law at the University of Wisconsin described the customary role of the JAG. "Technical and expert knowledge of the law," wrote William H. Page, "is supposed to be possessed by the judge-advocate." As with a civil jury, court-martial members "are not supposed to know the law as technical experts." Rather, they "should be guided by the opinion of the [JAG] on any questions of law or procedure that may arise during the trial," and they "must consider the grave consequences which may result from a disregard of legal advice given them by the [JAG.]" It was not too much even to describe the JAG as "the oracle of the law." According to Page, "the key to the development of military law is probably to be found in the position of the Judge Advocate General." His role was all the more important because the members of courts-martial are neither "a permanent court" nor a "technically trained body organized primarily for the purpose of adjudicating cases." In reality, "the court does not know the law in theory, and frequently does not know it in fact."

And so it was until 1951. Thus one can understand why the JAGs would be less than comfortable with USCAAF. A decision that found in favor of the defendant, whatever the specific grounds might be, could be seen as a condemnation of a JAG practice or procedure. The JAGs could conclude—with some justification—that the establishment of this court was, in reality, a reflection of their inability to provide what the civilian legal order deemed acceptable standards of military appellate review. This civilian tribunal could be seen as a lasting acknowledgment of JAG failure to provide real justice, and they resented it.

On the other hand, even the JAGs recognized political reality. Indeed, it may not be unreasonable to observe that no one becomes a judge advocate general without a working sense of such conditions. The code and the Court were not going to go away. Cooperation, if not consultation, was not only mandated, it was an operational necessity. For better or worse, judges and JAGs were partners in the process. In one sense, the more effective and thorough the JAGs were, the less work of correction there would be for the Court. While the judges appreciated this relationship immediately, the JAGs took somewhat longer.

Understandably, as the decisions against long accepted military justice practices came down, the JAGs sought somehow to confront the Court rather than their own commanders. But the judge advocate generals were also personally acquainted with the judges, and on paper at least, relations between them were cordial. Hence, they distinguished between the Court and its judges, seeking to force changes in the former without directly criticizing the latter. Their target, barely five months after USCAAF issued its first decisions, was nothing less than control of the Court's docket.

As enacted, the UCMJ provided three routes that could result in USCAAF review of a case:

1. All cases in which the sentence, as affirmed by a board of review, affects a general or flag officer or extends to the death penalty;
2. All cases reviewed by a board of review that the judge advocate general has certified to USCAAF for review;
3. All cases reviewed by a board of review in which, upon petition of the accused and on good cause shown, USCAAF has granted a review.

The first two criteria for judicial review were mandatory upon the Court. If the lower court's decision fell within either of these two categories, the judges had to review the case. Under the law, the Court exercised no discretion. The third criterion was very different. All that a petitioner had to do upon receiving an unfavorable board of review verdict was to file with the Court and show good cause.

The term "good cause shown" is capable of widely differing interpretations. If the petition raised questions or issues that were interesting, timely, and important, review could well be granted. Also, under all three of these provisions, the judges were able to specify issues on their own that they wanted argued—possibly in order to build a foundation for a statement of judicial intent in future cases. Moreover, it made no difference if the defendant's counsel had not raised these points on petition to the Court. Thus, the Court could compensate for what it might consider poor judgment by an attorney.

It was a matter of record, and the JAGs were only too well aware of the fact, that even in its first year USCAAF had been very selective in accepting cases under the third provision. Nonetheless, it was the only category in which the judges could pick and choose the cases in accord with their own inclinations. On March 14, 1952, the three judge advocate generals submitted a proposed amendment for the UCMJ to Quinn, Latimer, and Brosman, asking that it be included in the annual joint report for the period May 31, 1951, to May 31, 1952. It would have changed the third criterion as follows: "All other cases reviewed by a Board of Review in which, upon petition of the accused or his appellate counsel and on good cause shown, the Judge Advocate General, the

Assistant Judge Advocate General in charge of a branch office, or the board of review that reviewed the record issues a certificate of probable cause."

"In very strictest confidence," Brosman informed Morgan about the proposal. The judges had every intention of continuing their meetings with the JAGs. "I am, however, doubtful about very much accomplishment here." As to the proposed amendment, "I really regard the proposal as an insult to our intelligence. Of course, we shall have nothing whatever to do with it." Shortly thereafter, Brosman wrote again to Morgan, emphasizing the need for confidentiality. The letter indicates awareness on Brosman's part that there might be more behind the proposed amendment than just its words.

"We wish," he wrote, "to be entirely fair" to the JAGs, and "I for one do not wish to release their proposal so long as there is any chance of their withdrawing it. Although I have some doubt in the matter, they may ultimately come to do this." More important, "I may be able to break their ranks by talking Reg Harmon [air force JAG and Brosman's close friend] into withdrawing his approval." Finally, perhaps the proposed amendment "should be regarded as in the nature of a proposal made during the course of negotiations around a conference table, and should not at present be made public." In any event, "if it turns out that war must be declared, so be it."

Ultimately, this specific proposal disappeared, although, as will be seen, it reappeared in a different guise—one that the judges found as offensive as the first version. Exactly what the JAGs hoped to accomplish by their amendment remains unclear. But it may well be that they saw it as an effective source of pressure on the judges, a subtle suggestion of what might happen if USCAAF went too far in "tampering" with the traditional tools and techniques of military justice. This type of intimidation by intention would again be used against USCAAF in 1977–1979 and will be discussed later.

The judges had more to confront than JAG criticism. Although they refused to admit it, these officers attacked the Court for what they saw as excessive interference in military justice. At the same time, however, other lawyers criticized the new tribunal for not taking sufficient steps to improve military justice. Typical of this group was Cornell law professor Arthur John Keeffe, who published an article in *Reader's Digest* with the less than objective title "Drumhead Justice: A Look at Our Military Courts." Essentially a rehash of his earlier comments that military justice would be much improved if only the recommendations of *his* 1947 committee report on navy courts-martials had been followed, Keeffe's article described the UCMJ as "a step in the right direction, but an unfortunately short one." He repeated his objections to USCAAF as currently constituted and concluded that "a drastic improvement in our system of military law is needed."

Keeffe's strident spasms were, of course, nothing new. But previously they had been confined to law review articles that, in terms of public perception, were relatively insignificant. For better or for worse, the same could not be said about *Reader's Digest*. Perhaps Keeffe may have suffered from a lingering resentment both because he was virtually ignored during the drafting of the UCMJ and because no serious consideration had apparently been given to his possible candidacy for a seat on the Court. His frustration about military justice seems to have been shared by the Special Committee of the Association of the Bar of the City of New York.

It reported in October 1952 that the past year, "far from seeing further progress in the court-martial reform, has brought only regression from the advances that had been made in recent years." Coming after the first year of USCAAF, these comments irritated Frederick Bernays Wiener, former JAG officer and a well-known scholar on military justice, who wrote to the new chairman of that committee. "While your Committee is . . . frightening the bar with loose talk of regression," both JAGs and judges "are feeling their way through a new system, which has bad points as well as good." Unless the committee "is prepared to look at facts . . . and to eschew loose talk, instead of spewing forth unfounded exaggeration and, generally, working off its members' war-time frustrations, I submit that it would best serve the interests of the legal profession and of the nation by quietly disbanding."

These examples of court criticism for doing either too much or not enough were reminiscent of earlier comments about the UCMJ. They served to remind the judges, if any such prodding was necessary, that public interest in military justice had not totally abated. Disagreement among the judges themselves over how far the Court should go in "overseeing" the system reflected this tension.

In the *Clay* case, a unanimous Court had listed in unequivocal terms the due process rights held by members of the armed services. The extent to which such rights were self-defining increasingly was a source of disagreement between Brosman and Latimer. In a revealing letter to Ray Forrester, dean of Vanderbilt Law School, Brosman observed that in several of the due process cases, he had sought to articulate a concept that he called "general prejudice." It applied "whenever I was able to find a departure from some important and basic notion derivable from all four corners of the Code[,] although not in specific violation of any express provision." Brosman's point involved more than semantics. Finding a substantial lack of legal evidence as a basis for an error in fact-finding could bring the case within USCAAF jurisdiction, limited by the UCMJ to matters of law. It might, in other words, dramatically expand the scope of court authority—something that Brosman favored, but Latimer feared.

By early 1953, Brosman had concluded that Latimer was intent on undermining his earlier decision by insisting that in determining error during a court-martial, the Court also had to find prejudice rather than a purely unintentional mistake. "If *Clay* means no more than this," he wrote to Morgan, "it is reduced to the level of empty, pompous, almost spurious phrases." Even worse, "I think there has also been a recent tendency on the part of Bob Quinn to depart to some extent from the implications of *Clay*—not because of any fundamental change of heart but because I genuinely do not believe he realizes that some of George's opinions [which] he has been buying are really chipping away at *Clay*."

Morgan advised Brosman that his dissents "exhibit too much emotion." Referring to the Brosman rhetoric just quoted, that "one of the finest flowers of this Court's effort is reduced to the level of empty, pompous phrases," Morgan asked, "Does this add anything . . . except an implied accusation of insincerity in rendering the former opinion?" In his dissents, Brosman would benefit from brevity, "and a complete absence of adjectives and adverbs would make them much more effective as well as more dignified. It is needless to add that I should not have ventured these suggestions had you not invited them."

Brosman moderated his tone, but not his basic disagreement with Latimer, which involved differences in perception both of judicial philosophy and jurisdiction. Fearful that such judicial "flexibility" as exercised by Brosman might be seen as judicial aggrandizement, Latimer urged caution. His position built on the point that "unless opinions of this Court announce rules of law which can be applied practically by tribunals and other persons who are required to follow our decisions, its usefulness will be impaired." He objected to a rule of law "so incomprehensible and so lacking in identifiable standards that it can be measured only by the individual whims of appellate judges." The net result was that "a practical application of the principle is most difficult if not impossible." Moreover, he insisted that "we should not reverse a conviction unless we could find in the record of that case some prejudice to the substantial rights of the accused." Latimer's words may be contrasted with Brosman's concurrence in a different case: "Unless it is perfectly clear that the accused could not have been harmed, the present error should be regarded as reversible."

MORE CONFLICT BETWEEN JUDGES AND JAGS

In May 1952, Morgan received added evidence that the military—in this case the army—was violating the spirit if not the letter of the UCMJ. A cordial letter from Felix Larkin commented on the operation of the UCMJ: "I gather it is going along pretty well even though I also understand that the JAGs are giving the Court a little trouble." On the same day, Morgan heard from Robert Haydock, the young lawyer who had been Larkin's assistant in the Defense Department Office of General Counsel. Haydock wrote of a letter obtained from the ABA Special Committee on Military Justice to the effect that the "Army has sought to deprive accused personnel of their right to petition [USCAAF] for review by inducing them to sign waivers of that right. Indeed, this latter practice is so common that mimeographed forms are now being used for that purpose."

Haydock was also concerned with the need to "prevent frivolous appeals . . . which are taken merely because they are free and the defendant has nothing to lose." Obviously, the method employed by the army to discourage such appeals was unacceptable. But there was always the possibility that too much time would be taken by the need to consider all types of petitions duly filed. The issue of frivolous appeals troubled the judges and indeed still does. But it also served in part as a sort of doctrinal litmus test for sensing the relationship between jurists and the military.

Morgan promptly replied to Haydock that discouraging petitions for review was, "in my opinion, another indication of the interference and exercise of command control." If the petitions "are too numerous for the Court to sift . . . the solution certainly is not to cut down the right to petition or to put the sifting in the hands of the military. . . . We are certainly not going to sit idly by and see the Uniform Code emasculated . . . in the manner in which the Army weakened and to a large extent destroyed many of the reforms intended to be accomplished by the 1920 Act."

Morgan also sent a copy of this response to Larkin. "It seems apparent," he added, "that not only the JAGs, but the services also, are giving the Court considerable trouble and are attempting to preserve the kind of military control which we were all so anxious to prevent." The new code and court presented the services with "a fine opportunity to set themselves right with the Bar and the public with reference to the administration of military justice[,] and . . . those in control do not have enough sense to realize it." Even as Morgan wrote about waiver of the right of petition for review, however, so did the Court.

In an unsigned per curiam decision, the judges considered the validity of a waiver form prepared by the navy. They did not mince words: "This agreement between the accused and the [navy] complete to the extent of purporting to provide a consideration to the accused is, for appellate purposes a legal nullity." Moreover, "the execution of similar documents—however imposing in appearance or verbiage—will not be considered by us as in any way affecting his right to petition this Court for relief. We are anxious to make this conception crystal clear to the services." The Court reiterated the point that "the right of convicted persons freely and directly to petition this Court must be protected fully and in nowise abridged." Furthermore,

It is distinctly arguable that without a full, complete and careful explanation of the waiver and its legal effect, that its use is a legal trap for the uninformed. Despite the unenforceability of such a document, it is possible that an inadequately advised accused might attach legal validity or significance thereto and be misled as to his right to appeal. For these reasons[,] in any case coming before this Court which involves both a failure to petition timely and a waiver of the right, the surrounding facts and circumstances will be scrutinized by this Court with the greatest care to assure that the accused was fully advised of his rights, and was in no way misled into waiving them for the convenience of the Government.

A few months after this opinion was released, Alfred Proulx wrote about a lecture delivered by a Marine Corps general during Proulx's two weeks of training duty at the Naval School of Justice, to the effect that "there were just too many damn acquittals under the new Code. From conversations and other remarks I got the idea that the old time Navy spares no love for the UCMJ."

COPING WITH CRITICISM

The continued carping of the JAGs about the UCMJ and USCAAF, as opposed to criticism of its three judges, troubled the Court, although worse was yet to come. Quinn and his brethren hesitated to respond directly to the complaints if only because, as appellate jurists, it would be inappropriate to engage in public colloquy with the JAGs. On the other hand, they could not afford to sit still while the senior legal officers within the services used political contacts and publicity to press for changes in the UCMJ, changes that might directly affect operation of the Court. In the fall of 1952, the three decided to select, as Quinn put it, "a number of distinguished lawyers . . . to serve as a committee to study certain questions" that might later be referred to Congress. These included, among others, command control and the problem of limiting appeals to the Court.

The civilian "court committee" would be a consultive body separate from the Court, able to comment upon whatever it deemed appropriate, including— of course—JAG criticism. It would be composed of able and experienced civilian lawyers, all of whom strongly supported the concept of a civilian appellate court over the military. In a real sense, the committee was to run interference for the judges, to counter JAG comments with constructive proposals and to speak to the Court's concerns without appearing to speak for the judges. It included individuals such as Felix Larkin, Harvard law professor Arthur Sutherland, Whitney North Seymour, past president of the Association of the Bar of the City of New York and chair of the committee, and Joseph McClain, dean of the Duke University Law School. Quinn promptly asked advice from Morgan about the new committee, but the Vanderbilt law professor was less than enthusiastic about the proposal.

Concerning command control, "Is there," Morgan queried, "anything to be said now that wasn't said . . . before the committees of Congress and which was given full consideration? Are we to have rehashed the cases which occurred before the Code went into effect and new conclusions drawn as to the theoretical effectiveness or ineffectiveness of the Code provisions to cure the evil?" The possible limiting of appeals in wartime was "a proposal, I suppose, emanating from the services. It is the kind of thing that has a plausible appeal of practicability. In essence it is the first major attack on civilian control of military justice."

Those who supported such a scheme confused symptoms with causes. Morgan reminded Quinn that calls for the reform of military justice invariably took place not so much in time of peace as during actual war. This period would be the least desirable interval in which to attempt to curtail the right of appeal. The remedy for excessive petitions, he repeated, "is certainly not to limit civilian review." The only proposal for Morgan that "is feasible at present in my opinion is one to make the tenure of the judges for life instead of for terms of years." No response from Quinn to Morgan could be located, but Brosman did write a lengthy letter to his friend and mentor—one that reveals much about the rationale for the civilian committee and also the condition of USCAAF in 1953.

Brosman first pointed to a problem possibly even more serious than he indicated: "We are really working under a good deal of pressure—indeed too much to permit a finished job in our opinions." The Court's statistics supported Brosman's statement. By December 1952, USCAAF had delivered written opinions in 178 cases, with almost half of them (81) decided to the advantage of the accused. Proulx noted that more than 2,000 cases had been filed. He expected a schedule with "an average of 24 cases heard per month, or 8 opinions for each judge. Add this to the passing on of an average of 200 petitions per month, I doubt if they can do more."

Brosman admitted that one could "hold up publication until a really thoughtful and careful product is produced. Latimer is much more likely to do this than Quinn and I." But the chief judge believed that in this early period of the Court and code operation, "it is extremely important that we act promptly—and I agree with him in the main." Latimer, on the other hand, "is inclined to write more elaborate opinions and to hold up publication for a longer time. Actually, I suppose I am between the two, but I more nearly agree with Bob than with George." Brosman felt that "we are just playing into the hands of those critics who charge that a civilian court is an incubus if we do not get our opinions out as soon as we possibly can."

In retrospect, Brosman's position pointed to an extremely unfortunate situation. It can be argued that USCAAF commits a real disservice if it hands down decisions that are not well conceived, structured, or articulated. In the peculiar context of this court, however, the negative effects of such action can be still more destructive. Fairly isolated, as one distinguished scholar of military justice, Eugene Fidell, observed in 1982, from the civilian judicial system as well as the civilian bar, failing in general to attract sustained and thoughtful academic interest and critical scrutiny, limited in the extent to which its holdings are distributed, bound by the requirement for political balance in appointment to this bench—all these conditions make premature dissemination of decisions such as those described by Brosman even more inopportune. Such considerations "serve to deprive the court of many of the sources of institutional strength that furnish the mortar for a sound appellate structure."

Brosman went on to imply, accurately, that Morgan was "somewhat doubtful of the real utility" of the new committee. While the former chairman of the code committee might indeed be correct, Brosman and his colleagues were simply too busy to give much consideration to the proposals for code changes that were now coming forward. These proposals, "as you would suspect, come from . . . the services and the old-line service point of view on the one hand, and from what at least some people regard as the lunatic fringe on the other. In terms of our statesmanship at least, I genuinely cannot believe that our Committee will not serve a very useful purpose." When, for example, the JAGs propose changes, "some . . . will doubtless be of a minor nature and at the same time both safe and desirable. On the other hand, some are likely to be major and out of keeping with the spirit of the Uniform Code. We will certainly wish the advice of the Committee as to all of these proposals. . . . I think you will have no difficulty in seeing what I am driving at."

Suspecting that Morgan possibly had been disappointed not to be named himself to such a committee, Brosman wrote that "your name was the first one we thought of. . . . Ultimately we concluded that for a variety of practical rea sons it would perhaps be best not to have you on the Committee's membership—and I know you will understand fully what I mean here. We did not regard the loss as irreparable, however, for we were assured that you would be willing to advise us personally—as you certainly will be asked to do." Of course, "we deemed liaison with your committee important[,] and with this in mind we asked Felix [Larkin] to serve."

Finally, Brosman reassured Morgan that "although we tend to scrutinize service proposals carefully, we are doing our level best to maintain a cooperative attitude with the [JAGs]. Although there have been tough moments and there probably will be more of them, we have so far been able to maintain a sound working arrangement. Incidentally, the services do not at all like the appointment of our Advisory committee." Judicial awareness concerning the services' hostility to Morgan may explain the decision not to name him to the committee. A month later, Brosman told Morgan that the JAGs "appear to dislike us just about as much as they dislike you. I suppose the Services disapprove of Bob to the greatest extent; I come next; and George is most acceptable. However, he is merely an SOB and not a dirty one."

The Court Committee, so called to distinguish it from the Code Committee mandated by the statute, set to work with results that will be discussed in the following chapter. In the meantime, the Court finally was able to move into its new home, the building at 450 E Street having been vacated with the relocation of the U.S. Court of Appeals. By October 1952, the judges were holding forth in their own courtroom, but Proulx's office and the rest of the court staff did not move in until the end of the month. The move, Proulx observed, "is going to be chaotic enough without trying to get in before the painters and their scaffolding have pulled out. When they said we would move in October last summer, someone forgot to mention the year."

The years 1951–1953 represented a difficult period for the new tribunal. By the middle of this first segment in its history, external pressure had been initiated by the JAGs to change the code—as a means of placing pressure on the Court. Creation of the civilian advisory committee plus the first steps toward gaining life tenure represented the Court's initial response to JAG criticism. The JAG reaction and the results it produced were another matter.

15

Judges Versus JAGs, 1951–1955

Developments in USCAAF history that are traced in Chapters 15 and 16 must be seen in the context of the themes that link this entire book. How did the Court define and attempt to carry out its role? How did the military react, and how in turn did the Court respond? How would external political currents, such as appointment of a new judge, affect the tribunal?

Thus far, the controversy between JAGs and judges had been largely an internal matter. By 1954–1955, it burst wide open, although the services were very careful to distinguish between the code and the Court, criticizing the latter only by implication on the basis of "operational difficulties" with the former. Moreover, the JAGs sought to distinguish the Court as an institution from the judges as individuals, although their goal was obvious: to use criticism of the code as an indirect means to control the Court's authority. While concerned about this development, the judges were also involved in the first of numerous efforts to gain life tenure—a subject on which the JAGs likewise held views, markedly different from those of the Court.

TRAVAIL OVER TENURE

From the Court's viewpoint, it was appropriate that the first external call for life tenure after its establishment should come from Edmund Morgan, architect of the new tribunal. In April 1952—less than a year after the Court commenced operations—he wrote to Carl Vinson, still chairman of the House Armed Services Committee. Morgan reminded Vinson that his committee (with Morgan's enthusiastic approval) had stipulated life tenure for the Court, only to acquiesce in Senate substitution of limited terms: "If my memory is accurate, the sole reason for prescribing a limited term was the fear that the original appointees might be men poorly qualified for the position, whose selection might be dictated by considerations other than fitness for the office."

However, the concept of life tenure for this tribunal troubled the Senate Armed Services Committee, no matter how well qualified its first appointees were. Although the three nominations were approved without recorded opposition, both Senators Kefauver and Saltonstall supported limited terms, at least until the Court had had an initial trial period. There may also have been a question about whether or not there would be sufficient work for a tribunal with life tenure. Saltonstall and Kefauver had implied that the matter of life tenure could always be brought up later, after the Court had established itself. Now, the chairman need have no such qualms. According to Morgan, the first three judges "have made inapplicable all the reasons which induced the Senate and its Committee to amend the provision for life tenure."

Morgan received a reply not from Vinson, but rather from his chief counsel, Robert Smart. Diplomatic in tone, it quickly dampened any hope Morgan held that congressional support for life tenure might be easily obtained. "I seriously doubt," Smart observed, "if you are aware of the current attitude of the Congress . . . with reference to giving anybody anything. In every day vernacular, it's rough." The Court, after all, had been in existence "for less than one year. . . . I think that it is premature at this time to propose any [congressional] action." Better "to let the dust settle and get a happier Congressional atmosphere in being before any proposal on this subject should be presented." Smart had not yet gained an opportunity to discuss his response with Vinson, but "I think I know him well enough to predict that he would concur with my opinion."

There appears to have been more to Smart's view, however, than just consonance with his boss. Eager himself for a seat on the USCAAF bench, the last thing Smart wanted was for the incumbent judges to become frozen in their positions, the inevitable consequence of life tenure. This understandable and unstated preference indirectly raised a secondary issue related to life tenure. It had to do with the current judges. Morgan believed that Quinn, Latimer, and Brosman all merited life tenure, but how might this be accomplished? Could they be reappointed after an appropriate statute had been passed? How could one ensure that the president would reappoint these three individuals? Indeed, could the legislature compel the chief executive in the matter of a presidential appointment? Might, on the other hand, their current terms simply be extended to life by congressional fiat, bypassing the executive entirely?

Smart's implied negative advice to Morgan appears not to have dissuaded the judges from their goal. Less than two months later, and at Quinn's urging, Senator Green introduced a bill conferring life tenure on the USCAAF judges. It would have changed existing law in two ways: first, "the salary, retirement benefits, and other perquisites of the judges shall be the same as those provided by law for the judges of the United States Courts of Appeal," and second, "each

[USCAAF] judge . . . who holds office as such on the date of enactment of this Act shall continue to hold such office during good behavior." Thus, with one short bill Green sought to resolve both the question of legitimacy for the Court and the need for life tenure for its members. But his measure had a very brief tenure of its own and died in committee.

Undaunted, Quinn tried again during the next session. He may have realized, however, that there was little congressional interest in granting life tenure to new judges on a tribunal that had been deciding cases for less than a year. This time, the former governor sought to utilize his considerable charm and extensive political contacts in seeking legislative action.

In March 1953, Quinn wrote to another old friend, Congressman Philip Philbin, a Massachusetts Democrat on the House Armed Services Committee. He enclosed a copy of the revised proposal, essentially the same as the 1952 version. Given the magnitude of the Republican election victories in the fall of 1952, "we thought perhaps that the chances of passage would be improved if it were introduced by . . . some other Republican member of the Committee." Quinn also enclosed a memorandum explaining why changes to the Court should be enacted. He had sent copies to all members of the Rhode Island delegation, including Congressman Fogarty as well as Senators Green and Pastore, "but in the meantime if you can do any missionary work on the matter, I will appreciate it."

This explanatory memorandum, drafted by a court commissioner and revised by Quinn, drew heavily on an earlier analysis prepared by Daniel Walker during the debate over the civil service status of court personnel. Quinn catalogued a number of reasons for life tenure:

1. Congress had obviously created a court when USCAAF was established, but Title 28 of the United States Code defines a "Court of the United States" as "any court created by act of Congress *the judges of which are entitled to hold office during good behavior*" (emphasis in the original draft).
2. Quinn observed that for managerial purposes, USCAAF was administered by the Defense Department. Possibly because of this fact, the Civil Service Commission has "insisted on placing all personnel of the Court under its jurisdiction. . . . This not only wastes valuable time but interferes with the proper operation of the Court."
3. According to the existing statute, in case of sickness or a temporary vacancy on USCAAF, the president could designate a member of the U.S. Court of Appeals to fill in on a temporary basis. "This plainly indicates that Congress intended to put the judges of both courts . . . on the same plane."
4. Whatever may have convinced the Senate to delete life tenure from the UCMJ, its action "casts serious doubt upon the judicial stature of the court. It is undoubtedly looked upon in some executive circles as a cross between an administrative agency and a judicial entity."

These points were all drawn from the draft memorandum as first submitted to Quinn. However, he appears to have added a final summary paragraph. USCAAF, he noted, heads a judicial system "which currently administers approximately one-ninth of the criminal trials of the entire nation." In time of war, about one-third of such trials would reach its judges. "The jurisdiction of [the Court] is concerned not with mere property rights, but with the lives and liberties of Americans from all walks of life, all segments of society and all sections of the land. It was the clear intention of the Uniform Code to assimilate the administration of military justice as nearly as possible to that of the civilian community. All of these factors argue strongly for a Court of Military Appeals which is firmly integrated into the Federal judicial system." Indeed, Quinn insisted, in its sphere as the highest tribunal in military judicial hierarchy, USCAAF "should have the power, dignity, and prestige of the United States Supreme Court."

These arguments would be repeated with variations and changes in emphasis throughout the Court's continuing history. Quinn died without obtaining life tenure for his court, and as will be seen, Congress has consistently declined to grant this status to USCAAF judges. Nor is there any reason to believe that the immediate future will see a change in congressional sentiment. What is striking about USCAAF history, however, is the fact that absence of life tenure has not prevented the Court from exercising and augmenting its judicial authority. In other words, without life tenure, the judges have been able to accomplish some of what Quinn believed would be possible only *with* life tenure.

QUINN'S QUEST FOR CONSENSUS

In trying to build support for Green's proposal, Quinn drew on a variety of sources. Thus he sent the Rhode Island congressional delegation an excerpt from an article by New York University Law School professor John V. Thornton dealing with military justice under the new code and court. Thornton was impressed with "the combined scholarly and practical character of the Court's opinions. Their high caliber is particularly remarkable since the court has only three members and disposes of a tremendous volume of litigation. In a little more than a year[,] this bench has demonstrated that it deserves to be ranked with the elite of federal and state appellate tribunals."

Similar approbation came from a well-known senator, Margaret Chase Smith, a Republican from Maine. Writing in the *Boston Globe* about a recent USCAAF decision dealing with imposition of bread and water as punishment for certain military offenses, the senator lauded the Court even as she excoriated naval officials. This decision, according to Senator Smith, "surely gives real hope that this tribunal will not be the mere lackey of the naval and military brass." Further, she added, "there is considerable question in my mind whether [USCAAF] should be placed in the Department of Defense where its members can feel even the slightest feeling of being beholden to the military and civilian chiefs of the department." Immediately, Quinn sent excerpts to his Rhode Island congressional contacts. He emphasized that Smith's article "supports our bill for life tenure. She is a powerful member of the Armed Services Committee, and her help would undoubtedly be of great value."

The JAGs, of course, were fully aware that a bill to grant life tenure to USCAAF judges would be submitted to Congress. Brosman advised Morgan in April that "the Service people are planning to attack it on the ground that the provision freezing in the three incumbents is unconstitutional as an unwarranted exercise of the appointive power by the legislature." He further observed to Morgan that Quinn, "the judge they dislike most is untouched by any attack of theirs on a tenure bill. Given Bob's age, he has *de facto* life tenure now." Such opposition from the armed services, although not unexpected, would be unfortunate. Even worse, however, might be objections by the general counsel of the Defense Department, echoing the services' viewpoint. In July 1953, Brosman wrote Quinn that reservations—if not outright disapproval—from the Pentagon would be forthcoming. According to Brosman, there were several areas of difficulty.

"Actually," he wrote, "It appears that the comments of . . . Defense will not be nearly as favorable as we had been given to believe." The department would indeed reject the bills as submitted, offering instead "a substitute which omits the freezing-in provision." Moreover, the department declined to hold "that the Air Force claim of unconstitutionality is without support." Instead, it would submit an alternative bill "without the naughty language." The only possible benefit that occurred to Brosman was that at least the Defense Department "favors life tenure as a matter of principle."

Whatever enthusiasm the new Republican chair of the Armed Services Committee, Dewey Short, might have for USCAAF, according to Brosman, appeared to be more than offset by his general ignorance of military justice. "Short obviously knows very little about either the bill or the Court. . . . Actually he had so little background as not to know [that his own committee] had any finger in the confection [sic] and passage of the Uniform Code." Short— whom it is difficult to see as other than a lightweight—was even unaware that the House had originally provided life tenure for the judges. Aptly described by Forrestal's biographers as an "eloquent and bibulous congressman," at the conclusion of General MacArthur's speech to Congress in April 1951, Short had shouted that "we heard God speak here today, God in the flesh, the voice of God." His assessment may be contrasted with that of President Truman, who characterized the same speech as "a hundred percent bullshit."

Apparently, wrote Brosman, Short "thought the Uniform Code was a product of the Judiciary Committee!" Finally, there was the matter of Robert Smart, counsel to the House committee, who "is still interested in membership on the Court." Smart could therefore be expected to "do whatever he can to stall passage of any life tenure bill which will close the door on him." All in all, Brosman suggested, "maybe we had better start thinking about a five judge compromise." (Thirty-six years later, in 1989, Congress expanded USCAAF to five judges, its current size. But the lawmakers refused to provide life tenure.)

Within four days of Quinn's reply to Brosman, the Defense Department's general counsel forwarded a letter to the director of the Bureau of the Budget, one that confirmed Brosman's earlier conjecture: "It would appear more appropriate to amend the bill to provide that the indefinite appointments . . . should be made upon the expiration of the term of each judge who holds office as such on the day of enactment in order to avoid any legal question as to the validity of legislatively appointing certain individuals to office[,] thereby infringing upon [presidential] power . . . to appoint by and with the consent of the Senate." A revised draft listed the dates on which the three judges' terms were to expire and provided that "all successors, including any judge who is appointed to succeed himself and any judge appointed to fill a vacancy, shall hold office during good behavior."

The action of the Defense Department in supporting life tenure, but possibly not for the incumbents, left the judges uncertain as to their future course. Defense officials assured them that the Court would have ample opportunity to comment on the proposed changes prior to the next session of Congress scheduled to begin in January 1954. In the meantime, Richard Tedrow prepared a memo for the judges, explaining why the revised bill—even though it rejected life tenure for them but not for their successors—was so important.

The proposal "would resolve once and for all the confusion, at least in some quarters, as to our exact status." Its origins were less important than the fact that such confusion "should be dispelled without delay." Moreover, without the finality of a legislative act, questions could "arise as to the Court not being completely independent of the military establishment and of pressure groups, or of its being merely an Executive instrumentality." The great difficulty confronting USCAAF was that, in claiming to be a real court, it did not appear to fall within the various statutory provisions "affecting the Federal Judiciary generally." Unfortunately, the Court could not look to legislative intent as supporting its position. While the House had indeed provided for life tenure, the Senate had not, and the House had accepted the Senate action. If anything, legislative intent indicated a clear preference against life tenure. Thus, corrective legislation was even more necessary. Replete with citations, Tedrow's points apparently failed to convince the Justice Department, and although William Rogers, the deputy attorney general, was sympathetic to the Court's position, Green's bill troubled him.

At the outset, Rogers claimed that the bill "appears to be designed to place the judges beyond the removal power by the President." He based this contention on a portion of article 67 of the UCMJ. As enacted, this section provided that USCAAF judges could be removed by the president "upon notice and hearing, for neglect of duty or malfeasance in office, or upon the ground of mental or physical disability, but for no other cause." Because this provision obviously could not be reconciled with the principle of life tenure (which could end only by resignation, death, or impeachment), Green had deleted it from his bill. It was this deletion that bothered Rogers.

He summarized again the old controversy over the nature of a court-martial and pointed to the creation of USCAAF as a partial response to it. He also emphasized that the judges "are in large part free of command control." Conceding that courts-martial might in their nature be judicial, Rogers denied that this concession changed the essential character of such a proceeding from "a method of discipline exercised by the Commander in Chief and his authorized representatives." Further, he noted the limited jurisdiction exercised by USCAAF when compared to Article 3 tribunals. Finally, he questioned the need to change again what had itself been so important an innovation.

Indeed, "not only is the Code an experiment, but so too is the establishment of the Court and the use of independent civilians as judges." The entire system "has been in operation for . . . only slightly over two years. This seems to be hardly enough time for an informed judgment to be made as to whether the experiment has been a success." Unless "some imminent threat to the independence of the judges or some other immediate need exists, it is believed that the experiment should be given a further chance to be observed in action before so substantial a change is made." Here Rogers hints at the point raised earlier in this chapter. The obvious success of the Court in its early years without what it considered vital to its function—i.e., life tenure—in one sense made such a change all the more difficult to justify. Rogers concluded that when all was said and done, because USCAAF "is an instrument designed to carry out the President's . . . function as Commander in Chief, it would seem unwise to place any further restriction upon the power of the president to remove members of the Court." Accordingly he "is unable to recommend the enactment of the bill."

It seems incredible that the deputy attorney general could make such a fundamental error, especially in the light of more than two years of USCAAF reports. It may well be that Rogers had not informed himself of the earlier Ansell-Crowder controversy, the history of the UCMJ, or the state of military justice even as he wrote. At any rate, although he probably had so concluded even before receiving Rogers's memorandum, Quinn realized that the bill was stalled at least until 1954. Meanwhile, the JAGs had not been idle.

CONTINUED CONTENTION BETWEEN JUDGES AND JAGS

In their disagreements with the judges, the JAGs had an important tactical advantage: flexibility. They could articulate, adjust, and alter their positions, while the judges had to consider their roles as appellate jurists. In a real sense, while Quinn and his brethren had to wait for trouble to reach the Court, the JAGs were under no such constraints. Their response to the Court's outrage over the proposed change in review discretion, discussed in the previous chapter, illustrates the point.

Well aware of the hostile judicial reaction to their first proposal, the JAGs shifted ground. On March 30, 1953, they submitted a joint memorandum to Quinn, insisting that his court "should be protected against petitions for grants of review that are wholly lacking in legal merit. Under present law there is no means of regulating or eliminating these appeals, which may be initiated by the accused himself, who, though most frequently acting in entire good faith, generally has little or no knowledge of the points of law involved." In some instances, "petitions have been filed primarily for dilatory purposes." Finally, these undesirable conditions were exacerbated by the code's provision that gave an accused person thirty days to appeal to USCAAF from an unfavorable decision by a board of review.

This latter problem could be solved simply by reducing the time limit for such an appeal from thirty days to only ten. As to the primary difficulty of frivolous appeals, the JAGs offered a more subtle proposal than their first suggestion, which had been to condition an appeal to USCAAF upon JAG certification that such a step was warranted. Now they proposed to restrict USCAAF review to those cases where "counsel who represented the accused at trial . . . or appellate defense counsel appointed by the Judge Advocate General if the accused was not represented by [civilian] counsel before the Board of Review, shall certify that in his opinion the errors of law relied upon materially prejudiced the substantial rights of the accused." The report accompanying this proposal noted that "this particular means of regulation was selected because the accused's counsel may be expected to be fully cognizant of the circumstances of the case and because it does not permit arbitrary restriction of the right to petition in any case."

In a memorandum to the Court, Tedrow assessed the value of the JAG suggestion as minimal. "These fellows," he noted, "keep on trying." Seeking to protect the Court from cases "lacking in legal merit," the JAGs failed to understand that "we are unable to find whether there is merit until we have reviewed the record," exactly what the JAG revision would have restricted. Tedrow commented further that "in 25% of our cases of substance, we decided issues that counsel never saw fit to raise." Given this "lack of legal ability[,] I fail to see how . . . we could place such extreme reliance on counsel." Finally, "the requirement of such a certificate from one in the Service, to a greater or lesser degree makes the jurisdiction of this Court dependent upon the military." Tedrow described other sections of the report as "anachronistic if not atavistic." The chairman of the JAG Committee, General J. L. Harbaugh Jr., was one "whose progressive views are well known except they progress in the wrong direction."

About two weeks after Tedrow presented his comments to the Court, the JAGs submitted their report on recommended changes in the UCMJ. It included, among other suggested amendments, the provision for certification so soundly criticized by the chief commissioner. The language, however, indicated one intriguing change that may or may not have been another JAG adjustment to judicial hostility. The report stated that the code should be amended to provide that USCAAF "need only consider" petitions when certified by counsel. In the context of a statute dealing with possible actions, the word "need" as opposed to the word "shall" carries very different legal implications. By the change, the JAGs may have intended to retain USCAAF flexibility while pointing toward a way to avoid its utilization. Whatever the intent, this change utterly failed to assuage the doubts of the judges, who awaited findings from their own civilian Court Committee as a suitable basis for responding to the JAGs. Chaired by New York City attorney Whitney North Seymour, the committee submitted its report to the Court late in December 1953.

CONCERNS OF COURT AND COMMITTEE

Creation of the Court Committee, as distinguished from the Code Committee, had resulted from judicial awareness that an external group of distinguished lawyers, all selected because they were knowledgeable in military law and sympathetic to enactment and implementation of the UCMJ, could be a useful counterpoise in dealing with the JAGs. Not restricted by the constraints applicable to sitting judges, the committee could also bring a sense of objectivity to its deliberations. (The Code Committee was mandated by the UCMJ and included the judges and the JAGs. The code required annual reports to Congress from both. The Court Committee, however, was strictly the creation and responsibility of the three judges to whom alone it reported.) Quinn and his colleagues, on the other hand, were involved in the demanding routine of hearing, considering, and deciding cases, burdens that left them little time to consider—let alone confront—suggested changes in the UCMJ. All parties involved, judges, JAGs, and the committee, realized that the new code needed some improvements and changes. No one urged that the document remain completely unchanged. The extent to which it should be modified, however, was a different matter.

The JAGs had already achieved unanimity on a number of proposed changes. These included, among others, providing expanded jurisdiction for military courts with a single law officer serving alone. Further, they sought greater flexibility for themselves when taking corrective action in a court-martial where there was clear evidence of error, without having to refer the case to the board of review. The committee endorsed these changes. It declined, however, to support reducing the time available for petition to USCAAF from thirty days to ten, as the JAGs had sought. Instead, they recommended a fifteen-day period.

Moreover, as Quinn and his colleagues probably anticipated, it "definitely opposed" the JAG suggestion on limiting appeals to the Court. Although the members revealed concern with the workload of the three jurists, the committee declined to recommend any changes whatsoever in jurisdiction over their docket, especially since the judges had not sought any such modification. They pointed instead to the fact that "the Court has been able to function efficiently and justly under its present heavy workload." One suspects that the committee's purpose in raising this point was anything but subtle.

The judges had not complained about the ease of appeals to their court. It was the JAGs who suddenly demonstrated a novel solicitude for the Court in the wake of the allegedly excessive numbers of appeals that threatened to swamp the tribunal. From their perspective, Quinn and his brethren were wary of what they saw as the real motive for JAG concern—irritation over various USCAAF decisions that mandated new standards for due process and involved civilian judges in areas that previously had been the exclusive domain of the JAGs rather than aggravation over the supposedly high level of "frivolous" appeals.

Whether by accident or intent, the committee's recommendations reached the Court as Proulx was preparing the annual report, a document mandated by the code. It included separate sections by each of the JAGs, a section for USCAAF, and a joint report filed by the JAGs and the judges. Drafted during the first part of 1954, this report indicated where consensus had been achieved and where conflict could be anticipated. The JAGs and the judges unanimously recommended seventeen changes to the UCMJ, virtually all of which had already been endorsed by the Court Committee. Listed among them was the proposal to reduce the time for appeal from thirty days to fifteen. Conspicuous by its absence was the plan to limit the right of appeal.

The JAGs included as part of their report the August 1953 proposals that contained the ten-day limit as well as the certification requirement for appeal to USCAAF. More ominous, at least from the Court's viewpoint, was the statement by Ira Nunn, judge advocate general of the navy. Although he had signed the joint report replete with the seventeen recommendations unanimously supported by all parties, Nunn noted that the JAGs endorsed the August suggestions as well. Indeed, "proposed legislation implementing [them] has been drafted and will be submitted to the Department of Defense for inclusion in the . . . Defense Legislative Program for 1954." Although Nunn did not say so, the implication of his statement was that the JAGs were fully prepared to bypass both the Court and its committee and go directly to Congress through the Department of Defense. This, in fact, is exactly what they did, and Nunn's comment can be considered an early published indication of JAG irritation with USCAAF. Additional public examples of this displeasure would be forthcoming.

Nunn's move cannot have pleased the judges, but their immediate concern lay less with him than with the opposition of the Justice Department to Green's bill, still pending before the House Armed Services Committee. Quinn and his brethren had little doubt that continued opposition at this level would ultimately prevent its passage. In February 1954, therefore, Judge Latimer determined to speak with Deputy Attorney General Rogers "with the view of seeking to have the Department reverse its standing." Rogers assured Latimer that "as a matter of policy, there was no consideration of the patronage feature involved in the bill." Rather, Rogers apparently focused on the "newness" of the tribunal and the corresponding lack of a critical need to make a fundamental change after such a short period of operation. On March 17, Proulx received word that Rogers's "original comments would stand without amendment." Although the clerk did not know it, additional support for Rogers's position was circulating within the White House.

Given the facts that the Defense Department supported the bill if the provision for automatic tenure was deleted, that the Civil Service Commission raised no objection to the measure, but that the Justice Department opposed the enactment, the Bureau of the Budget appears to have been uncertain as to its recommendation and asked the White House for "guidance on the advice we should give Defense." Roger Jones, the assistant director for legislative reference, referred to the alternatives "of advising Defense that we concur . . . , or that we concur in the unfavorable Justice views, or we merely have no objection to the submission of both." With this less than enthusiastic response, Eisenhower's special counsel, Bernard Shanley, wrote to an old friend, Arthur Vanderbilt, chief justice of the New Jersey Supreme Court, asking his "views on the advisability of this Bill."

Vanderbilt replied with a confidential letter to "Bern." He had known one member of the Court—Paul Brosman— for the last fifteen years and had "the highest regard for him." Further, Vanderbilt had read some of the Court's opinions, "which impressed me favorably." Indeed, "I am told by some of my friends among the judges in the District of Columbia that the new tribunal has made a splendid record." Nevertheless, Vanderbilt was far from ready to advise that USCAAF "be transformed into a court with judges having life tenure."

He reminded Shanley that the tribunal "is still in an experimental stage." Moreover, "a very considerable proportion of the cases . . . involve offenses of a purely military character and breaches of military discipline, such as desertion, absence without leave, disobedience of orders, etc." Vanderbilt's point became clear after he recalled that shortly after World War II, he had chaired a committee to examine army military justice. "We considered the suggestion that there be created a court composed of civilians . . . but we rejected it and made no recommendation on the subject, because we felt that administration of military justice should remain within the Army, even though it should be independent of the Commanding Officer." Because he may have been unconvinced that it was fully appropriate for civilian judges to decide military cases, Vanderbilt "would not be in favor at this time of changing the tenure of members of the

Court." Even as Shanley pondered Vanderbilt's reply, the JAGs offered their own assessment of military justice.

GOING PUBLIC

Late in 1953, the navy released an assessment of military justice under the UCMJ and claimed that adoption of the code, "with its unwieldy legal procedure, has made the effective administration of military justice within the Armed Forces more difficult." The point was not lost on some of Quinn's friends in Congress. Representative John Fogarty spoke to his colleagues and lauded the work of the Court. He referred to an editorial in the *Navy Times,* which included the excerpt from the report just quoted. But it also contained an excerpt from a September 1953 speech delivered by the "able" chief judge. If the JAGs wanted to pick up the gauntlet, perhaps it was because the Court was willing to throw it down:

> We have not lost sight of the necessity for discipline in military law. We will not lose sight of the fact that the first obligation of armies and navies is to fight and win wars. We will never do anything to improperly interfere with the efficient operation of our military forces. But consistent with these objectives, we will do everything in our power to see that every member of the military forces accused of crime gets a fair and speedy trial, and an absolutely square deal.

Quinn's remarks, incidentally, were delivered to an audience that included the three JAGs.

The JAGs responded with public comments about both the code and the Court. Thus, on August 14, 1954, air force JAG Reginald Harmon addressed the annual meeting of the Judge Advocates' Association. Entitled "Progress Under the Uniform Code," his speech implied that little, if any, had resulted from its enactment. Harmon railed against three weaknesses inherent in its operation. First, the cost of administering military justice under one year of the code, he claimed, was "over a quarter of a million dollars, or approximately ten times the cost of operation under the Elston Act [the legislation superseded by the UCMJ in 1951]." Further, the air force JAG described the UCMJ as "unnecessarily laden with built-in delays." There are, he complained, "too many reviews on reviews indiscriminately granted to all offenders." Worst of all is the code's "tendency to destroy what once was the principal asset of the military justice system, that is, the swift and certain punishment of the guilty man." Now, Harmon lamented, "the certainty of punishment and the promptness of prosecution seem to be becoming a matter of historical interest." Without once mentioning the Court or its judges, Harmon in effect blamed both for the current condition of military justice.

When administering the UCMJ, "in many instances," claimed Harmon, "form has been elevated over substance. In case after case, convictions have been set aside for reasons that do not seem to the ordinary man to have the slightest bearing upon either the fairness of the trial or the fundamental rights of the accused." Yet, "when faced with . . . some really fundamental rights of the accused, like that of unreasonable search and seizure, the safeguards which the services have set up and carefully maintained under the earlier laws are struck down."

Previously scheduled to report to the JAG conference about the Court, Judge Latimer responded indirectly to Harmon's comments. He reminded his audience that congressional debate over the "present system of military justice as compared with its predecessor systems" had been lengthy, with the outcome that military justice—on the appellate level, at least—would "be governed to some extent by civilians." Possibly with Harmon in mind, Latimer observed that the Court "needs the support of all military and civilian lawyers and that that support has been forthcoming from most quarters." Speaking also for his colleagues, Latimer concluded that "he is satisfied that the Court has a place in our judicial system, and is here to stay."

The next entrant into the public commentary by the JAGs against the UCMJ was Admiral Ira Nunn. In 1953, he had sent Quinn an inscribed photograph as "an expression of my highest respect and esteem." Now, he reiterated Harmon's claims. Nunn predicted that the UCMJ "is bound to fall flat on its face in the event of mobilization. . . . Moreover, we think it is harmful and burdensome, even in times of peace, as at the present time." As for USCAAF, it is "in no way protected from frivolous appeals. . . . The result is our appellate bodies are badly crowded. The thing is badly bogged down, even now."

In August 1955 with the comments of the new army judge advocate general, Major General Eugene Caffey, the JAGs attained unanimity in their public critique of the code. Caffey essentially echoed the complaints raised by Harmon and Nunn. "Maybe," he concluded, "the time has come for a new look . . . to work over this system of military justice and try to speed it up some, try to cut out the useless parts of it, give the accused the protections they are entitled to, but work out a system that will be effective, which of course this one is not now. . . . The system we have now is very, very expensive, and time consuming, and about 95% of it accomplishes nothing."

COURT AND CONSTITUTION

As the JAGs intensified their attacks even as the life tenure bill languished in legislative limbo, USCAAF continued to decide cases and issue opinions. If by their tactics the JAGs sought to intimidate the judges, they seemed not to have succeeded. On the other hand, the judges continued to strive for balance between due process and the needs of the military. One example illustrates how difficult this challenge could be.

The question in *United States v. Sutton* was whether written depositions could be used in evidence against an accused who was not present when they were taken, if the accused had not waived the right to be present. It was not unreasonable to assume that the unanimous holding in *United States v. Clay* (1951) was dispositive. The Navy Board of Review so concluded and reversed Sutton's conviction. In *Clay,* Judge Latimer had noted that among the rights Congress granted the accused in the UCMJ was the right "to be confronted by witnesses testifying against him." Admiral Nunn certified the case to USCAAF, where it was argued in spring 1954.

A split tribunal reversed the board of review. Three years after *Clay,* Latimer now insisted that the code specifically sanctioned what Sutton sought to have proscribed. He argued that examination of earlier versions of American military law showed that—except in capital cases—where notice has been given to the other side in the litigation, a deposition "may be read in evidence." This well-established acceptance carried over into the UCMJ, which reiterated the same provision. Latimer held that due process privileges granted by Congress "had to be consider[ed] . . . in the light of any limitations set out in the Code. Surely we are seeking to place military justice on the same plane as civilian justice but we are powerless to do that in those instances where Congress has set out legally, clearly, and specifically a different level."

The judge noted further that the particular witness was in Korea, with the trial being held in California. To insist that the witness be returned in order to testify "might elevate the role of a witness to one of being a commercial tourist." Further, Latimer turned to the famous scholar on evidence, and a former member of the JAG Corps, John H. Wigmore. Cross-examination, Wigmore had written, is certainly a help to the tribunal hearing the case "if only it is available. But it is merely desirable. Where it cannot be obtained, the requirement ceases."

Finally, Latimer turned to the fact that "the right of an accused in all instances to be confronted by witnesses and the right of the Government to take depositions by written interrogatories are inconsistent." But rather than attempting to explore whether or not the Court could reconcile them under the code, he retreated into a dogmatic defense of the military viewpoint: "What may be desirable must give way to the absolute necessities of the services."

Early in June, Quinn wrote to his commissioner that Brosman "has serious doubts about the interrogatories." If so, Latimer must have convinced him otherwise. Of Latimer's opinion Brosman wrote that, while it "uses somewhat broader language than I would have selected, I concur generally in its terms, and warmly approve the result it reaches." It is possible that by 1954, given the JAG unrest about the Court and the code, Brosman and Latimer may have wanted to avoid finding a conflict between the code and the Sixth Amendment's confrontation clause. It was one thing to hold a military practice unconstitutional under the UCMJ. It was quite another to hold a portion of the code itself unconstitutional, and this from a new court that in some circles was not even considered to be a bona fide federal appellate tribunal.

Quinn, however, had no such hesitation. "I would be very reluctant," he wrote to his commissioner, "to indicate that we feel that men in the military service are deprived of the constitutional protections set forth in the 5th and 6th amendments, except in cases where the amendment itself excludes the protection." Sutton's conviction would have to be reversed "unless we admit the deposition. My view is that we should . . . forcibly assert the right of men in the military service to all constitutional guarantees not specifically excepted." If Brosman declined to accept this viewpoint, "then I desire to dissent and will proceed to prepare a dissent." And he did.

Quinn's position may be an example of his "hell yes, hell no" viewpoint discussed in an earlier chapter. "I have absolutely no doubt in my mind," he wrote, "that accused persons in the military service of the Nation are entitled to rights and privileges secured to all under the Constitution . . . unless excluded directly or by necessary implication." Quinn concluded that his brethren "would deny the accused the full measure of his constitutional right because of the mobility of potential witnesses in the military service. However, I cannot disregard a constitutional safeguard for reasons of expediency." Brosman appears to have been uncomfortable with his chief's claim of constitutional absolutism.

Quinn "has assumed the power to hold an act of Congress unconstitutional—at least in part. I say he has assumed this power, because he has not undertaken to demonstrate that we possess it. Perhaps he believes that the existence of such authority in the judges of this Court to be so evident as to dispense with exposition." The chief judge, complained Brosman, "is viewing the present problem with an eye single to one pan of the scales. Rather, I would urge a binocular approach here. . . . I find it genuinely difficult to understand why he will allow no place whatever to the claims of necessity, however pressing and however respectable."

In 1975, an anonymous writer of the official Army JAG Corps history observed that USCAAF "has felt its way carefully and, due to its small membership, the attitudes of individual judges have particularly affected its willingness to expand due process rights and grant relief." *Sutton* may well prove the point. The certainty of Latimer's conclusion was matched by Quinn's emphatic dissent. Brosman cast the deciding vote, and his term would expire in one year. Even though Quinn apparently supported Brosman's reappointment, with more than ten years left to serve, the former governor probably assumed that he would probably have another opportunity to reiterate his constitutional philosophy. He was correct.

CONTROVERSY OVER CHANGE

As 1954 passed into 1955, the future of the life tenure bill as well as the other suggested amendments to the UCMJ was doubtful—as was, still, USCAAF stature in the federal court hierarchy, and this in the third year of its history. The one thing that remained constant was JAG negativism toward the code and, by implication, the Court itself. Writing to Representative Philbin, Quinn insisted that "there would seem to be no good reason for refusing life tenure any longer. The resistance, if any, would undoubtedly come from the military establishment, which probably still resents the general idea of a *civilian* court acting as the court of last resort for the court martial system." A meeting between the JAGs and the judges only two days later illustrates the point.

The army JAG, Major General Eugene Caffey, called for expanding discretionary authority under nonjudicial punishment to allow commanders to award more than two weeks of confinement. He favored the use of bread and water as punishment and he recommended that military justice should be decentralized: "Do away with automatic review of death sentences." Rather, "power [should] be given to the convening authority in the field to carry out a death sentence without review at headquarters." Indeed, "speedy justice of this kind would prove to be an example to others." The "times have changed," noted Caffey, "and Congress may be receptive to his suggested amendments—in any event he feels it his duty to so advise . . . Congress."

For the air force, Harmon insisted that the JAG rather than appellate counsel should certify petitions to the Court. He "realize[d] that this suggestion would meet with criticism and also appreciate[d] the Court's reluctance to accept it." He "guarantee[d], however, . . . that it would still have a workload but that [his plan] would afford [the Court] more time to devote to the more important problems." Moreover, "if the [JAGs] abused their power, they would be subject to removal."

Latimer reiterated his opposition to any change in Court control of its docket. "He could not in good conscience appear before the Congress and support this provision which would, in effect, be an admission that the Court could not handle the job it had been assigned." Judges and JAGs should "build constructively within the existing framework of the Code rather than junking it as an unworkable law." Similarly, Brosman "could not see how the code committee could go to the Congress and suggest that we return to the old system within [only] three years after the enactment of the Code." As if to emphasize their differences, the JAGs and the judges agreed that, like the 1953 version, the 1954 report would have separate sections—"Joint Report–Court Report–Individual Service Reports."

Again, at the behest of Quinn, early in 1955 specific proposals for life tenure (and also expanding USCAAF to five judges) were introduced in Congress. Again, he communicated with various friends in Congress while Proulx labored to ensure that publicity favorable to the Court would be forthcoming. Again, the Court put forward the same arguments it had previously employed, often with only the date changed. And again, this time for Judge Brosman, Richard Tedrow prepared a comprehensive memorandum on the subject of life tenure. He concluded that "the military opposition to the Court, with or without life tenure, has been continuous." Whether such opposition to this latest measure "will be active or passive or indirect is not now known." The indirect approach—i.e., "we do not oppose it, but"—was, he recalled, used effectively against the 1953 proposal.

Proulx was also aware "that the latest attacks on the Code from various military quarters can cause a friend thereof to be concerned." He believed, however, that Congress would not restore the old system. "The point of no return was reached in 1950," with the passage of a comprehensive code. On the other hand, he wrote to a friend in the navy that "I know you will appreciate that the members of the Court will not engage in debate on this matter—but silence here is no indication of non-activity." Moreover, "the attacks have gone so far as to be looked upon as the best ammunition for the continuation of the Court and the Code. The sharper the criticism in some instances, the stronger the need for the Code."

By March 1955, the air force had become well versed in what Tedrow described as the "indirect approach" for opposition to life tenure. Its spokesman reiterated the point that "substantial doubt exists as to whether the Court accomplishes . . . the most effective appellate system possible in the administration of military justice." Until, therefore, "amendments are adopted, observed in action[,] and informed judgement made that the procedures as amended will function effectively in time of war and mobilization—only then can a determination on the life tenure feature be formulated." While waiting for responses from the army and navy, a delegation from the Court's civilian committee, along with Proulx, met with Deputy Attorney General Rogers, who had rejected the life tenure proposal in 1954. Proulx reported that this time Rogers would not object to the bill "should it be passed (this is very fine but it is the cart before the horse—actually we want the Department of Justice's approval prior to passage)."

Early in June, Proulx received word that "now the Navy has no objection on the five-man court or life tenure." The army, however, objected to USCAAF expansion. It also rejected life tenure if it was connected to "the freezing-in of the present incumbents." Like the navy, it did not object in principle to life tenure, leading Proulx to comment that "on the basis of present day affairs, I would peg this report as most favorable to the Court." For its part, the Defense Department saw no need for increasing the Court to five members and restated its support for life tenure "without infringing upon the power of the President to appoint by and with the advice of the Senate." Again, Quinn sensed the portent for postponement.

He informed Proulx that "I talked with Sen. Pastore and he is apparently waiting for Green to move. I told him time was running out. . . . He will go to [Senator Richard] Russell [chairman of the Senate Armed Services Committee] with Green if Green asks him to." Whether or not Pastore and Green visited with Russell is not clear. On June 21, Pastore talked with Majority Leader Lyndon Johnson and later the same day sent him a letter along with a Court-produced memorandum on the need for life tenure.

Aware of Johnson's influence, Pastore reminded the majority leader that Quinn, Latimer, and Brosman "have started from scratch. From the creation of the Court to the present time, they have decided well over six thousand cases . . . a phenomenal amount of work when you realize that these cases are indeed the precedents to be followed in the future." More important, "the present calibre of this Court is undisputed and I dare say unmatched. They have acted in a non-partisan fashion in the determination of all their cases." Even assuming that President Eisenhower would reappoint all three incumbents, "it is a matter of common principle . . . that this important judicial tribunal should have all the characteristics of our other important courts, namely, life tenure during good behavior." At this point, Pastore got down to the real reason for his letter: "I renew my appeal to you to urge our distinguished mutual friend, Dick Russell, to look favorably upon this legislation." Pastore admitted what Quinn had acknowledged—that unless and until Russell was willing to move, the bill would not. Neither did.

All during the summer, the bill awaited review by the Bureau of the Budget. Finally in November, word came to Proulx that the bureau had reported unfavorably on the bill. But by this time, the judges were concerned with another challenge that was indirectly linked to the matter of life tenure—Paul Brosman's future.

EXIT BROSMAN

The judge with the shortest term (ending on May 1, 1956) and holding a Democratic "slot," Brosman obviously understood what having a Republican president in office could mean. Very anxious for reappointment, Brosman apparently had the firm support of his brethren. One might expect a Republican to name one of his own party to Brosman's seat, giving the Republicans two of the three seats. Thus Quinn and Brosman, the two Democrats on the Court, were encouraged when Proulx reported on his meeting with Rogers, noted earlier: "Brosman's reappointment came up in the conversation and Mr. Rogers pointed out that the present administration has not allowed politics to enter into the judicial appointment picture in those cases where Democratic Judges have done a good job." Similarly, Senator Pastore also assumed that in the event that life tenure was enacted, "in all probability the present judges will be reappointed."

While the written record is scant, it is not unreasonable to assume that during the summer and fall of 1955, Brosman tried to gain support for his reappointment. Within the limits of his own keen sense of what was politically possible, Quinn helped where he could. Further, Brosman had the support of the Civilian Court Committee. Indeed, on December 20, he and Proulx traveled to New York to discuss the reappointment with some lawyers, possibly Whitney Seymour, the committee chairman. On December 21, Seymour wrote to Eisenhower's attorney general, Herbert Brownell Jr. By coincidence, most of the committee members were Republicans, "but we are unanimous in the view that Judge Brosman should be reappointed and that political considerations should not interfere with the continued service of the present Court team which has been so notable." Seymour reminded Brownell that in the earlier meeting with Rogers, "we emphasized the importance of Judge Brosman's reappointment, along with the desirability of ultimate life tenure for members of this Court."

We will never know whether Brosman would have been reappointed. Because his term did not expire until May 1, 1956, it is possible that no decision had been reached when Seymour drafted his endorsement. But his letter did Brosman no good. On December 21 (the day Seymour wrote), shortly after lunching with two of his staff the judge "complained of a pain near his heart and in his arm." A physician was summoned immediately from a nearby government building, but "before the doctor arrived within a few minutes, he was beyond medical attention."

Arthur Sutherland, professor of law at Harvard and a member of the Court Committee, well expressed the sense of shock that engulfed the Court community. He wrote to Quinn that if Brosman "had been twenty years older, such a sudden and easy end would not be so bad. But it is hard to see a man with whom we all spent such a happy day last week, suddenly laid low, comparatively young, with years of great usefulness ahead." Quinn in a note to Seymour added that Brosman "had the affection and esteem of everyone attached to this Court." Writing an official letter to the president, the chief judge called his late colleague "a fine man. He discharged his judicial obligations with unremitting energy, with dignity, and with fairness and devotion to the cause of justice."

The Court honored Paul Brosman during a brief but poignant memorial tribute on February 15, 1956. Brosman, recalled his chief, "was loved by every man and woman connected with this Court. He loved people, and was loved, and respected in return. He was a happy soul. He enjoyed life. He radiated cheerfulness, and he generated affection." He "was no respecter of rank. He was just as gracious to the most inconsequential shavetail as he would be to the most famous lawyer in the nation. He loved justice and struggled hard to attain it with both word and pen." The three JAGs also spoke briefly. But rereading the tributes in the light of half a century, the words of Frederick Wiener, speaking for the Judge Advocates' Association, remain especially apt.

As a member of the association, Wiener remembered, "we felt the glow of his outgoing personality; and we grieve now that his zest and sparkle are gone, leaving so much the losers those of us who remain." Brosman had consistently insisted that "the service lawyer's obligation is quite as rigid as that of his civilian brother." In his quest for the synthesis between "the lawyer's reason and the soldier's faith," Brosman's efforts were "unexpectedly cut short. Yet who, when the end comes, would not wish to be taken otherwise—without pain, without lingering, and at the height of one's powers? And so, in [Justice] Holmes' fine phrase, 'we end not with sorrow at the inevitable loss, but with the contagion of his courage, and with a kind of desperate joy we go back to the fight.' "

Paul Brosman's unexpected death came at an important time in USCAAF history. There was the obvious sense of loss, heightened by the suddeness of his passing. But his demise also created a sort of juridical void in that Brosman had tended to function as a pivot between Quinn and Latimer, both of whom on occasion took opposite sides of a judicial issue with an identical sense of certainty. More often than they, Brosman seems to have pondered—perhaps even struggled—to reach an outcome he felt warranted by the record. Finally, his death took from the Court a jurist who possessed personal charm and grace as well as the ability to remain on friendly terms with the JAGs even as they battled over divisive issues. With life tenure still only a dream, with Congress about to consider UCMJ revisions, some of which the judges believed quite harmful to the Court, with JAG criticism increasing in pitch, with uncertainty regarding the new appointment to the Court, Proulx was not guilty of understatement when he wrote of Brosman that "we certainly are going to miss him around here."

16

New Judge, Old Issues, Same Forum, 1955–1956

The extent of the disagreements between USCAAF and the judge advocate generals became even more evident with publication of the annual report for 1954, not distributed until May 1955. The judges and the JAGs could only agree to join in a very brief report of less than two pages, acknowledging that because "reconciliation of the different concepts has not been attained, the respective military departments have proposed their individually desired recommendations." The rest of the report consisted of a number of disparate sections, including not only the original seventeen recommendations but also drafts of two sets of UCMJ amendments separately urged by the navy and the air force. Although both retained the certification requirement for USCAAF review, there were substantial differences between the two versions.

The navy would have required defense counsel rather than the JAG himself to certify justification for USCAAF appeal. Moreover, it proposed reduction of the time limit for appeal from thirty days to ten. The air force pointed to what it claimed was a need to "lighten the work load of [the Court] and to eliminate excessive and frivolous appeals . . . [which result in] unnecessary waste of time, money and manpower with no benefit to an accused's substantial rights." Its version restored JAG authority to certify for a review but added an interesting twist, possibly as a result of USCAAF opposition already known to air force JAG Reginald Harmon.

Harmon called for the creation of a judicial appeals board to be set up within the JAG office, to consist of at least three officers above the rank of lieutenant colonel or commander who have "at least ten years legal experience, and who are members of the bar of a Federal Court or of the highest court of a State." (These requirements in terms of legal training went beyond those mandated by USCAAF for admission to its bar.) This panel would first consider all appeals for USCAAF review. If it unanimously agreed that the accused had not shown good cause for appeal from a board of review decision, no appeal would be allowed. If, however, there was no unanimity—even if a majority found no justification—the JAG was required to issue the certificate of cause and forward the case to USCAAF, which in turn would decide whether or not to grant review.

In that it apparently modified the JAG's absolute right to grant or not grant certification for USCAAF review that he had first proposed, Harmon's proposal had a superficial plausibility about it. On the other hand, it kept the appeals process insulated within the JAG office, contained no provision for civilians on his new judicial appeals board, and in no way guaranteed a defendant's right of appeal to the civilian court created by Congress. Harmon insisted that it would eliminate all those frivolous appeals, apparently so troublesome to the JAGs if not the judges, but at the same time would also "still guarantee an accused the right to appeal from the decision of the Board of Review." Despite such insistence, Harmon's proposal was nothing more than a transparent attempt to undercut civilian review.

By January 1956, with a new session of Congress under way, USCAAF had been informed that hearings on the proposed amendments to the UCMJ—first submitted by the Defense Department almost two years before—were to be scheduled. Seven years had passed since the House Armed Services Committee considered the new code. In those first hearings, the department had spoken on behalf of the military establishment. The fact that the armed services were less than enthusiastic about a uniform code had concerned but not controlled Larkin's efforts. This sense of single-minded purpose obvious in 1949 seems to have been lacking in 1956. Quinn and Latimer were justifiably concerned about what the hearings might produce.

The JAGs and the judges were not in full agreement, and the bill reflected this discord. The Court believed that some of the suggested changes went too far, while the JAGs desired to go further. Alfred Proulx observed that while all parties had agreed to support the original seventeen recommendations, "each JAG reserve[d] the right to plug for his individual amendments, if called upon to testify." But Proulx could not believe "that the uniformity of the Code would be sacrificed by allowing each JAG to pull away separately." Because they were not united, "their individual efforts will not succeed." On the other hand, the JAGs were united in their support of the proposed bill.

Their endorsement together with another factor contributed to USCAAF uneasiness. In their earlier efforts to gain life tenure as well as legislative enactment of the original seventeen amendments to the code, the judges had felt in control of their causes. They had drafted the tenure bill and lobbied for its passage; they had convened a committee that had considered and—in concert if not total harmony with the JAGs—recommended the new changes. But the legislation soon to be examined by the House Armed Services Committee came from the Defense Department at the behest of the navy, with the judges relegated to the position of any interested party—merely afforded the right to appear and be heard.

Writing to Judge Latimer as the hearings were about to begin, Tedrow was both perceptive and candid. He reminded Latimer that the UCMJ required not only regular consultation between the judges and the JAGs in the form of the code committee on the state of military justice but also a written annual report to Congress. And indeed, this code committee had reached consensus on seventeen proposed changes. But the legislation as submitted contained amendments, added with neither Court input nor endorsement. Thus, the judges were "forced to question that the present unilateral . . . Defense Bill can be construed" as a product of such consultation. Moreover, the bill itself "was never referred to the Court by the Department of Defense." Possibly with intentional understatement, Tedrow observed that "the Court has some difficulty with the positions of the Judge Advocates General who have apparently favored conflicting recommendations as appear from a comparison of the present Bill with the . . . Annual Report[s]." Unlike the earlier era of Felix Larkin, it seemed that USCAAF could no longer count, as it were, on having a friend at court.

A third reason for the Court's concern lay in the fact that its newest member was scheduled to take his seat on the bench even as the hearings commenced. Although Homer Ferguson chose not to testify before the committee, his appointment to the Court had the potential for a dramatic change in its future direction. Who was Homer Ferguson, and how had he come to USCAAF?

FERGUSON AND THE FRUITS OF DEFEAT

In 1954 Homer Ferguson, Republican senator from Michigan, was nearing the end of his second term. As a young lawyer, Ferguson gained public attention when he functioned as a one-man grand jury, investigating local corruption. While senator, he had served on the committee investigating the Japanese attack on Pearl Harbor—an experience, according to one correspondent, that left him "unawed by the military." During his second term, his senatorial career had been characterized by consistent and important support for President Eisenhower's domestic programs. Conservative and capable, if undistinguished, Homer Ferguson had also played a dominant role in amending the pledge of allegiance to include the words "under God." Such was the man who ran for a third term in November 1954.

As early as April 1953, Eisenhower was aware that Ferguson faced an extremely difficult campaign. During a cabinet meeting, the postmaster general warned that "we've simply got to be thinking of ways to help Ferguson. Give him a good bill to carry in the Senate. Or something." On September 9, 1954, the president was urged to visit Michigan during the campaign "to insure Sen. Ferguson's victory." Eisenhower's key aide, Sherman Adams, responded that "the President is well advised of the situation in Michigan . . . and will do all he possibly can within the limitations of time and energy to insure Homer's election." Eisenhower did visit Michigan, but to no avail. The result, although close, revealed the author of the patriotic "under God" to have been a political underdog.

A few days after the election, Secretary of State John Foster Dulles reported to Eisenhower that Ferguson "had been in." Dulles and the defeated senator "agreed that he would like a diplomatic appointment. The Pres. is looking for a judicial post. The Sec. said F. would like a Circuit Court of Appeals, but not a district." Dulles "suggested sending him to Belgium" and observed that the current ambassador—a Michigan native—"has not worked out too well." Eisenhower responded that Dulles "should do as he pleases."

A month later, Dulles and Sherman Adams discussed Ferguson's career alternatives. A former governor of New Hampshire, Adams functioned as Eisenhower's chief of staff, although that title apparently had not yet come into vogue within the White House. Adams indicated that the former senator could accept an appointment on the Civil Aeronautics Board (CAB). "A. suggested that he take the CAB for a couple of years and he would try to get him on the Court of Appeals." Dulles again referred to the possibility of sending Ferguson to Belgium. He then "asked if A. thought F. would take a post like the Philippines. A. said he might as this is just a stopgap. He [Ferguson] is calling the turn pretty arbitrarily. He wants this post but wants the Court of Appeals when there is a vacancy. A. thinks he should stay here and we should stand up to him to get him to take the CAB. A. has told the Pres. about this. The Sec. said that he wouldn't mind offering him the Philippines."

Early in January, Dulles informed Adams that there is "nothing new on Ferguson. Adams said we should just sit quiet and let him come around." Later that month, Dulles informed Adams that Eisenhower approved Ferguson's posting to the Philippines. However, since then Dulles "heard [that Secretary of Commerce Sinclair] Weeks is planning to ask him to be Under Secretary of Commerce for transportation. The Sec. would prefer that." Within twenty-four hours, however, Adams told Dulles that he was prepared "to sign off on Ferguson," who "wants to go to the Philippines. The Sec. thinks Mrs. F is [in] back of it." On March 11, Ferguson's ambassadorial appointment was announced.

Thus, at least four different posts for the defeated senator had been discussed within Eisenhower's administration, and while a federal appeals court position had been mentioned for Ferguson, it apparently was not the Court of Military Appeals. On the other hand, Eisenhower's administration was well aware that Brosman's term was to expire on May 1, 1956. As early as June 30, 1955, one presidential assistant—Bryce Harlow—noted that Democratic senator Walter George "is very desirous" that Brosman "be reappointed." A few weeks later Edward Tait, special assistant to the president, wrote to Judge John Minor Wisdom acknowledging Wisdom's enthusiastic endorsement of Brosman for reappointment.

Finally, Tait's office informed yet another of Eisenhower's assistants that "there have been no appointments made to the U.S. Court of Military Appeals by this Administration. The office of the General Counsel of the Department of Defense is primarily interested in any appointment to this Court. Recommendations should be submitted to the Secretary of Defense who then refers them to the office of the General Counsel." (Throughout USCAAF's history, this "procedure" for filling Court vacancies has never been consistently followed. Occasionally, the general counsel's office has been involved in selecting the judges. On numerous occasions, it has not.) This undeniable evidence of awareness concerning the USCAAF vacancy is noteworthy because at the time of his senatorial defeat, Ferguson received no apparent consideration within Eisenhower's inner circle as a possible successor to Brosman. In the meantime, Ferguson headed for Manila, USCAAF continued, and Brosman sought his renomination even as others saw themselves as his replacement.

Brosman's unexpected death removed whatever advantage the incumbent might have had and probably caused many more applicants to seek the post. Less than two weeks after the judge's death, Proulx wrote to a friend that "there are many rumors flying as to who will be nominated. . . . [W]e do know that the number of candidates for the position is increasing daily." A former commissioner was an applicant and also "Dick Tedrow is in there pitching. . . . Bob Smart is an avowed candidate and apparently he has very good backing."

One of Tedrow's pitches went to Maryland governor Theodore McKeldin, to whom he wrote one week after Brosman's death. "I am, of course, a Republican," he emphasized, and "I believe I am considered somewhat of an authority on military law." Tedrow further noted that "Chief Judge Quinn . . . will also recommend me for the vacancy insofar as he can do so with propriety." He "did not know when the vacancy will be filled but I understand it is a matter of some urgency due to the fact that the two existing members of the Court will have some difficulty in operating without a full bench." McKeldin promptly forwarded Tedrow's letter to Sherman Adams without his specific endorsement, stating merely that "I am sure that Mr. Tedrow . . . would be most appreciative of any consideration given him for such a position."

Meanwhile, members of the White House staff assembled basic information about the various candidates for appointment. A January 5 memorandum listed about a dozen names including the former Court commissioner, Francis Tappaan, the current chief commissioner, Richard Tedrow, and Robert Smart, still with the House Armed Services Committee. Smart apparently was supported by one of its Republican members, Dewey Short. One name, however, was not on the list, and its omission is noteworthy. Writing to Quinn a day later, Proulx reported that "for some reason Judge Latimer feels that Senator Ferguson is the strongest candidate." It remains unclear what information contributed to Latimer's conclusion, but he was correct.

The day before Proulx wrote to Quinn, Charles Wilson, Eisenhower's secretary of defense and an old acquaintance of Ferguson, spoke with Dulles.

"Homer Ferguson would make a good judge. W. wondered how the Sec. thought he was getting on where he is and whether it would be good to consider him for the appointment." Dulles replied that the move "might be worth thinking about. The Sec. does not think he is terribly happy there, and his wife has not been well." Dulles recalled that Ferguson had "wanted a judicial appt. at the time but nothing vacant. W. thought he could put his name in the hat if the Sec. thought it all right."

On the following day, Dulles conferred with both Wilson and Adams. He told Wilson that "he thinks well of the suggestion about Ferguson. He is doing well . . . and the Sec. thinks that he would probably like it and be good at it." A few hours later, Dulles called Sherman Adams about the Ferguson appointment. He had "checked with his people and as far as we are concerned, we would be happy to see him take it. He is doing all right but is not exactly a star of the first magnitude yet and his wife has been sick most of the time." Adams responded that "they will support it if that is what the Sec. wants." Wilson called Dulles again on January 10. "Has the Sec. found out if [Ferguson] wants it? The Sec. thinks he would. He talked with Adams and the Pres. and the Pres. thought it a good move. W. said the thing to do is to contact Ferguson" and asked Dulles "to sound him out."

Whereupon Dulles wrote an "eyes only" letter to Ferguson: "Charlie Wilson . . . is anxious to have you appointed to this Court. . . . I told Charlie that I would, of course, pass this information on to you right away. I do so with very mixed feelings. On the one hand, I am pleased (but not surprised) that such a possibility is available to you. On the other . . . I would be distressed to lose you from this post." Dulles realized that "because of the nature and importance of this Judgeship . . . you may wish to consider this matter rather carefully before giving us a reply." Asking that Ferguson give him and Wilson "an indication of your thinking in this matter" as soon as possible, Dulles commented of his cabinet colleague that "I need hardly add that our community of interests stops here. He shall be hoping for one reply and I another."

Ferguson cannot have deliberated very long. On January 18, he called Dulles at 6:30 in the morning "to say he would be glad to accept the judicial appointment but he didn't want to do it until April." Ferguson was concerned, however, "that he might not be confirmed for the full fifteen year term, as the Democrats would be able to block the confirmation and stall for the remainder of the year in the hopes that next year they would be able to fill the job with a Democrat." Ferguson's fears turned out to be groundless in part because of traditional senatorial support for one of their own (the Senate committee did not even request Ferguson to appear before it), to say nothing of Eisenhower's triumphant reelection in November 1956.

By this date, the inevitable rumors were beginning to circulate within Washington. On January 24, Proulx wrote to a member of the Court Committee that "the list of candidates is growing daily with the latest rumor . . . to the effect that the White House has made a commitment and that . . . Ferguson . . . [is] the man selected." Two days later he could not be much more specific on the subject to the chief judge. "I had thought," he wrote to Quinn, that by this date "there would be definite word on the appointment emerging from this mass of rumors and counter rumors." Latimer "is now convinced that Ferguson is the man . . . [and] for the sake of betting, I accepted one from Judge Latimer—a luncheon at the new Courthouse—he says Senator Ferguson, and I have the field." Proulx added that "I did learn that Senator Ferguson was Secretary Wilson's idea."

If Drew Pearson claimed to have uncovered the "inside scoop" about Truman's three choices for the USCAAF bench, Westbrook Pegler made the same assertion for Eisenhower's lone appointment. Noting, correctly, that Ferguson had provided essential support for the president in issues involving Senator Joseph McCarthy as well as the Bricker Amendment (a proposal that would have restricted presidential authority to conduct foreign policy), Pegler insisted that when Ferguson lost his Senate seat, "if there was any gratitude in Ike and the eastern claque which belittles the sovereignty of the United States and berates McCarthy for his 'methods,' he had little to worry about." The ambassadorship was "a stop-gap measure." Such positions usually "cost the occupant more than they pay and it was obvious that Ferguson couldn't last long." Instead, Eisenhower named him to USCAAF, "a soft spot for $25,000 a year. . . . The Court sits in Washington where Ferguson is really at home and Mrs. Ferguson knows her way to the supermarket, the movies and church."

Quinn and Proulx were both acquainted with the new judge, although Ferguson's personal experience with the Court may have been based on a very brief appearance by Quinn before the Senate appropriations subcommittee in June 1953. Ferguson had chaired the hearing, and his few questions were succinct, if not superficial. Proulx assured his chief that he would try "to learn how the Senator operated while he was on the Hill." In the meantime, the chairman of the Court Committee wrote that "Ferguson will be a valuable addition to the Court, particularly in its relations to Congress."

But his value would be based on his presence, and the new judge seemed in no hurry to return to Washington. Although unanimously confirmed on February 17, Ferguson indicated that he would not be available until the latter part of March because he wished to remain in the Philippines until after Dulles's long scheduled visit. Finally, the State Department informed Proulx that Ferguson "expects to arrive in Washington during the fourth week of March. . . . Judge Latimer had been on edge until this call came in for he was contemplating wiring him asking when he would be on the scene—he thinks the Senator is displaying very little interest in his new position."

Latimer and Ferguson would serve together for the next five years (all that remained of Latimer's term), and as will be seen, Latimer occasionally found himself at odds with Ferguson's interpretation both of the UCMJ and the role of the Court in its administration. Before his appointment expired, Latimer's dissents increased in number as well as stridency of tone. There may well have been another aspect to their relationship, however, besides doctrinal divergence. Latimer's son recalls that his father believed Ferguson to have been a "political hack" and as such, "a dismal choice for the position."

Quinn, on the other hand, enjoyed his new colleague. More than Latimer, Ferguson shared Quinn's conviction that involvement by officers of high military rank in no way implied superior military justice. Both men were "old-time" politicians, and both had held important elected office. Possibly because both had suffered from the exigencies of the electorate, Ferguson and Quinn remained very sympathetic whenever possible to the numerous requests for nonjudicial assistance they received as judges. Even before he arrived, Ferguson's past experiences indicated that he had more in common with Quinn than with Latimer.

A CONGRESSIONAL COMMITTEE REVISITS THE CODE

Although the primary purpose of the hearings before the House Armed Services Subcommittee was to consider the Defense Department omnibus bill, other interests lurked beneath the stated agenda. Judges Quinn and Latimer continued to push their life tenure proposal either as part of the omnibus bill or as a separate statute. While the proposed DOD legislation included the seventeen recommendations for changes that had been suggested three years before, Alfred Proulx observed that "each JAG has been plugging for individual items and the hearings might spill over into their respective areas." Realizing that the UCMJ would not be subject to extensive congressional revision, the service representatives instead elected to accentuate the positive about its effect—to offer constructive legislation that would make the overall statute even better. This strategy also included avoiding direct criticism of USCAAF while at the same time attacking specific provisions under which the Court operated.

In addition, spokesmen for services emphasized the importance of Congress in reforming military justice. Sometimes this tendency toward flattery verged on fawning. Thus, Vice Admiral J. L. Holloway said to one subcommittee member that "of course, . . . there is no one who leans more heavily upon the counsel of the Congress and the law than I do." The UCMJ "as it stands is a fine piece of legislation. It represents the synthesis and thinking of very devoted people." Holloway served as chief of naval personnel.

The first witness to appear before the committee, Assistant Secretary of the Navy Albert Pratt, argued that while the code provisions "to safeguard the individual are, for the most part, entirely proper and fine . . . [t]he complications of review have slowed the process of justice, which is always a disadvantage, and they have increased the administrative burdens in the number of people who are, in a sense, not productively employed. That has to be balanced against all the greater rights given to the individual." Vice Admiral Holloway specified what Pratt had suggested. The UCMJ "has not only hamstrung the commanding officer with administrative minutiae, but it has weakened his historic role . . . that of a wise, just, fatherly mentor, quick to punish the sinners and equally quick to help a man redeem himself and start afresh." (It would seem, given his rhetoric, that Holloway was not familiar with the celebrated 1842 incident involving Alexander Mackenzie, the commander of the U.S. Navy brig *Somers*. While at sea, Mackenzie ordered the execution of three young officers, including the son of the secretary of war. See Chapter 2.) Procedures mandated by the code have been carried out, "but with excessive delay and at a great unnecessary cost in man hours."

Holloway reminded the subcommittee that his service was neither a judicial nor a law enforcement agency. It, like the other branches of the armed services, existed "solely to provide an adequate national defense." And "when the procedures of courts-martial and other related legal matters become so cumbersome that officers must neglect . . . primary duties . . . then it is time that we take action to change the system." Such was the purpose of the measure under consideration, one drafted "without reducing in the smallest amount the features of the [UCMJ] that protect the rights of individuals."

The navy JAG, Admiral Ira Nunn (possibly regarded by Quinn as the nemesis of his premises), reminded the subcommittee that—unlike a civilian criminal code—the UCMJ "must not only maintain a good social order but we must foster and produce a dedicated fighting spirit." Like Holloway before him, Nunn insisted that "not many of these proposed changes have great significance. In fact, they are very mild, it seems to me." Nunn then summarized the key amendments but omitted any mention or description of the proposed requirement of certification by counsel as a condition for appeal to USCAAF. After two days of hearings, Tedrow reported to Latimer that "no witness has as yet criticized the Court in any way. Once or twice they were cornered and had to praise the Code and the Court." The attitude of the subcommittee, he felt, "continues to be pro-accused, pro-Code and suspicious of the military."

The awareness by military witnesses of this tendency may explain why they sought to minimize their differences with the judges. Thus, General Albert Kuhfeld, the air force deputy JAG, told the subcommittee that "this entire bill was worked out during conferences with [the Code] committee[,] and practically all of the provisions, all of the changes suggested, were approved by the three Judge Advocates General and the members of the Court." Here, Kuhfeld was disingenuous if not actually dishonest. In no way did the USCAAF judges accept, let alone approve, any version of the certificate requirement even though it had been modified in a vain attempt to mitigate their opposition. Both Quinn and Latimer were prepared to make their views very clear, but the subcommittee recessed the hearings for nearly a month, and they did not resume until April 16. Quinn and

Latimer testified on April 18, with Ferguson in attendance as an interested observer.

The chief judge did not mince words in his condemnation of the proposed legislation, submitted by the Defense Department at the behest of the navy: "It contains provisions which cannot be justified by experience, reason, or logic[,]" including "some proposed amendments which were either rejected by the Court members of the [Code] committee" or were not even presented to it for consideration. Of those that were presented, the worst, of course, was the certification requirement.

"This proposed change is so hostile to the spirit and intent of the code that I most earnestly oppose its adoption. It reads innocuously but it requires that an accused obtain a certificate of probable cause from counsel before the Court must consider his petition for a grant of review." The result of this amendment "is to return control of military justice to the armed services[,] for under its provisions they can prevent the flow of all but a relatively few cases to the court." Quinn reminded the subcommittee that 97 percent of the appeals coming to USCAAF were handled by military lawyers assigned by the JAGs: "If appellate processes can be controlled by the military, a good deal of the Court's influence can be eliminated." Lurking in the innocent words of the section "is the possibility that the services will choose the cases they desire to be heard."

Judge Latimer echoed the views of his colleague. The certification proposal represented the area where the two judges "clash head on with the services." Indeed, "if you want to render us impotent, and deny us the right to hear cases, that is the area in which you can do it. If the services can tell us what cases we can hear, those they do not want us to hear are not going to get to us." Latimer did "not know of any reason in the world why any man in the service should be denied the right to reach our court." As to the military's claim that USCAAF had to be protected from frivolous appeals, "let me worry about our workload." The JAGs, he added, "seem to take a deep interest in our postulated inability to perform. In my judgment . . . if the system fails to function properly . . . it will be because of difficulties encountered at the trial level or within the Services, not at the level of this Court."

The JAGs had modified the language of their certificate proposal, ostensibly to meet judicial objections. Nevertheless, every civilian who testified during the hearings condemned the certification proposal. The question can be raised as to exactly what the 1956 draft stated and whether or not the censure visited upon it by the USCAAF judges in particular was still warranted. The suggested amendment would have changed one category of USCAAF review as follows:

> All cases reviewed by a board of review in which upon petition of the accused and on good cause shown, the Court of Military Appeals has granted a review: but the Court must consider a petition for a grant of

review only if (A) counsel who represented the accused at his trial or before the board of review, (B) appellate defense counsel appointed by the Judge Advocate General if the accused was not represented by counsel before the board of review, or (C) civilian counsel retained by the accused, certifies that in his opinion a substantial question of law is presented and that the appeal is made in good faith.

It would seem from an examination of this language that USCAAF *must* review a case only under conditions set forth above as A, B, and C. However, the provision does not appear to alter the Court's ability to choose what it *may* hear as apart from what it *must* hear. If so, one wonders why Quinn and Latimer were so perturbed. Indeed, a spokesman for the Navy JAG Corps emphasized this point in a statement delivered to the subcommittee after the hearings had ended. It really was a rebuttal to all the negative comments, submitted by the service that was the moving force behind the proposed legislation.

There was no attempt to vitiate and circumscribe

the present power of the Court . . . and the proposal as drafted in fact would not permit such a result. The right of the accused to petition remains unchanged and the Court may consider any petition. [The amendment provides] that only in those cases wherein counsel certifies that a substantial question of law is presented and that the appeal is made in good faith is the consideration by the court mandatory. There is nothing in the language to prevent the court from reviewing every petition of an accused . . . should it determine to do so. Under these circumstances, it is difficult to see how this proposal can be characterized as an attempt to vitiate the present power of the court. . . . No such limitation on the present power of the Court was intended or in fact provided[,] but this point could easily be clarified by the addition of any language which is considered necessary.

Whatever the JAGs' original intent was in submitting this amendment, however they may have sought to explain, if not justify, their proposal, the judges would have none of it. On this issue, the JAGs and the judges appeared to be talking past each other. But Quinn had other matters on his mind besides certification. One was the issue of frivolous appeals, apparently of great concern to the JAGs. "We can," he insisted, "very easily take care of them under our rules." When one considered that some 33 percent of the cases involving errors, which were the basis for a grant of relief or reversal, "were errors never found by the services or by counsel for the Government or the defense, but were picked up by our law secretaries and commissioners, [it] seems to me that the court has nothing to worry about as far as frivolous appeals are concerned."

One of the witnesses before the subcommittee was John Finn, a lawyer and former navy JAG officer, who had previously testified in 1949 on behalf of the American Legion. He did so again seven years later and strongly urged that Congress postpone action on the UCMJ because, as he put it, "there are, frankly, many amendments to the code which we believe this committee should consider before it takes up a bill of this kind." Finn further informed Congressman Brooks that the American Legion itself was about to hold hearings on the state of military justice and the UCMJ, and to hear from a large number of witnesses whom it had invited to appear—including the three service JAGs and the judges of USCAAF. He asked that the legion be given an opportunity to appear again before the subcommittee after its own hearings, which were scheduled for the first week in May.

Finn also observed that the UCMJ had not been "in operation [for] a sufficient length of time to be the subject of amendment at this juncture." Moreover, it was not the code but rather the Manual for Courts-Martial (MCM), drafted by the military, that represented "the real difficulty." The MCM stood in relation to the code much as statutes stand in relation to the federal Constitution. It was (and still is) supposed to provide the specific rules and regulations under which the general precepts of the code are to be carried out. From a fairly concise volume rewritten in 1951, the MCM has expanded into what the late Frederick Wiener aptly decribed as "a literally monstrous book" that was three inches thick and weighed some five pounds. For Wiener, its "bulk and complexity" typified the "labyrinthine quagmire" in which he believed operation of the UCMJ is "currently entangled." (Without necessarily accepting his conclusion, this author readily agrees with Wiener's description of the MCM.) According to Finn, "if one were trying to sabotage the [UCMJ], one could not have devised a more artful or better means for so doing than is provided by the manual." It needed "amendment at this time far more than does the Code."

Although Brooks assured him that there would be no objection to "carrying the bill over" until after the American Legion's hearing, in fact the subcommittee adjourned on April 20 and apparently did not reconvene to hear from the legion. Later, in August, Proulx wrote that Congress had "adjourned without taking any action on the . . . Code." Indeed, "as a matter of fact, the House . . . Subcommittee never reported out the bill." With national elections imminent, adjournment, not amendment, took priority. The American Legion, however, did hold its hearings in May 1956, and a number of witnesses— including Judges Quinn and Latimer as well as Tedrow—appeared before it. Although all three JAGs were invited, only Air Force JAG Reginald Harmon and his assistant accepted the invitation. Some of the testimony offered warrants brief comment.

THE AMERICAN LEGION AND ITS PROPOSED REFORMS

In terms of political issues, it is an understatement to note that the American Legion is not regarded as liberal in outlook. Thus it is noteworthy that, in support for expansion of the UCMJ and the role of USCAAF in military justice, the legion was in the forefront of those groups that sought greater protection for members of the military in military justice matters, usually at the expense of its commanders' authority. Nor was this "progressive" outlook new. During the 1949 hearings that led to the code's adoption, Franklin Riter had testified on behalf of the legion and suggested among other things that command influence be listed as a federal crime, punishable in federal courts. Congress, however, has yet to make command influence a federal offense, and as Francis A. Gilligan and Frederic I. Lederer have noted, the UCMJ provision dealing with it has been ineffective. Justifiably concerned with the detrimental results that command influence has on military justice, with some regularity USCAAF has railed against it. On the other hand, as an appellate tribunal, the Court is ill-equipped to go after commanders who are guilty of the practice. It can and sometimes does mitigate the results, but can do little to punish its perpetrators.

Some witnesses who had not appeared before the House subcommittee contributed to the hearings, chaired by Franklin Riter. One witness—a former member of the Hoover Commission, Henry Shine Jr.—indirectly pointed to *the* critical problem in military justice. He spoke in terms of the navy, but his point applies to the entire military system, and it is as valid today as half a century ago. Commanders, he observed, find it difficult to accept the fact that a JAG officer has a dual responsibility, one side of which may be incompatible with the other. He must be a good officer under the chain of command, with all that the term implies, but at the same time must be professionally responsible as an attorney to be sure that the best possible justice and legal service are accorded to the accused in military justice affairs. Easier to articulate than assimilate, Shine's views raise a crucial issue. To the extent that military justice is scarred by the corrosive forces of rank and accompanying privilege, it has a built-in potential for failure. On the other hand, the military world cannot function without the dual forces of rank and discipline.

Ralph Boyd, who had been a member of the first civilian Court Committee appointed by Quinn, stated that the biggest problem in the services is "the ability to recognize where discipline leaves off and where justice should step in." Another witness, a member of the Reserve Officers Association, described certain military commanders as so narrow minded that "a mosquito could land on their nose and pick out both eyeballs without moving."

Former JAG officer Frederick Wiener offered his views to the committee. Five years after USCAAF had started operations, Wiener had changed his mind on some issues about which he spoken during the 1949 hearings on the UCMJ. Originally, he had strongly condemned removing the law officer as a member of the Court. Now, "I have completely changed my mind on that. I think the law officer should stay outside the court room." Like Riter, he felt that the role of the Court president had become obsolete. While Wiener still had "grave doubts about the Court," he concluded that USCAAF "has been a salutary influence" and that it "must be retained." Wiener's reaction to the certification proposal was typical of the man: unhesitating and forceful. The amendment was "vicious. I am unalterably opposed to it."

The committee appointed by the American Legion to study military justice, the UCMJ, and USCAAF submitted its report in September 1956. The Court had already received a sort of preview, possibly prepared by Tedrow. According to the memorandum, "needless to say, the military is and has been determinedly opposed to the Code, and particularly to the Court of Military Appeals." The JAGs had joined the Court "in approving a lesser number of suggested changes." But when the judges rejected other amendments, the military "in effect abrogated its agreement with the Court, and proceeded independently to sponsor the bill" through the DOD. Yet this conduct represented only a symptom of the underlying issues.

> The attacks on the Code, but actually it is the Court, have been continuous and are now increasing in tempo. All the Services are parties to this. When I say Services, I generally mean the Judge Advocates General as almost all attacks are made by them or inspired by them. . . . [T]he real object of the criticism, although they will not say so, is the civilian court that acts as a watchdog over the military and has the final say in exercising the control that formerly was the personal possession of the Judge Advocates General, and often abused by them. The JAGs resent the loss of this power. By way of substitute they make two basic claims: (1) that the Code is too expensive (meaning the Court); and (2) that it involves too much delay.

The Legion Committee report covered more than fifty pages, with one section devoted to USCAAF: "The movement to take the Court out of existence or to emasculate the Code to the extent that it would no longer be workable is probably much more deeply rooted in certain branches of the Armed Forces, than was realized by this Committee." Further, "we conclude . . . that the Armed Forces have definitely determined to abolish the Court of Military Appeals, or to so minimize its effectiveness that it would merely be a rubber stamp for the Military." This tribunal "is the most salutary advancement ever made in the field of military law."

Homer Ferguson had observed the House subcommittee hearings but participated neither in them nor in the sessions held by the legion. He cannot, however, have been unaware of the comments offered concerning the tribunal he had now joined. His presence, according to the legion, led to the hope that "time will congeal the legal rationale of the Judges . . . and that further years of experience with the Code will furnish decisions which are less likely to raise objections." The accuracy of this prediction remained to be seen.

17

Jurists Disagree, Congress Delays, a Judge Departs, 1957–1961

The period of Court history discussed in this chapter reveals several developments that often occurred simultaneously. An obvious realignment of judges
took place, with significant results for military appellate justice. Examination
of numerous USCAAF decisions during the first five years of the Court's history indicates a sense of common purpose among its first three judges. Perhaps
because they had been together from the earliest beginnings of the Court, and
possibly because they tended to seek consensus as they interpreted the UCMJ,
for the most part disagreements between Brosman, Quinn, and Latimer were
couched in relatively cool language. Dissents were concerned more with specific means to reach the goals mandated by the UCMJ than with the end results.
Further, while uncomfortable with Quinn's frequent absences from Washington, Latimer had accustomed himself to them—possibly because of his very
frequent contacts with Brosman, his neighbor as well as colleague.

All this shifted with Brosman's unexpected death in December 1955 and
the appointment of a new judge. Homer Ferguson's arrival brought subtle but
profound changes to the pattern of decision making as well as to the interrela-
tionship among the three jurists, a transition not made any easier by Quinn's
illness for about four months during the fall and winter of 1956–1957. More
frequently than in the Brosman era, the chief judge provided the pivotal vote
in a number of cases—choosing between the conflicting views of Ferguson
and Latimer. On some occasions he sided with Latimer, leaving Ferguson to
dissent—a practice the new judge apparently exercised more often than had
Brosman. Infrequently he dissented, in disagreement with both Ferguson and
Latimer. More often, however, Quinn joined with his new colleague, leaving
Latimer alone.

By 1960, Latimer's dissents had sharpened in tone, reflecting an increased
sense of judicial isolation and frustration. These feelings may well have been

233

exacerbated by Latimer's inability both to become chief judge after Eisenhower's reelection in 1956 and to gain reappointment in 1961. Also, Latimer apparently found it difficult to accept Ferguson as a colleague, possibly because of the latter's utter lack of exposure to a military environment. One of Latimer's sons recalled that his father thought that Ferguson "was a dismal choice for" the Court appointment, feeling that he was more a "political hack" than a qualified jurist with military experience. Latimer believed that Ferguson failed on both counts.

Nineteen fifty-six had ended with continued uncertainty in the face of congressional inaction on two matters of concern to the Court—proposed changes to the UCMJ and the question of life tenure for the USCAAF judges. Finally, the tensions between the judges and the JAGs that had appeared to lessen during 1956–1958 increased again in 1960, resulting in yet another effort by the military to alter the Court's jurisdiction. JAG irritation over several USCAAF decisions contributed to this development, and while unhappy about it, at the same time Latimer found himself joining them in vigorous criticism of an expanded activism for the Court as charted by his colleagues—one that was, in Latimer's view, way off course.

LINGERING LONGING FOR LIFE TENURE

The earlier efforts to gain life tenure for USCAAF have been discussed in a previous chapter. There seems little doubt that the judges, aided by Tedrow, had explored virtually every argument that could be advanced to justify this change. They saw no legal barrier to making USCAAF an Article 3 tribunal rather than its current status as an Article 1 court, or "legislative" tribunal. There was nothing sacrosanct in this designation. Tedrow informed Judge Ferguson that Congress had reestablished the court of claims under Article 3 in response to a Supreme Court decision that this court was an Article 1, legislative court—an action later affirmed by the high court (see *Glidden Co. v. Zdanok,* 370 U.S. 530 [1962]). If Congress could do this once, it could certainly do it again. Tedrow cited an additional reason for this conclusion. Article 3 courts exercise federal judicial authority as "to all controversies in which the United States shall be a party." In the court of claims, he added, "the United States is a party to all suits. . . . as a practical matter we can advance the same argument because the United States is a party to every case in this Court."

By 1957–1958, Quinn had realized that while life tenure apparently was not a feasible objective, other changes in the law governing his court might be more palatable to Congress. Thus he wrote to Senator Pastore and enclosed a proposed statute that did not give the judges life tenure. If, he noted, that goal "seems impracticable now, the proposed amendment would help considerably." Quinn's draft had three important provisions, and if life tenure could not be obtained, they would at least underscore the legitimacy of USCAAF as a federal tribunal.

The proposal listed USCAAF as a "court of record" and stipulated that its judges "shall be judges of the United States and shall be entitled to the same pay and shall have the same rights, powers, privileges, perquisites, and retirement benefits as judges of the United States Courts of Appeals." Quinn's draft also deleted the requirements that no more than two of the judges be from the same political party and that each judge be either a member of the bar of a federal court or of the highest state court. Finally, USCAAF "is authorized to appoint and fix compensation of such officers and employees as may be necessary to discharge its responsibilities without regard to Civil Service laws and regulations." Quinn repeated his contention that the Court "is undoubtedly looked upon in some executive circles as a cross between an administrative agency, and a judicial entity," thereby raising doubts as to its authority to issue various writs common to the judicial function.

In March 1958, however, Tedrow concluded that although life tenure might be highly desirable, it was not required in order for the Court to function as an independent judicial tribunal. He cited the U.S. Supreme Court decision in *United States v. Morgan,* which included a reference to section 1651 of Title 28, U.S. Code, the "All Writs Act." That section provided that the high court "and all courts established by Act of Congress may issue all writs necessary or appropriate in aid of their respective jurisdictions and agreeable to the usages and principles of law" (326 U.S. 502, 506 [1954]). USCAAF has not hesitated to issue extraordinary writs when deemed to be appropriate.

Short and seemingly uncomplicated in scope, after April 1958, the draft was seen by the judges as a feasible alternative to life tenure. At a meeting with several congressional staff members, the administrative assistant to Senator Richard Russell, longtime chairman of the Armed Services Committee, indicated that this powerful senator "was opposed to life tenure for any [federal] judge." Russell's opposition was apparently based on his very critical reaction to recent decisions by federal district judges regarding school integration in the South, following the 1954 Supreme Court decision in *Brown v. Board of Education.* (In 1958, Richard Russell's assistant was a young lawyer named William Darden. Ten years later, with Russell's enthusiastic endorsement, Lyndon Johnson appointed him to USCAAF—not, it might be noted, with life tenure.) In view of "this opposition, which would be practically unsurmountable," Quinn's bill seemed more feasible. Working with David Martin, the legislative assistant to Massachusetts senator Leverett Saltonstall, Quinn, Proulx, and Tedrow agreed that the bill would be presented to the Senate on a bipartisan basis.

Less than a week after this meeting with David Martin, Tedrow sent him a memorandum, explaining and clarifying some of the provisions in the proposed statute. Among other points he noted, correctly, that the political party provision was inappropriate for a federal court. Such a requirement "has always been limited to the administrative board or commission set-up." He also discussed the old issue of civil service coverage for Court employees. He explained to Martin that one section of the bill did indeed authorize USCAAF to "handle its personnel problems without regard to Civil Service." Tedrow added, however, that "no other Federal Court is subject to the requirements of Civil Service," a position that the Court had long maintained. "The present addition is to avoid all possible claims to the contrary." Even as Tedrow wrote these words, this issue—unresolved since the Court's creation—was again provoking controversy.

On March 28, Judge Homer Ferguson had asked the attorney general about his court's "status under Civil Service," a question of "great interest to the Court in its judicial function." "We would appreciate it," he concluded, "if your Department would make a search of the law as to whether or not we are in fact under Civil Service." Ferguson's letter resulted in a fifteen-page memorandum to the attorney general from Malcolm Wilkey, in the Justice Department's Office of Legal Counsel. Coming at a time when USCAAF prepared to seek legislation on exactly this issue, Wilkey's missive—which resulted in no less than four responses from Tedrow, plus one from Ferguson on behalf of the Court—requires some analysis.

USCAAF AND CIVIL SERVICE—ENVELOPING DARKNESS UNOBSCURED

Wilkey observed at the outset that the Court in his opinion "is subject to Civil Service" since it is in the executive rather than the judicial branch of government—a conclusion he assured his chief that "is certain to be controversial and subject to doubt." He added that "it may be preferable to consider the Court's request as a matter for legislative consideration, rather than a matter for authoritative determination by the Attorney General." In retrospect, one wonders why after making this very valid point, Wilkey did not do what he considered "preferable" and just leave the question for congressional solution. He next explored the legislative history of USCAAF, being very selective in his choice of citation. His conclusion "that the Court is within the Executive Branch is based on the view that the Court is part of the system of courts-martial, which traditionally is an instrument for aiding the executive properly to command the armed forces."

Wilkey went on to discuss a 1954 decision of the U.S. Court of Appeals for the District of Columbia Circuit, *Shaw v. United States*. It involved a defendant in a court-martial who, upon being denied relief by USCAAF, argued that the federal appeals court was required by law to hear his case because USCAAF was merely an administrative agency whose rulings were inherently subject to federal appellate review. Since 1954, the unanimous decision in *Shaw* rejecting this argument had been widely cited by USCAAF judges and staff as vindication of its claim to be a legitimate appellate tribunal. Nevertheless, Wilkey found the holding unpersuasive. The *Shaw* decision stated that USCAAF

> with the entire hierarchy of tribunals which it heads, may perhaps be considered as being within the military establishment; perhaps, whether or not that is so, it is properly to be viewed as a specialized legislative court, comparable to the United States Court of Customs and Patent Appeals. But, in any view, [USCAAF] appears to us to be a court in every significant respect, rather than an administrative agency. Certainly Congress intended that in its dignity and standards of administering justice the Court . . . should be assimilated to and equated with the established courts of the federal system.

Although wrong to dismiss these words as "dictum," Wilkey had a point in claiming that they did not definitively resolve the question whether or not USCAAF was within the military establishment. Certainly the words used by the Court indicated some doubt in the matter. For Wilkey, absent concrete proof to the contrary, the premise that the Court could be considered within the military led to the conclusion that because of the executive's role as commander in chief, the Court was within the executive branch—and thus subject to civil service.

Pointing to several examples of misquotation, Tedrow denounced Wilkey's statement as one that "contains so many inaccuracies [and] misstatements" that it is "apparently based on a basic misconception of our entire Constitution." He would be ashamed, Tedrow added, "to have my name on the [Justice] Department memo." He submitted another memo four days later, and apparently he was still very angry. The chief commissioner detailed Wilkey's misstatements, particularly an unfortunate twisting of the words of Edmund Morgan about the evils of the "traditional view" of courts-martial. He rebutted comments made by Wilkey concerning the *Shaw* decision. "These things," he fumed, "make a memo that is merely bad become ridiculous. If Wilkey's shoestrings ever break during office hours, he will fall four floors." Within a week Tedrow had calmed down sufficiently to submit a revised version of his comments, one that in fact became the basis for a formal response by Ferguson on behalf of his colleagues to the attorney general. As a practical matter, he wrote, "I consider the Justice memo over Wilkey's name as about as strong an argument as we could present to the Congress in support of any desired legislation."

More important, Tedrow emphasized, it would seem, correctly, that while Wilkey's memo was based on the traditional view of courts-martial, in fact "there is *no* legal basis for such view." Unless the Court was prepared to demonstrate this fact, Tedrow feared that "any memo will degenerate into a mere 'it is, it is not' argument." Apparently the judges agreed, because a letter to the attorney general written by Ferguson utilized Tedrow's arguments, although they were couched in a much less confrontational tone. The judges may have found it disquieting that so many years after Samuel Ansell had, or so he thought, effectively rebutted any claim to validity for the "traditional" view of courts-martial, this view still attracted support from officials such as Wilkey.

In July, Quinn addressed a letter to the chairman of the Civil Service Commission in which he asked him "to either rescind or reverse what we consider a rather hasty and erroneous holding." He added that the commission's ruling concerning USCAAF "was ex parte in nature, the Commission apparently making the determination in a closed hearing without notice to the Court." One possible reason for the Court's vigor in pushing the civil service issue may have been its sense that, as with the life tenure controversy, the tribunal was not being treated like other federal appellate courts. But the chief judge was not very optimistic, since most of the letter focused on the heavy burdens carried by Tedrow and Proulx and urged that these two employees be given a very high civil service rating. But the chief judge may have been inconsistent here. In the same letter, Quinn argued first that the CSC had made a mistake in claiming jursidiction over the Court, and second that it should give Proulx and Tedrow extremely high civil service ratings—a position that may have reflected his assumption that ultimately the commission would not retreat from its position. He was right.

In the meantime, the bill drafted by Quinn remained stuck in Senator Saltonstall's office, with Tedrow getting more and more restless. He saw David Martin rather than the senator as the main stumbling block. "With Saltonstall in the picture," Tedrow warned Ferguson, "we will have to forget about either Martin or the bill." He accused the assistant of "raising all kinds of objections (quibbles) about it." When Martin finally sent a "revised" draft of the proposed legislation, the chief commissioner concluded that most of "this suggested Bill is either unnecessary or undesirable." However, by the middle of July, Tedrow came to believe that the problem might be less the assistant and more Senator Saltonstall himself.

He reminded Ferguson that Saltonstall had been the prime mover in the Senate subcommittee to eliminate life tenure from the UCMJ chapter creating USCAAF. The Massachusetts Republican had also supported very short terms of three, five and seven years for the judges. Tedrow claimed that Saltonstall's overall attitude was "pro-military." Indeed, he concluded, "we may have placed ourselves in the hands of the enemy, or at least in the hands of one who is not completely in sympathy with the provisions and purposes of the [UCMJ.]" Even when one makes proper allowance for Tedrow's attraction to conspiracy theories, his comments about Saltonstall merit some attention. There is no doubt that he was unenthusiastic about life tenure, and his attitude may have been more the norm than the exception. There is some doubt, moreover, as to how strongly Quinn's senatorial friends such as Green and Pastore actively pushed for any significant change in the status of USCAAF beyond verbal assurances of support. To the present day, the Senate has yet to approve life tenure for the Court, to say nothing of the language Quinn had sought concerning the "rights, powers, privileges [and] perquisites" of its judges.

FERGUSON VERSUS LATIMER

Of course, the main purpose and responsibility of USCAAF was to review and decide cases raising serious issues of military justice. Even as it maneuvered for the objectives discussed above, the Court exercised these functions. By 1958–1959, it was clear that Ferguson's appointment had contributed to a significant expansion of judicial authority. There is no way to ascertain if its new activism specifically affected the chances for life tenure. There is no doubt, however, that this change split the Court and contributed to a new level of tension between Ferguson and Latimer, as well as between the judges and the JAGs.

According to USCAAF reports, Homer Ferguson first participated in deciding cases on June 1, 1956. At the outset, it may have seemed to Latimer that the new judge would support him rather than Quinn in key interpretations of the code. Thus in a case decided on August 31, Ferguson joined Latimer in reiterating the holding that certain due process provisions in the Bill of Rights did not apply to the military. Latimer announced that Ferguson had chosen to follow the precedent set down by Latimer and Brosman in the *Sutton* case, decided in 1953. Any expectation, however, that Latimer could count on Ferguson for consistent support was very premature.

On the same day, for example, the Court reversed a conviction because the trial counsel (prosecutor) had referred to an instruction issued by the secretary of the navy. "Reasonable men," ruled Ferguson, must "conclude that once the Secretary of a service enters the restricted arena of the courtroom, whether the members of the court are conscious thereof or not, he is bound to exert some influence over them." Although he concurred in this specific case, Latimer strongly rejected the idea that policy statements could not be called to the attention of court members "at the time they should be considered."

Early in January 1957, Ferguson and Quinn again joined together to reverse a conviction for drug use based in part upon evidence that the commander had ordered the defendant to provide a urinalysis—something he had refused to do. The Court held that such an order was illegal under the code, thus vitiating the resulting prosecution. Latimer dissented and warned that "if the sweep of the concurring opinion is as broad as it appears to me, then crime detection in the Services will be unnecessarily stifled." The concurring opinion was written by Ferguson.

Another area of judicial change effected by a Ferguson-Quinn vote concerned adequate client representation by defense counsel. In *United States v. Thornton,* the accused was represented by a lawyer who had previously represented a key witness in this case, an individual who earlier had pleaded guilty during his own court-martial. Thornton argued on appeal that this "dual representation" deprived him of "the effective assistance of counsel." Ferguson agreed. The legal "tightrope between safeguarding the interests of the accused . . . and retaining the prior confidences of [the witness] Fields" was unacceptable. "Such a rope is too narrow. Such a walk is too long. The possibility of falling is too real. The probability of prejudicing the accused is too great."

Latimer denounced his colleague's conclusion as one that "is, without doubt, based on the sheerest conjecture and speculation imaginable, for there is not the slightest shred of evidence in the record to support it." As for Ferguson's comments on tightrope walking, "they are merely diversionary arguments." The position of counsel, added Latimer, "must be on a rope and not on the Chesapeake Bay Bridge. Here there is nothing to show any reasonable probability that the boundaries between the interests of the accused and retaining the confidence of Fields had narrowed to the thickness of hemp."

Almost a decade before the U.S. Supreme Court had established rules of conduct to be followed when interrogating suspects in custody, Quinn and Ferguson had explored similar terrain. Another 1957 decision involved the refusal of the staff judge advocate to give any legal advice to the accused as well as his orders that the staff decline "to advise the accused on pain of having their 'heads roll.' " Consequently, the defendant was not informed "of his right to have a lawyer of his own selection present to aid him during the questioning." Latimer found the opinion inexplicable if not inexcusable: "I can only hope this is an ad hoc decision, for it contains a number of principles which make for bad law and difficult administration." Latimer listed at least seven flaws in the majority's opinion. He concluded by referring to the board of review decision, "a fully and carefully developed opinion. . . . It is unmentioned and not followed by the Court, but I commend it to those readers who may be interested in determining its logic."

An issue closely related to this case involved the right to counsel during an article 32 pretrial investigation, the military justice equivalent to a civilian grand jury. The UCMJ had provided safeguards for an accused that went beyond those normally found in grand juries. These included the right to be present during testimony and to have counsel available to assist in cross-examination. The question raised in the case of *United States v. Tomaszewski* concerned the qualifications of counsel in this pretrial procedure. Quinn and Ferguson concluded that counsel in an article 32 investigation had to have the same qualifications as those set forth for counsel in a general court-martial, i.e., be a graduate of a law school and a practicing member of a state or federal bar. It would defeat the purposes of such an investigation, in reality a sort of discovery process for the accused, "if a person unskilled in the requirements of proof, or knowledge of legal defenses, represents the accused."

Latimer rejected this latest example of what seemed to be rampant judicial activism. Echoing a treasured theme in American constitutional interpretation, he insisted that if Congress had wished to require the same qualifications for counsel in an article 32 matter as in a general court-martial, the preference would be found in the words employed, and they were not there. Not only had Congress remained silent on this issue, but "the history of military law argues to the contrary." Moreover, the majority failed to consider the implications of this new requirement in terms of costs to the military, and "we should not impose [it] in the absence of specific legislation."

Given the Ferguson-Quinn objection to the introduction at trial of policy statements from a service official such as the secretary of the navy, a logical corollary would be their hostility to examination by the court members of the Manual for Courts-Martial for use in closed sessions deliberation. The judges struck down this practice in *United States v. Boswell*. Ferguson noted an earlier holding that these individuals might not understand cases cited in the manual "and may well be confused by additional matter appearing in the text, not applicable to the case before them." In another previous decision, USCAAF had held that it was "error for the court members to consult cases" mentioned by the law officer "for the purpose of determining for themselves what law should be applied to the case." Court members, emphasized Ferguson, should not "consult 'outside sources' for information on the law."

To an observer familiar with modern standards of due process, Ferguson's conclusions do not seem unusual. One would not expect a jury to be given cases to read and examine as they consider their verdict, comparing and contrasting these decisions with the instant dispute. Latimer's vehement reaction to this holding is startling, even decades later. He may well have feared that, given the usual absence of legal training among court-martial members, the majority's ruling would deprive them of a valuable and necessary tool—an assumption possibly based on his perception of basic differences between civilian and military justice systems. While he emphasized the differences, Quinn and Ferguson accentuated the similarities of the two.

A majority of his court, wrote Latimer, "seizes upon this case as a foot-in-the-door method of laying down a far-reaching and devastating principle whereby it overturns the procedure used by all courts-martial since the adoption of the Code." It is hard, he added, "to conjure up a comparable instance where such a well established custom is buried with so little justification." If Latimer was correct in referring to one foot, Ferguson and Quinn positioned the other in the famous case of *United States v. Rinehart*.

Here, Ferguson ruled that use of the MCM by members of a court-martial "during the course of the trial or while deliberating on findings and sentence

[must] be completely discontinued." We "cannot sanction," he emphasized, "a practice which permits members to rummage through a treatise on military law . . . indiscriminately rejecting and applying a myriad of principles—judicial and otherwise—contained therein. . . . All the law a court-martial need know in order to properly perform its functions must come from the law officer and nowhere else." Ferguson made no bones about what this implied.

He traced the evolution of the law officer under the UCMJ. This individual had been fashioned "in the image of a civilian judge. . . . In a word, he was made a fountainhead of the law in the court-martial scheme of things." The various changes mandated by the code (and the Court) were intended "to bring court-martial procedure, wherever possible, into conformity with that prevailing in civilian criminal courts. We believe that military justice under the Code has come of age and the time has come when the use of the Manual by the court-martial must end." As Proulx later wrote, although the judges did not like having to choose between the code and the MCM, when they did, the choice was not difficult: "The terms of the law cannot be defeated by the terms engrafted thereon by an Executive Order and, if the two are inconsistent, the statute must stand alone."

By late 1957, Latimer must have been well aware of the judicial currents being stirred by his brethren. He seems to have sensed also that *Rinehart* represented a watershed in military justice since the introduction of the UCMJ, and he deplored not only the results of the decision but the reasons that had produced them. Latimer objected to "trying to force military law into the exact image of civilian law, [and] this case is a good vehicle to illustrate the folly of disregarding all differences between the military and civilian practices." Latimer saw no advantage in "forcing members of military courts to operate in darkness in areas where they must rule if we deny them access to the law that should guide them." He concluded with what had become a familiar theme in his numerous dissents: "Whether we like the law or not, until it is changed by Congress, it should not be emasculated by us." Latimer's increasing bitterness was reflected in his comment late in 1957 that while his associates considered *Rinehart* "as a worthy contribution to military law, I assert quite to the contrary. All I can say about [it] is that it fairly well establishes that the Court took an unnecessarily drastic measure when it threw away the Manual."

The Ferguson-Quinn "entente" showed little signs of weakening. Early in 1958, the Court reversed cases on the grounds of improper instructions given to court members by the law officer, as well as inappropriate advice offered by the staff JAG to the commander—who would normally place heavy reliance on it when approving or rejecting a court-martial verdict. In each case, Latimer dissented. In one, he accused his brethren "of veering away from a very substantial body of law. . . . We have written a series of cases dealing with this subject which may be swept away without mention by this holding." In the other, Latimer reiterated his objection to the sudden judicial condemnation of language employed by staff judge advocates "where the terms used had been in vogue for many years and we had affirmed hundreds of cases employing the same expressions. The language was stereotyped and the reviews just did not become misleading, confusing, or erroneous overnight."

Ascertaining the proper relationship between law and change represents an age-old judicial dilemma. How USCAAF viewed its connection to the military environment and how the judges viewed their role vis-à-vis the JAGs and Congress may well have affected their approach to these cases. With no military experience to draw upon, Ferguson brought a perspective very different from Latimer, who had served under combat. On the other hand, when the bottom line is reached, neither logic, consistency, nor continued reliance on precedent determine the outcome as much as votes do. Depending on the way one viewed USCAAF's functions, one could support or reject Latimer's position. From a perspective of almost fifty years, the changes ratified by Ferguson and Quinn were appropriate. On the other hand, result-oriented jurisprudence can always seem more palatable if one agrees with the results.

Latimer may have hoped that the decisions rendered between 1957 and 1959 represented the limits to his colleagues' judicial changes. If so, he was sorely disappointed with two decisions that were handed down during his last year on the Court. In *United States v. Russo,* Ferguson ruled that both the convening authority and the board of review could mitigate the severity of a death penalty sentence, thereby overruling an earlier decision by Brosman and Latimer—"a result," Latimer wrote, "that I am constrained to decry."

> I was hopeful that, in a field as critical as this, we would respect consistency, leave the law fixed, and rely on Congress to effectuate a change if it subsequently concluded that our construction was inappropriate. I was too credulous, for today's opinion sweeps the past aside, overturns a principle which has long been firmly imbedded in military law, refuses to follow prior decisions of this Court, and clothes two appellate agencies with power to impose an original sentence. . . . [T]he law is being changed because of Judge Ferguson's interpretation. No doubt he believes that he should undo the handicraft of Judge Brosman and the writer, but that position undercuts stability and offers comfort to those who assert that we are a court of men and not law. Certainly, if there is any merit to the doctrine of *stare decisis* and the argument that if Congress believes we misinterpret its enactment, the remedy is by corrective legislation, then this case is one of the best examples I can cite as a violation of those principles.

Ferguson replied indirectly to Latimer in what may still be described as one of the "great" cases handed down during the Quinn era. It will be recalled that in *Sutton* Quinn had insisted that all provisions in the Bill of Rights applied to members of the armed services unless excluded expressly or by necessary implication. It will further be recalled that shortly after Ferguson joined the bench, he had concurred with Latimer in rejecting the chief judge's position. By 1958, however, Ferguson had changed his mind. He waited until 1960 to join Quinn in scuttling *Sutton.*

Ferguson conceded that in the *Parrish* case, he had accepted Latimer's viewpoint "out of respect to the former holdings of this Court." Now, "critical re-examination . . . in the light of the Constitution convinces me that we erred in so giving effect to the doctrine of *stare decisis.*" The doctrine might have its uses, but "it should never be applied in order to perpetuate a mistaken view." Ferguson could have stopped there. Instead, and possibly to make the point very clear to Latimer, he added: "Indeed, it is our duty to overrule and modify decisions which are erroneous, although there has been no legislative change in the law as originally construed." In other words, changes in the statute were unnecessary to justify USCAAF's new holding because Latimer had been wrong. He concluded that in a court-martial, an accused had the right to be present along with counsel at the taking of written depositions concerning the case.

In a dissent that is almost twice as long as Ferguson's opinion, Latimer rejected the reasoning, rationale, and results reached by his associate. Although many of his points had already been made in previous dissents, Latimer implied that Ferguson either was unable or unwilling "to follow recognized and fundamental principles of constitutional law." More important, "in this instance, not unlike some others, my associates warp the Code to make military law on all fours with civilian law. It is impossible to take the military out of military law, and . . . there is a fundamental distinction between the two and recognition ought to be given by this Court to the differences." Ferguson and Quinn "should recognize that we are faced with issues which must be measured with regard to the necessities of the services and that a yardstick of civilian standards will lead us to false conclusions."

Latimer's dissents reveal a thoroughness in exploration of doctrine and case law that one sometimes finds lacking in Ferguson and Quinn. Given this predilection, he may have found their apparent ability to reach a desired judicial result by ignoring other factors—such as precedent—as offensive as their ultimate conclusions. Depending on one's viewpoint, Latimer may have had logic on his side but not the votes. Implicit in Latimer's words, of course, is the crux of the challenge facing a civilian court and code operating in a military environment. How the Court responded to it during the three decades since he left the bench is a matter of debate. This author believes that for all of Latimer's concerns—which any appellate tribunal ought to keep in mind— USCAAF has unquestionably helped rather than hindered military justice. While Latimer feared it was doing too much, the point can be raised with at least equal vigor that it was not doing enough.

JAGs VERSUS JUDGES

The JAGs had observed the Ferguson-Quinn "revolution" with concern if not anger. In his report for 1958, the army JAG briefly described eleven recent USCAAF decisions. (Of the eleven cases cited, Latimer dissented in all but one. There, he concurred only because the law had become fixed, in spite of his dissents.) "In many instances, these sharp departures from previous military practice have created difficult problems for military law enforcement authorities. In order to correct some of these deficiencies, proposed remedial legislation is under study." What that service had in mind became clear in the army JAG's 1959 report.

Major General Hickman noted "an increasing lack of confidence in the present system of military justice because of its growing complexity and difficulty of administration." Complaints from the field, he added, "indicate a growing concern over lack of stability in the law." Hickman reported that the secretary of the army had appointed a board of general officers "to study the present system of military justice and its impact on the administration of discipline in the Army as well as the essential fairness of the [UCMJ] both to the accused and to the Government." He cited eight additional USCAAF decisions and quoted from two of Latimer's dissents.

The Powell report, named for the board's chairman, General Herbert Powell, managed to be perceptive, partisan, provocative, and in two instances prophetic. Its recommendations that a court-martial could be conducted by a law officer sitting alone and that the court be expanded to a five-member tribunal ultimately became law. But the suggestion was couched in such terms as to ill conceal the army's animus toward the Court.

The report claimed that a three-judge court "is not sufficiently conducive to stable procedures and consistent administration of justice." Moreover, the replacement of Brosman by Ferguson "has caused a dramatic reversal in the law. A five-judge court would be much less susceptible to fluctuation." The two additional judges, however, would not be civilians but rather would be selected from a pool of military officers with at least fifteen consecutive years on duty in a JAG division. They would serve four-year terms and, unlike their three civilian counterparts, would not be eligible for reappointment. The intent was that "there would always be one judge not more than two years removed from military experience."

In his 1960 report, General Hickman noted "some twenty-five or thirty judicial decisions that . . . Army lawyers believe substantially hamper the operation of the Army." He also reverted to earlier complaints, claiming that the 1960 *Jacoby* case "has resulted in time-consuming delays in trials, undue expense to the government, as well as dismissal of charges for economic reasons." General Hickman, who had been a member of the Powell board, urged that the Defense Department bill be withdrawn and that the Powell report's legislative proposals be adopted. In their 1960 reports, however, none of the other services endorsed the Powell proposals.

The USCAAF judges refused to join a joint report with the service JAGs and denounced some of the Powell suggestions: "The Court is appalled by the proposals contained therein." To adopt them would be to return military justice to the conditions that had spawned both the UCMJ and the Court itself. In fact, the "difficulties experienced by the military . . . since the inception of the Code have resulted from their own attempts to revert to 'the old system' through manipulations of the [MCM], and departmental regulations." Close "scrutiny of all practices thereby introduced must be maintained." Probably inspired by the Powell report, the 1960 summary by the judges was the longest thus far in the Court's history and contains a useful summary of major cases decided between 1951 and 1960, as well as a cogent and at times eloquent justification for the Court's existence.

In 1989, F. B. Wiener aptly described the Powell proposed USCAAF expansion as "a court-packing plan more crass and more blatant" than the one urged upon the country by President Roosevelt in 1937. It is a pity, he added, that no member of the committee "possessed a sufficient sense of history to be aware of that damning analogy." If the army had hoped to bring about any changes in the UCMJ as a result of the Powell report, "approved glowingly" by Army Secretary Wilbur Brucker, it was disappointed. Moreover, it was about to lose its staunchest supporter on the USCAAF bench.

"SENATOR" QUINN AND "CITIZEN" LATIMER

It will be recalled that one of the reasons Quinn had insisted that he remain in Providence was his hope that he might yet be able to win election as a senator from Rhode Island. Senator Pastore showed no inclination to retire, but in 1960, Senator Green decided to step down. After some consideration, Quinn's close friend Congressman John Fogarty determined to seek an eleventh term in Congress. Thus in April 1960—even as USCAAF was dealing with the Powell report—a Senate race appeared wide open, and a number of potential senatorial candidates were identified by the Rhode Island press. One of them was, of course, Chief Judge Quinn. Now sixty-six years old, the former governor responded to a request that he comment on his political plans: "I am not a candidate . . . but I am available if the party is interested in me. I am at the command of the Democratic Party."

Old political operative that he was, Quinn did more than just respond to the newspapers. He prepared a short statement to be available to the forthcoming meeting of the state Democratic Committee. For nine years he had served as chief judge, protecting "the rights, the liberties and the honor" of members of the armed forces, "the guardians of our liberties and our first line of defense against a ruthless and implacable foe—the Communist Conspiracy." Again, Quinn denied that he was anxious to relinquish "that very important job." In truth, he had been prepared to relinquish it ever since he took the post, were an opportunity to run proffered him. Now, "if after careful consideration," party leaders concluded that "my energies and talents are of greater value to the State and Nation in the . . . Senate, I am ready and willing to stand for election in November."

The Quinn candidacy, observed Proulx, would go forward only if the judge was endorsed by the state Democratic Committee. "Otherwise, I do not believe he will enter the primary contest. No one to date has ever been able to beat an endorsed candidate, largely due to the manner in which the names of the candidates appear on the primary ballot." Proulx was both right and wrong. Denied the endorsement, Quinn declined to run. But the winner of the primary and later the election, Claiborne Pell, had also failed to gain endorsement.

While Quinn was willing to leave, Latimer was eager to stay. By December 1960 he began a belated effort to gain reappointment. There is little doubt that of all the USCAAF judges thus far, Latimer was the least political. He had little interest in politics and assumed that if he was performing appropriately, he would be reappointed. In retrospect, this may have been very poor judgment on Latimer's part, given his aggressive candidacy for the post in 1950. Also, as of 1960 no USCAAF judge had ever been reappointed. On the other hand, Latimer had served with devotion and dedication. Moreover, his opinions reflected a thoughtfulness and depth sometimes lacking in decisions handed down by his brethren. Nevertheless, by December 1960, Latimer appeared to be from the wrong party, seeking a choice appointment at the wrong time from the wrong administration.

He sought support from Felix Larkin, former general counsel of the Defense Department, "without knowledge of your political affiliation." Larkin responded favorably with a comment "that your services to the Court have been in the finest tradition of the American judiciary." Although himself a Democrat, "I would certainly hope that the political requirements of the [UCMJ] would not prevent your reappointment." Despite this hope, with a Democrat and a Republican already on the Court and with a new Democratic administration taking office, Latimer had little chance. When his term expired on May 1, he still had heard nothing concerning either his replacement or reappointment. "The lapse of time," he wrote to Larkin, "leads me to believe that my chances are remote." And so they were.

Latimer was the first USCAAF judge to go into retirement, in his case involuntarily. His record seems to have been a mixed one. Especially in his early years, he contributed to important doctrinal interpretations of the UCMJ. His last three years on the bench, however, found Latimer more and more unhappy not only at the pace of change from his colleagues but also with some of the changes themselves. The debate over the relative importance of stare decisis in appellate jurisprudence will never be settled. It is true, however, that the holdings that so disturbed him remain good law, and while Congress would in the future overrule USCAAF decisions by statute, as will be seen, it would not be based on those decisions that he had decried. As Latimer prepared to return to Salt Lake City, interest centered less on his accomplishments than on his successor. By early June, Quinn and Ferguson were still waiting. But their contact with Latimer was not over. Among all the former USCAAF judges, he appears to have been the only one who ever returned as attorney of record to argue several cases before his old court. Latimer's most famous case was probably that of Lieutenant William Calley, the leader of the My Lai "massacre" during the Vietnam War (see Chapter 20).

18

Assessing Military Justice, Attempting Life Tenure, Attaining Reappointment, 1961–1966

A NEW JUDGE

On March 9, 1961, Proulx informed Quinn that "Judge Latimer had seen the President . . . regarding his reappointment." Such news surprised neither Proulx nor Quinn, who knew that Latimer had been increasingly active in his efforts to retain his seat. More important was Proulx's discovery that Texas congressman Paul J. Kilday "was [also] seeking the appointment and had Congressman Vinson [chairman of the House Armed Services Committee] personally see the President on his behalf." First elected to Congress in 1938, Kilday had continuously served on the House Armed Services Committee since 1939. Although deeply interested and involved in military affairs, he had not been part of the subcommittee that drafted the UCMJ and had no direct experience with the administration of military justice. On the other hand, he consistently supported both the Court and the code, and over the years Kilday had apparently gained the confidence of senior military officials. After his appointment to the Court was announced, an air force general wrote that "I know that we have never had, and never will have, a better representative on [USCAAF,]" while a navy JAG noted Kilday's "demonstrated ability to hold the services 'at bay' in their repeated efforts to amend the code virtually out of existence and into the limbo of the last century."

By May 1, Latimer's term had officially ended, thus temporarily reducing USCAAF to a two-member court. Although, according to Proulx, Latimer "has not given up hope[,] the realities of politics being what they are, the fact that word was not received before the expiration of his term, I would have to say that his chances grow dimmer every day." When Kilday's appointment was finally announced in June, it came more as a finale to what had become a foregone conclusion. In his quest for reappointment, Latimer was supported by the armed services but not his two colleagues. Yet, as he himself realized, given the time and political context, reappointment was too much to expect.

President Kennedy nominated Kilday on June 28, 1961, and the Senate unanimously confirmed the appointment on July 17. Thus far in its history, all five nominations to USCAAF had received unanimous approval from the Senate. As had been true of Homer Ferguson, in Kilday's case as well the Senate Armed Services Committee did not even trouble to ask him to appear at the pro forma confirmation hearing. Normally, the presidential appointment files carry some indication of the selection process by which judges were appointed to the Court. Diligent research by the Kennedy Library staff in the 1960–1961 files failed to locate any such papers on Kilday's appointment, indicating that the nomination was probably decided by informal agreement between Kennedy's staff and Kilday. Kilday not only had the support of Vinson but also that of his old Texas colleagues Vice President Lyndon Johnson and House Speaker Sam Rayburn. With such backing, documentation on the appointment process was hardly necessary, and its absence is not surprising. On June 5, Kilday had written to Lyndon Johnson "to express my very sincere thanks for the recommendation you gave me and for the very material assistance you have rendered me in this connection."

Kilday informed the Court that he did not plan to join his new colleagues until the fall. Whether or not Quinn realized that lobbying for life tenure with a congressman soon to be a judge on the very court to which this change would apply might be questionable, he did not hesitate. Very shortly after Kilday's appointment was announced, Quinn and Proulx visited the new nominee. Kilday mentioned to the chief judge that a constitutional question about life tenure had already been raised. Quinn replied that "this obstacle if it did exist could easily be overcome," and he promised to send Kilday a memorandum on the subject within three days. He did.

Quinn conceded that opposition to life tenure for his court rested on the ground that the modification, as applied to the incumbent judges, "would usurp or contravene the President's right to nominate the Judges of the Court, with the advice and consent of the Senate." This objection, he insisted, "is contrary to established practice and law. Tenure of office is a matter separate and apart from the right to appoint and the manner of appointment." Quinn emphasized that "there is a genuine need to assure the Court's independence as a judicial tribunal and to eliminate the possibility of interference by administrative agencies with the full discharge of its judicial obligations."

Although Quinn was saying nothing new, the issues to which he referred were still current. During the summer of 1961, the Bureau of the Budget again received one of the congressional proposals for USCAAF life tenure. So did the chairman of the Senate Armed Services Committee, Richard Russell, who sought the reaction of the Defense Department. Again—this time speaking through the air force—the department objected. Neither its rationale nor the rhetoric on this subject had changed. It was as if everything the Court had presented on the need for life tenure during the last decade had been ignored.

It is "well settled," according to the air force department memorandum, "that courts-martial are instrumentalities of the executive power provided by Congress for the President in his capacity as Commander in Chief, to aid him in properly commanding the armed forces and enforcing discipline therein." Conceding that USCAAF "is considered to be a court in every significant respect, not merely an administrative agency," the department "is opposed to any legislation which would make the court part of the judicial branch, since the court, by virtue of its functions, should remain part of the executive branch." Further claiming that the proposed bill "contains a number of provisions which might be interpreted as tending to convert the Court into an Article III court," the memorandum argued that such action "could create an anomaly without predecent, possibly producing problems of greater moment than the benefits it purports to bestow." Concealed in this verbiage was exactly the point to which Kilday had already been alerted.

If USCAAF became a U.S. court, could it still remain under the jurisdiction of the Defense Department? More important, what about presidential power to remove judges from this tribunal? Would such a change not infringe "upon the President's authority to remove members of a court that is part of the executive branch"? Flying in the face of federal judicial history since 1789, the memorandum insisted that this authority "should not be deleted; otherwise, the judges could only be removed by impeachment." However, "the Department of Defense would not oppose legislation designed to enhance the dignity and prestige of the Court of Military Appeals." It proposed no such legislation in this memorandum. Nor, of course, did this glib reassurance solve the questions that had troubled the Court from its inception. Moreover, the memorandum utterly failed to consider whether Congress could grant life tenure to the judges of an Article 1 court that it had created. One might have expected the department to offer some new arguments in rebuttal to the claims made by proponents of extended terms for USCAAF. But merely to repeat and rehash past assertions put forth by the armed services displayed a knee-jerk reaction rather than reasoned reflection.

Quinn wasted little time in replying to the Defense Department memorandum. Again he had a draft from Tedrow, which he may well have used in its preparation. He cited federal judicial precedents, one of which had been noted more than forty years before by Samuel Ansell. The "fallacy of the Air Force Report's basic premise is established by the foregoing authoritative pronouncements." Nevertheless, added Quinn,

the theme of "instrumentality of command" is constantly reiterated by those charged with enforcing the law and professing to supervise discipline within the Armed Services! It was just such declarations that led to the abuses which caused the repudiation by the Congress of the administration of military justice under the Articles of War and the [regulations to govern] the Navy. It was just such spurious reasoning which created the need for the establishment of this Court as the civilian overseers of the system of military justice contemplated by the Uniform Code. Are we to regard the reiteration of the oft-rejected premise [as] a precursor of further attempts to restore a repudiated system?

For his part, Quinn reiterated the arguments in favor of life tenure. But his response also reflected some deeper issues that went beyond the usual comments about the need to be protected from undue political influence. "If this Court," he wrote, "is to secure for the future personnel equal in professional capacity and standing to that from which other Federal Judges are recruited, it is essential that the members of its bench enjoy similar treatment in this particular." Precisely the same point had been raised by former army JAG officer and Washington attorney Frederick B. Wiener testifying about the proposed UCMJ in 1949: "I think we should face it frankly—the appointments to the specialized courts of our judicial system haven't attracted the same sort of talent that the courts of general jurisdiction have attracted." While it remains true that the quality of federal judges depends in large measure upon the care and importance that the president attaches to their selection, it may also be true that the prospect for life tenure as a federal judge might well attract better qualified candidates than an offer for a fixed number of years. Predictably, Quinn concluded that both the premises and the conclusions of the air force position were erroneous, "and approval should be withheld."

THE SENATE SUBCOMMITEE AND THE CODE

Even as the House subcommittee prepared to consider life tenure for USCAAF judges and the related problems of pension and retirement benefits, a joint Senate Armed Services–Judicary Subcommittee on Constitutional Rights scheduled hearings between February and March 1962 and focused in particular on the rights of personnel in the armed services. Unlike the 1956 hearings, Senator Samuel Ervin's group had no specific bill under consideration. Rather, the panel as well as those who appeared before it probably saw the sessions as an opportunity for a general assessment of military justice after eleven years of operation under the UCMJ.

One of the first witnesses before Ervin's subcommittee was Reginald Harmon, recently retired after a record number of years (twelve) as the air force JAG. In an earlier appearance during hearings held in 1956, he had argued essentially that both the Court and the code were unnecessary. Six years later, recalling his old description of the UCMJ and the system of military justice it mandated as "unwieldy and cumbersome in peacetime, and . . . probably unworkable in the event of a major large-scale war," Harmon stated that "I have not been presented with any new evidence which would change that opinion." He added that the "greatest single objection to the [UCMJ] is its tendency to destroy what was once the principal asset of the military justice system: that is the swift and certain punishment of the guilty man." Indeed, the "certainty of punishment and the promptness of prosecution seem now to be only a matter of historical interest."

This was so because the UCMJ is "unnecessarily laden with built-in delays." Even worse, "in many instances, form has been elevated over substance in the administration of the code." Comparing the old Articles of War, the short-lived Elston Act, and the UCMJ that had superseded both of them, Harmon called the UCMJ "the most expensive, the least efficient and the most ineffective system of the three." The solution to this undesirable situation was simple: "I recommend the repeal of the [UCMJ] in its entirety." Kilday, fresh from more than twenty years in Congress, recalled Harmon's good reputation even as he dismissed his recommendations: "We have progressed further than that in modern times. . . . I think under the code you have come a whole lot nearer the Anglo-Saxon concept of justice and there has been great progress made."

No stranger to congressional hearings involving the UCMJ or USCAAF (he had already appeared at three of them), Wiener supported the Court. He was less enthusiastic about the UCMJ, observing that "the matter of military justice is a dilemma . . . that arises out of the need for reconciling essentially irreconcilable concepts." A military organization "is and must be an authoritarian organization because its job is to send men obediently to death if need be." Punishment in the military, he added, "is primarily deterrent. Punishment in the civil courts is, of course, primarily reformatory." And "an army is not a deliberative body."

Thus military justice should be limited "to situations where the standards and techniques and procedures of military justice are necessary, and it shouldn't attempt to parallel civilian justice." Here, Wiener took issue with those—among them the USCAAF judges—who argued that military justice wherever possible ought to be identical to its civilian counterpart. Indeed, the UCMJ "introduces what I think are unsuitable civil concepts, civilian concepts [sic]." Even worse "is that the uniform code divorces the administration of military justice from the consciousness of the services. Instead of the services disciplining themselves and taking a precise interest in seeing that the guilty are convicted and the innocent go free, the whole thing is turned over to the cops and the lawyers." On the other hand, Wiener endorsed USCAAF because "it is impossible to expect the services without [its supervision] to stamp out the endemic existence of command influence." Moreover, the Court was necessary "to look over the shoulders of those people who just can't be relied upon to do a completely decent job by themselves."

Ervin's hearings failed to produce any immediate legislation, although he did propose a number of bills to address some of the issues that were raised. His subcommittee did not resume the hearings until 1966, when they considered no less than eighteen bills, including those drafted in 1962. In the meantime, the House Armed Services Subcommittee turned to the issue of life tenure for Quinn and his colleagues. Eleven years after USCAAF's establishment, Quinn felt he had reason to be optimistic.

THE HOUSE, THE CODE, AND THE COURT

It will be recalled that spokesmen for the defense establishment as well as the executive branch had opposed previous life tenure proposals essentially because they believed them to be incompatible with the power of presidential removal, a UCMJ provision in effect since the original enactment of this legislation in 1950. And indeed, under Article 3 auspices, federal judges can be removed *only* by impeachment. The 1962–1963 House hearings centered on an attempt to provide life tenure for USCAAF judges while at the same time keeping the presidential removal power intact.

Only one witness, Air Force JAG Albert Kuhfeld, appeared before the subcommittee on July 26, 1962, and he spoke for the Department of Defense. This time, Kuhfeld emphasized, "the status of the Court as an article I, or a legislative court, would be clearly retained." Its judges, moreover, would not be "judges of the United States," because that term applied to Article 3 courts, created under federal judicial authority. They would have life tenure, although they would remain subject to presidential removal. This provision, which apparently was sacrosanct to the Defense Department, could not be applied to an Article 3 court because "one of the very basic characteristics of an article III court is that a judge can only be removed by impeachment." Nevertheless, as the committee counsel put it, "We are trying to give all the elements of a U.S. judge, without making it an article III court."

The subcommittee also wrestled with the problem of mandatory retirement for the judges, something that Kuhfeld quickly reminded its members "is not done in any of the other [federal Article 3] courts." L. Mendel Rivers, subcommittee chair, replied that "the other courts do not compare with this. We want to get away from that." To which his own counsel responded, "No, Mr. Chairman, we do not want to get away from it. We are trying to get away from it as little as we can. That is the whole point." Of course, Russell Blandford added, with a legislative court, the Congress "can do about whatever you want to do. But every time that you make this court different with regard to its privileges, its rights of resignation, and its rights of retirement, then you detract from its dignity."

As Rivers put it, the subcommittee had difficulty "in trying our best to get away from article III and carry on the philosophy of article III" at the same time. Possibly with the views of Senator Russell in mind, Rivers noted further that "if there is a fallacy in the Constitution, it is to let the Federal judges sit during good behavior. I see a lot of good fellows turn from gentlemen to tyrants overnight, when they put on that shroud." Even so, the future chairman of the House Armed Services Committee supported life tenure for USCAAF judges along the lines discussed above. Like many of his southern colleagues, Rivers was uncomfortable with both civil rights legislation and the expanded role for federal judges regarding integration cases in the years since *Brown v. Board of Education* (1954).

Because of some questions concerning retirement pensions, the subcommittee put off final action on the life tenure bill question until June 1963. Reintroduced by Congressman John Fogarty, this bill reiterated essentially what the Armed Services Committee had decided one year before—life tenure subject to presidential removal, with the incumbent judges also eligible for reappointment. In addition, USCAAF judges would be entitled "to the same salary, allowances, perquisites, retirement, and survivor benefits as judges of the U.S. court of appeals." Again, General Kuhfeld stated that the Defense Department supported the bill, and again Russell Blandford emphasized that USCAAF was "a legislative court, as opposed to a constitutional court." Moreover, under this bill, "the jurisdiction of [the Court] is not intended to be enlarged. . . . It is not intended to set up a new court of the United States as a result of the enactment of this legislation." Without even a voice vote, the panel reported the bill favorably to the full committee. The entire hearing apparently took less than one hour.

During a session on July 16, 1963, the House Armed Services Committee considered a number of pending measures, including the USCAAF tenure bill. Speaking for the subcommittee, Mendel Rivers emphasized anew that the judges "ought to have the dignity of life tenure." At which point, a committee member reminded Rivers that "you have not given [USCAAF] the dignity, because the President himself can remove them, and he cannot remove Federal Judges. . . . If we have a right to go this far, we have a right to go and say the removal should be on the same basis as any other Federal [judge.]" As he had attempted numerous times before during the other hearings, Blandford sought to explain why it was not that simple.

"We are attempting," he noted, "to exercise the authority of the Congress to establish a legislative court. This gets into a great realm of constitutional law. . . . [W]e are trying desperately to avoid using the same language, which would then be construed as clothing this court with all of the aspects of a constitutional court, where then we lose our jurisdiction. . . . We had to bend over backwards, otherwise we wouldn't even have jurisdiction over this bill to make it a legislative court." In other words, the committee sought to give judicial tenure without involving the Senate Committee on the Judiciary. A year earlier, Rivers had been a little more candid when he observed that "I do not want to get mixed up with the Judiciary Committee. That is why I want to stay clear, as far as possible, of the jurisdiction of the Judiciary Committee." Again, without even an informal vote, let alone a roll call, Chairman Carl Vinson noted that the "bill is unanimously reported." Within three weeks, it reached the House floor.

In his report accompanying referral of the bill to the entire House, for a third time Mendel Rivers explained what the measure entailed. Drawing heavily on material furnished to the committee by the Court, he cited the need to "free the judges from the danger of political and other pressures" and to assimilate the USCAAF bench "to that of a U.S. court of appeals, thereby bringing the administration of military criminal law closer to complete accord with that obtaining in Federal civilian courts." Finally, life tenure would "assure for the future personnel equal in professional capacity and standing to those recruited as judges of other Federal courts." However, Rivers made no mention of the thorny issue concerning the need for the court's "dignity" on the one hand and life tenure being terminated by presidential removal on the other. He also extolled the accomplishments of USCAAF to date: "Its insistence upon high professional performance by all legal personnel involved in trials by courts-martial, and upon strict compliance with the provisions of the [UCMJ], has resulted in the elimination of many of the justified grounds for the complaints lodged against the earlier procedures."

In discussing the bill before the House, Rivers raised his level of rhetoric. He claimed that since its inception, USCAAF "has been on trial and the experience has been very good. They have earned this distinction and it gives them a dignity to which they are entitled." As to the three incumbents—Quinn, Ferguson, and Kilday—"there are no three finer men in the judiciary." Congressman Harold R. Gross, Republican from Iowa, responded that "I am not aware that we are in the business of passing laws giving people jobs for the rest of their natural lives on the basis of their being nice fellows."

Democrat John Fogarty offered some eloquent historical perspective. Reminding his colleagues first of the fact that "the best method of keeping our courts independent is through a tenure basis" and also of plenary congressional authority to regulate the armed services, Fogarty called the UCMJ "the most revolutionary change in the court-martial system this country has ever contemplated." But, he added, "of what profit is confidence, of what worth is justice, of what use is judicial excellence if these attributes are purchased at the price of discipline. . . . The necessary balance, we were sure, could be struck by dedicated, mature, judicious minds applying, interpreting and explaining the law." Shrewdly emphasizing the fact that two of the three current judges were former congressional colleagues, Fogarty singled out Quinn for special attention: "This pioneer of civilian supervision of military courts has established for [USCAAF] its judicial tone, its orderly administration, the currency of its docket, and its faithful conformity to the spirit as well as the letter of the uniform code."

Rhetoric notwithstanding, Congressman Gross was "still unable to understand why this bill is before the House." Regarding the claim that tenure was necessary in order to give the judges the dignity they deserved, Gross was blunt: "I am not aware that you can legislate dignity. If this is the excuse for this bill . . . that you are lending dignity by giving these three judges lifetime tenures, then you have not very much to stand on." In reply, Carl Vinson claimed that the intention of the legislation was "to remove Executive influence." Gross asked, "What evidence is there that there has been executive interference with this Court?" Vinson responded, "Not one particle at all." Then, commented Gross, "that argument does not stand up very well, does it?" Vinson insisted that a court should not be "dependent upon reappointment" and that it "should be given the same prestige and the same standard, at least, as other Federal courts."

Possibly aware that his opposition was futile, Gross persisted: "I see no similarity between a judge of [USCAAF] and a Federal appeals court judge. I see no real comparison in the type of work they do. A judge in the court of appeals is confronted with every conceivable kind of case, whereas the gentlemen on this court are confronted with one type of case and one type of case only, if I understand their duties." Nevertheless, Vinson summarized the Court's history and added the point that enactment of the statute would "eliminate once and for all the baseless contention that the court is an instrumentality of the Executive by confirming its identity as a legislative court established under article I."

Noting that the bill had unanimous support from his committee, Vinson called for the vote. Final passage by an overwhelming margin followed, with 314 in favor, 82 opposed, and 37 abstaining. With such a favorable vote, Proulx was understandably optimistic about life tenure for his court. "We're half-way home," he wrote, "and a good start time-wise for passage during the 88th Congress. We have high hopes that this will come about." But it was not to be. As early as June 26, Proulx had been warned that Senate action might be delayed, as it "has just received from President Kennedy his Civil Rights proposal package, which could tie up the Senate for the balance of the session." Indeed it did, and when one adds to this Richard Russell's continued intransigence plus the tragedy of Kennedy's assassination in Dallas a few months later, one can understand why the Senate failed to consider the House bill.

Thus, in spite of all that had gone before, life tenure for USCAAF judges remained remote. Quinn had hoped that Senator Ervin's subcommittee might represent a viable detour around the Russell roadblock. Early in 1964, he observed that Senator Pastore was "collaborating with Senator Ervin . . . in our behalf." But Ervin was unwilling to break with his southern colleague. A year later, Proulx conceded that Ervin "would not be disposed to introduce the life tenure bill in the Senate if it did not meet with prior approval of Senator Russell—being aware of the latter's opposition to life tenure for any court, we cannot look to Senator Ervin for assistance at this juncture."

Although understandable, Ervin's decision not to oppose Russell—thus again leaving the Senate as a unmovable barrier to the measure—seemed even more unfortunate because there had appeared to be clear sailing for the proposal in the lower chamber. Fogarty assured Proulx that "there would be no difficulty in getting the bill through the House." In the meantime, Quinn's term was drawing to a close, and if he could not attain life tenure, he would have to seek reappointment, something that had not yet occurred in USCAAF history.

QUINN'S QUEST

As Quinn considered his options, he could only have been well aware of Latimer's fate. Yet the former Rhode Island governor hoped to capitalize first on his many congressional friends and contacts as well as the fact that Lyndon Johnson had been elected by a landslide. Indeed, Senator Pastore suggested that the entire Rhode Island delegation (all four of them) join in a letter to Johnson requesting reappointment and solicited a memorandum from Quinn's office to help him in its preparation. Proulx promptly complied.

The memorandum listed a number of reasons for Quinn's reappointment. They included the point that this would not be a new nomination, "thus age [seventy-one] discounted." His record as the first and only chief judge in the Court's history warranted retention. Proulx quoted various encomiums from military personnel as well as Senator Sam Ervin. He added that Quinn had resigned from a lifetime judicial appointment in Rhode Island to accept his current position. Finally, he noted of his chief judge: "health excellent and capacity for work undiminished—mentally and physically sound."

A few weeks later, the secretary to former Rhode Island senator Theodore F. Green wrote President Johnson that "the Senator is definitely interested in having you consider [Quinn] for reappointment." Apparently Green's stature warranted more than the usual acknowledgement from a presidential assistant. Instead, Cyrus Vance, the deputy secretary of defense, drafted a proposed reply for "Special Presidential Assistant" Jack Valenti. Noncommittal at best, the letter merely stated that "the President appreciates Judge Quinn's outstanding career both prior to and after appointment to the Court . . . and recognizes the distinction with which he is serving." In his covering letter to Valenti, Vance had stated, "I think it is significant to note that Judge Quinn will shortly be 72 years old and the term of a Judge of [USCAAF] is 15 years."

Upon learning from House Speaker John McCormack, another Quinn booster, that Valenti would be dealing with the Quinn matter, Pastore addressed a personal letter to him. He reminded "Jack" that Quinn had long been a symbol among Democrats in Rhode Island and that as "Fighting Bob," he had been minority leader in the state senate "when you could count Democrats on the fingers of both hands." On a "very personal note," added Pastore—himself a former governor of Rhode Island—"when I was a young boy . . . working as an errand boy in a tailoring establishment which made Bob Quinn's clothes, it was there that I was so impressed by his vigor and progressiveness in the Democratic cause that, I can humbly say, gave me the inspiration to follow a public career in the Democratic Party."

Even before receiving Pastore's letter, Valenti had asked the White House personnel director, John Macy, for a "reading" on Quinn's status. On February 25, Valenti heard from Macy's office that the director would recommend two or three persons for the Court position but not Quinn, "mainly because he is 72 years old." Valenti was further informed that "the President is fairly firm on such appointments over the age of 60," and "even in view of the strong desires of the R.I. delegation, they are still not going to recommend reappointment." Whereupon Valenti sent a short note to the president, enclosing Pastore's letter and reporting on the negative recommendation from Macy's office. "For all that I can determine, Judge Quinn's advanced age is the only reason that Macy is not recommending him." Should, he asked, "we go forward with the nomination anyway?" Johnson replied with a notation scrawled on the bottom of the letter, "See me. Get Pastore in to see me."

In the meantime, Macy's office submitted its own memorandum to Johnson, noting that Quinn would be "87 at the termination of a second term if reappointed." Macy urged that "a younger man be appointed" to USCAAF, and "that Quinn be named to the existing vacancy on the American Battle Monuments Commission." (In a very real sense, the Battle Monuments Commission might have been a graveyard for Quinn, if only because it was responsible for the operation and maintenance of some thirty-seven overseas military cemeteries and memorials. Its eleven members "serve at the pleasure of the President, without compensation except travel expenses and a $20 per diem when engaged in Commission business." In short, the commission was a "do nothing, dead-end" type job.)

Pending Johnson's decision, Macy's office also continued lining up potential candidates for the president's consideration. Two of them warrant brief discussion because they reveal the way Macy's office went about locating candidates for such a position as well as a concern for expertise in the appropriate field. The availability of the Macy files at the Johnson Library offers a good opportunity to study some of the actual options offered to a president in appointing USCAAF judges. Neither in Eisenhower's nor Kennedy's administration were these candidates screened as thoroughly as Marsh and Macy appear to have done for Johnson. Besides having to respond to the usual potential office seekers, Macy's office also actively sought them out. Had he wished to do so, in other words, Johnson could have appointed very distinguished legal scholars and practitioners to USCAAF positions.

In March, Macy's assistant, James Marsh, contacted Phil C. Neal, dean of the University of Chicago Law School. Neal responded with a letter proposing several names. One was Frederick Bernays Wiener. A former army JAG officer as well as an able legal historian, Wiener had presented testimony at both the House and the Senate hearings in 1949 on the proposed UCMJ and USCAAF and currently practiced law in Washington, where he argued extensively in the federal appellate courts, including USCAAF. Apparently, Wiener's potential candidacy went no further. In the margin of Neal's letter appears the comment, "Brilliant but lacks temperament." Marsh had also discussed a nomination with Russell Fairbanks, at the time a professor of law at Columbia University Law School, and soon to become the first dean of the new Rutgers Law School at Camden. Although retired from the regular army, Fairbanks felt that a possible position on USCAAF was so important that "I would be prepared to resign my commission."

As is not unusual with presidential options, in the Quinn case Johnson found himself getting conflicting signals from some of his staunchest Democratic supporters and his own personnel office. Macy's notes of a meeting with the president on April 4 well reveal his ambivalence: "The President is torn on this one. He would like to please Pastore[,] but he is clearly opposed to reappointing a man who is 72 years old to a 15 year term. When I left him, he had a call in to [Judge] Kilday to ask what the burdens of this particular Court might be."

Later on the same day, Valenti reported to Johnson that he had talked with Pastore: "He understands your position . . . but he finds himself in a bind." Pastore wanted to discuss the matter with John Fogarty, a Rhode Island congressman and a close friend of Quinn. Pastore "was sympathetic to the President's dilemma, but he kept saying 'what can I tell Quinn?' " On the next day, Valenti again talked with Pastore, who had discussed the matter with the former governor. The chief judge was concerned about the fact that "he will not be eligible for federal retirement for a little under three years from now." According to Valenti, Pastore "is hopeful of getting a resignation from Quinn that would go into effect the moment that he becomes eligible for federal retirement. I remonstrated against the President's difficulty in the appointment for even a restrictive period of time."

For a third day in a row, Valenti and Pastore wrestled with the Quinn quandary. Pastore observed that if Quinn could remain on the bench until spring 1968, he would apparently be entitled to a federal pension that was four thousand dollars greater than if he were to retire in May 1966. Valenti then paraphrased some of Pastore's comments: "Look, I am with my President. He can always count on me. . . . Whatever the President does in the Quinn matter will make no difference to my loyalty. I am the President's man. . . . But it would be so heartwarming to me if in this difficult moment, the President would reappoint Quinn—and get from Quinn a resignation dated" on the appropriate day that his pension is secured. Even if Johnson refused him, "it will not make one iota of difference in my continued support all the way for the President—but, God, it would be so good for me to say the President had a difficult decision, but he resolved it in favor of Pastore."

Upon receiving Valenti's third memorandum in as many days, apparently Johnson agreed to see Pastore, and with the desired results. Although dealing with a potent politician, Pastore was no amateur either. Emphasizing his loyalty to the president even as the Vietnam quagmire deepened could not have hurt his cause. Valenti later well described the atmosphere of crisis concerning Vietnam that affected the White House from spring 1966 until 1968: "No matter what we turned our hands and minds to, there was Vietnam, its contagion infecting everything that it touched, and it seemed to touch everything." Thus the Quinn matter simply was not a primary object of concern. One week later, Pastore wrote to Valenti to "thank you for your cooperation in the Quinn matter. Frankly, this could have had a very disappointing result without your understanding and help, and I want you to know I appreciate it very, very much. I hope that someday you will grant me the opportunity to do something for you."

Whether or not Macy was aware of Pastore's actions is not clear. He continued to gather names for submission to Johnson, and what stands out is the apparent candor with which he evaluated them. He described one candidate who enjoyed the support of "most of the Democratic leadership in Maryland" as a man who "would probably do [the job] acceptably, but his career has not been at a sufficiently high level to effectively compete with other candidates." Five days later, Macy submitted his first three choices for Quinn's seat to the president. His leading contender was Fairbanks, whom Macy described as "the best candidate I have found." He characterized another of his choices as a man "who would make a good, but not outstanding judge." But when Macy discussed his candidates with the president on April 23, Johnson told Macy that Quinn would be reappointed "with the understanding that he will only serve until the Spring of 1968. The details [with] respect to this condition will be worked out by Mr. Valenti through Senator Pastore."

With Quinn's term expiring on May 1, Macy urged that we "proceed as rapidly as possible, because USCAAF judges *do not* continue to serve after the expiration of their terms." The resignation letter from Quinn was drafted in the White House on April 25. Its key provision stated that "I hereby submit to you my resignation from the Court to become effective at such time as you may see fit to accept the resignation." Two days later, the formal notice to the Senate of Quinn's reappointment had been prepared, but Valenti recommended to Johnson that "you allow me to call Senator Pastore and ask him to forward the undated resignation letter from Judge Quinn to you." Johnson's assistant Jake

Jacobsen reported to the president that Pastore "told me that Judge Quinn would deliver the letter of resignation to him tomorrow and that he assures us that he will have it here. . . . he gave me his word that the letter of resignation would be forthcoming."

On April 28, Valenti's office received Quinn's handwritten resignation, dated June 20, 1968, whereupon the nomination went forward to the Senate. Apparently, the fact that Quinn had dated his letter caused some concern, since one of Johnson's aides had assumed that the letter would be undated, as was the usual practice with "blanket resignations." However, Valenti's office made it clear that "June 20, 1968 is the date to which, under the present understanding, Judge Quinn will serve, and that on that basis the nomination . . . can go forward to the Senate."

Although the Armed Services Committee had not bothered to invite either Ferguson or Kilday to appear at their confirmation hearings, the panel insisted on a formal session with Quinn present because, as Russell put it, "we have had some additions to the Committee since Judge Quinn's original appointment." Ordinarily, he added, "we do not hear those who are up for reappointment." During the very brief hearing, Quinn gave no indication of the previous events concerning renomination. In a response to a question from Massachusetts Republican Leverett Saltonstall—and like the nominee a former governor of his state—Quinn did remark, however, that he would "be glad" to continue "if the committee would like to have me . . . I would be glad to serve at least for a few years, as long as the law will let me."

But Quinn had dated his letter June 20, 1968, thus making his resignation impossible prior to that date. Moreover, he resigned "at such time as you see fit to accept it." Therefore, unless Johnson, or his successor, moved to activate the resignation, theoretically Quinn could continue in office until his term expired, in 1981. It might also be noted that the letter was addressed "to the President," not to Lyndon Johnson. After superficial questioning, Quinn's nomination went forward to the full Senate, where he was confirmed on May 16, 1966. On the same day, Johnson again designated Quinn as chief judge.

The president had assumed that with Quinn's resignation in hand, he would have a new USCAAF appointment in 1968. Ultimately he did, but it would not be to replace Quinn. Moreover, Johnson probably did not anticipate that the tragedy of Vietnam would overtake both him and his administration. Disappointed and defeated, LBJ left the presidency while Quinn remained on the bench. Richard Nixon would have to deal with the next segment of the Quinn saga, which, it turned out, was far from over. Indeed, because of disgraceful conduct, Nixon would also leave the presidency in defeat and disappointment—and when he did, Quinn *still* sat as a USCAAF judge.

19

Litigation, Legislation, and Longevity for Quinn, 1965–1968

Robert Quinn was the first of only two USCAAF judges appointed to a second full term. President Johnson, however, did not intend that the chief judge should serve out his fifteen-year renewal, an understanding that apparently had been accepted by Quinn. In the meantime, Ferguson, Kilday, and Quinn continued to function as the Court, and the various machinations concerning reappointment of the chief judge must be seen in the light of other developments between 1965 and 1968. While the three judges appear to have had mutual respect and regard for each other as colleagues, they strongly disagreed concerning several new developments in military justice. Not surprisingly, these divided opinions reflected the vigorous reactions among lawyers and judges triggered by the Warren Court's "revolution" in criminal law—a process well under way even as Quinn gained reappointment.

DOCTRINAL DEBATES AND DIVERGENT DECISIONS

In 1964, by a vote of 5 to 4, the Supreme Court held that an incriminating statement made by a defendant during police interrogation "was inadmissible because the defendant had been denied the right to consult counsel." Whether or not the Warren Court "revolution" started with this famous decision, *Escobedo v. Illinois,* is less important than the fact that USCAAF had grappled with its issues on a number of previous occasions. In 1957, for example, Quinn and Ferguson concluded that while "an accused is not entitled to appointed military counsel prior to the filing of charges . . . he is not thereby precluded from obtaining necessary legal advice." One year later, the same two judges sought to clarify the important distinction between "no right to appointed counsel as distinguished from no right to consult counsel."

These cases involved interrogation of a suspect who was later formally accused.

Two years before the *Escobedo* decision, over a dissent by Ferguson, the Court held in *United States v. Petty* that "an accused is not denied the assistance of counsel unless he requests and is refused the right to consult counsel during the interrogation, or is misinformed as to his right to counsel." Two years after *Escobedo,* in *United States v. Wimberley,* a unanimous Court declined to extend the right of counsel "to include the investigative processes." Indeed, according to Chief Judge Quinn, "nothing in the [UCMJ] or in the decisions of this Court, and nothing in our experience with military methods of interrogation, indicate that the only feasible way to give maximum effect to the constitutional right to the assistance of counsel is that the accused have counsel beside him during police questioning."

During the interval between *Petty* and *Wimberly,* Paul Kilday wrote a letter to his brethren expressing "my concern about the number of divided opinions in this Court." A surprising number of persons, he noted, have "expressed to me the hope that we could do something about the high incidence of divided opinions." Indeed, "other than the diehards who want no civilian court, this constitutes the major criticism that I have ever heard" concerning it. Kilday added that this objection had been expressed to him "in jocular terms," leading him to conclude that "this means that people are not likely to express criticism to members of a court. It does not mean that there is no strong criticism rampant." The newest USCAAF member probably agreed with this viewpoint, all the more so because his brethren were the cause for such a condition.

"I believe," he wrote, "[that] divided opinions militate against the prestige of any court." Moreover, "I believe it to be a very serious matter to any court and, especially, a three judge court." Worst of all, "divided opinions are most confusing in the field. Persons charged with the administration of military justice are left in a quandary as to the statement of the law and what should be followed." Particularly because USCAAF normally acted only after a case had already been considered both by a JAG and a court of review, any judicial split "arms our critics with powerful ammunition."

Coming from a perspective of more than twenty years as a congressman, one who had repeatedly sought to fashion consensus whenever possible, Kilday's views were understandable, although somewhat naive. From his perception, "there are not basic differences between the Judges. Our divisions . . . are on the facts or the application of the law in a particular case." (Where, it might be asked, could there be more fundamental areas of juridical disagreement than over facts and law?) Nevertheless, he concluded, "our divisions have increased rather than diminished." Indeed they had, and the minimal role Kilday played in this trend is very clear.

An examination of several USCAAF volumes during the seven years Kilday served on its bench confirms the paucity of his major dissents. In two sample periods, Quinn dissented at least twenty-six and sixteen times; Ferguson, fourteen and twenty-one times; but Kilday did not dissent at all. In the vast majority of controversial cases, Kilday appears to have been the pivotal swing vote. The 1967 case in which the Court adopted the Miranda rules for criminal interrogation is an excellent example of this trend. *Miranda* established that an individual held for custodial interrogation must be informed of the right to counsel; of the fact that, in the case of indigency, counsel will be provided through the Court; and of the right to remain silent, having been advised that anything stated thereafter could be used in evidence.

Speaking for himself and Judge Kilday, Judge Ferguson noted that in this case, involving an accused who had requested counsel, the JAG for the navy had filed an amicus brief which urged that "military law is in nowise affected by constitutional limitations." Thus, the principles in *Miranda v. Arizona* were both irrelevant and inapplicable. The air force JAG, under whose jurisdiction the case arose, conceded the primacy of the Constitution to military justice. He argued, however, that the Supreme Court "has no supervisory power over military tribunals." Therefore, it was neither necessary nor desirable that USCAAF follow its lead. Ferguson did not find any merit in the navy's position. "The time," he wrote, "is long since past . . . when this Court will lend an attentive ear to the argument that members of the armed services are, by reason of their status, *ipso facto* deprived of all protections of the Bill of Rights."

To be sure, military justice had evolved as a field of jurisprudence somewhat separate from its civilian counterpart. While the extent of such separation remained controversial, by 1967 both USCAAF and the high court were "satisfied as to the applicability of constitutional safeguards to military trials, except insofar as they are made inapplicable either expressly or by necessary implication." Nor was there validity to the contention that *Miranda* represented a supervisory function rather than one of constitutional adjudication. Calling the air force JAG's position an "ingenious argument," Ferguson reiterated the assumption that U.S. Supreme Court views on constitutional issues "are binding on us." Because the defendant in this case had been informed "that no counsel would be appointed for him [contrary to the Miranda rule], it follows that the statement thereafter taken from him was inadmissable in evidence."

Although Kilday agreed with Ferguson that "this Court is bound by the Supreme Court on questions of constitutional import," Quinn insisted that the Supreme Court had not intended to apply *Miranda* "to the military legal system." He pointed to the well-established doctrine against self-incrimination set forth in the UCMJ, arguing that its provisions in article 31 "satisfy all constitutional requirements." Quinn further claimed that although not specifically required by the code, the actual military practice of "according the individual faced with in-custody interrogation the right to consult the staff legal officer . . . is fully as effective a safeguard" as what is set forth in *Miranda*. To demand more, as did his brethren, "is to legislate, not adjudicate." Although in this case

Quinn had found himself in dissent, on numerous occasions he joined with Kilday, leaving Ferguson as the dissenter. On the other hand, the combination of Quinn and Ferguson, with Kilday in dissent, was very rare.

THE TENUOUSNESS OF TENURE

It will be recalled that in 1963, the House of Representatives had passed the bill granting USCAAF judges life tenure, only to see it stalled in the Senate—a victim both of Richard Russell's unyielding opposition and the legislative logjam of statutes proposed in the wake of President Kennedy's assassination. It will further be recalled that during 1965–1966, Quinn's concern had shifted to the question of his reappointment. With that goal attained, the Court sought yet again to gain equal tenure status with other federal appellate judges. Indeed, Court efforts toward this goal had been ongoing even before Quinn began his campaign to retain his seat.

Thus, Judge Kilday had visited with his friend Lyndon Johnson on October 23, 1963. He also urged Quinn to ask Senator Pastore to see both Johnson and Russell. By the time Quinn talked with Pastore in January 1964, Johnson had become president, and Russell had made it clear to House Speaker John McCormack—a close friend of Quinn's—that he "is definitely opposed to the bill—to life tenure for any court." Kilday also believed that Maine Republican senator Margaret Chase Smith "has great influence with Senator Russell." In other words, as Quinn observed to Rhode Island Congressman John Fogarty, "There is work to be done." By April, however, Kilday and Quinn had conceded that "any further effort to get Senator Russell to buy life tenure would be useless."

Being no novices to political behavior, the next question may well have occurred to both Quinn and Kilday simultaneously. Since Russell "would not budge, would he buy the bill without life tenure[?]" The recalcitrant senator agreed. His House counterpart, Carl Vinson, immediately indicated that the House bill would be revised, cutting out life tenure but retaining the fifteen-year terms plus other pension benefits in the original measure. Thus by April 13, instead of gaining ratification for life tenure, in reality Quinn and Kilday faced its requiem.

Within ten days, Proulx met with William Darden, a staff member of Russell's committee and longtime aide to its chair. Shortly thereafter, he prepared a summary of the benefits included in the House bill, albeit without life tenure. The measure would "confirm the Court of Military Appeals as a legislative court established under Article I of the Constitution." Moreover, "it would make explicit what is now implicit": that its judges "are entitled to the salary, allowances and perquisites of judges of the U.S. Courts of appeals." It would give USCAAF judges the same retirement rights as their Article 3 counterparts.

Finally, "it will enhance the standing and prestige of the court by providing security for those serving as judges thereof. . . . Currently, a federal district judge of proven ability would not aspire to membership on [USCAAF] because of the diminished security and lesser retirement rights." Rhetoric aside, while fixed terms were desirable, the question can be raised as to what judicial security could mean to USCAAF judges without its most basic component, life tenure. Moreover, there is validity to the conclusion that by its refusal to grant USCAAF judges equal standing with other federal appellate judges, Congress denigrates its own creation.

Even though this measure was apparently acceptable to Russell, no efforts appear to have been undertaken to enact it until 1967. The delay was due in part to the vicissitudes of political action in Washington, including the lengthy debate and three-month-long Senate filibuster over the 1964 Civil Rights bill. In September 1967, Senator Pastore wrote to Quinn, reminding him once again of Russell's "antipathy to life tenure. Right or wrong, that's the way he feels not only to the military court, [but] I suppose to all courts." His view represented "a feeling," added Pastore, "quite prevalent among the southern senators and here again I suppose it stems from the Civil Rights issue."

The next day, Darden sent Pastore a draft of a statute based on the old 1963 House bill but stripped of its life tenure provision. He also provided an additional reason why USCAAF may not have urged that the 1963–1964 "compromise" bill be adopted. Darden noted that although "in 1964 this version of the bill was acceptable to Senator Russell, I think . . . it produces so little change that the Judges of the Court apparently were in disagreement over whether such a bill was worth enactment." For reasons that are unclear, by November 1967 Quinn and his colleagues may well have decided to accept what they could get, even though it was much less than had originally been sought. After satisfying himself that both Quinn and Russell would support it, Pastore introduced the new proposal, which cleared Russell's committee in less than three weeks. No further hearings were held on the bill, possibly because there was so little of substance that remained in it.

Similarly, in reporting the bill favorably to the Senate, Russell could not point to any major legislative innovation contained in the measure. His statement emphasized "the congressional intent . . . that the Court of [Appeals for the Armed Forces] be a court in every significant respect." But "despite this clear intent, there have been contentions that the court is not a court at all but is an instrumentality of the executive branch or an administrative agency within the Department of Defense." The report further noted that while the tribunal is "located for administrative purposes in the Department of Defense," this phrase referred only to its function of furnishing the court with "such things as telephone services, transportation facilitites, and to purchase supplies. The court justifies its own budget and funds are appropriated for its operations with no control exercised by the Department of Defense."

For about the first twenty-five years of its history, this statement was apparently true. But during the controversial tenure of Albert Fletcher Jr. as chief judge between 1975 and 1980, the department actively interfered in the Court's budgetary procedures (see Chapters 21 and 22). By reaffirming its creation under Article 1 of the Constitution, the legislation would "reaffirm the congressional intent that the court be the civilian supervisor of the administration of military justice and the final interpreter of the requirements of military law."

As if to leave the matter beyond all doubt, Russell added that "the bill proposes no change either in the term of offices or the retirement benefits of the judges." It did provide, however, for the possibility that a USCAAF retired judge might be recalled to active status if needed and could occupy offices in a federal building. Without formal discussion or recorded vote, the Senate passed the bill the next day. Almost seven months later, and without serious debate or a recorded vote, the House concurred. Thus far, the current congressional action concerning USCAAF had been of such limited significance that earlier considerations within the Court about not even bothering to endorse such a bill become understandable.

THE EXTENDED EFFORTS OF SENATOR ERVIN

After the 1962 Senate hearings, Ervin had introduced a number of bills to reform military justice. The senator, who served in the U.S. Senate from 1954–1974, represented an intriguing amalgam of liberal and conservative views. Thus he was very supportive of due process protection for members of the military. Upon hearing that a navy petty officer had lost his confidential security clearance because he criticized American policy in Vietnam, Ervin wrote a strong protest to Secretary of Defense Robert McNamara: "That a citizen should suffer any penalty because he dared express views contrary to official policy, is an affront to the most basic principles that we as free individuals and American citizens hold supreme." On the other hand, Ervin denounced civil rights legislation with equal vigor. He did not believe that "the Federal government may constitutionally preempt the criminal jurisdiction of the States to punish private acts of discrimination." The Civil Rights Bill of 1968 was "another futile exercise in attempting to solve racial problems by the coercive power of the law instead of through increased understanding and cooperation of the races."

The bills never left the Senate committee to which they had been referred, and in 1965, Ervin submitted them again, reintroducing the measures with virtually the same comments he had used before. In 1966, a special subcommittee drawn from both the Senate Armed Services and Judiciary Committees held hearings on the proposals. Many witnesses who had appeared previously came forward again to reiterate their views. But the 1966 hearings differed from the 1962 sessions in two important ways.

In the first place, all parties concerned were well aware that there was now a much greater public interest in military matters even as the Vietnam War intensified. Moreover, the 1966 hearings revealed a well-orchestrated effort by the military to transform certain of Ervin's bills into a format acceptable to them. Ultimately, as is so often the case, neither the objects of the intended legislation nor its sponsor obtained all they wanted. But in retrospect one is impressed with the way in which the military, in particular the army, employed compromise rather than confrontation.

Among Ervin's bills were several that would have made changes in USCAAF jurisdiction within military justice. Based upon his 1963 proposals, they sought to: strengthen the means for penalizing unlawful command influence; provide a pretrial conference in certain courts-martial; provide military judges for special courts-martial; give USCAAF the authority to review administrative discharges and dismissals from the services; prohibit a senior board of review member from evaluating another member; set up a civilian board to correct military records; increase the authority of the law officer, now to be called the military judge; and finally, replace the existing boards of review with new tribunals—to be called courts of military review—to be appointed by the service secretary instead of TJAG and to have a civilian as chief judge. Taken as a whole, again these changes would have made major alterations in the operating procedures for military justice, although Ervin emphasized that it was not his purpose "to do anything whatever which would impair in any way the capacity of the Armed Forces to maintain discipline." Rather, he hoped to "ascertain whether or not we can bring that necessary function and the administration of military justice into harmony with each other."

Ervin was genuinely concerned with this goal. He sought, through his proposals, to enable the military justice system to "attain, insofar as human wisdom can, the closest approximation to true justice." There was no intention to interfere with the "prerequisites of the national safety. Rather, it has been to maintain the integrity and prestige of the military judicial system, while at the same time, incorporating the essential legal safeguards which have been nurtured and severed through centuries of our history. It is of the utmost importance that the arm of our society which is entrusted with the defense of our liberties and our freedom not be found lacking in one of the most valuable aspects of our civilization, judicial protections of individual rights."

Although not directly addressed in any of Ervin's measures, the issue of life tenure for USCAAF could not be ignored. The well-known opposition of Richard Russell notwithstanding, Ervin remained troubled by the disinclination of the Senate to consider Court tenure—even though he declined to push the proposal: "I think it is a great mistake. I certainly think the other Federal courts rather look down their noses at the Court . . . and are inclined to think that it is not a court in every sense of the word."

All three judges appeared before the subcommittee, and all endorsed legislative efforts to deal effectively with command influence. But they insisted that Congress, not the judges, had to solve this problem. Quinn urged prosecution for "deliberate attempts to exercise command control," stating that "just because a general or admiral commits the offense should not make him any less amenable to prosecution than a private." Ferguson pointed to the inherent impropriety of a staff JAG officer retaliating "against counsel's efforts to serve his client by giving him a totally unsatisfactory efficiency report." Such a scenario, one that he claimed had actually occurred, represented a serious threat to military justice.

"If the defense counsel, in the best traditions of our bar, ignores the efforts to influence him and stands up and fights for his client, he gets a bad efficiency report which can absolutely ruin his military career." If the influence is ineffective, the court can do nothing because "the accused has had his day in court and there is no basis for reversal. . . . If, on the other hand, counsel is in fact fearful for his career, we will hear nothing about it, for the record will be totally silent in the matter. The dice, therefore, are loaded in favor of the sycophant, and something should and must be done by the Congress."

The military position on the subject of command influence, especially as it concerned improper evaluation of the lower appellate court judges, generally consisted of outright denial that such incidents occurred, let alone that they were inappropriate. It simply was not true that the chairmen of the various judicial panels were unable to rate fairly and objectively. To say otherwise, as the legal officer to the Marine Corps commandant noted, "misjudges the caliber and devotion of our people to the point almost of being slanderous." No officer sitting as a judge, he added, "who has devoted his entire adult lifetime to the service of the law is likely to put an accused in and out of jail just to please his boss." Listening to the witness, Ervin could not resist pointing to "a human element which I admit I succumb to. I am always inclined to think that the wisest members of the Senate are those who share my sound views on questions." As to the extent of command influence, while the military now conceded that the practice "is not legal[,] . . . our problem with [it] is really a question of the exercise of judgment, and we cannot legislate good judgment."

Earlier, Ervin had scoffed at the idea of a total absence of command influence in any court-martial, saying that such a claim reminded him of the story about a lawyer "summoned down to the jail to see his client. The lawyer asked him, 'What have they got you here for?' And the client told him. The lawyer said, 'Well, they can't put a man in jail for that.' And his client said, 'Well, I am here.'"

Ervin's joint subcommittee concluded its hearings in March 1966, but it was not until June 1967 that he reintroduced the Military Justice Act of 1967 in the Senate. Recognizing the corrosive effect of the lengthening Vietnam conflict, Ervin reminded his colleagues that "more and more private citizens are being called to service in an ugly war. . . . We cannot wait, as we did a generation ago, until these men return to civilian life with their stories of injustice." He claimed that, with few exceptions, the new proposals incorporated the provisions introduced earlier. The exceptions, however, reflected legislative realities—and they were more significant than Ervin acknowledged.

Thus, Ervin had sought to abolish the summary court-martial. The unanimous opposition of all the armed services, joined by the Defense Department—which, unlike the 1948–1949 period, appeared increasingly inclined to speak for the military rather than to it—doomed this provision. Ervin was able to retain a stipulation giving a service member an option to decline a summary court, thus ensuring that "no citizen would be forced to stand trial against his will in an American court . . . where the same man is judge and jury, prosecutor and defense counsel." Nevertheless, although the summary court "is an inferior court in concept, procedure, and in the quality of justice it dispenses," it remained part of the UCMJ. Taken as a whole, however, Ervin's proposed Military Justice Act of 1967 represented a significant and far-reaching transformation of the UCMJ. Promptly referred to the Senate Armed Services Com mittee, for reasons that remain unclear the omnibus bill never reached the Senate floor. Further impetus for changes in the UCMJ shifted to the House.

Aware of the significant changes desired by Ervin, the military—aided by a special ABA committee—drafted an alternative measure. Submitted to the House Armed Services Committee in April 1967, it had the unanimous backing of all the services as well as the Defense Department. Compared to what Ervin had sought, one can easily understand why.

The bill focused primarily on increased participation of law officers on courts-martial. On the other hand, it made no changes in the courts of military review, provided no increase in Court authority, and barred trial before a military judge alone without the consent of the convening authority. Moreover, it made no mention of any civilian board to correct or review military records. Although the legislation blocked a special court-martial from awarding a bad conduct discharge unless the accused was represented by legally qualified counsel, this safeguard was waived in time of war. Representative Philbin was not guilty of exaggeration when he later claimed that the bill was merely "an attempt to make a few changes that are non-controversial." Even so, its supporters worried that any modification of its provisions might block ultimate enactment.

One member of Congress observed, correctly, that "when you give a man a bad conduct discharge you are putting a stigma on him for life, and I think he should have adequate protection." As written, the exception in time of war would give the military the "opportunity for people in the field to say, 'Well, we just couldn't find a legal counsel.' They will find a way of justifying the reason they couldn't find it, even if they could have gotten one by going a hundred miles down the road." Indeed, "in my experience, the most unfortunate cases arise in time of war[,] and where the most damage and harm and lack of consideration is given is in time of war. This is where they need protection the greatest." Before sending the measure to the full House, the committee decided not to make any changes but to add "a very strong statement in the report" that counsel should be readily available.

Within a few weeks, however, the committee reconsidered the issue and deleted the exception. As amended, the proposed bill cleared the House on June 3, 1968, without change, debate, or recorded vote. Promptly introduced into the Senate, the enactment was duly referred to the Armed Services Committee where Senator Ervin was ready and waiting. Although Ervin later submitted a committee report of more than thirty pages endorsing a heavily amended version of the House bill, he insisted that his revisions were only "an attempt to make a few changes that can be agreed upon by the Congress and the armed services," and that he was trying "to improve some of the procedures and increase the substantive safeguards in courts-martial." Ervin can be pardoned for his disingenuousness. But one need only compare the bill as originally passed by the House with the alterations adopted by the Senate and later concurred in by the lower chamber to see that the revisions incorporated many of the "reform" measures of concern to him for more than six years. In both his written correspondence and his later remarks to the Senate, as that body prepared to vote on the amendments, the North Carolina senator was more candid.

Writing to Army TJAG Kenneth Hodson only a few weeks after passage of H.R. 15971, Ervin claimed that the measure did not contain "the minimum reforms of the [UCMJ] necessary to return the military system of criminal justice to the leading position it so recently occupied in American Law." Therefore, he concluded that "a number of amendments are necessary . . . and I shall offer them when the bill is considered by the Senate Armed Services Committee." In a letter to his fellow southerner and chairman of the Armed Services Committee, Richard Russell, Ervin described the eight changes he desired in the legislation. Among the most important were: redesignating the "law officer" as the "military Judge," creating an independent field judiciary, requiring legally qualified military counsel in all special courts-martial, facilitating the option by a serviceman for trial by a summary court-martial, strengthening the ban against command influence, and providing that a military judge must preside at all special courts-martial empowered to adjudge a bad conduct discharge.

Conceding that the House bill was a "far cry" from his measure, Ervin had to consider the warning from his House counterpart that the entire chamber "would not accept much more than the reforms" contained in its version. Rather than find out how true this assertion was, instead Ervin determined to "beef up the House bill" as previously noted. Several of the committee staff "had extensive discussions" with army representatives from the JAG Corps, with a resulting agreement that the military would not oppose six out of the eight Ervin changes. The military balked, however, at Ervin's insistence that legally qualified military counsel be available at all special courts-martial. Apparently, Ervin had agreed to meet with Army TJAG Hodson to see if "some of these differences can be worked out."

The meetings between Ervin and Hodson did indeed take place, and as Ervin later wrote to all the members of the Senate Armed Services Committee, "I have modified some of the amendments . . . and have withdrawn others." The result was Defense Department acceptance, if not enthusiastic endorsement, of Ervin's revised revisions, apparently a sine qua non for House approval. The senator from North Carolina could now assert that his colleagues need have no fear that "acceptance of my amendments will jeopardize enactment of the bill this year." Ervin was fully aware that if the House endorsed the Senate amendments without change, "no conference will be necessary," hence his concern that the changes be acceptable to the military prior to reconsideration by the House. Following pro forma approval from the Senate committee, Ervin described some of the key changes to his fellow legislators.

He emphasized that his proposed alterations had been accepted—some with marked reluctance—by the military. One such provision, one of the very few deletions from the House bill, eliminated the need for the commanding officer to approve a court-martial before a military judge alone. Ervin explained that "the command structure in the military presents a possibility of undue prejudicial influence over the Court that is not present in civilian life. . . . [T]he military judge, having heard arguments from both trial and defense counsel concerning the appropriateness of trial by a military judge alone, will be in the best position to protect the interests of both the Government and the accused." Because Ervin shrewdly had retained virtually the entire House bill, adding rather than altering, he placed the military in the unpleasant position of either accepting his changes or seeing the entire measure, replete with all they had sought, face probable defeat. Ultimately, the Defense Department accepted Hodson's recommendation that "there were so many good aspects in the legislation that we really shouldn't turn it down" because of military opposition to certain of Ervin's additions, especially this one. Another change preserved the right of a defendant to decline a summary court-martial, a forum "which affords literally no safeguards to the defendant."

A third revision sought to strengthen the existing UCMJ ban against command influence by ensuring that the performance of a court-martial participant either as a member, trial, or defense counsel "could not be evaluated in preparing an effectiveness, fitness, or efficiency report . . . nor could he be given a less favorable rating because of his zeal in acting as defense counsel in a court martial." Nevertheless, just as Ervin had to concede the impossibility of abolishing the summary court, so here he had to accept an exemption to this amendment that permitted "general instructional or informational courses in military justice if such courses are designed solely for the purpose of instructing members of a command in the substantive and procedural aspects of courts-martial."

With no discussion or recorded vote, on October 3, 1968, the Senate accepted Ervin's amendments. When properly greased, the legislative process can be remarkably swift. One week after Senate action, the House concurred in a similar manner. Thus, the most important changes to the UCMJ since its adoption in 1950 were enacted by Congress without any sort of floor debate, let alone a formal roll call. Two weeks later, President Johnson signed the measure into law. The thoroughness of congressional consideration was conspicuous by its absence.

One suspects that the paucity of legislative attention was due to external circumstances as well as a traditional—although unfortunate—lack of sustained congressional interest in military justice. The bill passed as Congress rushed toward adjournment in the midst of a contentious presidential campaign that followed the disastrous (and bloody) Democratic Convention in Chicago. With Johnson's administration mired in the miasma of the Vietnam tragedy and with the election one month away, the lawmakers had little interest in debating the nuances of court-martial procedures. Even as Johnson signed the bill, however, his attention had been called once again to the question of Chief Judge Quinn's continued presence on the USCAAF bench.

THE QUINN SAGA CONTINUES

It will be recalled that in 1965 as a condition of reappointment, Quinn had submitted a postdated letter of resignation to Johnson. He would step down in June 1968, when he became eligible for federal retirement. As this time drew nigh, however, it became clear that the chief judge did not wish to leave office. At his request, Senator Pastore again wrote to Johnson, seeking an extension of Quinn's tenure. "If it doesn't happen," he later noted to Quinn, "it certainly won't be because I didn't try for one of the greatest men I know."

On May 9, Johnson's aide, Jack Valenti, reminded Pastore's office of the agreement for Quinn to resign. He also stated that "the President had made a commitment to a longtime friend for the Court." His assertion probably referred to Johnson's old friend and former congressional colleague, Paul Kilday. Kilday had been a judge since 1961, and while Johnson could have designated any of the three sitting jurists as chief, he had made no change; Quinn had continued to hold the center seat on the bench. Even though he had Quinn's resignation in hand, for reasons that remain unclear but that might be related to Pastore's concerns, Johnson hesitated to activate Quinn's retirement.

Another of Johnson's aides, Larry Temple, informed the president that he had specifically asked Kilday if "there would be any problem—legal or practical—with permitting Judge Quinn to continue to serve as a member of the Court and naming Judge Kilday as Chief Judge. Judge Kilday knew of no legal prohibition of this." But he was concerned that "this might prove embarrasing both to himself and the President—and might cause some conflict on the Court. He did not want to cause any problems [and] had indicated his interest in being Chief Judge only because he understands Judge Quinn was resigning." According to Temple, Kilday indicated that "if Judge Quinn is to continue on the Court . . . it would be a preferable working situation for Quinn to remain as Chief Judge and Kilday to retain his present status." Temple summarized Kilday's attitude as "whatever the President wants to do is fine with him."

Johnson's hesitation may signify that the president had not yet decided what he wanted to do, if only because an additional candidate now surfaced. Early in June, William Darden, the chief of staff for Senator Russell's Armed Services Committee, indicated his interest in succeeding Quinn. Indeed, as early as 1965, Darden had expressed similar sentiments, anticipating Quinn's exit at the end of his first term. After Darden made known his latest aspirations to join the Court, John Macy received information indicating that Darden was "very able, and very close to Senator Russell." His interest, according to Macy, "is in response to the Intelligence that Judge Quinn . . . will in fact retire some time this summer. In all likelihood, there will be a number of voluntary candidates for this post. It pays well. It has a long term. The work is not very demanding. This is low priority."

One can appreciate Macy's candor while deprecating his conclusions. His views regarding the low priority of this appointment reflected a perception widely held in administration circles about USCAAF since its inception. Truman, if not his staff, may have been the exception, because he placed great emphasis on the appointment process. As far as can be determined, no other president since Truman has troubled to interview any potential USCAAF members. At the bottom of Macy's comments is a handwritten notation referring to the anticipated USCAAF vacancy: "Justice Department has no interest. Leaves it to us and to DOD." It is noteworthy that in December 1966, when the Justice Department issued a four-page press release extolling the record-breaking number of federal judges selected by Johnson since assuming office—seventy in all—no mention was made of Quinn's reappointment. While it is true that Macy had sought outstanding candidates for USCAAF appointments and would do so again, overall his attitude appears to have been all too typical and cannot have been helpful to the continued development of USCAAF as a judicial institution of distinction.

Late in June, Quinn's impending resignation received wide coverage in the Rhode Island press. The *Warwick–Pawtucket Valley Evening Bulletin* reported that Quinn had submitted a resignation "about a week ago, but that he has heard nothing from the President." According to a White House staff member, however, "There is a possibility that [Quinn] may retire this year. . . . If the President does not act to give him an extension, he must leave the bench." But the staff member appears to have been mistaken. Although Quinn had indeed submitted a letter dated June 20, 1968, in order for the resignation to go into effect, the president would have to act on it. Put another way, for Quinn to stay where he was required only that the president do nothing, which is exactly what happened.

During the summer months the matter remained unresolved as the Senate grappled with a related issue, that of a replacement for Chief Justice Earl Warren, who had retired. At least one newpaper writer commented that Johnson "has decided not to act on Judge Quinn's resignation because of Senate opposition to Justice [Abe] Fortas," Johnson's choice to succeed Warren. There is, however, no evidence to justify such a conclusion. Indeed, it is based on the dubious assumption that Senate interest in the USCAAF chief judge was in the same league as appointing the chief justice of the United States. A Senate filibuster blocked Fortas's confirmation as Quinn's resignation lay pending. When both courts opened their fall terms, Warren and Quinn presided as usual.

By September, with the issue of the chief judge's position still unresolved, Kilday and his supporters were becoming restive. His former colleague on the House Armed Services Committee, Representative Philip Philbin, wrote to Johnson extolling Kilday's qualifications. Johnson's assistant acknowledged the letter, adding that "as far as I can determine, the present Chief Judge has not submitted a resignation." More accurate was Macy's reply to a writer supporting a candidate for USCAAF: "There is a widely held impression that a vacancy on this Court exists. . . . However, no vacancy exists and, at this point, it does not appear probable that one will occur in the near future." It is reasonable to conclude that by September, Johnson may have decided to leave the Quinn matter alone. Two days later, Johnson's assistant was informed that "Kilday had called again to urge that we accept or get Quinn's resignation so that he, Judge Kilday, can be named Chief Judge before court convenes for its fall session."

On October 3, Johnson received a memorandum concerning what now might be called the Quinn caper. First, the president was informed that the White House had "received no letter of resignation from . . . Chief Judge Quinn." Moreover, "Kilday called to say that the Court will open its fall term on October 8. He said that Quinn apparently thought he had submitted a resignation which would be accepted." One can only wonder what Johnson concluded upon receiving this missive.

There are at least two copies of Quinn's resignation letter in the Johnson papers. Also, as was noted in the previous chapter, correspondence related to the agreement reached on Quinn's reappointment clearly indicates the parties' knowledge of the resignation. Finally, Quinn's resignation had been announced, confirmed by Quinn himself, and indeed had been *the* sine qua non for renomination by the president two years before. Perhaps the confusion on this issue arose because of internal communication problems within the administration as it grappled with a number of critical matters in its last months, including Vietnam and the 1968 presidential election campaign.

The *Washington Examiner* stated that "some thought [Quinn] had actually written a letter to the White House about [resigning,] but five offices in the White House which handle such matters report they never saw the letter and the President knew nothing about it." To make matters even more confusing, if possible, Quinn was quoted as saying that "I considered resigning but actually I had not resigned." Whatever the reason, Quinn sat as chief judge when the fall term began. Four days later, Paul Kilday died of a massive heart attack.

Shocked by the tragedy, Johnson telegraphed Mrs. Kilday that he had "lost a friend and colleague. America has lost an outstanding public servant. Our men and women in uniform have lost a champion." Kilday's widow asked that her husband be buried in Arlington National Cemetery. A newly adopted rule, however, restricted burials therein to "Medal of Honor winners, active duty and retired members of the armed forces, and honorably discharged veterans who have also served in high positions in the federal government." Kilday fit none of these criteria. Nevertheless and with Johnson's approval, his assistant Joseph Califano instructed the Pentagon to "find a way to bury Judge Kilday in Arlington."

As commander in chief, Johnson could have ordered the burial, "but this would be an unwise departure from practice." Instead, the army authorized the interment "based on the unique role which judges of [USCAAF] play as the ultimate tribunal in the military justice system." On the day the ceremony was to take place, Califano was informed that a veteran's group "was so incensed over the burial . . . that it threatened to file suit in the District Court to require the disinterment of Kilday." A White House operative "immediately got in touch with the National Committee of the VFW and told them to stop acting like children." The end result was that the VFW National Headquarters "called the local office here and told them to immediately stop all harassment and to [f]orget the entire matter." White House Press Secretary George Christian emphasized that "there had been no pressure from the White House." When Paul Kilday was laid to rest not far from the president who had named him to the Court, Lyndon Johnson attended the graveside service.

The administration wasted no time in searching for a replacement. One day after Kilday's burial, Johnson's assistant Mike Manatos reported to the president that Richard Russell was in line to become chairman of the Senate Appropriations Committee: "This means that Bill Darden will be left hanging since there is no room for him on the Appropriations Committee[,] and chances are Senator [John] Stennis would want his own Chief of Staff on the Armed Services Commmittee." Perhaps "Darden might be considered as a replacement for Kilday." "I suppose," concluded Manatos, that "Bill Darden has qualifications equal to or better than any one else in this area. When both Bob Quinn and Homer Ferguson are pushing the high 70s perhaps an infusion of young blood could be worked out for the Court."

In the meantime, John Macy went about preparing his own recommendations for Johnson. He submitted four names to him—two judges and two law professors. All of these individuals had been considered during the 1966 search for a nominee who Macy had assumed would replace Quinn. Again, Russell Fairbanks headed the list. He was "the best qualified candidate I know of at this date." But Johnson probably gave little—if any—consideration to Macy's choices. Scrawled on the memorandum, although not in Johnson's hand, is a notation that "I would like to name Bill Darden."

Macy's assistant checked with the Defense Department concerning Darden, since some doubt had been been expressed that a "Senate staff man would measure up to the quality" of other individuals previously mentioned either by Defense Secretary Clark Clifford or Macy as potential Court nominees in the event of a vacancy. Macy's informant "couldn't recall such unanimous enthusiasm for any candidate for any office in the past. Every one, from the Secretary on down, has the highest regard for Darden." Another of Macy's correspondents, perhaps inadvertently, offered an accurate assessment of Johnson's choice. Compared with some other candidates, Darden might be "no great brain," but there were other factors to consider: "He has some 20 years experience with Defense legislation, and as Dick Russell's boy all these years, he is sure to be confirmed."

Having just lost a bruising and bitter battle with the Senate over the ill-fated Fortas nomination to replace Earl Warren, one can understand why Johnson was drawn to Darden as a nominee, since he apparently was a "sure thing" for confirmation. Promptly informed of the Defense Department's positive recommendation, Johnson formally nominated Darden on November 5. In a typical example of the famed Johnson style, the president personally called Darden to congratulate him on his selection.

With Darden on the Court and with Richard Nixon elected as president, the Quinn matter remained unresolved. On December 4, a member of Johnson's staff wrote a fitting epilogue for a fascinating and still unfinished episode:

> This is a screwed up case. . . . Quinn was reappointed in 1966 on the condition that he resign in 1968. [The letter of resignation] is in the White House files . . . but it has never been acted upon. Part of the problem, I am told, was that it was misfiled for a long time and nobody could find it. It is now found . . . but there is no plan to accept it. The matter is complicated by news stories this year indicating Judge Quinn has submitted his resignation. No one is too sure of the source of the stories. If you want to be judge of the Court of Military Appeals, Quinn's resignation is in the files.

When Richard Nixon left the presidency in 1974, the resignation was still in the files, and Robert Quinn was still on the bench.

20

Disagreements, Departures, and Decisions, 1969–1975

Richard Nixon took office in January 1969, inheriting both the Vietnam problem and Judge Quinn's continued presence on the Court. It may well be that Johnson's preoccupation with the former crisis had prevented resolution of the minor problem. Within a matter of months, Nixon's new administration took up the issue of USCAAF appointments even though, as Nixon aide Bryce Harlow wrote to Republican Senator Everett McKinley Dirksen, "there will not be another vacancy until May 1, 1971," the expiration of Ferguson's appointment. Unless, of course, Robert Quinn resigned. Now it was Nixon's turn to cope with the ongoing Quinn caper.

THE CASE OF THE DISAPPEARING RESIGNATION

By June 1969, it had been ascertained that "apparently . . . Quinn submitted his resignation during the Johnson administration, but it was not acted upon. He, therefore, resolved it." A staff member would try to "see if the resignation is still kicking around somewhere." The new administration's interest in a USCAAF opening had to do not so much with the age or quality of the incumbents as with the fact that such a vacancy "would greatly assist in carrying out the President's desire to give a highly visible job to a VFW type." In addition, the Republican members of the House Armed Services Committee informed Nixon that they "strongly recommend" the appointment of their committee counsel, William Cook, to the Court. The problem for Nixon was the lack of a position rather than politically suitable candidates to fill it.

    The White House staff ascertained that Johnson had reappointed Quinn to a full fifteen-year term "on the understanding that an undated resignation would be offered by Quinn" when he had served sufficient years to qualify for a federal pension. A search of the White House files turned up "no evidence of an undated resignation," but Quinn's letter of June 20, 1968, had been located. Whether the effective date for retirement benefits was June 20, 1968, or August 1, 1969, "it would appear that on any theory [Quinn] soon will have fulfilled his service requirement for the full pension. Is there any way we can pursue this matter with [Senator John] Pastore, so as to open up Quinn's job? Otherwise, we apparently will have him with us until 1981, at which time he will have achieved the ripe old age of 97." Quinn's letter, although clearly dated July 20, 1968, stated that "I hereby submit to you my resignation from the Court to become effective at such time as you see fit to accept it." Since the letter had been written to "Mr. President" and not President Johnson, and since it had never been formally accepted by Johnson or—apparently—withdrawn by Quinn, the question arises whether Nixon could have acted to accept the resignation during 1969 or thereafter. As will be seen, however, he did not.

Asked by Harlow to contact Pastore, another staffer responded later in July that according to Pastore, "Johnson had agreed to leave [Quinn] on the Court and that Quinn's letter of resignation had been withdrawn and was no longer in effect." (It should be noted that a diligent search through both the available Johnson and Quinn papers has turned up no evidence whatsoever of any such withdrawal. On the other hand, as pointed out in the previous chapter, Johnson's inaction was the only action necessary for Quinn to remain where he was.) Furthermore, Pastore stated that "Quinn was very important to him in his State . . . and that he, Pastore, would vigorously oppose any change. Pastore made his position very clear." Harlow was also informed that Congressman Les Arends, the Republican whip and a senior member of the House Armed Services Committee, "asked me to tell you that the members of [this Committee] would stand behind their recommendation that [William] Cook be given the next vacancy on the Court." On July 28, Harlow wrote to Arends that "your emphatic views in behalf of Bill are rightly and fully known and, of course, will not be overlooked." A staff memorandum stated that "when we finally get an opening on [USCAAF] it will have to go to Cook, minority counsel, as Les Arends has made it clear this is one of the things he's really strong on." Cook ultimately would be named to the Court, but not by Nixon.

In the meantime, USCAAF had other problems to confront. Even as replacements were proposed and Quinn's resignation was pushed, the U.S. Supreme Court handed down one of its most far-reaching and controversial decisions concerning military justice. It resulted in major contention between the high court and the military, with USCAAF caught in the middle. This case and its aftermath deserve some discussion.

THE ODD ODYSSEY OF O'CALLAHAN

On its surface, the case of Sergeant James O'Callahan was similar to many incidents in military justice. During the evening of July 20, 1956, while on leave from his post at a fort near Honolulu, O'Callahan apparently entered a hotel room and tried to rape its occupant, a fourteen-year-old girl. Arrested as he sought to flee the area, he was turned over to the military police, confessed to the attempt, faced court-martial for a number of offenses, and was convicted on all of them. Along with other penalities including a dishonorable discharge, O'Callahan was sentenced to ten years' imprisonment at hard labor. For almost his entire prison term, military justice heard nothing from this defendant.

Toward the end of his incarceration, O'Callahan sought a writ from USCAAF on the grounds that he had been denied certain constitutional rights at his court-martial. The Court required only two paragraphs to deny his plea. Even as it did so, however, O'Callahan awaited response from a petition for habeas corpus that had been filed earlier on his behalf in federal court. Rejected by both district and appellate courts, he appealed to the U.S. Supreme Court. That tribunal agreed to consider the issue of court-martial jurisdiction to try a member of the armed forces for "a crime . . . having no military significance, alleged to have been committed off post and while on leave." In June 1969, a bare majority of the Court decided this question in favor of O'Callahan.

Speaking for the Court, Justice Douglas criticized military justice, noting—correctly—that the court-martial judge was not one "whose objectivity and independence are protected by tenure and undiminishable salary and nurtured by the judicial tradition." Quite aside from the potential for real abuse through command influence, he added, "Courts-martial as an institution are singularly inept in dealing with the nice subtleties of constitutional law." Finally, he emphasized the "unusual" factors in this case. The defendant was "properly absent" from his installation. There "was no connection—not even the remotest one—between his military duties and the crimes in question. The crimes were not committed on a military post or enclave; nor was the person whom he attacked performing any duties relating to the military." Hawaii was not the occupied zone of a foreign country, but was under civil authority with functioning civil courts. In short, "the offenses did not involve any question of the flouting of military authority, the security of a military post, or the integrity of military property."

What, then, was a "service connected" offense? The decision gave the military virtually no guidance. Moreover, Douglas failed to mention, let alone resolve, the issue of retroactivity. Aware, if only from Justice Harlan's dissent, that the O'Callahan decision could create a strong sense of uncertainty in military justice, within two years the Court agreed to consider the issue again. In the meantime, a great deal of commentary about the decision—much of it negative—appeared, sparing neither Douglas nor his opinion. For its part,

USCAAF confronted the implications of *O'Callahan* only four months after that case had been decided.

As had been true when USCAAF applied the *Miranda* warnings to the military, the tribunal split 2 to 1 concerning application of the *O'Callahan* doctrine. Again, Judge Ferguson, joined by Judge Darden, spoke for the Court, while Chief Judge Quinn wrote a lengthy dissent, marked by bitterness and frustration. Ferguson noted that the defendant lived off post, that he committed crimes against "civilian victims, unconnected to the military," and that the "accused's horrid acts, like those of O'Callahan, did not flout military authority, breach military security, or affect military property." Simply put, the *O'Callahan* holding "requires us to set aside the findings of guilty . . . and order the charges dismissed."

Judge Quinn tried to reject the reasoning of the *O'Callahan* decision even as he conceded that "I am constrained to accept its premise and its conclusion, but I hope that the searching criticism of the bench and bar may . . . convince a new or future majority" of its error. As for Douglas, Quinn commented that "I have looked askance at what I regard, rightly or wrongly, as the incontinent disorder of some of the constitutional opinions of the justice who authored the *O'Callahan* opinion." Seeking, apparently unsuccessfully, to minimize the decision's scope, Quinn emphasized that it "cannot be read with the literalness of a first grade primer. . . . I read *O'Callahan,* therefore, not by rote, but in light of the experience and reason of nearly two hundred years of American Government." He insisted that the Douglas list of service connection variables "was not, in my opinion, intended to be definitive or exclusive. Other circumstances can establish the military significance of the offense or demonstrate its service-connection."

Quinn ended his lengthy dissent with an angry rejection of the Douglas "fossil-like canard that military justice is institutionalized injustice." Here, responding to the markedly antimilitary justice tone of *O'Callahan,* the chief judge emphasized the not insignificant contributions of his own court since its creation. Dissenting in a 1962 case, Douglas had made unfavorable comparisons between federal judges appointed under Article 3, such as himself, and federal judges appointed under Article 1, such as USCAAF jurists: "Men of highest quality chosen as Article I judges might never pass muster for Article III courts when tested by their record of tolerance for minorities and for their respect of the Bill of Rights—neither of which is as crucial to the performance of the duties of those who sit in Article I courts as it is to the duties of Article III judges. . . . Judges who sit on Article I courts are chosen for administrative or allied skills, not for their qualifications to sit in cases involving the vast interests of life, liberty or property. . . . Judges who might be confirmed for an Article I court, might never pass muster for the onerous and life-or-death duties of Article III judges."

At the urgent request of Army TJAG Hodson, Solicitor General Erwin Griswold—the former dean of Harvard Law School—argued the high court sequel to *O'Callahan*. The decision may have sought to "clarify" the earlier holding, but in retrospect it seems that the 1971 holding represented the start of a retreat from *O'Callahan* that did not end until its complete abandonment in 1987. The 1971 opinion was authored by recently appointed Justice Harry Blackmun, who spoke for a unanimous court. Blackmun, possibly with a sense of understatement, began his opinion in *Relford v. Commandant, U.S. Disciplinary Barracks* with an observation that the 1969 holding "already has occasioned a substantial amount of scholarly comment." He also listed more than fifty-five USCAAF cases citing *O'Callahan*, stating further that the Court would not reconsider that decision: "Our task here concerns only its application."

Relford involved a member of the military on active duty but in mufti who was accused of raping two civilians. The offenses "took place on the military reservation consisting of Fort Dix and the contiguous McGuire Air Force Base." One of the two victims was the sister of a serviceman on duty at the base, while the other was the wife of another serviceman, also stationed there. In other words, both were "properly at the base." Taking all these facts together, "we readily conclude that the crimes with which Relford was charged were triable by a military court."

Blackmun added a somewhat cryptic comment that "*O'Callahan* marks an area, perhaps not the limit, for the concern of the civil courts and where the military may not enter. [*Relford*] marks an area, perhaps not the limit, where the court-martial is appropriate and permissible. What lies between is for decision at another time." As to the issue of retroactivity, of particular concern to the military, this "issue is better resolved in other litigation where, perhaps, it would be solely dispositive of the case. We take some comfort in the hope that the present decision should eliminate at least some of the confusion that the parties and commentators say have emerged from *O'Callahan*."

Despite Blackmun's "comfort," the Court returned to the issue of retroactivity in the confusing case of *Gosa v. Mayden, Warden*. By a bare majority, the justices declined to apply *O'Callahan* retroactively, but as Solicitor General Griswold put it, "You have [to] read rather closely to find that out." Justice Blackmun's plurality opinion was joined by three other justices, "but that was just four votes out of nine." The fifth vote came from Justice Rehnquist, who felt that *O'Callahan*, "if it stood," should be applied retroactively. But he also believed that that case had been wrongly decided and should be overruled. Thus, "we do not have a majority against the retroactive application of *O'Callahan*, but we do have a majority against *O'Callahan*, retroactively."

In 1987, six justices overruled *O'Callahan* in an opinion authored by Chief Justice Rehnquist that seemed as critical of Douglas's 1969 opinion as Douglas had been of military justice. During the interval between the two cases, it had been left to USCAAF—with some difficulty—to explore the reaches of the service connection requirement. For its part, during the same period, the high court had handed down a number of rulings that severely limited the reach of constitutional protection to members of the armed forces, and the decision overruling *O'Callahan* should be seen in this context. This notable trend appeared to justify Justice Marshall's plaintive dissent in *Solorio* that now "members of the Armed Forces may be subjected virtually without limit to the vagaries of military control." The Court's action "reflects contempt, both for the members of our Armed Forces and for the constitutional safeguards intended to protect us all."

So eager was the majority to overrule the Douglas decision, that in *Solorio* it acted without even a specific request from the United States that it do so. Indeed, *Solorio* was a case in which, without actually saying so, the high court endorsed the lower court finding of a service connection and went on to overrule *O'Callahan*, an action it considered far more important. Justice Stevens protested that "today's unnecessary overruling of precedent is most unwise." Because the Court did not disagree with USCAAF, "it has no business reaching out to reexamine [*O'Callahan* and *Relford*]. . . . The fact that any five Members of the Court have the power to reconsider settled precedents at random, does not make that practice legitimate." While Stevens declined to agree with the opinion, concurring only in the judgment, three other justices dissented. The opinions in both *O'Callahan* and *Solorio* reflected the narrowest of margins, a bare majority of the Court.

COURT CHANGES

The question of Quinn's resignation remained unresolved as the *O'Callahan* and *Relford* line of cases was litigated. But Nixon received word that an opening on USCAAF would soon be available, as Homer Ferguson came to the end of his term. Almost eighty-two years old, in February 1971 the former Michigan senator asked to see Nixon in order to inform him "of his plan to resign." Nixon's aide advised the president that "there will be no press involvement." However, "you may want to give the Judge a set of Presidential cuff links."

A leading candidate to replace Ferguson appeared to be Albert Watson. A conservative from South Carolina, a former member of Congress, and strongly identified with southern segregation policies, he claimed support from Senator Strom Thurmond and Gerald Ford. Nixon, however, received a warning from Senator Hugh Scott, the minority leader, that "a considerable head of steam is building up against" Watson's nomination. The situation, he wrote, "is tailor-made for [Indiana] Senator Birch Bayh and for some of those in adversary positions on the Armed Services Committee," and the appointment would come at a time "when every effort would be made to link the nomination with Mylai and other military furores [*sic*]." As if to confirm Scott's prediction, three days later Senator George McGovern (Democrat from South Dakota) publicly denounced the proposed appointment. The plan "again demonstrates the Administration attempt to shape the judicial system to its own purposes without a real regard for the needs of justice and for courts which should merit the respect of all Americans." Nothing came of Watson's proposed nomination.

While the question of a successor to Ferguson—who had assumed the position of USCAAF senior judge—remained unanswered, Nixon did solve the problem of Chief Judge Quinn. Judge William Darden later recalled that a Nixon aide, Fred Buzhardt, had asked him if Quinn would resign "if he [was] not Chief Judge." Darden does not recall his answer, but without any notice to Quinn, Nixon's staff prepared a presidential document naming Darden as chief judge. Drafted on June 10, 1971, and hand delivered to Darden by a White House messenger on June 24, it fell to the new chief judge to inform the seventy-seven-year-old Quinn, who had served in that post for more than twenty years, of his sudden replacement: "It was embarrassing to me to have to tell Judge Quinn that I had that letter."

The free transferability of the chief judge's position was abolished by a recent amendment to the UCMJ. Now—as is the case with other federal appellate courts—it rotates, with a nonrenewable five-year term as chief judge going to the jurist with the most seniority. If, on the other hand, that judge has less than five years of his appointment remaining, the term as chief judge is similarly limited. According to Darden, Quinn "was shaken" by the event. His immediate reaction was to ask Darden "whether I thought he should resign." Darden urged him not to take such a step, and Quinn remained on the bench.

Darden declined to force Quinn from his rather ornate chambers, where he had been ensconced for almost twenty years. Nixon's sudden move can be described as underhanded, if not vicious. On the other hand, Quinn had agreed to resign in 1968 but had later declined to do so, and Nixon—not unreasonably— was unwilling to have him continue as chief judge with the potential to remain in that post until Quinn's term ended in 1981. This step, of course, did not solve the matter of Quinn's continued occupancy of a seat on the Court. If Nixon's strategy was aimed at somehow pushing Quinn into leaving, it failed. Nixon would leave Washington before Quinn left the Court.

If "shaken" privately, publicly Quinn reacted to the announcement with typical aplomb. No stranger to politics, according to Fred Proulx who wrote to a former USCAAF commissioner shortly after Darden's elevation had been announced, "the passing of the baton to Judge Darden was his wish." With a Republican president, Quinn was under no illusions concerning his continuance as chief judge. The timing and manner of the appointment, however, was another matter, and Quinn's supporters were critical of both. Proulx also commented on the proposed Watson nomination calling it a "trial balloon" that the president sent up "before he ran the risk of being involved in another Carswell situation, which he can ill afford." (The reference to Carswell concerned Senate rejection of Nixon's nominee to the U.S. Supreme Court.) More important, "we hear rumors from time to time tossed around, including a black colored

Judge on the Supreme Court of Ohio by the name of Duncan." Indeed, "the consensus of opinion seems to be [that] it will be a black appointment in the light of the Watson flak and also as a promotion piece for an all volunteer Army, which you know, will have a higher percentage of blacks than that which obtains in the overall population." As often happened, Proulx was correct.

A young attorney from Columbus, Ohio, Robert Duncan had come to the attention of William Saxbe, the state attorney general, who later became a senator and then from 1974 to 1975 was the U.S. attorney general. Duncan served as Saxbe's chief counsel in 1965. Three years later he was appointed to fill an unexpired term on the Ohio Supreme Court, to which he was reelected for a full term in 1970. At the behest of Senator Saxbe, Duncan was also named to the White House Fellows Commission. As a black member of a state supreme court and with the Nixon administration "interested," as he later recalled, "in some black presence as it were," Duncan was in the right place at the right time. Moreover, as the *Navy Times* put it, unlike prior USCAAF selections, Duncan "is neither a practicing politician, nor a defeated one." Unanimously confirmed by the Senate after a brief and superficial hearing before the Senate Armed Services Committee, on November 29, 1971, he took the oath of office from Supreme Court Justice Potter Stewart.

Duncan's appointment heralded a period characterized by rapidly changing personnel on the Court. Indeed, he served the shortest term thus far in the Court's history, less than three years. During his tenure, however, the Court decided one of the most notorious cases in its history, the court-martial that resulted from the My Lai massacre, *United States v. Calley*. The defendant, William Calley, had hired former USCAAF judge George Latimer to represent him. Quite vocal in his contention that the extensive publicity engendered by the massacre and its aftermath had rendered the army incapable of providing his client with a fair trial, Latimer found himself criticizing the very system that he had defended for ten years—an irony not lost on Proulx, just completing his second decade as clerk of the Court. "By the way," he wrote to a former USCAAF commissioner, "how did you like Judge Latimer running down the system which he strongly defended for 10 years? [Do you have] any suggestion as to what I should do with the first ten volumes of our reports where all the statements he made were diametrically opposed?"

The publicity cited by Latimer also affected the Court. Proulx noted that during early April 1971 the Calley case "has flooded our office with approximately 1800 letters received during the last five days. A week ago . . . we had a demonstration at our front door." The letters, many of which apparently came from Texas, all carried the same message, and two brief excerpts will indicate their general tone: "In regards to the disgusting trial of Lt. Wm. Calley—I think it stinks. Here is a man who killed the enemy in the act of defending his country, only to have the same country to put him on trial for it. The whole rotten mess makes me sick to my stomach. . . . I am *not* [emphasis in original] a radical of any sort[,] only a betroden tax payer [*sic*] who is fed up with all this nonsense. Turn him loose"; and "If he is going to be punished why not arrest former President Truman who ordered the atom bombs dropped on Hiroshima and Nagasaki? They too, killed millions of innocent children, babies, women, old men, old women, young innocent boys and girls, etc., etc."

Altogether, Latimer represented Calley three times—his original court-martial, his appeal before the Army Court of Military Review, and the final appeal before his old court on which one of his original colleagues, Judge Quinn, still sat. Observers noted, however, that the seventy-year-old Latimer "seemed often to be out of his depth . . . losing his place among papers or repeating himself." Another observer was even more harsh in his assessment of Latimer's performance as counsel. Latimer had apparently represented Calley without fee, "a fact that led some wits to remark after it was over that Calley had gotten his money's worth. The defense was confusing and confused, rambling, directionless, contradictory, and totally ill-prepared."

For his appeal, Latimer asked the Court to rule on thirty issues drawn from a transcript of more than twenty volumes. The initial memorandum to the judges from the central legal staff member charged with examining the case recommended that every one be rejected. The staff director concurred but recognized that "the seriousness of the crimes" (Calley had been convicted of murdering at least twenty "oriental human beings") might "warrant something more than a simple order of 'Deny.' " The judges agreed and ordered argument on three issues: excessive publicity, insufficient evidence, and prejudicial error concerning the way in which Calley's defense of superior orders had been submitted to the trial court.

Writing for himself and Judge Duncan, Quinn rejected all three issues and emphasized that the instructions of the military judge "on all issues were comprehensive and correct. Lieutenant Calley was given every consideration to which he was entitled and perhaps more." The court-martial findings, reached after more than eighty hours of deliberation, "represent the truth of the facts as they [the court members] determined them to be and there is substantial evidence to support those findings. No mistakes of procedure cast doubt upon them." Duncan later recalled that "I didn't think the *Calley* case was very difficult, either factually or legally. It was not a difficult case at all in my judgment. . . . There were some issues in *Calley* which weren't before the Court that I think were extremely important but the record we had to deal with, I thought, wasn't difficult at all."

Several months before the *Calley* decision was announced, Judge Darden had written to Nixon expressing his desire to resign from USCAAF. He had served for five years of a term—originally Kilday's—to end in May 1976. More than two decades later, Darden recalled that he had become "a little weary with the Court's routine." He had found that the issues were not "really stimulating" nor was "dealing with them very satisfying." Darden's candor was not new. In 1971, he had stated publicly that "I can't honestly say I enjoy the job. I haven't felt that I was good enough at it yet. I don't really have the confidence yet that I'd like to have."

Not until December 29 did Nixon's staff send Darden a graceful letter of acknowledgment. "For more than five years," Nixon wrote, "you have met the challenges of your office with great skill and dedication." Within a few weeks, Nixon appointed Duncan as the new chief judge—possibly because of Quinn's continued resolve to remain and Nixon's consistent refusal to restore him to the position he had held for twenty years. For his part, on February 17, 1974, Duncan utilized a legislative provision enacted in 1968 and again requested Ferguson to resume full-time judicial duties as a "senior judge" until further notice. Thus, USCAAF could function with a full bench, although Ferguson and Quinn were eighty-five and eighty years old respectively.

This judicial stability was short-lived, however, for within six months Duncan resigned to accept appointment as a federal district judge in Ohio. Although he recalled that his old sponsor and mentor, William Saxbe, urged him to accept such an appointment, which unlike the USCAAF seat included life tenure, Duncan had personal reasons for making such a move. Work on USCAAF was not "the sort of challenge that I felt presented itself to me intellectually as a professional. . . . After all, you are talking criminal jurisprudence . . . , and although I certainly don't want to minimize to any degree or make any comment which dilutes the importance of that Court[,] in my own view . . . if you examine the agenda of matters that come before a district court and what comes before [USCAAF] then the restrictions [are] with the Court of Military Appeals." One intriguing conclusion that can be drawn from Duncan's comments is that limited terms in office might be more desirable for USCAAF judges than tenure, if only because a regular turnover of judicial personnel would help contribute to a sense of newness and intellectual stimulation on their part.

With two vacancies to fill, the Nixon White House turned to consideration of candidates. Since even in normal times such selections were not considered urgent, in Nixon's case they received even less attention than usual. As the selection process got under way, the Watergate crisis was in full flower. President Johnson, occupied by Vietnam, had failed to act on Quinn's resignation. President Nixon would resign his office before final action on the USCAAF vacancies could be completed. Gerald Ford (and later George Bush) would subsequently make three appointments to that Court, more than any other president since Truman.

THE PROCLIVITY FOR PREFERENCES AND POLITICS

On March 14, 1974, Vice President Ford received an "eyes only" memorandum from a White House staff member, Jerry Jones. He reported that Defense Secretary James Schlesinger had proposed Kenneth Pye as Darden's replacement. Currently dean of Duke University Law School and later to become president of Southern Methodist University, Pye's credentials remained as impressive as they had been when John Macy first called them to the attention of Lyndon Johnson in 1965. Indeed, Schlesinger "feels Pye is the most outstanding candidate he has seen." His background "will allow Pye to provide the necessary leadership to bring the Court back to a position of prominence and efficiency." However, there were some problems "in proceeding with his nomination."

In the first place, Pye "is a self-admitted Kennedy/Johnson Democrat. . . . Senator Helms has indicated he will not clear him, considers |Pye| a very hard-line anti-Nixon man and threatens to 'go off the reservation' if Pye is nominated." Moreover, there were a number of other candidates for the position—"several are Pye's equal and all have strong Republican credentials and support." In "order to give Al Haig the best input possible," Jones asked Ford "whether or not we should go ahead." (Al Haig was General Alexander Haig Jr., a former member of Secretary of State Henry Kissinger's staff who had become White House chief of staff in May 1973.) Haig and Schlesinger discussed the nomination, and "while not wedded to Pye, the Secretary is very anxious to have him as a member of the Court, and to have him named Chief Judge." Without comment, Ford rejected Schlesinger's proposal.

Two months later, Ford received another "eyes only" memorandum from David Wimer, a White House staff member. This time, Schlesinger proposed the appointment of a current Colorado Supreme Court justice, William Erickson, "an extremely skillful juridical administrator, well able to take charge, intellectually and managerially, of a Court badly in need of repair." Again the availability of numerous other candidates came up, and Wimer noted that "we are faced with the traditional interrelated dilemma of (1) more candidates than opportunities, (2) the potential disappointment of Members of Congress whose candidates are not selected, and (3) balancing substantive requirements against necessary political concerns."

Wimer attempted to solve this problem by recommending that Erickson replace Duncan as chief judge. For the Darden vacancy, he revived the name of William Cook, still serving on the staff of the House Armed Services Committee and still receiving "the highest regard" for his "abilities and loyalties" from the Republican members of that committee. On the other hand, Wimer conceded that the Defense Department "is not in favor of Cook's appointment and consider him a 'hack.' At the same time, they have indicated that if they get Erickson, they can probably live with Cook." Ford approved Wimer's recommendations possibly because he felt that these two choices balanced the need for expertise with political realities.

At this point, another major figure in the Nixon Administration provided differing input into the USCAAF selection process. In May 1974 Air Force Major General Brent Scowcroft, serving as Kissinger's deputy on the National

Security Council, was asked about Wimer's recommendations. Scowcroft's aide, Jan Lodal, drafted a response that endorsed Erickson but rejected Cook, whose "experience and other qualifications are less than adequate for the Court of Military Appeals." Lodal further explained his opposition to Cook: "Currently we have two specific problems with [USCAAF]. First, the system is antiquated and needs modernization; Congress and the DOD have emphasized this fact. Second, the current Court needs to have its stature upgraded and reinforced; its rulings have been continually challenged by other courts. There is no indication that Mr. Cook has the background and wherewithal needed to resolve these problems."

Lodal urged that Scowcroft "strongly pursue this matter. We cannot tolerate less than highly qualified individuals on the Court, particularly in this period of special morale and discipline problems, the transition to the all-volunteer force, and urgent needs of minority members of the Services." He assured Scowcroft that the Defense Department "would wholeheartedly agree with the non-concurrence. . . . At a minimum, we owe it to Secretary Schlesinger to have his full views brought to the attention of General Haig and the President."

Scowcroft sent a "revised" memorandum to Wimer. It endorsed Erickson's nomination as chief judge, calling him "clearly well qualified for that important position." He made no mention of Cook but noted that "the success of the all-volunteer force is related to the perceptions held by those who are potential volunteers. The equity with which discipline is maintained is important in forming those views[,] and it is essential that military justice and those responsible for it be of the highest caliber." He recommended that "efforts be made to solicit additional recommendations from the Defense Department and elsewhere in the interest of selecting a nominee whose experience and qualifications are more in keeping with the high standards and difficult demands to be expected of [USCAAF] judges in the years ahead."

Shortly thereafter, the general counsel of the Defense Department, Martin Hoffmann, suggested two additional candidates to complete Darden's term, one of them a sitting judge from Minnesota, Judge Stephen Maxwell. Unlike Scowcroft, Hoffmann did not mince words concerning William Cook: "We do not agree that William Cook is an acceptable candidate. In our view the Court as presently constituted and the necessity for revitalization of the military justice system require appointments in the spirit of excellence. In view of the age and disposition of Judge Quinn, the appointment of Cook would place an undue burden on Justice Erickson that would probably preclude his assumption of a full range of necessary activities the Chief Judge should undertake and pursue."

In the meantime, on June 21, the White House formally announced Nixon's intention to nominate Erickson as Duncan's successor and also to designate him as chief judge upon Senate confirmation. Duncan resigned effective July 11 and in his formal letter to Nixon described the Court as "a strong and healthy judicial installation." Shortly thereafter, Wimer submitted Cook's nomination to Nixon for final approval, informing him that "all necessary checks have been completed." On August 2, the White House formally announced Nixon's intent to name Cook to the Court. After he had retired from the bench, Cook candidly summarized his path to the Court: "I began thinking what job am I qualified for . . . and not many people agreed to want to go on the Court of Military Appeals. . . . now it doesn't lead any place. I mean truthfully it is kind of a last job. So I followed up, I thought I was fairly qualified to serve on that Court[,] so I began talking to various friends and I became a candidate out of the committee to go on the Court."

Even as Wimer sent his memo, the House Committee on the Judiciary passed the third and final article of impeachment against Nixon for his obstruction of justice in seeking to cover up the Watergate incident. Nevertheless, it appeared that Nixon had filled the two existing USCAAF vacancies, and that the Court would return to full strength, including Quinn, of course—now in his twenty-fourth year of service.

Nixon began what would turn out to be his final week in the White House by receiving an unusual letter from Erickson. He had expected to maintain his residence and chambers in Denver, "devoting so much of my time to work in the District of Coumbia as the Court might require." Apparently the Defense Department officials with whom he spoke had accepted such a stipulation, which, Erickson added, "was deemed to be proper and workable in the light of the history of the Court." Moreover, "a substantial majority of the Chief Judges of the [U.S.] Courts of Appeal maintain chambers and perform a large part of their judicial work at a place other than that at which the Court sits." Nevertheless, Erickson had "become aware of the strong objections of some members of the Congress, and of others who were closely related to the Military Court."

The nominee was "forced to conclude that the objections to my maintenance of a Colorado residence were well founded. In my opinion, it is necessary for the Chief Judge . . . to maintain his residence . . . where the Court sits." Erickson was well aware of Quinn's pattern of "commuting" to the Court only for oral arguments and conferences, spending most of his time in Providence. Therefore, it became necessary for Erickson "to determine whether I could give up my life-long residence, friends and family ties in Colorado to move to Washington." He "concluded that I could not, and regretfully must request that you withdraw my name from further consideration." On August 6, Wimer drafted the formal withdrawal for the president's signature. Three days later, Nixon resigned.

Having made his preference for Cook clear on several occasions as vice president, the new chief executive saw no reason to change his mind. Indeed, even before Nixon resigned, Cook had informed the USCAAF clerk that the Senate Armed Services Committee had scheduled a hearing on his nomination for August 15. The hearing went off as scheduled, and it produced more than the usual superficial banter. The nominee submitted a brief statement, concluding with the comment that "there is something unique about military law in a disciplined society and, as I view the role as a Judge on [USCAAF], it is to preserve and protect individual liberties while, at the same time, assuring that the military establishment is able to function in an orderly fashion. Obviously, this is a fine line which can only be determined on a case-by-case basis."

The committee chair, Mississippi senator John Stennis, responded, "You will remember, I know, that justice is blind. But you don't have to be blind yourself, and you don't want to be blind. . . . I have a feeling that out among the services maybe we have too much law and too little discipline." Cook replied that he had said much the same thing in his statement but expanded his point in a later comment to Senator Strom Thurmond: "I do think that there has been a tendency in the immediate past to forget discipline and forget the establishment and to think of the individual. We must think of the individual, but I think probably in my opinion the Court has gone overboard." Thurmond then asked Cook, "Do you feel that all the benefits of our civil law are applicable to those serving in the military uniform?" Cook replied, "Insofar as we can do it within this discipline society of which I was just speaking."

Stennis observed that "if I didn't believe you would do your duty . . . as you saw it I wouldn't vote to confirm you, but I think we are up against some practical realities of life. . . . In the military, I think we have leaned over backwards trying to decide these military discipline cases . . . too much as a civilian court would decide them." Senator Thomas McIntyre told Cook, "I had come into the Army, and I believed very much in the civil authority that you are innocent until you are proved guilty. So I hope you will remember that part. I believe in discipline as the Chairman is talking about. But you must not consider those guys guilty the minute they are charged." Responding to McIntyre, Senator Taft recalled his days in the navy when serving as a recorder on a naval court. The captain "called me in . . . and said, 'Look, I think you are doing fine, but your sentences are a little light. You are interfering with my prerogative to reduce them.'" Cook made no reply, but McIntyre stated that "that is the military attitude in its worst form."

Unanimously confirmed by the Senate a day later, Cook joined Robert Quinn on the USCAAF bench. The record of his opinions and dissents indicates that Cook seems to have taken the Stennis warning to heart. They reflect a notable tendency to support the military's position. Indeed, one army JAG colonel described a Cook dissent as "one of many that rank him among the finest jurists to sit on the Court of Military Appeals, or perhaps any court." Of course, one's perspective determines how one perceives a given decision. Other Court observers took a less charitable view.

The Quinn saga had a final touch of irony. As Nixon left office, the man he had removed as chief judge resumed that position. Quinn would remain in the center seat until President Ford designated another judge to fill it. With 1974 drawing to a close, Ford's aides indicated that they had found one.

FORD FINDS FLETCHER

In 1974, Albert Fletcher Jr. served as a state judge in Kansas, a position he had held for almost fourteen years. He had received a law degree from Washburn University, where one of his classmates and acquaintances was a future U.S. senator and presidential hopeful, Robert Dole. Coauthor of two studies on state judicial administration, Fletcher later recalled that in 1974 he had been under consideration for selection as a federal district judge. Instead of such an appointment, Fletcher received a phone call from Martin Hoffmann, still general counsel of DOD but soon to be named secretary of the army. Hoffmann asked if Fletcher would be interested in being considered for a seat on USCAAF, a court about which Fletcher was frank to admit he "knew nothing."

Fletcher's expression of interest resulted in two letters to Ford from Senator Dole strongly recommending not only Fletcher's appointment but also his immediate designation as chief judge. For his part, Hoffmann interviewed Fletcher. In considering his appointment, Hoffmann later recalled that he had wanted to see on the Court judges with "some really high visibility, strong modern-type people that would have the empathy of the military justice system in them, but have—you know—the flexibility to build the Court and modernize the Code." Fletcher "was obviously a dedicated, hard working sort of guy."

Hoffmann also had been concerned "about the stature of the people that were going to go on the Court." He described Fletcher as a person with "a terrific temperament," one who "didn't appear to have much of an agenda." Indeed, "I never saw an agenda and we didn't have a specific agenda that said you have to civilianize this thing. The agenda was, it's got to be a military thing, and the more it gets kind of eccentric and crabbed and mechanistic and too conservative for the times[,] the Supreme Court is going to step in there and straighten the God damn thing out and that's not what we want." Hoffmann's comments are of special interest in the wake of what happened to the Court between 1975 and 1980 (see Chapters 21 and 22).

On February 12, Ford's staff forwarded Fletcher's name to him for consideration, although the White House counsel's office observed that "there is no evidence of quality." Ford responded with a handwritten note that "I have no objection *but* [emphasis in original] this seems like a very choice appointment to someone I don't know or seems to come out of nowhere. Talk with me." Given this response, one wonders if Ford ever saw Dole's letters.

One week later, Ford's personnel director replied to the president. Fletcher's recommendation "is the result of an effort by Secretary Schlesinger and Marty Hoffman [*sic*] to substantially upgrade the calibre of personnel on this Court which, historically, has been composed of retired congressional staffers." Furthermore, "the prestige of the court is generally thought now to be at an all-time low at a time when there is increasing pressure on the military justice system. . . . Finally, the department wishes to improve the quality of decisions by the Court. Apparently there has never been an opinion conference among the three judges." This memorandum warrants a few comments.

Thus far in USCAAF history, of eight appointments to the Court, only two "congressional staffers" had been named, one of them by Ford himself. It is true that two former members of Congress (Ferguson and Kilday) had also been among its members, but to state that the Court "historically has been composed of congressional staffers" is incorrect. Moreover, at the time of the memo, Quinn had suffered a severe stroke and was unable to communicate. While he would not resign until late April, he never again sat on the bench. Further, the comment that "apparently there has never even been an opinion conference among the three judges" is a striking example of ignorance. If it referred to the past twenty-five-year history of the Court, the statement is utter nonsense. If, however, it was based on the fact that in early 1975, with only one full-time judge (Cook) and one senior judge (Ferguson) and with Quinn incommunicado in Providence, formal conferences were probably considered unnecessary if not impossible, then the statement seems more reasonable. At any rate, the memo—replete with its reference to the fact that Fletcher and Dole were classmates—must have satisfied Ford, because shortly thereafter Fletcher's nomination went to the Senate.

The April 10 confirmation hearing before the Senate Armed Services Committee may well have set a record for brevity. Senator John Stennis submitted a letter on Fletcher's behalf from Senator Dole. Dole observed that "the American people, for a variety of reasons, no longer repose an automatic trust and confidence in their institutions whose ability to inspire confidence, only a short time ago, was unquestioned." What was needed, he added, "is the appointment to responsible positions of men and women who are perceptive enough to appreciate the dimensions of this problem and innovative enough to deal with them." It "pleases me to assure this committee," Dole concluded, "that [Fletcher] is such a man."

Stennis asked Fletcher why he would accept the appointment "that is to come." Fletcher replied that "this is the court wherein that fine line which the judiciary and the court have to walk in order to balance individual rights against society's rights becomes particularly important. This is because in the Armed Forces you have a disciplined society to balance against the individual's rights. It is the court's purpose to protect both and to preserve both[,] and this particular area is a great challenge in the law." No other senator beside Stennis even bothered to ask any questions of Fletcher, and the committee unanimously approved his nomination. The entire hearing lasted fifteen minutes. Four days later, the Senate confirmed him by voice vote.

With his designation as chief judge that followed very shortly, the Fletcher era began. No one knew it at the time, of course, but Fletcher's term as chief judge would generate more controversy between the Court and the military than any other period in USCAAF history. Rancor, resentment, and recrimination would characterize his tenure. But all this was yet to come. In the meantime, a more pressing matter confronted both the Court and President Ford. The Quinn era was at last drawing to a close, and before 1975 ended USCAAF would consist entirely of new judges.

21

Conclusion, Confrontation, and Culmination, 1975–1980, Part I

FAREWELL TO QUINN AND FERGUSON

Although Robert Quinn's resignation was submitted to President Ford in April 1975, in fact the Quinn era had come to an end that January when he had suffered a stroke. While the letter bearing his resignation requested status as a senior judge, its subject lay comatose in a Rhode Island nursing home. Nevertheless, the first USCAAF chief judge was honored during a Court ceremony on April 25, 1975. Rumors had already circulated as to the seriousness of his condition, lending an almost surreal atmosphere to the proceedings—a foreboding that accentuated the possible with acquiescence in the probable. The ceremony, according to Judge Cook, who presided, was "being videotaped and transcribed so that Judge Quinn will know the very high esteem that is held for him."

Among the highlights of the brief ceremony were the comments of Senator John Pastore, who had first met Quinn more than fifty-five years before. As Rhode Island's senior senator, Pastore had aided Quinn on numerous occasions, not least of which was the campaign for Quinn's reappointment in 1966. Now Pastore emphasized that his former governor "was a good man. He loved people, knew people and that is why he was successful as a judge. He knew people and knew how to serve people." Another member of the Rhode Island congressional delegation added that "there isn't a day that goes by that Robert Quinn does not do something for somebody." General George Prugh, army TJAG, commented on Quinn's ability to interpret the new UCMJ so as to make "the Code come alive," and this in a context "that set the highest standards of professional performance." Perhaps William Darden best captured Quinn's essence when he described Quinn's "historic prescription for making a great judge—he should be first a gentleman, and it helps if he knows a little bit of law."

A few weeks later, on May 19, 1975, Quinn passed away. His twenty-three-year tenure as chief judge will stand as the record, since in 1992 Congress mandated a five-year term based on seniority. More instinctual than intellectual in his judicial approach, he emphasized in his opinions what he had often articulated during his political career: that law be both practical and practicable. He was a man of great personal charm, and with the politician's gift for "people relationships" he had managed to remain on cordial terms with the JAGs even when rejecting the military position in specific cases. On the other hand, especially in his later years, his frequent absences from the Court had deprived it of effective administrative leadership. And when a new chief judge sought both to revitalize the Court and to expand its role in military justice, the military would find the differences between the Quinn and Fletcher approach disturbing, as will be seen.

The tributes to Quinn had temporarily obscured the urgency for a third Court appointment in that the incoming Fletcher along with Cook and Ferguson, temporarily sitting as a senior judge, could keep the tribunal operational. Even before Quinn's retirement ceremony, Senator Strom Thurmond urged that Ford offer an incumbent South Carolina Democratic congressman "a position on a second or third level basis," if only because the South Carolina Republicans have—according to Thurmond—an "outstanding" candidate who "would have an outstanding chance of being elected" to fill the seat. It is interesting that Thurmond considered a USCAAF seat as "a second or third level." In this, he was not alone.

With the possible exception of Truman, virtually every president who has made appointments to this Court has considered them less important than other federal judicial positions. At this point, it seems that Thurmond was much more interested in the Republicans winning a local congressional campaign than in seeking a well-qualified candidate for USCAAF. He is neither the first nor the last congressional figure to have considered such appointments in terms of political preference and advantage rather than judicial qualifications. His candidate was a conservative South Carolina Democrat who had served in Congress for about eight years. James Mann had the advantage of "strong support" from Thurmond, the senior Republican on a committee where seniority remained—and still remains—very important. Although Ford signed off on the appointment in early June, Mann's nomination never reached the Senate.

By the middle of June, rumors concerning Mann's "imminent" elevation to the bench had circulated among the local South Carolina newspapers. Again Thurmond wrote to the White House, urging that "since the news is out, I think it would be advisable for the announcement of the appointment to be made as soon as possible. . . . This would hold down speculation and enable us to get on with the job of determining who the successor is going to be." Apparently, Mann and Thurmond had differing perceptions as to what "as soon as possible" implied. On July 23, Mann indicated that Ford had agreed "*not* to nominate

him . . . until after the Congressional recess," in part because of unfinished legislation and a pending congressional trip to the Far East. Ford's director of personnel joined Thurmond in urging again that the "nomination be made
immediately." Possibly resentful of the implication that he was manipulating
the timing of the nomination for partisan purposes, on August 6 Mann abruptly
asked that Ford withdraw his name.

Strom Thurmond wasted no time in urging yet another nomination upon
Ford. Less than a week after Mann's withdrawal, he wrote "personal attention"
at the top of his letter to the president extolling the qualifications of Matthew
Perry. A young but experienced trial attorney and also a director of the
NAACP, Perry had already come to the attention of local Democratic politi-
cians in the possible context of the forthcoming congressional elections. From
Thurmond's perspective, it becomes very clear why he might be so eager to
see Perry removed from local politics to the safe haven of a federal court in
Washington. Perry, he assured Ford, has "successfully represented defendants
in many significant cases relating to civil rights."

It may indeed be that part of the "understanding" reached by Perry and
Thurmond included an assurance of later appointment to the federal district
court in South Carolina. What better way to remove a potential candidate from
effective political candidacy than by appointing him not only first to a federal
judgeship but later to a judgeship with life tenure as well. In fact, this is exactly
what happened to Matthew Perry. When urging his appointment, Strom Thurmond had the happy opportunity to merge political expediency with aspirations toward racial harmony and a "fairer" system of military justice.

Reminding the president that there had been only one black jurist in the
history of USCAAF, Thurmond concluded that Ford would "have the opportunity to restore balance to the Court with a Black American who is eminently
qualified and greatly respected by all who know him." South Carolina governor
James Edwards telegraphed Ford that Perry "would make an outstanding member of the Court." Other individuals in Ford's administration joined in support
for Perry, with newly appointed Secretary of the Army Martin Hoffmann being
"particularly impressed with Mr. Perry's reputation, stature and ability." On
December 10, Ford sent Perry's nomination to the Senate. Within a week, the
Senate Armed Services Committee briefly considered four presidential nominations, one of them for Matthew Perry, to USCAAF.

Thurmond extolled Perry's qualifications, whereupon the committee chair,
Mississippi senator John Stennis, noted that "your endorsement will go a long
way in helping Mr. Perry." Indeed, it appeared that Perry might not be asked
even one question until Senator Goldwater inquired if "moving from the state
bar into the military bar is going to present . . . you with any problems." Perry
replied that "I do not perceive of a great deal of difference except to the extent
that there is indeed some principal difference in the philosophy certainly of the
military as distinct from the civilian sector." Reiterating a theme raised in ear-

lier hearings, Stennis noted that "I do not believe that we can have an effective, dependable, military service unless there has been some real discipline drilled into these men." Perry responded that "there are some basic differences in the philosophies in the civilian sector as against the military sector. . . . [T]here has to be some device by which the command authority can induce the obedience, the allegiance of those whose duty it is to carry out the military purpose."

Apparently satisfied with this reply, the committee unanimously approved Perry, as did the Senate shortly thereafter. As Perry prepared to take his seat in January 1976, Ford quietly authorized the reappointment of William Cook to a full fifteen-year term on the USCAAF bench. Thus, Ford's final USCAAF appointment was in fact a reappointment, and with it the president had completely reconstituted the Court—something no other chief executive has done since Truman. In 1976, none of its judges had served for even two years.

STORM CLOUDS GATHER

The growing antagonism between Fletcher and the military justice "establishment" from 1976 until his replacement as chief judge in 1980 sometimes resulted in the accusations that he possessed a hidden agenda for change concerning military justice and that he had assumed his office with instructions from an unnamed civilian official within the Defense Department to transform it. One example of this viewpoint claimed in 1984 that "there is a plan which has been in existence since the 1950's and which has dictated the course of movement in military justice matters over the years. . . . [I]t closely parallels the British system in which limited power is held by command with significant offenses being handled in civilian courts by civilians." Indeed, this officer prefaced his comments with the statement that for some time he "had felt that those who were pressing 'military justice reform' had a game plan supporting a specific objective." Even though Fletcher had not been chief judge for four years, the writer believed that "we are apparently at war and don't know it. . . . The success of the 'plan' was viewed . . . as being inevitable (I think largely because of its backing and our being asleep)."

It matters less whether such claims had any basis in fact. As will be seen, they did—but nowhere near to the extent assumed. On the other hand, what people believe to have happened may well affect their perception of what did utimately occur. Thus in exploring Fletcher's relationship to the military justice system, it becomes important to ascertain what changes he proposed, when, and in what context.

It should also be remembered that Fletcher was only the fourth chief judge in the history of the Court and that two of his predecessors, Darden and Duncan, had held this office for very short periods. Neither had made any significant changes in administrative policies that had evolved over a twenty-five-year period and that were largely based upon a frequently absent chief judge. Moreover, the comments of the White House staff member who explained to President Ford why Fletcher had been recommended should be recalled: "It is the result of an effort . . . to substantially upgrade the calibre of personnel on this Court. . . . The prestige of the court is generally thought now to be at an all-time low. . . . Finally, the [Defense] department wishes to improve the quality of decisions by the Court." In other words, there can be no doubt that Fletcher had been given an indication that changes were needed, if not a specific mandate to undertake them.

Fletcher had been in office for barely two months when on July 15, 1975, he addressed an eight-page memorandum to the JAGs, stating that he had discussed a number of ideas with his fellow judges, and that they had "concluded that it would be desirable at this time to offer some of our thoughts for discussion purposes. The enclosed memorandum reflects these concepts in very general terms." Adding that the Joint Committee on Military Justice "already has done substantial work in this area, producing a series of recommendations which warrant careful consideration," Fletcher invited the JAGs to a meeting on July 21 to "discuss your proposals as well as to hear your views."

Giving the military one week to absorb a number of proposals that were controversial may well have been unwise. A conservative institution within an even more conservative environment, the military justice system over the years has developed an almost reflexive hostility to proposed change, especially from a newly appointed civilian. On the other hand, to claim that Fletcher's conduct revealed a hidden agenda or some masterminded plot to promulgate major changes—ill-disguised to conceal their radical nature—is unwarranted. Indeed, examination of the memorandum reveals a number of proposals for change that should be noted, but with the benefit of hindsight seem more prophetic than provocative. Among ideas "warranting discussion," Fletcher proposed the following:

1. Statutory powers of the convening authority to overrule trial judges on certain matters of law should be abolished.
2. The power of the convening authority to appoint judges and counsel should be eliminated.
3. Staff judge advocates should be rated by someone other than the convening authority.
4. There should be a truly independent judiciary at both the trial and appellate levels. One way might be to appoint military judges for a term of years "with removal by appropriate authority for good cause only."
5. Trial and appellate authority should be vested with continuing jurisdiction, replete with authority to exercise a contempt power comparable to that wielded by federal trial judges.

6. The authority of military tribunals to exercise extraordinary writ jurisdiction should be clearly mandated.

7. Trial judges should determine sentences, since sentencing "is, in essence, a judicial function."

8. Random selection of court members rather than appointment by the convening authority "should be considered as a means of enhancing the perception of fairness in the military system of justice."

9. The power to promulgate procedural rules to govern courts-martial ought to be vested in the judiciary rather than the chief executive.

10. Codification of the supervisory role for USCAAF "over the entire system of military justice would insure uniformity and enhance control" over the entire system.

11. The U.S. Supreme Court should be able to review USCAAF decisions based on the petition for certiorari, which "would enhance the prestige of [both the Court] and the system of military justice as a whole."

What unified most of these proposals was a marked emphasis on expansion of judicial authority both for USCAAF and—to an even greater extent—the military judge. Although Senator Ervin had sought to enlarge that official's powers and the Military Justice Act of 1968 had done so to a limited extent, Fletcher's suggestions went much further. Even as they increased judicial responsibility, it would be at the expense of the convening authority's jurisdiction. Thus, military hostility to such changes is understandable.

Given the informal, irregular, and frequently inconclusive nature of Court and TJAG meetings that had previously prevailed—with very few exceptions—during the Quinn era, Army TJAG Wilton Persons probably did not expect to receive such a memorandum from any USCAAF chief judge, let alone a jurist with very limited experience in military justice newly arrived from a state court. He responded with a diplomatic note to Fletcher and sent along reprints of articles dealing with the UCMJ. Fletcher replied that "after you submitted to me articles concerning the Code, I thought it only fair that I read them since they could influence my thinking as to what my priorities should be. I believe that they have made me reconsider some of the suggestions initially made." Essentially, however, they reiterated what Fletcher had already proposed.

But Fletcher urged Persons to consider that "the military courts should be parallel to the courts in the federal court system." Some of his proposals "must be done by statutory enactment." Others, he noted, "could be accomplished by court decision." At the July meeting, Persons noted that the services "would need a reasonable amount of time to consider an extensive change." Fletcher commented later that "he would like to believe that moves could be made toward an independent judiciary, not necessarily one outside of the service, but a judiciary that has no susceptibility to pressures from any part of the chain of command."

The military reply took the form of a memo for all TJAGS from the Joint Service Committee on Military Justice. It well reflected the military viewpoint, and although more temperate in tone, the reaction still brings to mind the army's Kernan Committee report concerning the old Ansell reforms proposed in 1918–1919. Unlike the Code Committee, this group had no civilian members. Fletcher had urged that military judges should be appointed for specified terms. The committee, while agreeing that such tenure "tends to create the impression of an impartial judiciary," insisted that it should not be be required by statute "in view of the inherent limitations in the application of tenure to the judiciary of the various services." The services would be denied "a necessary flexibility in the personnel area."

Polite rejection of virtually all of Fletcher's proposals was accompanied by a comment that might be called prophetic in the light of later events. The committee reminded Fletcher that the UCMJ specifically gives the JAGs responsibility for the administration of military justice. Nowhere, it may be added, does the code indicate that this responsibility is also to be exercised by USCAAF. On the other hand, it was certainly not unreasonable for its judges to assume that the highest appellate tribunal in the military should indeed exercise some supervisory authority over military justice. Whether by accident or by design, for the most part both the judges and the JAGs had avoided a clash over the issue of supervisory jurisdiction during the Quinn era. The potential for conflict remained, however, if only because both parties could legitimately claim similar responsibilities. Nevertheless, to the JAGs in 1976 and thereafter, Fletcher's statement that USCAAF was similar to the U.S. Supreme Court for the military justice system went much further than what seemed warranted by existing law and practice.

The tone of the committee report, although critical, was definitely not confrontational. Fletcher had only been on the bench for a few months. Yet, the new chief judge had made it clear that some of the changes he proposed could be made through judicial decision rather than congressional enactment, the latter frequently guided by military and JAG input. They might, in other words, be implemented by the judges themselves. If his initial proposals were indicative of his intended policies, Fletcher and the JAGs seemed to be on a collision course. And, in fact, impact was not far off.

CASES AND CONFLICTS

Several decisions handed down by the Fletcher court during its first year should be noted. As individual outcomes, they might not have been so important, but when taken together they portended dramatic changes in military justice. In August 1975, Fletcher spoke for a unanimous court in striking down the voluntary enlistment of a dyslexic soldier who had been given "a list of numbers and letters" by a local recruiter to ensure his eligibility for service. Holding that "a government agency must abide by its own rules and regulations where [their] underlying purpose . . . is the protection of personal liberties or interests," he concluded that the "recruiter's misconduct" rendered the enlistment void, thus nullifying any attempt by the army to court-martial the defendant for alleged wrongdoing. "The result we reach will have the salutary effect of encouraging recruiters to observe applicable recruiting regulations while also assisting the armed forces in their drive to eliminate fraudulent recruiting practices." This decision basically reaffirmed an earlier unanimous holding. As will be seen later, both the military and Congress would act to reverse USCAAF's unanimous findings—in which six judges (Quinn, Darden, Duncan, Cook, Fletcher, and Ferguson) had concurred.

Three weeks later, the Court overruled a twenty-year precedent dealing with search and seizure. It restricted authorization for such a procedure when conducted on a foreign military base, in this case by local British authorities. Fletcher pointed to the 1961 landmark ruling by the U.S. Supreme Court, *Mapp v. Ohio*. He emphasized its holding that no evidence could be admitted that had not been "seized in compliance with the [Fourth] Amendment's conditions." The new chief judge concluded that "from the military standpoint, we see nothing burdensome in also requiring for American prosecutions that the military authorities comply with our constitutional standards."

In what would later become a fairly frequent practice, Cook dissented. To say, he argued, "that the Constitution operates against a foreign government in its own country is . . . in my opinion, quite wrong." He claimed that the Fourth Amendment protected only against action by federal or state authorities: "A foreign government, like a private person, is just not subject to these provisions." Indeed, "the majority's repudiation" of "settled constitutional doctrine . . . is . . . unjustified and unsound."

Early in February 1976, a unanimous Court forbade the convening authority to reverse a decision taken by a military judge, in this case to dismiss a charge on the basis of denial of a speedy trial. In one of his last opinions for the Court, Ferguson noted that the 1968 Military Justice Act had amended the UCMJ to create a military trial judiciary "independent of the line of command." In this context, to allow a "*lay* convening authority to *reverse* a ruling of *law* by the trial *judge*" seemed inherently inconsistent, and "we decline to do so" (emphasis in original).

The convening authority could indeed direct reconsideration, but "the judge to whom the record is returned is not to presume himself reversed thereby." On the contrary, he "is charged to reexamine his own ruling . . . and to rule thereupon once again, which ruling will be the product of his own, independent legal judgment." Thus the Court struck down the section in the Manual for Courts-Martial that required the military judge to "accede to the view of the convening authority." Ferguson's opinion remains an excellent example of the Fletcher court's determination to enhance the authority of the military judge, even if it came at the expense of the convening authority.

Finally, in August 1976, in *McPhail v. United States,* another unanimous decision authored by Cook resoundingly reaffirmed Court authority to issue appropriate writs in aid of its jurisdiction. "Drawing on boastful passages from earlier opinions, relying on analogies in Supreme Court practice and raising anew its congressional mandate to insure fairness in military justice," Cook had no doubt about USCAAF's role in such cases. To deny its authority, he wrote, "to relieve a person subject to the [UCMJ] of the burdens of a judgment by an inferior court that has acted contrary to constitutional command and decisions of this Court is to destroy the 'integrated' nature of the military court system and to defeat the high purpose Congress intended this Court to serve."

Undoubtedly, "there are limits to our authority . . . [w]hatever those limits are," and Cook declined to discuss them in any way; "as to matters reasonably comprehended within the provisions of the [UCMJ,] we have jurisdiction to require compliance with applicable law from all courts and persons purporting to act under its authority." Although within two years Cook recanted this position, believing then that congressional action had limited his court's jurisdiction, his fellow judges have never overruled *McPhail.* In 1999, however, a unanimous Supreme Court decision seemingly endorsed Cook's 1978 "recantation," holding that USCAAF's authority under the All Writs Act was limited to issuing process only in aid of its existing statutory jurisdiction.

For Court watchers, accustomed to the slower pace of the Quinn era, cases like these (and many more could be cited) portended a new sense of both USCAAF activism and aggrandizement. A few statistics illustrate the trend. In 1974, less than 6 percent of petitions for review were granted. By December 1975—eight months into Fletcher's term—almost 17 percent had been granted. In 1974, less than 49 percent of the decisions had favored the accused. By the end of 1975, that number had risen to almost 69 percent.

Writing less than one year after Fletcher took his seat on the USCAAF bench, a former JAG officer who became a civilian lawyer, John Willis, concluded that the Court has "exhibited a rather free tendency to subordinate precedent to its perception of justice by expressly overruling prior decisions affecting search and seizure, command influence and court martial jurisdiction. . . . Civilianization through and of the judiciary," he added, "should improve military justice particularly when led by the example of its highest appellate court."

But Willis also was aware that this new activism contrasted markedly with the Supreme Court's clear intent to "accept broadly stated claims of military necessity or difference." This intent could be contrasted with Fletcher's insistence that "the simple utilization of the terms 'security' or 'military necessity' cannot be the talisman in whose presence the protections of the Sixth Amendment . . . must vanish. . . . [T]his Court once again must state that analysis and rationale will be determinative of the propriety of given situations, and that the mere uniqueness of the military society or military necessity cannot be urged as the basis for sustaining that which reason and analysis indicate is untenable."

Willis concluded that USCAAF surely "has rejuvenated military justice. But how long can the court continue its energetic resurgence?" In fact, "implementation of its rules and suggestions will require the cooperative efforts of others," and when "cooperation ceases," the tribunal "may again find itself floating without direction. The positive contribution of the present court can be negated, and its enthusiasm dissipated."

Possibly by inclination, the military establishment rarely responds favorably to sudden change. Moreover, its organizational structure is such that doctrinal changes in military justice procedures typically go unnoticed by much of the command. But the JAGs, especially those who unsuccessfully argued case after case before Fletcher's court, realized by mid-1977 that a new era was upon them. The best explanation from their perspective came from a young JAG officer, Captain (later Brigadier General) John Cooke. In a lengthy exploration of USCAAF decisions for 1975–1977, the first two years of the Fletcher era, he discerned two precepts that in turn led to several basic trends.

In the first place, Cooke found that the Court was "reevaluating the balance between 'justice' and 'discipline' in the military justice system." Claiming in effect that military justice is too important to be left to the commanders, the Court "feels that considerations of justice must be given greater emphasis." Thus it has tended "to distinguish and separate functions exercised by the commander. . . . [He] is permitted to retain his disciplinary functions. but his . . . judicial functions have been taken away from him." However, Cooke added, "This tendency deserves close scrutiny, for it must be recognized that justice and discipline are properly but two sides of the same coin; to the extent that the court separates them unnecessarily, it risks devaluing the whole system."

More important, Cooke sensed a determination by the Fletcher court "to play a dynamic leadership role in the [military justice] system." Indeed, USCAAF "sees itself as the only institution capable of bringing to the system the type of constant leadership it believes necessary." Absent regular congressional scrutiny—which was possible but very improbable—"only [the Court] is in a position to interpret the Constitution and the UCMJ for the entire military justice system and to supervise it on a constant basis." Hence, the Court "will exercise extensive authority over the entire system." (Although written in 1977, Cooke's words are very relevant in a contemporary context. The continued disinclination of Congress to practice any meaningful and regular scrutiny over the military justice system, matched with a noticeable lack of judicial interest in rigorous inquiry, may raise serious questions as to the actual effectiveness of civilian oversight concerning military justice.)

These two assumptions formed the basis for three noteworthy trends demonstrated by the new Fletcher court. First, the role of the military judge must be expanded, even as the convening authority's influence over trial proceedings was to be restricted, with a restructuring of "the military justice system along lines closer to its civilian counterparts." Second, USCAAF will supervise the entire military justice system, not only for all personnel within it but to the extent of making rules and establishing policies to be followed by its practitioners—especially the judges on the intermediate courts of military review appointed, it might be noted, by the JAGs. Indeed, according to Cooke, Fletcher's court viewed the JAGs "as playing only a limited role in the supervision of military justice." One can see that this assumption, quite apart from the numerous cases that reflected it, was an early basis for the friction between Fletcher and the JAGs that characterized his tenure as chief judge.

Cooke commented on the tendency—already evident in 1977—for the courts of military review to reject the analysis set out by USCAAF in particular cases. He emphasized that such action "will not only lead to reversal by [USCAAF] in many of such cases. More importantly, it is likely to reinforce [USCAAF's] distrust of military courts and may as well lead the court to impose more rigid rules in this and other areas to reduce the maneuvering space available to lower courts." Finally, in a number of areas, such as search and seizure, jurisdiction, and self-incrimination, the Fletcher court "will interpret broadly the rights of individuals."

Cooke could not help but be aware of the strains that such activism had placed on the military justice system. "It is often difficult," he observed, "for military members, including lawyers, who are trained to execute the commander's desires, not to give undue weight to the commander's needs, be they explicit or implicit." Yet Fletcher's court now insisted that the commander's needs, like any other element that may affect the outcome of a case, must "be proven, not presumed." Now the burden of proof for showing that military conditions or necessity required a different rule than that prevailing in the civilian community was increasingly upon the military, not the accused.

Moreover, Cooke was troubled by the potential isolation of the commander from military justice. It was one thing to bar a commander from the exercise of judicial functions because of his disciplinary role. It was quite another "to say that [his] interest in discipline should play no part in judicial determinations." The system should indeed be insulated from command control, but it "should not, and cannot be insulated from the basic elements of the military society it serves without seriously distorting the results it produces."

Finally, Cooke noted that "courts are not, ordinarily, the best mechanism through which to institute widespread revision of the law." Trying to change attitudes as well as law involves "an educational function which the court has occasionally neglected in its desire to move quickly. This has, not surprisingly, generated much uncertainty and distrust." But Cooke's conclusion was very dissimilar to the knee-jerk military reaction to USCAAF holdings of an earlier era. For practitioners of military justice, the Court's new direction "should generate reevaluation, not retrenchment. . . . It should now be clear that the status quo is an unavailable alternative."

Other critics of USCAAF's activism joined Cooke in urging reevaluation—but from the Court, not the military—with an emphasis more on retraction than reevaluation. They criticized the premise from which Fletcher's tribunal had acted—the very basis for its claim to supervisory jurisdiction over the system. Thus, during a speech delivered in early 1977, Navy TJAG William Miller insisted that USCAAF "is not a constitutional Supreme Court and is not an Article III court, and its proper relationship to the military justice system cannot be deduced from the model of the judicial relations in our constitutional system."

Indeed, he added, whatever role it fulfills, "or even its very existence, is not *constitutionally* mandated" (emphasis in original). Rather it came from the UCMJ, which, Miller reminded the judges, "specifically and purposefully" assigned supervision of the military justice system "to a military official, the Judge Advocate General." It seemed clear to this JAG, "therefore, that in evaluating its role and its authority, the Court must do so in the context of the Code itself, and not by analogy to the far different role of the Supreme Court." Finally, Miller claimed that making changes in the UCMJ "is the province of Congress, not of the Judge Advocates General, *and not* of the Court of Military Appeals" (emphasis in original).

But not all JAG officers agreed with Miller's assessment of the Fletcher court, and at least one member of the navy appellate defense division, Carl Horst, took "strong exception [to] the substance of your remarks." They reminded him "of what I perceive as the Navy's continuing refusal to accept the UCMJ." As to Miller's negative reaction to the recruiting abuse decisions (discussed earlier), they were in fact "a most logical outcome of the recruiting abuses which the military has tolerated too long. . . . The result is, however, long overdue." Finally, the claim of "great instability to which you refer results as much from the intransigent reaction of the Navy and a Marine-like orientation, end justifies the means, Nixon-like attitude of damn the law, full speed ahead."

Chief Judge Fletcher did not respond to Miller directly, and, indeed, this author has been unable to locate any correspondence between Fletcher and the JAGs dealing with their critical reactions to the decisions of 1976–1978. In November 1977, the *Army Times* published an article based on an interview with Fletcher. If the chief judge was upset by the growing criticism of his Court, he gave no indication of it. Indeed, his comments bristled with a confident and aggressive tone that could only exacerbate the situation. The remarks appeared in a series of newpapers devoted to the military and widely distributed within it. "Military persons," Fletcher warned, "should not expect [the Court] to sit on its hands and wait for change. . . . We have been left by default as the actor to bring about change."

Fletcher acknowleged that the Court was interested in "civilianizing" military justice: "I think the Court has only one standard to look toward for change and that is the civilian system." As a result, "the changes being made are probably those which result from similar concepts found in the civilian system." But Fletcher immediately added that "always foremost in our minds are the unique necessities of the military system." Nevertheless, "the military is only a second society, not the primary." Rather, it had to function under the larger civilian world whether the JAGs liked it or not.

Fletcher emphasized that "we don't serve the military. The civilians created us. We have no responsibility to the military. Our responsibility is to the civilian community called Congress. We are guided by their electorate which wanted civilian supervision of military justice after World War II." Possibly with Miller in mind, the chief judge observed that "you've got to talk about who is responsible to whom. And we're responsible to Congress and the civilian society, not to the Judge Advocates General."

According to Fletcher, military enlistees "are a more exact mirror of the civilian community today, and they expect to have more of the rights they had out in the civilian community." The military "just has not reckoned with this pattern yet. I think the Court has." As to any agenda that he supposedly had upon assuming office, Fletcher was candid and confident. "Those who interviewed me," he recalled, "expressed a desire to look at reorganization of the military justice system to see if it could be improved or enhanced and [to] attempt to raise the status of the system." Fletcher's recollections tally with the documentation circulating within the Ford administration at the time of his appointment.

Whether he intended to do so or not, by going public with comments about his court's conflict with the JAGs, Fletcher had upped the stakes. It was one thing to issue decisions within the confines of an appellate tribunal. It was quite another to assert in the military press that USCAAF did not serve the military and indeed had no responsibility to the JAGs. For their part, in their continuing dispute with Fletcher, the JAGs found new allies, and if Fletcher had raised the ante, the JAGs were increasingly inclined to call the hand.

22

Conflicts and Culmination Concluded, 1975–1980, Part II

Even as the military's hostility to the Fletcher court's activism in military justice intensified, the chief judge faced additional attack from two unexpected sources—the Court's own staff and the Office of the General Counsel to the Defense Department. While the dispute concerning the staff resulted in a lawsuit against the judges, it was easily resolved. By 1979, however, tensions between Defense Department General Counsel Deanne C. Siemer and Fletcher had escalated to the point where her office coordinated and encouraged JAG criticism of USCAAF—an action without precedent. Both developments deserve attention.

JUDGING THE JUDGES

The litigation between the three USCAAF judges and their staff originated from the jurists' long-standing desire to control the employment and discharge of their own employees. Since 1951, the staff had been under the jurisdiction of the Civil Service Commission (CSC). As was noted in earlier chapters, this policy had resulted from an assumption that the Court was part of the executive branch of government. While the judges had consistently disagreed, claiming juridical independence identical to that exercised by any federal appellate tribunal, in actual practice their staff had been under CSC administration for almost twenty-five years.

At Fletcher's request, the commission had obtained an advisory opinion to the effect that his Court was "beyond a doubt" a "proper component of the judicial branch of government." Therefore, wrote CSC director Joseph Damico, "We now consider your agency outside the Commission's purview, subject only to your own personnel authority." Upon receipt of this advice,

Fletcher, Cook, and Perry signed two resolutions that all existing CSC schedules, life insurance, retirement and health programs, as well as other provisions and regulations "are hereby adopted as our own on an interim basis until such time as a contrary intent is expressed by resolution of the judges." Whatever the intent of these resolutions may have been, they failed to assuage fears of USCAAF staffers who suddenly had been informed that they were no longer under CSC jurisdiction and protection. As one observer noted, "They retain only temporary rights subject to the whim of the court." The staff promptly filed suit against the judges.

The suit was of short duration. The CSC assumed that the Military Justice Act of 1968 had somehow changed the status of USCAAF employees, a position that the Justice Department rejected. It noted, correctly, that the legislative history of the 1968 statute contained "no express discussion of the civil service status" for such employees. Indeed, "there is no indication whatsoever that the Congress either contemplated or intended in 1968" to change such status. There was absolutely no reason "to reopen the question now." In other words, as the U.S. attorney for the District of Columbia informed the assistant attorney general, "We do not believe the position now taken by the Civil Service Commission's staff can be successfully defended." The solution was "that we be authorized to negotiate a settlement." Its terms were virtually self-evident. The plaintiffs would have to dismiss the judges as defendants, while the government would stipulate that "the Court's employees will retain their civil service status."

Within a week, the assistant U.S. attorney had gained the concurrence of all three judges concerning their dismissal from the litigation. Fletcher, however, "takes no position on whether the [CSC claim] is correct or whether . . . our memorandum is correct." With the disinclination, if not outright refusal, of the Justice Department to defend the judges, in reality they had little choice but to agree to the proposed settlement. By August 29 all parties had so acquiesced. In thanking the three judges for their cooperation, Assistant U.S. Attorney Royce Lamberth observed that he could "no longer agree with the old adage that judges make the worst clients." On the other hand, a reporter for the *Washington Star,* while possibly less tactful than Lamberth, may have been as truthful. "You might say one moral of this tale is," he observed, "that wise judges know when not to go before a judge." Today, the Court functions under a sort of compromise—its staff is still under CSC jurisdiction, but the judges may appoint a part of their chambers personnel on a rotating basis. The arrangement thus ensures both stability and change.

From their perspective, the JAGs may well have viewed published accounts of the internal strife within the Court as further evidence of Fletcher's apparent disregard for well-established practice as well as his capacity for aggressive self-aggrandizement. Thus, in November 1977, the *Army Times* reported that USCAAF, "already criticized by military officials for 'civilianizing' the military justice system, has proposed 50 major changes," some of which give the Court "more control over the system." According to Fletcher, "The military has seen fit to ignore all 50 aspects by making no comment." He thought "they would say, 'Yes, some of these are good ideas and we will go ahead with them.' "

The chief judge further added that about half of the fifty recommendations "are being resolved by opinions in the Court." Once again, Fletcher's comments could only have worsened the tensions between him and the service JAGs. In a widely distributed "service" publication, he had acknowledged a list of major changes desired by the Court, denigrated the military response to them thus far, and stated that many of the changes would be—if they had not already been—implemented by the judges themselves, with a clear implication that acceptance or rejection by the JAGs was irrelevant.

Although from its beginning USCAAF has been a part of the Defense Department for "administrative purposes only," until 1976–1977 there had been little, if any, friction between the Court and civilian Pentagon officials as opposed to occasional clashes between the judges and the uniformed TJAGs. It seems accurate to state that since 1951, the Office of the General Counsel had demonstrated minimal interest in the Court. Moreover, the annual appearances by Chief Judge Quinn before the Senate Appropriations Committee to justify the Court's budgetary requests reflected a similar lack of external concern, with the very brief sessions characterized by a tone of conviviality between the former governor and the few senators in attendance. All this changed during the Fletcher era.

Deanne Siemer, the recently appointed general counsel, was an articulate and aggressive Washington attorney with ties to Lloyd Cutler, a highly visible adviser to senior officials in the new administration of President Jimmy Carter. Siemer took office just as the tensions between Fletcher and the JAGs became more evident. For a variety of reasons, including mutual animosity, relations between Fletcher and the general counsel's office soon became equally tense; and by 1978–1979, the general counsel was actively involved in efforts to monitor the Court budget, to coordinate JAG criticism of Fletcher, to gain congressional rejection of certain USCAAF decisions, and to replace Fletcher as chief judge. With Fletcher on one side and Siemer on the other, relations between the general counsel's office and the Court reached a level of hostility never before experienced in its history.

In 1977, Fletcher had sought an additional $150,000 "to fund a neutral and independent study by leading consultants to assess the qualitative . . . impact resulting from dispersion of military justice roles and responsibilities among military commanders, trial and appellate judges and multiple service courts." An assistant to Siemer, Manuel Briskin, advised her that "it is of dubious propriety and doubtful wisdom for the Court to exercise an administrator's function rather than a judicial one by contracting to study the operation of the military justice system below them. There is at best bare support for this expansion beyond the Court's judicial role."

Anticipating Fletcher's insistence that, like other Article 3 federal courts, USCAAF's budget should be submitted intact to Congress without modification from the Pentagon, Briskin informed the general counsel that there was no such comparable statutory provision for this court. Thus, there was no "legal impediment to the President submitting a reduced budget estimate for the Court." But the memorandum warned that "if the [Defense Department] reductions to the Court's request become a public issue, . . . there is a likelihood the issue would be perceived as another deficiency in the military justice system and an attempt by the Department to thwart the Court."

Faced with the decision to delete these funds from its budget, USCAAF Court Executive Ward Mundy dispatched a protest to Harold Brown, Carter's new secretary of defense. As to the general counsel, "with due respect, I fear that your office has been gravely misled by some of your subordinates who have virtually no experience in military justice, a system whose integrity demands independence from command pressure at all levels. I urge you to consult counsel outside your department before taking a move which will have the most serious consequences for your administration and the independence of the military justice system and this Court." No reply to Mundy has been located, but a memo to Siemer suggested that a proposed letter from Defense Secretary Brown should emphasize that "the reduction of $150,000 for a duplicative management and policy study of military justice roles and responsibilities within the military departments does not in any way interfere with the Court's ability to perform its judicial functions."

By January 1978, Siemer's office had become actively involved in the dispute between Fletcher and the JAGs. A memo to her from an assistant general counsel noted that the army and navy JAGs "are separately to attack" USCAAF in speeches before appropriate ABA committees at the ABA February meeting: "These speeches were reviewed and approved in our office this week." They would criticize the tribunal "as an activist court bent on mandating changes in military jurisprudence through judicial decisions which contravene the clearly expressed will of Congress. . . . As a result of these alleged judicial excesses[,] military discipline is said to be in the process of being undermined and the perception of military justice as an effective instrument of law is being eroded. Support of remedial legislation is to be urged."

As far as this author has been able to ascertain, never before in the history of the civilian office of the general counsel had that department allied itself with senior JAG officials in preparing public criticism of the U.S. Court of Appeals for the Armed Forces. Issues of propriety to one side, Siemer's conduct raises some very troublesome questions concerning not only the perception of civilian control over the military but also how the general counsel's office had evolved to the point where it could actively pressure a civilian court to render decisions more in conformity with the military's desires. As will be seen, in later months Siemer went even further in this direction, utilizing an interesting mixture of bullying and bombast against the Court.

The next round in the fulminations over the Fletcher court came from another civilian source, a federal district judge. An admitted conservative Republican appointed to the bench by Lyndon Johnson in part—as he recalled—"because I voted for Barry Goldwater and willingly admitted it," Oliver Gasch had been a JAG officer in World War II. Active in the Judge Advocates Association, he was well acquainted with senior army JAG officials. It was at their suggestion that he agreed to visit the Judge Advocate General's School of the Army in March 1978 to present a lecture entitled "Who Is Out of Step?" Gasch had no doubt about the answer.

Critical of the Court's activist course, Gasch claimed that Fletcher had "openly stated that the Court will continue to make changes until the services decide to get in step with it, at which point the judges will 'lay down their mantle of the stimuli and put on the robes of response.'" As other Fletcher critics had noted, Gasch insisted that the object of the civilian community differed dramatically from that of the military, where discipline was indispensable. "In the disciplined military environment," he said, "there is only a very narrow margin, for there is *no* payoff in *placing* or *showing* in war. There is no substitute for victory" (emphasis in original).

Gasch's comments seemed relatively mild when compared to the criticism leveled at some decisions of the Fletcher court by judges serving on the courts of military review, the intermediate level of military appellate justice. These judges, it might be noted, are appointed by and serve at the pleasure of the judge advocate general, without established terms. This practice, which to many—including this author—seemed of doubtful utility, was upheld by the U.S. Supreme Court as constitutional (see *Weiss v. United States,* 510 U.S. 163 [1994]). The unanimous and seemingly superficial opinion gave little comfort to those who support a judicially secure and independent appellate bench for the military.

Thus, Senior Judge John Dunbar described recent Fletcher findings as opinions that lacked "clarity and accuracy of expression . . . [and] logic and meaning." One case, *United States v. Booker,* that raised the issue of a right to counsel for relatively minor military justice offenses, particularly irritated Dunbar. He labeled it as "pseudo-rational manipulation" that "smacks of a sort of youthful, one-sided idealism . . . devoid of the slightest realization that the services might have a stake in the matter." Fletcher's "leaky logic" represented an instance where "we do have a duty to make discriminating, critical, and level-eyed analyses of questionable opinions and to register our objection to them." Indeed, Dunbar insisted, if *Booker* was accepted "as representative of communicable and credible legal reasoning, then, in my opinion, there can be no further honest thinking in military law."

Such comments may have been instrumental in leading USCAAF to reconsider and modify its *Booker* holding. Dunbar remained unimpressed, commenting on the Court's continued failure "to render its opinions in clear, accurate and communicable language." (Cursory examination of Fletcher's written opinions indicates some justification for Dunbar's comment.) In his opinion, the language in the second *Booker* case remained "elusive and, in areas, woefully unintelligible." This was due to USCAAF's "continuing efforts to civilianize the military justice system," an approach "fashioned by persons lacking broad and balanced military backgrounds." Never before, he added, "has there been such a tremendous gap between the decisions of [USCAAF] and their interpretation by the service appellate courts. Previously, the guidance of the High Court, however objectionable, was respected and by common consent accepted." Now, "the present Court's irreverent rejection of many military values" had created tensions that were both unfortunate and unnecessary.

Of course, this is not the way most intermediate tribunals write about decisions from their high court. That they occurred is evidence that Fletcher's course, however laudable in intent, had produced very serious internal friction within the military justice system. If Fletcher felt intimidated by these new attacks on his court from fellow judges, he gave no indication of it. In April, when he appeared before the Senate Appropriations Committee, he first turned to the still ongoing dispute with Siemer and Brown. Without mentioning either by name, the chief judge took the offensive.

Fletcher stated that "the budget request before you does not represent the Court's desires but rather those of the Secretary of Defense. For the first time in the history of the Court, the Secretary of Defense has tampered with the Court's budget as well as its statutory responsibilities, both in violation of congressional mandates." Unlike other federal tribunals, Fletcher added, "the military justice system literally has no one to turn to for consulting work, particularly when the Secretary of Defense takes it upon himself to meddle in the Court's internal affairs." Indeed, he asked the Senate committee "to take whatever action it deems appropriate, to include consideration of future criminal sanctions, to restore the Court's budgetary independence from the Department of Defense."

During his 1979 appearance before the Senate committee, Fletcher noted that in spite of the committee's statement that "the [Defense] Department has no authority or prerogative regarding the Court's budget or operations," the additional funds had not been authorized. Moreover, he claimed that Siemer had issued several "coercive statements . . . regarding the Court's operation." She had also tried to interfere with a court-initiated promotion for Ward Mundy. "This abnormal interest in and unwarranted control of the Court's internal operation by the General Counsel coupled with her prior tampering with the Court's attempts to request funding . . . suggests that something drastic is necessary to end this David and Goliath relationship."

Siemer probably agreed with this comment. Her next proposals, although indeed drastic, were far from what Fletcher had in mind. Privately, she undertook to replace the controversial chief judge as soon as possible. Publicly, she had already initiated a widely disseminated proposal to abolish the Court of Military Appeals in its entirety.

SIEMER'S SOLUTION

On April 3, 1978, the *Army Times* reported that Siemer "has proposed abolishing [USCAAF] and assigning the judges to other positions until their terms with the Court expire." She further suggested that the intermediate military appellate courts take over as the final source of appeal "for most military cases." Controversies raising constitutional questions "should be referred to the Fourth Circuit Court," sitting in Richmond, Virginia. Siemer had previously warned Fletcher that "if the current [military justice] system is unsatisfactory in any respect, we may have to consider a legislative solution." The general counsel expanded on her scheme during an interview published in the *Navy Times*.

Siemer observed that one major question is "whether the military justice system needs a court at the top or whether it can function as other justice systems do, feeding into the regular court system. We are looking at that." She had picked the Fourth Circuit Court not because it was more conservative than its D.C. counterpart, but because the D.C. Circuit "is just loaded down with extra duties. . . . Those poor folks are just over their heads." The reporter also asked Siemer, "Is this a plan to civilianize the military justice system?" Her answer did not mince words.

"That is such a misnomer. [USCAAF] is a civilian court. There is not a military person on it. It could not be more civilianized no matter what it was. [USAAF] is a civilian court just like the Fourth Circuit is a civilian court." (More than twenty years later, Siemer's point seems strained, at best. To be sure, all USCAAF judges are civilians. But the central legal staff includes former career military officers, while a number of its judges have elected to have as their advisers, or "commissioners," recently retired JAG officers whose legal experience, though extensive, has been largely limited to the military justice environment.)

Again, Siemer questioned "whether the military justice system needs the protection of a special court. Military decisions on constitutional questions are as forthright and forthcoming for individual rights as are so-called civilian courts. The impression that is created by having a special court to deal with this is that somehow they are different. That's not true. You don't need to trust [treat?] military constitutional issues any differently." Finally, the general counsel implied that Fletcher's court was overinvolved in legislative and administrative matters. This court, she said, "is a strange animal. . . . It may be that the judges can spend their time better at being judges than worrying about administrative matters." Every other court, she implied, "is run differently."

Not suprisingly, Fletcher rejected the proposed participation of the Fourth Circuit in military justice. It would only add "another layer of appeal before a criminal conviction becomes final . . . with no appreciable benefit to the accused or the government." Moreover, "it is highly questionable whether a federal circuit court should wade into the military justice thicket to review 28 years of decisions interpreting the [UCMJ]." Instead, the embattled chief judge called first for the expansion of his court to five judges, and second, that either the plaintiff or the government be able to "petition the Supreme Court . . . to review any [USCAAF] decision . . . involving a constitutional question." Ultimately, Fletcher's proposals became law, one in 1983, the other in 1991—both after he had been replaced as chief judge.

Siemer later explained to this author the tactic she employed. She claimed that an effective way to force the JAGs to "consider whether they really wanted this Court was to propose that we get rid of this Court." In other words, her plan was more a "trial balloon" than a serious suggestion intended to become law. Reaction to it would indicate whether JAG concern was due more to the personality and philosophy of a particular judge or to a fundamental flaw in the structure of the military appeals system in general.

Yet Siemer insisted that "if [abolishing the Court] was the only solution, I certainly would not have hesitated to do it." In spite of Siemer's comments, this author remains very skeptical that there was ever a serious intent from the general counsel to abolish USCAAF. On the other hand, as will be seen, her office generated a lengthy study on the workings of the Court. Her tactics forced the JAGs to consider whether the alternatives she proposed might be worse than what they had had for almost thirty years; and they may well have led USCAAF in 1979–1980 to modify some of the doctrinal positions that had generated such controversy. Indeed, from her perspective, "putting out the alternative of abolishing the Court brought forth lots of proposals with respect to what else could be done[,] and it worked splendidly in my view." Siemer had noted that "an activist General Counsel is just as difficult for the JAGs as an activist court. They would prefer no action anywhere."

By the spring of 1979, Siemer's office had prepared a thorough and reasonably unbiased analysis of USCAAF and its relation to military justice. Colloquially called the "rainbow book" because each of its sections was printed on a different color paper, the project—according to Siemer—"was written for the purpose of shaping the issues and providing the necessary background for decision making." As such it did not endorse or represent any "official point of view of the Department of Defense." The report did, however, describe the origins and transformation of the Court after almost thirty years of operation— and in language that reflected the general counsel's earlier comments about the current state of the tribunal and its relationship to military justice.

The first section detailed the "need for reform." Noting, correctly, that USCAAF's creation had represented a compromise between those in favor of civilian review of military justice and those opposed to this practice, it stated that while a civilian court had emerged, it was "entirely within the Department of Defense with no direct access to the federal courts of appeal or to the Supreme Court." Its judges had limited terms instead of life tenure, ensuring "the possibility of replacing judges who proved unsuited to the task of applying military principles within a judicial system." By 1979, judicial review had become "the accepted mode in the military justice system." Moreover, "because the military justice system has outgrown the compromise reached in 1951," critical examination of it was needed in order to assess what improvements might be appropriate.

The report found two fundamental flaws in USCAAF's current operation. First was the fact that "the appellate process is shut off almost completely from the Supreme Court." The alternative use of collateral attack to obtain such review was in reality "a judicial trek that has been criticized as inefficient, costly, time-consuming, and redundant." Even worse was the unavailability of any other tribunal to which the government could appeal an adverse ruling. Although not mentioning Fletcher by name, the report stated that the current tribunal "has ruled against the government on cases considered by the military . . . to be of direct importance to the maintenance of order and discipline in the armed forces," citing a number of decisions as evidence. When USCAAF "declines to follow Supreme Court precedent, the government has no recourse." And when it follows civilian precedent "despite unique military considerations, the government also has no recourse."

Without federal appellate review, the Court "is the final arbiter of its own powers . . . and when the court expands its powers into areas where there is substantial disagreement that Congress ever intended it to be," such action "creates a tension that adversely affects all operations of the military justice system. Over the past five years the Court has steadily sought to expand its powers. . . . That result ultimately may be judged right or wrong, but the instability in the military justice system that it produces is unmistakable. There is always available the alternative of a legislative solution to correct the substantive errors . . . or to correct the results that the Congress finds inappropriate, but that is an unacceptable way to administer a justice system."

The second major flaw in USCAAF's current operation is its "considerable turnover. During the last ten years, eight different judges have held the court's three seats. Within a four-year period, there were seven judges who sat at various times in nine different combinations. Only two of the vacancies . . . resulted from illness or death, suggesting that there are fundamental problems with the court that are causing this turnover."

The report made no effort to explain what "these fundamental problems" might be. However, three come to mind. First is the relative insecurity of a judicial appointment that in this period frequently was made to complete a predecessor's unfinished term, a practice later banned by Congress. Second is the relative boredom that inevitably sets in for judges who can only consider cases involving a highly specialized and limited field of criminal law. Third is the unfortunate application of political considerations, such as with the cases of Judges Duncan and Perry, which resulted in the use of USCAAF as a mere stepping-stone to a lifetime appointment as a federal district judge.

Whatever the fundamental causes, the results have been "to introduce substantial instability and unpredictability into the military justice system . . . and the state of the law has become more uncertain." Such uncertainty not only makes the teaching of legal doctrine difficult. It also creates an impression "that the military justice system is arbitrary and capricious," and "in a system where respect for the law is of such paramount importance, it is imperative that such a development be avoided."

The major cause for preparation of the rainbow book was the military reaction to the Fletcher court. Also beyond doubt is that the report generated the wide interest and varied discussions that Siemer had sought in ordering its production. Some specific proposals that resulted from it will be noted in the epilogue of this book. In the meantime, however, Siemer turned her attention toward encouraging congressional rejection of several Fletcher court holdings concerning recruiter misconduct. But even as some hearings were scheduled, more conflict erupted between USCAAF and its military critics.

Indeed, two months before the hearings, Fletcher acknowledged that his court had become somewhat beleaguered. In an address to the Pentagon chapter of the Federal Bar Association, he lauded its accomplishments. "The present Court," he said, "has proceeded to bring and maintain the word justice into the court-martial system." It "has provided a series of decisions that make the military justice system a criminal justice system second to none." But "we are too successful. Apparently our system cannot stand the light that has been allowed to come into military justice. . . . All of a sudden the closed shop was no longer closed."

This had transpired because "the Court acted like a Court. The regulations promulgated by the services mainly for perception purposes but seldom followed were now being enforced. The light that blinds is that the Court by decision was making the individual services follow their own devised regulations." "Have you," Fletcher asked in conclusion, "seen or read any critical review of the last four years' decisions of [USCAAF] by any one other than a military person?"

CONGRESSIONAL INTERVENTION

Early in his tenure as chief judge, Fletcher had spoken for the Court in a unanimous opinion dealing with recruiter misconduct, one that essentially reaffirmed a prior holding—also unanimous—by three other judges. These decisions held that "defects in the enlistment of a military member, including recruiter malpractice, could be raised by an accused after the commission of an offense and could defeat court-martial jurisdiction." In another case, Judge Ferguson had observed that while presidential authority to make rules and regulations for the conduct of courts-martial was indeed lawful, the same might not be the case for such regulations governing pre- and post-trial matters. To the JAGs, the Catlow-Russo holdings had created unreasonable and unworkable demands for monitoring of recruiter conduct. Ferguson's comment, even though it had no force of law, seemed to imply a questioning of a long held executive function based upon constitutional authority as commander in chief.

Speaking before a House subcommittee, Siemer emphasized that "courts tread on difficult and uncertain [terrain] when opinions are based on public policy grounds." She detailed three tests that could justify such action, all of which had been supposedly ignored by the Fletcher court in reaching its conclusion concerning recruiter actions: (1) a mistaken assumption of "little guiding legal precedent"; (2) "when there has been a careful weighing of the benefits and costs to the public of the proposed outcome, and when on balance the benefits so far outweigh the costs that there can be really little question about where the public intent lies. That is not the case here"; and (3) "when the rights involved rise to the level of importance that justifies judicial intervention in the normal policy prerogatives of the Legislative Branch in declaring public policy and in the Executive Branch in [its implementation.] We believe that is also not the case here." Echoing the JAGs who had denounced the Fletcher court's holding in these cases for the last four years, Siemer insisted that the choices imposed by the findings resulted in "an undue strain on the procedures that are essential for the maintenance of military order and discipline."

Following Siemer's brief presentation, all three TJAGs appeared, almost as if in lockstep, all following the lead of the general counsel in calling for congressional intervention against the Court. Army Major General Persons claimed that USCAAF had focused to an excess on the "illegal actions of the recruiter and ignored the enlistment misconduct of the [defendant.]" The navy JAG commented on a related "aberrant interpretation" by the Fletcher court of well-established presidential authority as commander in chief to establish rules of procedure for courts-martial. One way, he noted, to solve this difficulty might be "by transferring this authority to [USCAAF.] This may be what two members of the court would desire, as this would coincide with the court's present activist posture." But Rear Admiral Charles E. McDowell did not "believe, however, that the tribunal has the experience, resources, or basic understanding of or appreciation of the military justice system, especially in the light of some of their recent decisions."

Chief Judge Fletcher also appeared as a witness, although it seemed an exercise in futility. He emphasized that the "integrity of the military justice system and, yes, the military services cannot withstand the condonation in any way of . . . recruiter criminal acts." Moreover, he questioned the need for urgency in congressional intervention as reiterated by the JAGs. If recruitment tactics were having a considerable negative effect on military discipline, "reason dictates that if the problem is substantial, then fraudulent recruitment practices must be the rule rather than the exception." In fact, the Court had published eight decisions in four years on this topic: "We average about 2,000 petitions a year, so it seems reasonable to draw the conclusion that either few cases of this nature are reaching our Court or, if they are, we are denying the petitions. Thus, if there is a substantial problem, then it must be through some regulatory procedure promulgated by the services themselves or through misinterpretation of our decisions by other military judicial tribunals." Concerning the proposal to reaffirm presidential authority to issue rules for courts-martial, Fletcher viewed this step as evidence that "Congress is willing to wash its hands of military justice legislation and is turning the reins over to the Defense Department [the agency that actually drafts the great majority of the regulations "imposed" by the President]. That is not unlike asking the fox to guard the chicken coop."

The concerns raised in 1979 by Fletcher are just as valid today. Indeed, it would not be inaccurate to characterize the contemporary attitude of both Congress and the U.S. Supreme Court toward critical oversight of military justice as one of simple disinterest. In 1990, for example, Congress quietly deleted the requirement that changes in military justice regulations had to be reported to that body. The implications of such disinterest for effective civilian oversight of military justice speak for themselves. It might be noted that in 1996, the ABA Standing Committee on Armed Forces Law strongly recommended that the UCMJ be amended to provide for a broadly constituted, predominantly civilian advisory committee on rules of procedure and evidence at courts-martial; a method of prescribing rules of procedure and evidence at courts-martial; and a reporting to Congress concerning rules of procedure and evidence at courts-martial. Such changes have not yet occurred.

Besides Fletcher, only one other witness came forward to oppose congressional action. Eugene R. Fidell, a Washington attorney with a great deal of experience in military justice litigation, represented the American Civil Liberties Union. Fidell mentioned that recent USCAAF decisions had already "narrowed the scope of [Fletcher's] *Russo* holding," evidence that "the law has been growing, [and] is continuing to grow. . . . I would question the need for Congress to intervene on a spot basis now. . . . and I would say that the law should continue to go on its usual case by case basis, and further growth and evolution can be anticipated." Moreover, unlike the JAGs, Fidell believed that the recruiter misconduct cases "were properly decided."

Resolved "after full briefing and oral argument," congressional overturning of such decisions from "any federal court by legislation is not something to be undertaken lightly." The current instance was even more undesirable, as the JAGs had sought to change the law by amendments incident to the authorizing process rather than by extensive congressional hearings and investigation. Indeed, the suggested UCMJ amendments had not even received scrutiny from the Code Committee, a body established by the UCMJ as "a forum for the exchange of views. That purpose has not been served here."

The outcome of the very short hearings, spread out over portions of only two days, was never really in doubt. The proposed UCMJ changes quickly and quietly became law. Judicial relief for alleged recruiter misconduct by members of the armed services was curtailed, and presidential authority to establish policies for virtually all aspects of military justice was reaffirmed. Even as the hearings took place, however, both Deanne Siemer and the Carter White House had become involved in the process of selecting a new Court member. The ultimate choice, Robinson Everett, is the only USCAAF appointment ever recommended to the president by a nominating commission. The process that ensured not only his selection but also the way in which it took place is noteworthy.

THE APPOINTMENT OF EVERETT

By September 1977, rumors of Judge Perry's "imminent" departure from USCAAF were circulating in Washington, although he had only been on its bench for a year and a half. In fact, Perry would not leave until September 1979. California congressman Ronald Dellums wrote to President Carter, expressing his concern that "representation from the minority community be retained given the increasing number of minority military personnel and the high proportion of appeals from minorities that reach this Court." In fact, no USCAAF judge from a minority community has been selected since Perry, and no woman served on its bench until 1991, when President Bush appointed Susan Crawford, who had been the inspector general for the Defense Department. Another consideration focused on the presidential nominating commission "that is in the works to recommend judges."

Thus, David Addlestone, director of the ACLU Military Discharge Review Project, wrote to the associate counsel to the president that his "major concern is that appointees in the past, with few exceptions, have been selected on the basis of whom they knew on the Armed Services Committees." Addlestone recommended a number of well-qualified individuals to serve on such a commission, none of whom were currently employed by the Defense Department. Addlestone's fears that the nominating commission might be too intimate with the Defense Department were shared by the White House. Carter's counsel wrote to his assistant that while DOD "wants to have a major input, to which I have agreed, . . . I also think that we should have a great deal of interest in the selection . . . of this commission, so that it will not be completely dominated by the Department of Defense."

The nominating commission was duly established by President Carter's executive order of June 5, 1978, and would consist of six members, including Deanne Siemer as the chair. The order required the commission to submit "the names of no more than five persons whom [it] considers well qualified to serve in the position." Although the basic rationale for the commission was to screen up to five suitable candidates so that Carter could choose among them for his ultimate selection, in fact the order failed to require a minimum number. As will be seen, this omission was of great significance because the commission ultimately submitted only one name.

Not until April 26, 1979, however, did Siemer move to select the commission members, informing the White House that "I think we have covered all the bases." Her choices consisted of two officials in the Defense Department plus an attorney, a federal judge, and A. Kenneth Pye, who at that time was the chancellor of Duke University and would later assume the presidency of Southern Methodist University. Siemer explained that she had not selected any representatives from the JAGs, "and we made that decision after consultation with them." Her nominations included "one black and one woman in the group of five." Although Siemer claimed to have provided for "representation from the academic community, from the private bar, [and] from the federal bench," in fact half of her proposed panel—including its chair—came from the Defense Department.

It turned out that both the Defense Department and the White House insisted that Siemer's slate be modified. An internal note within the counsel's office staff stated, "Let's come up w[ith] alternatives.—then discuss." Writing again to the White House counsel's office, David Addlestone claimed that Siemer's list "is totally unrepresentative of the practitioners in the field." Even worse from his viewpoint was that it "seems to contain a majority of persons who would, or have taken a public position against, the current philosophy of the Court." The net result would be akin to "having DOD in effect select the members of the Court," which "of course violates the intent of the [UCMJ]." As finally constituted, the commission consisted of six lawyers—including two representatives from DOD [both women] and one black attorney.

Within two months, the commission was ready with its report. It examined thirty-nine applications and interviewed eleven candidates, including three blacks. Out of this number, however, the commission suggested only one nominee for Carter's consideration, despite the wording of its mandate. In explaining this step to senior administration officials, Siemer sought to place the proposed nomination of Robinson Everett in a very broad context. She was both forceful and candid.

"When I first came to office," she wrote, "there was such strong, consistent criticism of the Court . . . that I undertook a lengthy study of the situation. This was an attempt to quiet the criticism and lack of respect for the Court temporarily by demonstrating active interest in reform." Regardless of the "rainbow book" findings, "my private view is that this Court has such serious problems with basic scholarship, use of precedent, and written expression of decisions that very substantial changes are necessary to bring military justice at the appellate level up to rudimentary federal standards of acceptable performance." While a number of long-term "solutions" to "a very difficult problem with [USCAAF]" were under consideration, "this appointment is a key to the short-term solution."

A number of factors had persuaded the commission to put forth only one name. There were only fourteen months left of Perry's term, a limitation that "makes finding qualified, much less outstanding candidates very difficult." Moreover, in accordance with the statute, the nominee had to be a Democrat, and the vacancy needed to be filled quickly. "The two incumbent judges [Fletcher and Cook] have widely differing views on most issues and there will be no majority until the new appointment is made. Military justice will be at a standstill at the appellate level." Further, the short term made it "vitally important that the nominee be a recognized expert in military law. There is no time for the lengthy education process necessary for persons not familiar with the field."

Here, Siemer may have had in mind the number of USCAAF judges who had been appointed for political expediency rather than practical experience in military justice. Although they served with dedication if not distinction, they all had a much longer period in which to familiarize themselves with military justice, to say nothing of the role that their legal staff in chambers might have played in such an education. Most important, however, was the availability of a candidate who "was by far the best qualified."

Siemer listed Everett's qualifications, which were impressive and satisfied all the needs just noted. An academician as well as a practicing advocate who had appeared before the Court, Everett had published widely in the field of military justice. As a law student at Harvard, he had been taught evidence by Edmund Morgan, the professor who chaired the committee that drafted the UCMJ and proposed the very Court that his student would later join. An imposing figure with a sleepy smile that concealed a sharp legal intellect, Everett "knows both of the incumbent judges on the Court . . . and gets along well with them." But Everett possessed more than experience and expertise. He had served as an air force JAG, and he "deals very successfully with the Judge Advocates General, even though he often takes positions contrary to theirs." Indeed, he enjoyed the enthusiastic endorsement of all the service JAGs, who were eager to see a nominee with a broad knowledge of military justice. Siemer also noted, accurately, that Everett had not sought this appointment, and "indeed, it would be a hardship for him to take it."

Having justified her panel's decision to nominate only Everett to President Carter, Siemer further urged that he be designated chief judge as soon as possible: "Many of the Court's problems . . . can be solved from within. A new

Chief could quiet the rhetoric against the [DOD] and the [JAGs] that has been pouring forth in the current Chief Judge's impromptu speeches and could create an atmosphere more conducive to respect for the Court." In a separate memo to Secretary of Defense Harold Brown, Siemer emphasized Everett's personality: "He is both strong and diplomatic. I am confident that both his appointment and his leadership will greatly increase the stature of this beleaguered Court." "You know," she added, "that in my view the current Chief Judge has been a major cause of the Court's problems."

Conceding that the commission's mandate might not extend toward recommending in effect the replacement of the current chief judge, Siemer obtained unanimous agreement from her panel that it "is of the opinion that Mr. Everett would serve with distinction as Chief Judge of the Court." True, his designation "might cause temporary problems with [Fletcher,] but Everett has both the character and stature to meet that challenge well." Indeed, Everett and Fletcher served together for the remainder of Fletcher's time on the Court in an atmosphere utterly free from any personal rancor.

Finally, Siemer reminded Brown that DOD would be recommending "a number of reforms in the current Court," and in all probability the president "may have two new appointments to make to this bench." Here Siemer was mistaken. Although DOD urged that USCAAF be increased to five judges, that did not happen until 1990. Within fourteen months (the remainder of Perry's term), Carter had been defeated for reelection, and Everett would be his only appointment to the Court. Recognizing its importance, Congress by special statute designated a ten-year term for him. After 1990, on numerous occasions Everett has returned to USCAAF temporarily as a senior judge.

Siemer's draft of Brown's recommendation to Carter, one that essentially repeated what she had reiterated, concluded that "if [USCAAF] has stability, consistency of doctrine, and an appreciation of the special problems of the military, we should reap substantial benefits in areas of military discipline. It is my belief that appointment of your nominee as chief judge would help achieve those objectives." Carter's designation of Everett as chief judge was drafted on February 25, 1980, ten days after his nomination had been sent to the Hill, "to be submitted upon his confirmation by the Senate."

Formally nominated on February 15, 1980, all that remained was the traditional perfunctory hearing before the Senate Armed Services Committee. Considering seven other Carter nominations, it spent minimal time on Everett's. The nominee did, however, have a chance to offer several comments both on USCAAF and military justice in general. Everett appears to have been the only judge in USCAAF history who, during the confirmation hearing, criticized a line of cases that had come from the very court he was about to join. He noted that while the Court has "some unique responsibilities" concerning military justice, "basically it is a court and should behave as a court."

The nominee added that "it certainly is unfortunate when there are three opinions by three judges going off in different directions." Here, Everett referred to a Supreme Court case, which he could not identify, where supposedly "they had ten opinions with nine justices . . . which obviously introduces some elements of uncertainty." One senator responded: "I know the clerks are powerful; I didn't know they were that powerful." Everett mentioned the need "to produce a more predictable result," a goal that could be reached in part by "self-restraint as well." Indeed, he would not view his confirmation "as an opportunity to implement in an opinion my personal predilections or things I have advocated over the years but which are completely at odds with the precedent of the Court. I think that it is important to maintain continuity and to be aware of precedent in rendering decisions."

Even before the formal hearing, rumors concerning Everett's appointment had already dampened JAG enthusiasm for any radical changes to USCAAF. Thus the navy JAG noted that abolition of the Court was "too drastic a measure to overcome the more easily remedied faults. . . . I think the approach of abolishing the Court is like buying a new car when the old one only needs a tune-up." Moreover, added Admiral C. E. McDowell, Siemer's proposed change "could result in the judiciary committees of the Congress becoming involved in military justice matters." Finally, McDowell was aware that Article 3 judges usually held their appointments for life. Replete with his deficiencies, at least Fletcher's term was finite. One can easily understand why the thought of such a judge remaining on the Court with indefinite tenure might well persuade the JAGs that minor change rather than radical transformation would be appropriate.

Major General George Prugh, recently retired as army TJAG, had been even more critical of Siemer's proposals. All too often, he noted, motivation for change "stems from disenchantment with the people involved, rather than the procedure itself." In fact, Siemer's draft memorandum "simply does not make out a convincing need for the various remedies it considers." Can it be fairly said "that the Court has not properly done its job as Congress intended it to do? Before such a charge can be made there has to be a lot better justification evident than the weak arguments advanced in the [rainbow book]."

Promptly confirmed by the Senate and immediately designated chief judge, Robinson Everett took the oath of office on April 16, 1980, almost thirty years after Harry Truman had signed the statute creating both the UCMJ and USCAAF. Under his leadership, the Court reached out to the JAGs, emphasizing a commonality of justice rather than a clash of jurisdictions. Thus, his appointment signaled both the end of an era and the advent of a new chapter in the Court's history. At some future date, perhaps another volume can chronicle its later developments. In the meantime, however, the Everett selection provides an appropriate occasion from which to offer a final overview of USCAAF's history during its first thirty years. As my book concludes, what can be said of this tribunal when measured both by its potential and performance?

Epilogue

In 1951, Felix Larkin observed that the highlight of the Uniform Code of Military Justice was its new appellate procedure. It was intended, he emphasized, to resemble a civilian system, replete with appropriate counsel and civilian judges—"men of high caliber and judicial experience." Two years earlier, Representative Philip Philbin had stated that "this Court will be completely detached from the military in every way. It is entirely disconnected with [*sic*] the Department of Defense . . . [and] completely removed from any outside influences." Similarly, Larkin and Edmund Morgan expected this new federal tribunal to take its place as an independent appellate court, with the perquisites, procedures, and stature of its sister institutions. So much for intentions and expectations.

In fact, the history of the United States Court of Appeals for the Armed Forces has been unlike any other federal appellate bench. For a number of reasons explored in this book, the results have been impressive as far as they go, yet at the same time both disappointing and a source of concern for the future. What kind of picture emerges of this court? What are students, observers, and practitioners of military justice to make of its history? A few conclusions based on the preceding chapters may be appropriate here.

The very nature of USCAAF's purpose, to serve—with few exceptions—as the final interpreter of *military* law was undercut from the beginning by the repeated emphasis on the unique *military* environment within which the Court operated. No other federal appellate bench has functioned both in the shadow of the huge defense establishment and the Senate Armed Services Committee. Indeed, by keeping this tribunal under the jurisdiction of that committee rather than the Senate Judiciary Committee, Congress has ensured that the Court's future rests with a body for whom qualifications of legal ability and judicial distinction may be secondary to political considerations and expediency.

326

It is in no way intended as disrespect to the Armed Services Committee to point out that whatever its considerable contributions to the American military mission may be, careful and judicious screening of potential federal appellate judges has not been one of them. Ample indications have been given in these chapters of the superficiality that has sometimes characterized such considerations. The fact that such practices may not be uncommon does not make their occurrence any less unfortunate. Moreover, unlike the Judiciary Committee, this panel has consistently declined to seek outside evaluation, such as ABA input, concerning the qualifications of USCAAF nominees.

While it certainly is to be expected that members of the Senate Judicary Commitee might inquire of judicial nominees concerning their judicial and constitutional philosophy, the Armed Services Committee rarely does so. Typically, its chair warned the first USCAAF judges in 1951—even before they took office—that "any abuse of the powers of this court will be disastrous to this Nation." Richard Russell emphasized that "this will indeed be a court of military justice, [not] an agency that will be damaging to the observance of discipline in the armed services." Russell saw no choice betweeen the need for discipline and the demand for justice. He believed that insistence on the former had to guide administration of the latter. After half a century of Court decisions, it can be argued to the contrary that emphasis on justice can make military discipline more effective.

Moreover, no other federal appellate tribunal has had to deal with a group of military lawyers, JAG officers who had been the principal operatives of the military justice system for more than a century before the Court's creation, and who under the new code retained supervisory responsibility for it. The first three decades of USCAAF's existence from 1951 to 1980 were characterized by serious conflicts between the judge advocate generals and the judges. The JAGs repeatedly sought to curb the influence or authority of the Court—either by limiting its jurisdiction, altering its composition, or seeking congressional or civilian support to force a change in its decisions. The tension between the JAGs and the Court is a dominant theme in this book, and one that has not yet been played out. In fact, it may never be resolved.

Finally, no other federal appellate tribunal has sought to attain for so long and with so little success what its early members believed so essential to judicial independence—life tenure. It can be argued, as Senator Wayne Morse did in 1950, that insisting that the new court be on a par with the U.S. Courts of Appeal while at the same time refusing to give its judges that security and tenure common to their federal counterparts was inconsistent. It can further be asserted that the absence of life tenure has diminished the stature due this federal court, resulting in frequent turnover of its judges, unfortunate congressional lobbying for judicial candidates, and possible unwillingness of outstanding candidates to seek or accept appointment to its bench.

Although the jurists changed over the years between 1951 and 1975, the

Court itself did not. The procedures put in place by Chief Judge Quinn, who did not resign from the bench until 1975, and his first clerk, Alfred Proulx, who served for more than twenty years, remained essentially the same. Also, while there were a few significant changes to the UCMJ in the Military Justice Act of 1968, they did not directly affect either the Court or its relationship to the system. It was not until 1975 that Chief Judge Fletcher proposed a number of significant alterations in the way military justice had been administered.

Encouraged by those most responsible for his appointment to reinvigorate the Court, Fletcher's course of action resulted in controversy that involved clashing personalities, antagonism between judges and JAGs, and vigorous disagreement over judicial doctrine. When the smoke cleared, he had been replaced as chief judge, and the opportunity for major reforms in military justice had been lost—an occasion that at this writing has not reoccurred. For what could have been, as well for the denouement that actually took place, the Fletcher years remain tragic in their long-term institutional results.

Given the level of bitterness that existed between Fletcher and the JAGs by 1979, it is ironic that any of his proposals for judicial reform came to pass. Seized upon by his severest critics, nevertheless the controversies he engendered may well have been the catalyst for enacting some of the changes he sought. The convening authority can no longer overrule trial judges. This official has also lost the power to select both the judge and counsel in a court-martial. Every service now has a separate appellate defense division. Certain USCAAF decisions may now be appealed to the U.S. Supreme Court, and the number of its judges has been increased from three to five.

Yet, many of his suggestions failed to become law, with unfortunate results for military justice. "For administrative purposes only," USCAAF is still linked to the Defense Department. The two catchall articles in the UCMJ remain unchanged. The quest for intermediate military appellate judges to have specific terms of office has gone unheeded, and unfortunately the Supreme Court has endorsed this policy. Random selection of court members by lot rather than appointment by the convening authority is still rare, if practiced at all. Most important, the legitimacy and parameters of USCAAF supervisory jurisdiction over military justice remains uncertain. With the 1999 Supreme Court decision in *Clinton v. Goldsmith,* it may well have been circumscribed. Not only do senior military justice officials continue to resist both civilian involvement and input in the field, but effective civilian oversight of military justice by both the Court and Congress has diminished in the years since Fletcher's term as chief judge.

In retrospect, the fate of Albert Fletcher's proposals for reform stands as a stark testament to the limits of the judicial function. Wherein, one might ask, beyond the UCMJ does USCAAF authority exist? How can it enforce its decisions? What moral force attaches to its pronouncements? When the Court speaks in several separate voices, as it often did between 1975 and 1980, how can it achieve the tone, eloquence, and insights so vital for judicial and moral authority? It may be that the net effect of the Fletcher era ultimately was to retard the process of reform and embolden the forces of reaction, a development aided by the election of three consecutive conservative administrations between 1980 and 1992.

There is no doubt that USCAAF has made a real difference in military justice since 1951. As indicated in this book, to a greater extent than ever before, the Court linked the Bill of Rights to military justice, sought to insulate the courts-martial from improper influence, and worked to ensure the independence of the military judge, albeit with limited success. In spite of these dramatic contributions, however, its ultimate performance has not matched its potential. Traditionally and unnecessarily clothed with a reputation for the arcane, contemporary appellate military justice still suffers from a lack of critical civilian interest and scrutiny. How often, for example, is the subject taught in law school and subjected to the type of analytical scrutiny found in the pages of the best law reviews? Moreover, appellate military justice lacks constructive interplay with civilian jurisprudence as well as an effective and functioning bar. Its decisions, especially in the post-Fletcher era, have tended to benefit the prosecution. While continuation of USCAAF as a federal tribunal seems certain, its effectiveness cannot be taken for granted.

Ultimately, much will depend on how all parties—Congress, the military establishment, the judges, and the bar—perceive the Court and its high function. Homer Ferguson and Albert Fletcher saw their roles in very different terms than did George Latimer, William Darden, William Cook, or even Senator Richard Russell. These differences have not resulted from party identification. Indeed, the two judges who were the most vigorous critics of "abuses" in military justice and the recipients of the sharpest complaints from the JAGs were both Republicans (Ferguson and Fletcher) appointed by Republican presidents (Eisenhower and Ford).

Given both the legacy of Fletcher's years and the selection since then of less aggressive jurists, to some extent USCAAF has shifted course. On the other hand, this more conservative tendency since 1980 is not necessarily permanent. Judicial holdings are not carved in stone, and what is dissent today may well become doctrine tomorrow. Perhaps the history of the Court since 1950 will embolden future USCAAF judges, to paraphrase George Bernard Shaw, to see military justice not as it is and ask, Why? but to envision the process for what it can become and ask, Why not?

Bibliography

MANUSCRIPT COLLECTIONS

American Legion Hearings, May 1956, USCAAF Archives
Newton D. Baker Papers, Library of Congress
Tasker Bliss Papers, Library of Congress
Reva Beck Bosone Papers, University of Utah Library
Jimmy Carter Papers, Carter Presidential Library
George E. Chamberlain Papers, Oregon Historical Society
John Cooke Papers, USCAAF Archives
Enoch Crowder Papers, University of Missouri Library
Dwight D. Eisenhower Papers, Eisenhower Presidential Library
Samuel Ervin Jr. Papers, Southern Historical Collections, University of North Carolina
    Library
Homer Ferguson Papers, Bentley Library, University of Michigan
Gerald Ford Papers, Ford Presidential Library
Felix Frankfurter Papers, Library of Congress
Gordon Gray Oral History, Columbia University
Gordon Gray Papers, Military History Institute
Gordon Gray Papers, University of North Carolina
Kenneth Hodson, Oral History, Military History Institute
Lyndon B. Johnson Papers, Johnson Presidential Library
Judge Advocate General of the Army Department Files, Judge Advocate General's School,
    University of Virginia
Judge Advocate General of the Army Records, National Archives and National Archives
    Records Center
Estes Kefauver Papers, University of Tennessee
Felix Larkin, Oral History, Truman Presidential Library
Felix Larkin Papers, USCAAF Archives
George Latimer Papers, USCAAF Archives

Marx Leva, Oral History, Truman Presidential Library
William Miller Materials, USCAAF Archives
Edmund Morgan Papers, Vanderbilt University and Harvard Law School
Richard M. Nixon Papers, Nixon Project, Washington, DC
George Prugh, Oral History, Military History Institute
Robert Quinn, Oral History, Providence College Library, Special Collections
Robert Quinn Papers, USCAAF Archives
Leverett Saltonstall Papers, Massachusetts Historical Society
Deanne Siemer Materials, USCAAF Archives
Henry Stimson Papers, Yale University
William Howard Taft Papers, Library of Congress
Harry Truman Papers, Truman Presidential Library
Millard Tydings Papers, University of Maryland
John Henry Wigmore Papers, Northwestern University

UNPUBLISHED MATERIALS

Annual Court Reports Files, 1951–1980, USCAAF Archives, USCAAF Clerk's Office Clerk
    Chronological Files, 1951–1969, USCAAF Archives
Legislative History of the Military Justice Act of 1968, USCAAF Archives
Life Tenure Files, USCAAF Archives
Speech File, USCAAF Archives

GOVERNMENT DOCUMENTS

Committee on a Uniform Code of Military Justice. *Uniform Code of Military Justice: Text,
    References and Commentary.* 1949.
Full Committee Consideration of H.R. 3179, Armed Services Committee, 88th Cong., 1st
    sess., 1963.
*Hearings Before the Committee on Armed Services of the United States Senate: Nomina-
    tion of Albert Fletcher, Jr.,* 94th Cong., 1st sess., 1975.
Hearings Before the Subcommittee of the Armed Services Committee on H.R. 6583, 84th
    Cong., 1st sess., 1956.
Hearings Before the Subcommittee of the Committee on Appropriations on H.R. 5969, part
    1, 83d Cong., 1st sess., 1953.
*Hearings Before the Subcommittee on Constitutional Rights of the Committee on the Judi-
    ciary,* U.S. Senate, 87th Cong., 2d sess., 1962.
Hearings Before Subcommittee No. 1 of the Armed Services Committee on H.R. 3179, 88th
    Cong., 1st sess., 1963.
*Joint Hearings Before the Subcommittee on Constitutional Rights of the Committee on the
    Judiciary and a Special Committee of the Committee on Armed Services,* U.S. Senate,
    89th Cong., 2d sess., 1966.
Senate Armed Services Committee. *Nominations to the Court of Military Appeals.* June 16,
    1951. SRrt-T, 34.
U.S. Air Force. *Oral History Program. Interview of Major General Reginald C. Harmon.* 1987.

U.S. Army. *Oral History Program. Interview of Major General George S. Prugh.* 1975.

U.S. Army. *Oral History Program. Interview of Major General Kenneth Hodson.* 1971.

U.S. Army. *Report to Honorable Wilber M. Brucker, Secretary of the Army.* Committee on the Uniform Code of Military Justice, Good Order, and Discipline in the Army. 1960.

U.S. Congress. *Abridgement of the Debates of Congress* 14, 1842–1844.

U.S. Congress. *Congressional Record* 57, 1919; 49, 1948; 109, 1963; 113, 1967.

U.S. Congress. *Journals of Congress.* 1786.

U.S. Court of Military Appeals. *Interim Report.* 1952.

U.S. Court of Military Appeals. *Report.* 1953.

U.S. House of Representatives, Committee on Armed Services. *Report, Amending the Articles of War to Improve the Administration of Military Justice.* Report no. 1034. 80th Cong., 1st sess., 1947.

U.S. House of Representatives, Committee on Military Affairs. *Report, Judicial System, United States Army.* Report no. 2722, 79th Cong., 2d sess., 1946.

U.S. House of Representatives, Subcommittee of the Committee on Armed Services. *Hearings to Amend the Articles of War.* 80th Cong., 1st sess., 1947.

U.S. House of Representatives, Subcommittee of the Committee on Military Affairs. Hearings. *Courts-Martial, Amendments to Articles of War.* 69th Cong., 2d sess., 1920.

U.S. Navy, Office of the Judge Advocate General. *Legislative History—Uniform Code of Military Justice.* 1950, 1985.

U.S. Senate, Committee on Military Affairs. *Hearings on Trials by Courts-Martial.* 65th Cong., 3d sess., 1919.

U.S. Senate, Subcommittee of the Committee on Military Affairs. *Hearings on [the] Establishment of Military Justice.* 66th Cong., 1st sess., 1919.

U.S. War Department. *Proceedings and Report of Special War Department Board on Courts-Martial and Their Procedure.* Washington, DC: Government Printing Office, 1919.

PERIODICALS

Anderson, Thomas. "Is a Court-Martial a Criminal Court?" *United Service* 6 (1882): 297–301.

"Andrew Jackson and Judge D. A. Hall." *Louisiana Historical Quarterly* 5 (1922): 538–70.

Ansell, Samuel. "Military Justice." *Cornell Law Quarterly* 5 (1919), 1–17.

———. "Some Reforms in Our System of Military Justice." *Yale Law Journal* 32 (1922): 146–55.

Association of the Bar of the City of New York. *Report on Pending Legislation for the Revision of the Army Court-Martial System.* New York, 1948.

Avins, Alfred. "New Light on the Legislative History of Desertion Through Fraudulent Enlistment: The Decline of the United States Court of Military Appeals." *Minnesota Law Review* 46 (1961): 69–116.

Benson, Daniel. "The United States Court of Military Appeals." *Texas Tech Law Review* 3 (1971): 1–21.

Bogert, George Henry. "Courts-Martial: Criticisms and Proposed Reforms." *Cornell Law Quarterly* 5 (1919): 18–47.

Brown, Terry W. "The Crowder-Ansell Dispute: The Emergence of General Samuel T. Ansell." *Military Law Review* 35 (1967): 1–45.

"Can Military Trials Be Fair? Command Influence over Courts-Martial." *Stanford Law Review* 2 (1950): 547–58.

Connor, William M. "The Judgmental Review in General Court-Martial Proceedings." *Virginia Law Review* 32 (1945): 39–88.

Cooke, John S. "Recent Developments in the Wake of United States v. Booker." *Army Lawyer* 71 (1978): 4–13.

———. "The United States Court of Military Appeals, 1975–77: Judicializing the Military Justice System." *Military Law Review* 76 (1977): 43–163.

Cox, Walter T., III. "The Army, the Courts, and the Constitution: The Evolution of Military Justice." *Military Law Review* 118 (1987): 1–30.

Douglass, John. "The Judicialization of Military Courts." *Hastings Law Journal* 22 (1971): 213–35.

Droddy, J. D. "King Richard to Solorio: The Historical and Constitutional Bases for Court-Martial Jurisdiction in Criminal Cases." *Air Force Law Review* 30 (1989): 91–133.

Everett, Robinson O. "O'Callahan v. Parker—Milestone or Millstone in Military Justice?" *Duke Law Review* 69 (1969): 853–96.

Fairman, Charles. "The Law of Martial Rule and the National Emergency." *Harvard Law Review* 55 (1942): 1253–1302.

Fidell, Eugene R. "The Culture of Change in Military Law." *Military Law Review* 126 (1989): 125–32.

———. "If a Tree Falls in the Forest . . . ; Publication and Digesting Policies and the Potential Contribution of Military Courts to American Law." *JAG Journal* 32 (1982): 1–29.

———. "Judicial Review of Presidential Rulemaking Under Article 36: The Sleeping Giant Stirs." *Military Law Reporter* 4 (1976): 6049–59.

———. "Military Justice: The Bar's Concern." *American Bar Association Journal* 67 (1981): 1280–82.

Fidell, Eugene R., and Linda Greenhouse. "A Roving Commission: Specified Issues and the Function of the United States Court of Military Appeals." *Military Law Review* 122 (1988): 117–48.

"Free Speech in the Military." *New York University Law Review* 53 (1978): 1102–23.

Gasch, Oliver. "Who Is Out of Step?" *Army Lawyer* 66 (1978): 1–9.

Griswold, Erwin. "Appellate Advocacy." *Army Lawyer* 3 (1973): 14.

Hansen, Donald W. "Judicial Functions of the Commander." *Military Law Review* 41 (1968): 1–54.

Henderson, Gordon. "Courts-Martial and the Bill of Rights: The Original Practice." *Harvard Law Review* 71 (1957): 293–324.

Hodson, Kenneth. "Courts-Martial and the Commander." *San Diego Law Review* 10 (1972): 51–71.

Holtzoff, Alexander. "Administration of Justice in the United States Army." *New York University Law Review* 22 (1947): 1–18.

Illinois State Journal-Register. October 27, 1990, 24.

Keeffe, Arthur John. "Universal Military Training With or Without Reform of Courts-Martial?" *Cornell Law Quarterly* 33 (1948): 465–87.

Landman, Bernard, Jr. "One Year of the Uniform Code of Military Justice: A Report of Progress." *Stanford Law Review* 4 (1952): 491–508.

Lurie, Jonathan. "Military Justice 50 Years After Nuremberg: Some Reflections on Appearance v. Reality." *Military Law Review* 149 (1966): 178–86.

Margulies, Herbert F. "The Articles of War, 1920: The History of a Forgotten Reform." *Military Affairs* 43 (1979): 85–89.

Miller, Joel. "Three Is Not Enough: Some Tentative Thoughts on the Number of Judges on the United States Court of Military Appeals." *Army Lawyer* 45 (1976): 11–14.

New York Herald. 1882.

New York Times. 1917–1920, 1945–1946, 1948–1950.

New York Tribune. 1919.

New York World. 1919.

Page, William Herbert. "Military Law—A Study in Comparative Law." *Harvard Law Review* 32 (1919): 349–73.

Pasley, Robert, Jr., and Felix Larkin. "The Navy Court Martial: Proposals for Its Reform." *Cornell Law Quarterly* 33 (1947): 195–234.

Providence Daily Journal. 1941, 1946, 1960.

Prugh, George S. "Introduction to William Winthrop's *Military Law and Precedents.*" *Revue de Droit Penal Militaire et de Droit de la Guerre* [Review of Military Justice and the Law of War] 27 (1988): 437–59.

Reader's Digest. 1951.

Royall, Kenneth T. "Revision of the Military Justice Process as Proposed by the War Department." *Virginia Law Review* 33 (1947): 269–88.

Scheiber, Harry, and Jane Scheiber. "Constitutional Liberty in World War II: Army Rule and Martial Law in Hawaii, 1941–1946. *Western Legal History* 3 (1990): 340–78.

Scheisser, Charles, and Daniel Benson. "A Proposal to Make Courts-Martial Courts: The Removal of Commanders from Military Justice." *Texas Tech Law Review* 7 (1976): 559–600.

Sherman, Edward F. "The Civilianization of Military Law." *Maine Law Review* 22 (1970): 3–103.

———. "The Military Court and Servicemen's First Amendment Rights." *Hastings Law Journal* 22 (1971): 325–73.

Silliman, Scott. "The Supreme Court and Its Impact on the Court of Military Appeals." *Air Force Law Review* 18 (1976): 81–93.

Smith, Matthew. "The Real McCoy in the Bloodless Revolution of 1935." *Rhode Island History* 32 (1973): 67–85.

Van de Water, Frederick. "Panic Rides the High Seas." *American Heritage* 12 (1961): 20–23, 97–99.

Wacker, Daniel. "The 'Unreliable' Court-Martial Conviction: Supervisory Relief Under the All Writs Act from the United States Court of Military Appeals." *Military Law Review* 100 (1975): 609–59.

Washington Herald. 1919.

Washington Post. 1918–1920, 1948–1950.

West, Luther. "A History of Command Influence on the Military Justice System." *UCLA Law Review* 18 (1970): 1–156.

White, Robert J. "The Background and the Problem." *St. John's Law Review* 35 (1961): 197–214.

Wiener, Frederick Bernays. "American Military Law in the Light of the First Mutiny Act's Tricentennial." *Military Law Review* 126 (1989): 1–88.

———. "Book Review." *Cornell Law Review* 56 (1974): 748–58.

———. "Courts-Martial and the Constitution: The Original Understanding." *Harvard Law Review* 72 (1957): 1–49, 266–304.

————. "The Seamy Side of the World War I Court-Martial Controversy." *Military Law Review* 123 (1989): 109–28.

Willis, John T. "The United States Court of Military Appeals—Born Again." *Indiana Law Journal* 52 (1976): 151–66.

BOOKS

Adams, John. *Diary and Autobiography.* Ed. L. H. Butterfield. New York: Atheneum, 1964.

Army Lawyer: A History of the Judge Advocate General's Corps, 1775–1975. Washington, DC: Government Printing Office, 1975.

Ashton, J. Hubley, ed. *Official Opinions of the Attorneys General of the United States.* Washington, DC: W. H. and O. H. Morrison, 1869.

Auerbach, Jerold. *Unequal Justice: Lawyers and Social Change in Modern America.* New York: Oxford University Press, 1976.

Bassett, John S. *The Life of Andrew Jackson.* New York: Doubleday, Page, 1931.

Bates, Edward. *Diary.* Ed. Howard Beale. Washington, DC: American Historical Association, 1930.

Beaver, Daniel R. *Newton D. Baker and the American War Effort, 1917–1919.* Lincoln: University of Nebraska Press, 1966.

Buell, Augustus. *History of Andrew Jackson.* New York: Charles Scribner's Sons, 1904.

Chafee, Zechariah, Jr. *State House Versus Pent House.* Providence: Booke Shop, 1937.

Chambers, John Whiteclay, II. *To Raise an Army: The Draft Comes to Modern America.* New York: Free Press, 1987.

Clompton, Beverly. *Her Honor the Judge.* Ames: Iowa State University Press, 1980.

Coffman, Edward M. *The Hilt of the Sword: The Career of Peyton C. March.* Madison: University of Wisconsin Press, 1966.

————. *The Old Army: A Portrait of the American Army in Peacetime, 1784–1898.* New York: Oxford University Press, 1986.

————. *The War to End All Wars: The American Military Experience in World War I.* New York: Oxford University Press, 1968.

Cooper, James Fenimore. *Letters and Journals.* Ed. James F. Beard. 4 vols. Cambridge, MA: Belknap Press, 1964.

Crackel, Theodore J. *Mr. Jefferson's Army: Political and Social Reform of the Military Establishment, 1801–1809.* New York: New York University Press, 1987.

Cramer, C. H. *Newton D. Baker: A Biography.* New York: World Publishing, 1961.

Davis, Burke. *Old Hickory: A Life of Andrew Jackson.* New York: Dial Press, 1977.

Edwards, Jerome E. *Pat McCarran: Political Boss of Nevada.* Reno: University of Nevada Press, 1982.

Fairman, Charles. *Reconstruction and Reunion, 1864–1888, Part I.* New York: Macmillan, 1971.

Feld, Benjamin R. "The United States Court of Military Appeals: A Study of the Origins and Early Development of the First Civilian Tribunal for Direct Review of Courts-Martial, 1951–1959." Ph.D. diss., Georgetown University, 1960.

Fontenay, Charles L. *Estes Kefauver.* Knoxville: University of Tennessee Press, 1980.

Frankfurter, Felix. *Felix Frankfurter Reminisces.* New York: Anchor Books, 1960.

Friedman, Lawrence M. *History of American Law.* 2d ed. New York: Simon and Schuster, 1985.

Fry, James B. *Military Miscellanies*. New York: Brentano, 1889.

Gayarre, Charles. *History of Louisiana*. New York: Armand Hawkins, 1885.

Generous, William T., Jr. *Swords and Scales*. New York: Kennikat Press, 1973.

Grossman, James. *James Fenimore Cooper*. New York: William Sloan, 1949.

Hayford, Harrison. *The Somers Mutiny Affair*. Englewood Cliffs, NJ: Prentice Hall, 1960.

Hersh, Seymour. *Cover-up: The Army's Secret Investigation of the Massacre at My Lai 4*. New York: Random House, 1972.

———. *My Lai 4: A Report on the Massacre and Its Aftermath*. New York: Vintage Books, 1970.

Hodgson, Godfrey. *The Colonel: The Life and Wars of Henry Stimson, 1867–1950*. New York: Alfred A. Knopf, 1990.

Hoopes, Townsend, and Douglas Brinkley. *Driven Patriot*. New York: Alfred A. Knopf, 1992.

Hughes, Emmet John. *The Ordeal of Power*. New York: Atheneum, 1963.

Ives, Rollin. *A Treatise on Military Law*. 4th ed. New York: D. Van Nostrand, 1886.

Jackson, Andrew. *Correspondence*. Ed. John Bassett. Washington: Carnegie Institution, 1927.

Karnow, Stanley. *Vietnam: A History*. New York: Penguin Books, 1991.

Klement, Frank L. *The Limits of Dissent: Clement L. Vallandigham and the Civil War*. Lexington: University Press of Kentucky, 1970.

Kohn, Richard. *Eagle and Sword: The Federalists and the Creation of the Military Establishment in America, 1783–1802*. New York: Free Press, 1975.

Lane, Jack. *Armed Progressive: General Leonard Wood*. San Rafael, CA: Presidio Press, 1978.

Lewis, Walker. *Without Fear or Favor*. Boston: Houghton Mifflin, 1965.

Lieber, G. Norman. *The Justification of Martial Law*. Washington, DC: Government Printing Office, 1898.

Lincoln, Abraham. *Collected Works*. Ed. Roy Basler. New Brunswick, NJ: Rutgers University Press, 1953.

Lockmiller, David A. *Enoch H. Crowder: Soldier, Lawyer, and Statesman*. Columbia: University of Missouri Press, 1955.

Manchester, William. *American Caesar*. Boston: Little, Brown, 1978.

Meador, Daniel J. *Criminal Appeals: English Practices and American Reforms*. Charlottesville: University Press of Virginia, 1973.

Millett, Alan R., and Peter Maslowski. *For the Common Defense: A Military History of the United States of America*. New York: Free Press, 1984.

Moyer, Homer F., Jr. *Justice and the Military*. Washington, DC: Public Law Education Institute, 1972.

Neely, Mark E., Jr. *The Fate of Liberty*. New York: Oxford University Press, 1991.

O'Neil, William L. *American High: The Years of Confidence, 1945–1960*. New York: Free Press, 1986.

Parrish, Michael. *Felix Frankfurter and His Times*. New York: Free Press, 1982.

Philbrick, Thomas. *James Fenimore Cooper and the Development of American Sea Fiction*. Cambridge, MA: Harvard University Press, 1961.

Pitman, Benn. *The Assassination of President Lincoln and the Trial of the Conspirators*. New York: Funk and Wagnalls, 1954.

Polenberg, Richard. *Fighting Faiths: The Abrams Case, the Supreme Court, and Free Speech*. New York: Penguin Books, 1987.

Pound, Roscoe. *Criminal Justice in America.* New York: Da Capo Press, 1930.

Proceedings of the Naval Court-Martial in the Case of Alexander Slidell Mackenzie. New York: Henry G. Langley, 1844.

Rearden, Steven L. *The Formative Years, 1937–1950.* Vol. 1 of *The History of the Office of the Secretary of Defense,* ed. Alfred Goldberg. Washington, DC: Government Printing Office, 1984.

Remini, Robert. *Andrew Jackson and the Course of American Empire, 1767–1821.* New York: Harper and Row, 1977.

Roalfe, William R. *John Henry Wigmore: Scholar and Reformer.* Evanston, IL: Northwestern University Press, 1977.

Schlesinger, Arthur. *War and the Constitution: Abraham Lincoln and Franklin D. Roosevelt.* Gettysburg, PA: Gettysburg College, 1988.

Smith, Page. *John Adams.* New York: Doubleday, 1962.

Turner, Thomas. *Beware the People Weeping: Public Opinion and the Assassination of Abraham Lincoln.* Baton Rouge: Louisiana State University Press, 1982.

Weigley, Russell F. *The History of the United States Army.* Rev. ed. Bloomington: Indiana University Press, 1984.

Welles, Gideon. *Diary.* Boston: Houghton Mifflin, 1911.

White, G. Edward. *Warren: A Public Life.* New York: Oxford University Press, 1982.

Winthrop, William. *Military Law and Precedents.* 2d ed. Washington, DC: Government Printing Office, 1920.

Index